Brian Glanville was football correspondent for the *Sunday Times* for thirty-three years, and then sports columnist for the *People*. He has covered the last thirteen World Cups, and wrote and co-edited *Goal!*, the official film of the 1966 World Cup. He has written many short stories and novels about the game, including *The Rise of Gerry Logan, The Dying of the Light* and, for children, *Goalkeepers are Different*.

The Story of the World Cup

The Essential Companion to South Africa 2010

Brian Glanville

faber and faber

First published in 1973 as *The Sunday Times History of the World Cup*
by Times Newspapers Limited, London

Revised editions published in 1980 and 1984 as *The History of the World Cup*
by Faber and Faber Limited
Bloomsbury House, 74–77 Great Russell Street, London WC1B 3DA
Revised editions published in 1993, 1997, 2001 and 2005 as *The Story of the World Cup*
This revised edition published in 2010

Typeset by RefineCatch Limited, Bungay, Suffolk
Printed in England by Mackays of Chatham plc.

A CIP record for this book is available from the British Library

ISBN 978-0-571-23605-3

10 9 8 7 6 5 4 3 2 1

Contents

List of illustrations

The author and publishers are glad to acknowledge the following copyright-holders of illustrations reproduced in this book:

Colorsport, 13
Keystone Press Agency, 1–7
S & G Press Agency, 8, 11, 12
Syndication International, 9
Bob Thomas, 10, 14–21
Popperfoto, 22–25
Pedro Ugarte/AFP/Getty, 26
Damien Meyer/AFP/Getty, 27

Preface

As the World Cup finals in South Africa draw closer, we can only hope and pray. This alarming venue was avoided only at the eleventh hour when the elderly New Zealand representative, defying his brief, abstained from voting and thereby enabled Germany rather than South Africa to stage the 2006 tournament. And very well they did it. No escape this time, alas. The World Cup voters have been Blattered, you might say, into handing South Africa the finals. A country where criminality runs riot, murders are commonplace, robbery endemic. The whole alarming prospect exacerbated by the fact that the tournament now involves an overblown quantum of 24 clubs.

There were ominous portents when South Africa put on, in June 2009, the far less populous Confederations Cup. Alarming testimonies from what you might call the battlefront by respected correspondents painted a grim picture of the perils. Not that much official concern was shown. Fikile Mbalula, the deputy minister responsible for security, showed no concern for those outside the magic circle of officialdom—meaning players and blazer wearers. One correspondent told an alarming tale of being obliged to drive four hours through the night from Bloemfontein to Johannesburg in pitch darkness along a two lane road. Another, *The Times*' Owen Slot, toured the country looking at stadia and accommodation, or the preoccupying lack of it. He reported that in at least two cases, new stadia were built at vast expense though others already existed. And that in one crazy case, a new stadium was built almost alongside a perfectly viable predecessor.

Accommodation, especially outside the largest cities, is bound to be a problem. Hotels are at a premium. Private families can provide only limited accommodation. Blatter himself was warned against camping sites in the bleak South African winter, yet at Polokwane, the farthest north venue, it has been suggested that a camping site for 2000 fans be erected on school grounds. Fans have been warned not to travel by train or bus for fear of molestation. During the Confederations Cup tournament, various journalists were robbed. One was even subjected to extortion by police when he tried to park his car. Panglossian as ever, Blatter will no doubt continue to assure us that everything is for the best in the best of all possible worlds.

Mastercard will maintain their official role in the tournament but only after a bitter battle in a New York court against Visa, to whom FIFA were trying to transfer the long held contract. The presiding woman judge accused both FIFA representatives of lying. On return to Zurich, one of them was briefly suspended, then re-emerged as FIFA's chief executive.

As for the contestants, the money would seem largely to be on Spain and Brazil. In winning the 2008 European Championship, the Spaniards played much delightful football, with a splendidly inventive midfield of little men such as such as Xabi Alonso and Fabregas, though even he, with all his talents, had to fight for a place. In attack, Fernando Torres came to full splendid maturity, displaying power, pace, skill and supreme opportunism.

The Brazilians have become less dour under Dunga, previously criticised in his own country for a negative approach. They made a poor beginning to the ludicrously over-populated South American qualifying tournament—oh for the little groups of yesteryear! —but gradually picked up and had the great satisfaction of accounting for the old foe Argentina in Rosario. Yet though they won the Confederations Cup, they had their difficulties on they way, and for all the jewelled presence of those such as Kaka, one remembers how they disappointed in Germany when so strongly favoured.

Argentina, or more precisely their autocratic leader, Julio Grondona, in a moment of madness appointed Diego Maradona as their manager. The all too predictable consequences were a string of catastrophic results, worst of all the 6-1 drubbing in La Paz by humble Bolivia—Maradona having neglected to take any precautions against the breathless altitude, which meant that the pursuit of qualification went right down to the wire.

England, after the fiasco of the Wally with the Brolly, appointed Fabio Capello as their leader and kept a 100% record in the eliminators till the ill-fated penultimate group game in Ukraine. This they lost 1-0 after surviving a penalty which led to their keeper Robert Green being sent off. But defeats in friendly matches by both Germany and Spain have led to doubts amidst the general euphoria, while it became increasingly difficult to understand Capello's magnificent obsession with a diminished David Beckham. Not least when a crop of fine fast young right-wingers had emerged: Aaron Lennon, Theo Walcott (hero of a remarkable five goal win against Croatia in Zagreb), James Milner and Shaun Wright-Phillips.

Things seemed to tremble on the edge of farce as Beckham was awarded one cheap cap after another as a short-term substitute. Fiasco loomed when Beckham was proclaimed to have overtaken Bobby Moore's splendid haul of 108 caps. But Bobby won them over 90 minutes; except when as in the 1966 World Cup Final, he played another half hour of extra time. I've known, liked and admired Fabio since first meeting him after he'd helped Italy to their first ever win against England in Turin in 1973 and found him a man of charm, humour and intelligence. But his severe attack of Beckhamitis is still baffling.

Meanwhile, England's goalkeeping position has been troubling. It did look for a time as if Manchester United's Ben Foster, putting long months of injury behind him, would be the belated answer, but this season, Foster's form has dipped vertiginously. None of the other rivals to the 39-year-old David James has been convincing. Long ago the revered French novelist André Gide was asked who was the greatest French poet to which he replied, '*Victor Hugo, hélas.*' Victor Hugo, alas. If you asked me who is the best English goalkeeper I'd have to answer, 'David James, alas.' Fresh in my mind being a glorious flying one-handed save at Wolves to give Portsmouth their first points of the season at the eighth time of asking. But oh, the inconsistency!

And so to South Africa. Let us pray.

URUGUAY
1930

Background to 1930

Like so many of the best ideas in football, that of the World Cup was conceived in France. Its true parents were, indeed, two Frenchmen: Jules Rimet, after whom it was eventually named, and Henri Delaunay. Rimet was President of the French Federation, FFF, for thirty years from its beginning in 1919, and President of FIFA, the Fédération Internationale des Football Associations, from 1920 to 1954; an extraordinary record. Delaunay, who had been concerned with running French football from 1908, was officially Secretary from 1919 till his death in 1956, a little before the death of the 83-year-old Rimet.

These two men complemented each other: Rimet the persuader, the diplomat, sometimes intransigent, always devoted to the game; Delaunay the worker, visionary and energetic. Sometimes they quarrelled, but they were the pioneers of French football, European football—and the World Cup.

The very first meeting of FIFA took place in Paris in 1904—without the benefit of British attendance—and decided rather grandly that it alone had the right to organise a world championship. This right was not to be exercised for twenty-six years. In 1920, at FIFA's Antwerp congress, concurrent with the Olympic Games, the idea of a World Cup, previously much debated, was accepted in principle. In 1924, at the Paris Olympics, the FIFA meeting discussed it in more serious detail, while a dazzling and hitherto obscure Uruguayan side walked off with the soccer tournament.

Two years later, at FIFA's congress, Delaunay proclaimed: 'Today international football can no longer be held within the confines of the Olympics; and many countries where professionalism is now recognised and organised cannot any longer be represented there by their best players.'

This had always been true of Britain, which even before the war had been represented by genuine amateurs and which in a couple of years would withdraw from FIFA over the question of broken time payments. Now, it was keeping out such rising countries as Austria and Hungary, while many of those which competed were professionals in all but name. In 1928, in Amsterdam, where Uruguay retained their title against a strong challenge from Argentina, Delaunay's resolution that the World Cup be set on foot at once was adopted. But where should it be played?

There were five aspirants: Italy, Holland, Spain, Sweden and Uruguay. Tiny Uruguay, with its proud footballing tradition—'Other countries have their history,' their team manager, Viera, would say at the 1966 World Cup, 'Uruguay has its football'—made an offer extraordinary for a country of merely two million people. They would pay all travelling and hotel expenses for the visiting teams, and they would build a new stadium for the tournament. It would be in central Montevideo, and would be called the Centenary Stadium, for Uruguay in 1930 would be celebrating a hundred years of independence. It would be built in only eight months, three of which included the rainy season.

Faced by such transcendent enthusiasm, what could the European countries do but withdraw—altogether? None of the four disappointed hosts made the trip to Uruguay, which in those days took a wearying three weeks.

The Contenders

Allotted the World Cup at FIFA's 1929 congress in Barcelona, Uruguay found themselves, two months before it was due to kick off, without a single European entrant. In addition to the four we have mentioned, the Austrians, Hungarians, Germans, Swiss and Czechs said no; the British were out of FIFA. Belgium, Romania and Yugoslavia vacillated, as did France, though after Rimet's appointment to the FIFA presidency, and Uruguay's 1924 appearance in Paris, the moral imperatives were strong.

Embittered, insulted, the Latin American federations threatened to withdraw from FIFA; a threat they would be making many times in the years to come. Belgium and Romania at last adhered—Belgium under the pressure of the veteran FIFA Vice-President, Rodolphe William Seeldrayers, Romania under that of King Carol himself. Though the German-speaking king was never popular in Romania, he had always had much to do with Romanian sport. One of his first acts, on coming to the throne, was to grant an amnesty to all suspended Romanian footballers. Now he picked the Romanian team himself and brought pressure on the companies which employed them to give them time off for Uruguay. Yugoslavia also agreed to go, so there would be four European entrants; but not even by the greatest feat of imagination could they be ranked among the élite. The bitterness in Montevideo was scarcely assuaged.

In the 1924 Olympics Uruguay had thrashed Yugoslavia 7–0 and France 5–1. In 1928, Belgium had been beaten by Argentina 6–3; and now they were travelling without three of their best players, including Bastin.

Argentina, traditional rivals of Uruguay in the Lipton Cup, would be there, however, and would be doughty rivals. In 1928, it had taken a replay before they succumbed 2–1 in the Olympic Final.

The United States would be there too; moreover, they were one of the teams seeded in the four qualifying pools, which had been set up only when it was realised there wouldn't be enough countries to make a knock-out competition possible. At this time there was still professional football of a sort in the States, the rump of the attempt by such as Bethlehem Steel to put the sport on its feet in the 1920s. The American team, managed by Jack Coll of Brooklyn Wanderers, was made up largely of British and Scots pros: Alec Wood, James Gallacher, Andrew Auld, James Brown and Bart McGhee from Scotland, George Moorhouse from England. They were powerfully-built men whom the French players nicknamed 'the shot-putters'.

Brazil were present, but it was not long since the gates had been opened to the black player and the game there was still somewhat in a condition of inspired anarchy. Chile and Mexico, who made up Pool I with Argentina and France; Bolivia, in Pool II with Brazil and Yugoslavia; Peru, in Pool III with Uruguay and Romania; Paraguay, in Pool IV with the USA and Belgium completed the entry of thirteen. The four Pool winners would go into the semi-finals.

Uruguay were unquestionably the favourites, though their fine team of the 1924 and 1928 Olympics was fractionally past its peak; in the image of its famous centre-forward, Pedro Petrone. Nevertheless, it had home advantage and its still abundant talent in its favour, and it is arguable that it would have won the tournament whatever European teams had come, even England, Scotland and the formidable Austrian Wunderteam.

The Earlier Matches

The four European teams, whose boat had picked up the Brazilians en route, were tumultuously welcomed in Montevideo, though none had been seeded head of a group; a distinction reserved for Uruguay, Argentina, Brazil and the USA. The Centenary Stadium was, alas, still unfinished, thanks to heavy rain; early matches had to be played on the grounds of the Penarol and Nacional clubs, Pocito and Central Park. On Sunday afternoon, July 13, France opened the tournament against Mexico with a 4–1 win; although their admirable and unspectacular goalkeeper, Alex Thépot, was kicked on the jaw after ten minutes, giving way to his left-half, Chantrel. (There would be no substitutes for another forty years.) The French team was a good and lively one, with Etienne Mattler, who would play so well for France for so long, at right-back, Pinel as pivot, and a captain, Alex Villaplane, the right-half, who would ultimately be shot by the French Resistance for collaborating with the Nazis.

Two days later, France faced the gifted Argentinians—and were most unlucky to go down by 1–0. Monti was at his most ferocious, hurting the ankle of Lucien Laurent, France's inside-left, early in the game, and giving Pinel, who largely overplayed him, some kind of a knock every time they met. Monti it was who scored the goal, nine minutes from time. Argentina were given a free kick, twenty yards out. As Monti took it, Pinel stepped to his right, unsighting the excellent Thépot—and the shot flashed into the net.

Three minutes later, with Maschinot, the centre-forward limping after another tackle by Monti, Marcel Langiller raced the length of the field. It might have been the equaliser, but Almeida Rego, the Brazilian referee, suddenly blew for time. Instant chaos. While Argentina's fans invaded the field of Central Park, the French players assailed the referee, insisting there were six minutes left. Mounted police galloped on to the field, Senhor Rego consulted his watch and his linesmen, and at last, raising his arms, cried to the heavens that he had erred in good faith. Cierro, the Argentinian inside-left, fainted, the game resumed, and the remaining minutes petered uneventfully away.

Afterwards, Uruguay's watching players declared that France deserved to win, Thépot and Pinel were carried off shoulder high, and the Argentinians complained accordingly to the Organising Committee, threatening to go home; thus sounding what would become another tediously familiar note.

In their next match, against Mexico, deprived of Manuel Ferreira, taking a university exam, they brought in young Guillermo Stabile, *El Enfiltrador*, destined to become the competition's leading scorer and eventually his country's team manager.

This was a match in which the Bolivian referee, Ulysses Saucedo, gave no fewer than five penalties—Monti was not playing!—of which perhaps two were justified.

Stabile, who had scored three goals against Mexico, kept his place for a tempestuous game against Chile, Ferreira coming in as inside-left. Two minutes from half-time Monti, back again, kicked at Torres, Chile's left-half, as he jumped to head the ball. Torres retaliated, and both teams indulged in a protracted brawl, broken up with great difficulty by the police.

Argentina, Stabile scoring twice more, won 3–1 and advanced to the semi-finals. A tried France had anti-climactically gone down 1–0 to Chile, managed by the old Hungarian star, George Orth.

Uruguay did not enter the fray till July 18, when the Centenary Stadium was at last ready to receive them. Not unexpectedly, perhaps, the game against Peru was a disappointment. Peru's defence held out well, and where Romania had scored three against them, Uruguay could manage only one; a late one by Castro—a player who had lost the lower part of one arm.

For their next match, against Romania, Uruguay brought in

Scarone and their new star, Pelegrin Anselmo, for Castro and Petrone, respectively, winning 4–0 in a canter to qualify.

In Group II, Yugoslavia unexpectedly toppled Brazil 2–1 in their first game. Brazil were individually cleverer, collectively inferior. Two of the Yugoslav team, Beck and Stefanovic, had just helped Sète win the French Cup. Tirnanic and Beck scored in the first half-hour, another goal was disallowed for offside, and Brazil could muster but one reply through their captain, Neto. Each team then beat Bolivia 4–0, and the Yugoslavs went through.

So did the United States, their strong defence and breakaway attacks routing Belgium and Paraguay in turn by 3–0. In the semifinal, alas, the much greater pace and sophistication of the Argentinians simply overwhelmed them and they crashed 6–1; precisely the score by which Uruguay trounced Yugoslavia. The half-time score was only 1–0, a goal credited to Monti, but in the second half the Americans simply fell apart, conceding five more, the last three within nine minutes, two to the swift right-winger, Peucelle. Brown, their own outside-right, got their only goal.

Eighty thousand spectators watched Uruguay despatch Yugoslavia after sustaining the shock of a fourth-minute goal by Seculic. Cea and Anselmo made it 2–1 by the interval, and Yugoslavia were then refused, on a controversial offside decision, what would have been their equaliser.

So, in the second half, Uruguay scored four. Fernandez caught the Yugoslav defence off guard with a cleverly lobbed free kick which Iriarte converted, then Cea, the inside-left, scored two more, the first after a mistake by Yugoslavia's captain and right-back, Ivkovic. Next day, Argentina joined them in a Final which would be a repetition of the Olympic Final of 1928.

The Final   Uruguay v. Argentina

In Buenos Aires the excitement was phenomenal. Ten packet-boats were chartered to take fans across the River Plate to Montevideo, but they were insufficient; thousands of desperate supporters thronged the centre of Buenos Aires, clamouring for more boats. When they eventually sailed, at ten o'clock on the eve of the Final, a great crowd thronged the quayside to see them off, letting off fireworks and chanting, '*Argentina si, Uruguay no!* Victory or death!' Arriving in Montevideo, the Argentinians were searched for revolvers by customs and police; and searched again at the entrance to the Centenary Stadium. The kick-off was scheduled for two o'clock; the gates were opened at eight in the morning, and by noon the ground was packed. Though it could take 100,000, the attendance was limited to 90,000—with memories of an inaugural day when the police had been overwhelmed by the crowds and the ticket offices, now closed with metal grilles, were assailed.

John Langenus, chosen, as had been expected, to referee the match, demanded that the safety of himself and his linesmen be guaranteed, and only a few hours before kick-off did his fellow referees authorise him to preside. The Argentinian players had been under a police guard day and night, mounted police escorting their coach to and from each training session. Around the stadium, soldiers with fixed bayonets kept the crowds moving; and after all this there was still the question of the match ball.

Each team insisted on a ball of native manufacture; a point which had not been covered in the regulations. It was finally decided that Langenus should toss up on the field. To a fusillade of firecrackers, he did. Argentina won.

Though Uruguay clearly had to be favoured on their own stadium, before their own crowd, the team had not played with the assurance of its predecessors. Moreover, Pelegrin Anselmo was unfit and was replaced at centre-forward by Castro; Petrone's sun had definitely set. Argentina might have missed Orsi, but they had found Stabile, and their forward play had been excellent; full of fast, sweeping, intelligent movements, the traditionally fine ball control allied to subtle positioning. In goal, however, there was a manifest weakness. Angelo Bossio's flashy, unreliable play had led to his being dropped from the semi-final, but his replacement, Juan Botasso, was no great improvement.

The first half was pregnant with surprises. After only twelve minutes, Pablo Dorado, the Uruguayan right-winger, gave his country the lead, but Peucelle, his opposite number, equalised, and ten minutes from half-time John Langenus boldly sanctioned a goal by Stabile which Nasazzi, Uruguay's captain, fiercely insisted was offside. Crowds being unpredictable organisms, there was no attempt to invade the pitch this time, merely a stunned acceptance.

The crowds came to life again ten minutes after the interval, when Pedro Cea capped an insidious dribble with the equalising goal. Uruguay had broken the spell. Ten minutes more and the young Uruguayan outside-left, Santos Iriarte, put them ahead, and finally Castro, Anselmo's understudy, smashed the ball into the roof of the net in the concluding seconds. Uruguay had won an exciting and surprisingly good-tempered game.

But what of Monti, alias 'The Man Who Strolled'? Long, long afterwards, at the age of 92, sole survivor of Argentina's team, Pancho Varallo, then the inside right, accused Monti of being in a state of panic after receiving death threats. Varallo, who played ten years for Argentina and in his old age ran a lottery ticket shop in the city where he'd begun his career with Gimnasia y Esgrima, declared that in the dressing-room before kick off in the final, Monti feared he'd be killed, threatened not to play, and had to be reassured by Varallo and the other players.

But throughout the match, Varallo recollected, Monti was in such a state of terror as to be virtually a passenger. When Varallo himself was injured and had to limp on the wing, Argentina were effectively reduced to ten men.

Motor horns blared in triumph, ships blew their sirens in the port, flags and banners flew, the next day was proclaimed a national holiday. The golden, 50,000-franc Cup, designed by a French sculptor, Abel Lafleur, was consigned to Nasazzi by Jules Rimet.

In Buenos Aires, the Uruguayan Consulate was stoned by an infuriated mob until the police dispersed it by opening fire. The World Cup was well and truly launched.

RESULTS: Uruguay 1930

Pool I

France 4, Mexico 1 (ʜᴛ 3/0)
Argentina 1, France 0 (ʜᴛ 0/0)
Chile 3, Mexico 0 (ʜᴛ 1/0)
Chile 1, France 0 (ʜᴛ 0/0)
Argentina 6, Mexico 3 (ʜᴛ 3/0)
Argentina 3, Chile 1 (ʜᴛ 2/1)

	P	W	D	L	GOALS F	A	Pts
Argentina	3	3	0	0	10	4	6
Chile	3	2	0	1	5	3	4
France	3	1	0	2	4	3	2
Mexico	3	0	0	3	4	13	0

Pool II

Yugoslavia 2, Brazil 1 (ʜᴛ 2/0)
Yugoslavia 4, Bolivia 0 (ʜᴛ 0/0)
Brazil 4, Bolivia 0 (ʜᴛ 1/0)

	P	W	D	L	GOALS F	A	Pts
Yugoslavia	2	2	0	0	6	1	4
Brazil	2	1	0	1	5	2	2
Bolivia	2	0	0	2	0	8	0

Pool III

Romania 3, Peru 1 (ʜᴛ 1/0)
Uruguay 1, Peru 0 (ʜᴛ 0/0)
Uruguay 4, Romania 0 (ʜᴛ 4/0)

	P	W	D	L	GOALS F	A	Pts
Uruguay	2	2	0	0	5	0	4
Romania	2	1	0	1	3	5	2
Peru	2	0	0	2	1	4	0

Pool IV

United States 3, Belgium 0 (ʜᴛ 2/0)
United States 3, Paraguay 0 (ʜᴛ 2/0)
Paraguay 1, Belgium 0 (ʜᴛ 1/0)

	P	W	D	L	GOALS F	A	Pts
United States	2	2	0	0	6	0	4
Paraguay	2	1	0	1	1	3	2
Belgium	2	0	0	2	0	4	0

Semi-finals

Argentina 6
Botasso; Della Torre,
Paternoster; Evaristo, J.,
Monti, Orlandini;
Peucelle, Scopelli,
Stabile, Ferreira (capt.),
Evaristo, M.

United States 1
Douglas; Wood,
Moorhouse; Gallacher,
Tracey, Auld; Brown,
Gonsalvez, Patenaude,
Florie (capt.), McGhee.

SCORERS
Monti, Scopelli, Stabile (2), Peucelle (2), for
Argentina
Brown for United States
ʜᴛ 1/0

Uruguay 6
Ballesteros; Nasazzi
(capt.), Mascheroni;
Andrade, Fernandez,
Gestido; Dorado,
Scarone, Anselmo,
Cea, Iriarte.

Yugoslavia 1
Yavocic; Ivkovic
(capt.), Milhailovic;
Arsenievic, Stefanovic,
Djokic; Tirnanic,
Marianovic, Beck,
Vujadinovic, Seculic.

SCORERS
Cea (3), Anselmo (2), Iriarte for Uruguay
Seculic for Yugoslavia
ʜᴛ 3/1

Final

Uruguay 4
Ballesteros; Nasazzi
(capt.), Mascheroni;
Andrade, Fernandez,
Gestido; Dorado,
Scarone, Castro, Cea,
Iriarte.

Argentina 2
Botasso; Della Torre,
Paternoster; Evaristo,
J., Monti, Suarez;
Peucelle, Varallo,
Stabile, Ferreira
(capt.), Evaristo, M.

SCORERS
Dorado, Cea, Iriarte, Castro for Uruguay
Peucelle, Stabile for Argentina
ʜᴛ 1/2

ITALY
1934

Background to Italy

It would be twenty years before the World Cup returned to South America—and to Uruguay. The 1934 tournament was altogether more high-powered and highly competitive, though for the first and only time so far the holders did not defend. Uruguay, still piqued by the defection of the European 'powers' in 1930, plagued, too, by one of those periodic players' strikes which would still torment them over forty years later, stayed at home. Italy organised it, Italy won, prompting the reflection of John Langenus: 'In the majority of countries; the World Championship was called a sporting fiasco, because beside the desire to win all other sporting considerations were non-existent, and because, moreover, a certain spirit brooded over the whole Championship. Italy wanted to win, it was natural, but they allowed it to be seen too clearly.'

Given the Fascist climate of the times, it was perhaps inevitable. The Italian team, the *azzurri* (blues) were 'Mussolini's *azzurri*', the Duce himself would appear, heavy-chinned and smirking under a yachting cap, at Rome's Stadio Nazionale. Vittorio Pozzo, the Italian *Commissario Tecnico*, a great anglophile but a great authoritarian, unquestionably used the inflated spirit of the times to promote an atmosphere, a discipline, which subsequent Italian managers have envied, and which would never have been possible without it; any more than Pozzo himself, the revered father figure. 'Kind, but with a strong hand,' he reminisced. 'If I let them make mistakes, I'd lose my authority.' He did not hesitate to make use of *oriundi* South American stars of Italian origin. Three of them, all Argentines, played in the final. One was Monti, whom Pozzo wanted as a roving centre-half in the image of Manchester United's Charlie Roberts, whom he'd known and admired when a poor student before the First World War. Pozzo's tactics would be firmly based on pre-Third Back Game days.

'If they can die for Italy, they can play for Italy,' he grandiosely claimed, meaning that *oriundi* were liable for Italian military service. But when, in 1935, war was declared on Abyssinia, Enrico Guaita, the World Cup outside-right, was caught trying to slip across the Swiss border with other *oriundi*. Play yes, die, no.

Pozzo and the equally authoritarian anglophile Hugo Meisl of Austria, were the dominant figures in European football between the wars, sharing the friendship of Herbert Chapman, the remarkable Yorkshireman who built up Arsenal. The 'natural' final would have been between Italy and Meisl's so-called Wunderteam, fractionally past its peak but still a fine side, which had whacked Italy 4–2 in Turin only months before the World Cup began. They would meet in the semi-final.

This time, it would be a knock-out competition with sixteen teams in the first round; a dispensation which meant that Brazil and Argentina came some eight thousand miles to play just one game. There had been, besides, a qualifying competition, in which, curiously, even the Italians were obliged to take part. They beat Greece in Milan, a match in which Nereo Rocco of Triestina, later the outstanding manager of Milan, played his only (half) game for his country.

The tournament had been assigned to Italy at the Stockholm congress of 1932. It was realised that it could no longer be confined to a single city, nor to a country without huge resources. Uruguay had in fact paid everyone's expenses and still made a comfortable profit in 1930, but the scale was growing. 'The Italian Federation', promised its delegate, *Avvocato* Mauro, 'is capable of sustaining these burdens, and even in the case of an adverse balance wants to hold the entire final stages of the tournament, using as its theatre the numerous and flourishing Italian cities, all provided with magnificent stadiums.' Behind the hard-working Mauro and his pleasant energetic colleague, Engineer Barassi, the Fascist government stood ready to pick up the cheque.

The Opening Games

There was still, curiously, an eliminating match to play before the tournament proper could begin; curiously because it took place in Rome between two countries as distant as Mexico and the United States. The Americans, with only two survivors from their 1930 semi-final team, won, but were thrashed 7–1 in the same Stadio Torino by Italy in the following game. Thirty-two teams had entered the qualifying tournament; twenty-two from Europe, eight from the Americas, one each from Asia and Africa— none from Britain.

Both South American teams went out at once. In Genoa, Spain were 3–1 up against Brazil at half-time, a score which did not change. Argentina went down 3–2 to Sweden, their team including not a single member of the 1930 side.

In Turin, France provided the chief surprise of the round, doing far better than had been expected against the Austrians, who had most of the luck that was going. Austria won only in extra time with a most dubious goal.

The Germans, who had prepared thoroughly, were startled by Belgium in Florence, but recovered strongly. The Belgians scored twice in the first half to give them a 2–1 lead; then the team blew up. Conen, Germany's centre-forward, completed a hat trick, and his side won 5–2.

In Trieste the fancied Czechs were troubled by the Romanians. Dobai scored for Romania after eleven minutes, but Puc, the thrustful Czech left-winger, and Nejedly, their dangerous, graceful inside-left, replied in the second half. The winner was rather a lucky goal, for Nejedly received the ball after Sobotka won it in a bounce-up.

Hungary were given a surprisingly hard time of it by Egypt in Naples, winning only 4–2. Switzerland beat the Dutch 3–2 in Milan; one of their goals, by the bespectacled centre-forward Kielholz, came from a shot which hit a bump in the ground and was crazily diverted.

The Second Round

The second round included two fascinating pairings: Italy would play Spain in Florence; Austria and Hungary, those old foes, would meet at Bologna.

Italy were rough, the referee weak. Spain took the lead with a goal which might have demoralised a less resilient team than Italy. When Langara, the centre-forward, took a free kick, Regueiro—whose son would play for Mexico in the 1968 Olympics—swung at the ball, miskicked it utterly, and in miskicking beat the wrong-footed Combi. A minute after the interval, Italy were lucky to equalise when Pizziolo, the right-half, took another free kick. Zamora, obstructed by Schiavio, could only push the ball out, and Ferrari drove it home.

In extra time, Pozzo switched Schiavio and Guaita, as he would in the Final, but now it was unproductive. After the game he called each of his players, one by one, into the salon of the hotel where they were staying on the Lungarno. For the replay the following day he wanted only volunteers, and there were three changes. Pizziolo had broken his leg—another blow Italy had ridden with aplomb—and gave way to Ferraris IV, while de Maria and Borel had their only game of the competition, in attack. Spain by contrast were able to use only four of their previous team. Noguet, a young reserve, stood in for Zamora, and Bosch, the left-winger, was hurt as early as the fourth minute. Eight minutes later Meazza, always dangerous in the air, rose gracefully to Orsi's corner and headed Italy into the semi-finals.

In Bologna, Hugo Meisl picked the busy little inside-forward Horwarth and he, though no Sindelar, gave the team fresh drive in what Meisl described as 'a brawl, not an exhibition of football'. After only seven minutes, Horwarth raced in to convert Zischek's cross, and with Sarosi well under form Hungary found it hard to get back into the game.

Six minutes after half-time, Zischek, in the centre, drove in Bican's pass to make it 2–0, and the match began to get rough. Sarosi reduced the lead from a penalty, things grew rougher still, and Markos, Hungary's right-winger, foolishly got himself sent off just when his team threatened to equalise. As it was, they pressed gamely on till the end, though the most dangerous shot was Sindelar's, gloriously saved by Szabo. Austria, calmer and better together, had deserved their win, and had found new life.

In Milan, heavy rain did not prevent a large crowd, mushroomed with umbrellas and chequered with swastika flags, from attending the Germany–Sweden game. Germany, with one inside-forward lying deep, the other upfield, met in Sweden a team of similar Nordic propensities, solid rather than skilful, and had slightly the better of the first half.

Twelve minutes after the break, Rosen, the Swedish centre-half, found Kroon, his left-winger, unmarked ten yards from goal. Kroon shot wide, and Sweden's chance had gone. Three minutes later, when Rydberg, who had made two fine saves in the first half, could only push a ball out, Hohmann, Germany's inside-right, scored. Another three minutes and he got a far more spectacular goal, beating both Swedish backs and drawing Rydberg out of goal before placing his shot coolly past him.

Sweden soon afterwards lost their left-half, E. Andersson, who was hurt, but they kept on gamely and Dunker scored them a consoling if irrelevant goal.

At Turin, the Czechs won the best match of the round against the combative Swiss. The game swung and swayed, but the Czechs always seemed to have the resources of skill, stamina and confidence to regain the lead, running out winners by 3–2.

The Semi-Finals   Italy v. Austria

The semi-finals now brought together Italy and Austria in Milan, and Germany and the Czechs in Rome. By all rights, the Italians should have been tired, the Austrians favoured, but Hugo Meisl would have none of it. Italy, he said, had better reserves that Austria, were better prepared and would be better supported. Perhaps his pessimism would have been confounded again had not Horwarth, the lively catalyst, been injured, his place going to Schall; and had it not been for a deluge creating just the heavy surface which the Vienna school found anathema.

Zischek and Sindelar—sternly guarded by Monti—were particularly disadvantaged in the heavy conditions, but Smistik had a magnificent game at centre-half. The only goal was scored by the Argentinian right-winger Guaita after eighteen minutes, in a clever move that followed a corner. Later, he missed another chance to score, and Austria, who looked much more tired than the surprisingly lively Italians, did not have a shot at goal until the forty-second minute. Ferraris was in dominant form, which was as well for Italy when the Austrians turned on pressure for a quarter of an hour after the interval. In the last minute, with Italy again calling the tune, Zischek picked up a clearance by his goalkeeper, Peter Platzer, and tore through Italy's defence while the crowd watched, silent and aghast. But he shot wide, and Italy had reached the Final.

Czechoslovakia v. Germany

So did the Czechs, who beat Germany in Rome, showing clearly that the W formation, like patriotism, was not enough. They frolicked round the muscular, well-organised but uninspired Germans like Lilliputians round a Gulliver, while a curious weakness of the Germans was poor finishing. Rahn, Seeler and Muller were far away. The Germans, moreover, began the game most cautiously, both inside-forwards, rather than just one, lying deep; Hohmann, their talented inside-right, was seriously missed.

The crowd, including Mussolini in his yachting cap, was neutral and restrained as the Czechs gladly took up the initiative the Germans gave them. After twenty-one minutes Junek, the right-winger, concluded an attack which swept all the way across the forward-line with a shot which Kress could only beat out. Nejedly scored; and Czechoslovakia became a little complacent.

The second half, however, saw them regain their grip, and victory seemed inevitable—when Planicka made one of those errors which remind one of Disraeli's epigram that the defects of great men are the consolation of dunces. He simply stood and watched as a long shot by Noack, Germany's inside-left, sailed over him into goal. 1–1.

Germany, thus reprieved, pressed fiercely, and Ctyroky almost put through his own goal. Ten minutes after the equaliser, however, the forceful Puc belted a free kick from just outside the area against the bar. Krcil, the left-half, sent it back into the net. Germany collapsed, and Nejedly, taking Cambal's pass, dribbled fluently through to add the third.

Three days before the Final, Germany consoled themselves with victory in the third place match in Naples against a dejected Austria. Both teams made several changes, and Germany scored after only twenty-four seconds; another save-rebound-shoot affair, scored by Lehner. Conen got a second, Horwarth, fit again, made it 1–2, and for a while Austria made the Germans look ploddingly inadequate. But Lehner eventually scored again for Germany, and the only goal of the second half came from the Austrian left-back Seszta's thirty-yard free kick. Play became rough, but Germany survived.

The Final   Italy v. Czechoslovakia

Rome had been curiously phlegmatic about the tournament, and even for the Final there were surprising gaps on the terraces. It was perhaps a pity the game was not played in the north, for the Stadio Nazionale, with its pitch of less than regulation size, its less than 'capacity' crowd, was hardly an ideal arena.

It was known that Italy had the stamina and the power, not to mention home advantage and support, but the Czechs had wonderful skill and subtlety. The Czechs, indeed, began with some splendid, characteristically short-passing 'Danubian school' football, with Cambal, the centre-half, everywhere, Puc a great trial to the Italian right flank, Svoboda a clever inside-right. Planicka, though fate would be cruel to him again, looked authoritative in goal, ably abetted by his right-back, Zenisek. Pozzo felt that both teams were keyed up, not least his goalkeeper, Combi, and that the game was a disappointing one in consequence.

There was no goal till twenty minutes from the end. Then Puc, who had been off the field with cramp, returned to take a corner. When the ball finally came back to him, he struck a long shot to Combi's right, the goalkeeper dived late—and Italy were one down. How near the Czechs then came to making the game sure! Sobotka missed a fine chance, Svoboda banged a shot against the post. The Italian attack was stuttering: Schiavio looked tired, Guaita moved into the middle to confuse matters.

Things looked black for Italy till eight minutes from the end, when a goal dropped out of the blue. Raimondo Orsi, the Argentinian left-winger, received the ball from Guaita, ran through the Czech defence, feinted with his left foot and shot with his right. The ball, swerving crazily, brushed Planicka's desperate fingers and curled freakishly into the net. Next day, Orsi tried twenty times to repeat the shot for the benefit of photographers, with no goalkeeper in goal; and failed!

So there was extra time. Pozzo decided he wanted Schiavio and Guaita to keep switching, but such was the tumult of the ecstatic Italian fans that he was unable to make himself heard. At last he rushed around the pitch and managed to tell Guaita. The second time the switch was made it produced a goal.

Ninety-seven minutes had been played when a limping Meazza got the ball on the right wing, where the Czechs had tended to neglect him. He crossed to Guaita, who made ground and in turn found Schiavio. He, with a final effort, beat Ctyroky and shot past Planicka. When asked afterwards what strength he had called on, he said wryly, 'The strength of desperation'.

Italy had not only won the World Cup; they had made a profit of a million lire in the process. The more sceptical wondered if they would have won anywhere else. Four years later, they would get their answer.

RESULTS: Italy 1934

First round

Italy 7, United States 1 (HT 3/0)
Czechoslovakia 2, Romania 1 (HT 0/1)
Germany 5, Belgium 2 (HT 1/2)
Austria 3, France 2 (HT 1/1, 1/1) after extra time
Spain 3, Brazil 1 (HT 3/1)
Switzerland 3, Holland 2 (HT 2/1)
Sweden 3, Argentina 2 (HT 1/1)
Hungary 4, Egypt 2 (HT 2/1)

Second round

Germany 2, Sweden 1 (HT 1/0)
Austria 2, Hungary 1 (HT 1/0)
Italy 1, Spain 1 (HT 1/0, 1/1) after extra time
Italy 1, Spain 0 (HT 1/0) Replay
Czechoslovakia 3, Switzerland 2 (HT 1/1)

Semi-finals

Rome

Czechoslovakia 3	Germany 1
Planicka (capt.);	Kress; Haringer,
Burger, Ctyroky;	Busch; Zielinski,
Kostalek, Cambal,	Szepan (capt.), Bender;
Krcil; Junek, Svoboda,	Lehner, Siffling,
Sobotka, Nejedly,	Conen, Noack,
Puc.	Kobierski.

SCORERS
Nejedly (2), Krcil for Czechoslovakia
Noack for Germany
HT 1/0

Milan

Italy 1	Austria 0
Combi (capt.);	Platzer; Cisar, Seszta;
Monzeglio, Allemandi;	Wagner, Smistik
Ferraris IV, Monti,	(capt.), Urbanek;
Bertolini; Guaita,	Zischek, Bican,
Meazza, Schiavo,	Sindelar, Schall,
Ferrari, Orsi.	Viertel.

SCORER
Guaita for Italy
HT 1/0

Third place match

Naples

Germany 3	Austria 2
Jakob; Janes, Busch;	Platzer; Cisar, Seszta;
Zielinski, Muenzenberg,	Wagner, Smistik
Bender; Lehner,	(capt.), Urbanek;
Siffling, Conen, Szepan	Zischek, Braun, Bican,
(capt.), Heidemann.	Horwath, Viertel.

SCORERS
Lehner (2), Conen for Germany
Seszta for Austria
HT 3/1

Final

Rome

Italy 2	Czechoslovakia 1
(after extra time)	
Combi (capt.);	Planicka (capt.);
Monzeglio, Allemandi;	Zenisek, Ctyroky;
Ferraris IV, Monti,	Kostalek, Cambal,
Bertolini; Guaita,	Krcil; Junek, Svoboda,
Meazza, Schiavo,	Sobotka, Nejedly,
Ferrari, Orsi.	Puc.

SCORERS
Orsi, Schiavio for Italy
Puc for Czechoslovakia
HT 0/0

FRANCE
1938

Background to France

By 1938 and the third World Cup, Europe was in turmoil. The *Anschluss* had swallowed up Austria, whose best players had been greedily snatched by the German national team, while Spain was in the throes of civil war. From South America, meanwhile, Uruguay, still piqued by the refusals of 1930 and troubled by a continuing crisis of professionalism, declined to come to France; as did Argentina. The Argentinians were still sulking because France's candidature for the World Cup had been preferred to their own at FIFA's 1936 Congress at the Opera Kroll, Berlin. After coquetting with the organisers for months, they at length decided to stay at home; a decision which provoked a riot outside their federation's offices in Buenos Aires that the police had to quell.

The tournament included—for the first and only time to date—the Cubans, Poles and Dutch East Indies, while the Swedes, Romanians and Swiss were again present. The Czechs, runners-up in 1934, still had Planicka in goal, the classic Nejedly at inside-left and Kostalek at right-half. Otherwise they, like Italy, had rebuilt. Once more, despite distances and early eliminations, the competition was to follow a knock-out pattern.

The First Round

Italy were very nearly knocked out at once: in Marseilles, by the Norwegians, who had given their Olympic team an arduous run for their money. Norway, playing with six of the team which had lost only 2–1 to Italy in the Olympic semi-final, were a goal down in only the second minute. Piola found Ferrari, whose shot was dropped by the Norwegian goalkeeper. Ferraris II, the left winger, shot the ball home. R. Johansen, the Norwegian right-back, now indicated Piola to his centre-half, Eriksen, who nodded and dropped back to dedicate himself successfully to the big centre-forward, Henriksen, the little right-half, taking his place in midfield. The pendulum swung.

Brunyldsen, the mighty centre-forward, now began to set dreadful problems for the Italian defence. He was well abetted by his fast, direct left-winger, Brustad, and Kwammen, a composed inside-right. Three times post and bar were hit, and finally Brustad, in the second half, received from Brunyldsen, cut inside Monzeglio, and equalised. Soon afterwards, Brustad had the ball in the net again, to be given offside; and just before time, Olivieri made his famous save from Brunyldsen, whom Pozzo called 'a cruel thorn in my crown of roses'.

Five minutes into extra time, Piola at last evaded the Norwegian defence, when Paserati shot. Again H. Johansen could only block, and the centre-forward scored. Italy had survived their hardest match of the tournament.

The Brazilians were drawn against Poland, in Strasbourg. The game turned out to be an extraordinary one, with extra time, eleven goals, and infinite swings of the pendulum. Brazil had the classic, coloured full-back, Domingas Da Guia and the wonderfully elastic black centrefor-ward, Leonidas, scorer of four goals; the Poles had their blond inside-left Willimowski, himself the scorer of four.

At Strasbourg it was wet and muddy, but Leonidas was as dangerous as ever. In the second half, he once took off his boots and threw them dra-matically to his trainer, but the Swedish referee, Eklind, made him put them on again.

Surprisingly, the Brazilians chose no fewer than six debutants in their team, but by half-time Leonidas already had a hat trick, and his team were leading, 3–1. After this, the Polish half-backs took hold of the game, and it was Willimowski who ran riot. He scored twice, forcing extra time. Willimowski got another in the supplementary period, but goals by Leoni-das and Romeo, a coruscating inside-right, took Brazil narrowly through.

In Paris, at the Parc des Princes, it took a replay before the brave Swiss put out the Germans. In the first half, Gauchel gave Germany the lead, but Trello Abegglen, a popular figure in France after much success with Sochaux, headed in Wallaschek's centre. The second half and extra time produced no more goals.

Five days later—World Cups moved at a more leisurely pace in those days—the Swiss fielded an unchanged team. The Germans now picked three Austrians.

There were now six goals. Germany were actually 2–0 up by halftime, Hahnemann, their Austrian centre-forward, and Loertscher, with an unfortunate own goal, having scored. Wallaschek made it 2–1, and when Aebi, the Swiss left-winger, temporarily went off injured, his team increased rather than relaxed their pressure. Aebi came back, Bickel equa-lised, and the splendid Abegglen scored twice more to give Switzerland victory.

In Toulouse, Cuba, who were only there because Mexico had with-drawn, astonished the Romanians, who still had three members of their 1930 team. The result was an exciting 3–3 draw and the Cubans, unimpressed by fervent praise for their fine goalkeeper, Carvajales, dropped him from the replay. Undaunted, Carvajales called a Press conference of his own at which he promised that Cuba would win the replay: 'The Romanian game has no more secrets for us. We shall score twice, they will only score once. *Adios, caballeros.*' He proved right, though some, including the linesman and Final referee,

Georges Capdeville, thought the Cuban winner was offside.

Stalemates, indeed, proliferated. There was another at Le Havre between Czechs and Dutch; this was, however, resolved in extra time, when the loss through injury of van der Veen finally proved too much for Holland.

France, the hosts, were another team with plenty of experienced World Cup men. Thépot—who, with Delfour and Aston, had been 'chaired' by the crowd at the Gare de Lyon on his return from the 1934 World Cup—had gone. But a superb new goalkeeper had emerged in Laurent di Lorto, who had played brilliantly against the Italians earlier that season at the Parc des Princes. Delfour and Aston were still there; so was Etienne Mattler. Alfred Aston, indeed, was recalled to the right wing when Roger Courtois dropped out ill, and had a magnificent game against Belgium at Colombes. So did Jean Bastien of Marseilles, a young right-half making his debut in place of the injured Bourbotte.

France scored against their old foes in forty seconds when Badjou, Belgium's surprisingly recalled 1930 World Cup keeper, could only parry Jean Nicolas' shot, and Veinante, yet another 1930 veteran, shot home. After ten minutes, Nicolas slipped through for a second, but Isemborghs scored for Belgium in a breakaway, and it was twenty-five minutes into the second half before France made the game sure, Aston taking out two defenders and making a second goal for Nicolas.

At Reims, Hungary brushed aside the Dutch East Indies 6–0, Sarosi and Zsengeller scoring a couple each.

The Second Round

Now Italy, the holders, met their French hosts in Paris. Pozzo brought in Foni for Monzeglio, and Amedeo Biavati and Gino Colaussi on the wings, but he kept Serantoni, who had had a dreadful game in Marseilles. His confidence was rewarded, for Serantoni played with robust aplomb for the rest of the World Cup, an inspiring figure to the team.

Played at the enlarged Colombes Stadium before 58,000 fans, the match at first found both teams uneasy, remembering perhaps the 0–0 draw of the previous December. It was Piola who turned the tide. He not only threatened the French goal, but distributed the ball superbly with head and both feet, and moved cleverly to the flanks, lithe and explosive. When his opponent, the naturalised Austrian Gusti Jordan, was presumptuous enough to leave him in the second half, it proved disastrous.

Colaussi put Italy ahead after only six minutes, swerving round Bastien and sending over a cross-ball which made its way through Di

Lorto's hands and into the net. But within less than a minute Delfour found Veinante with a delightful pass, praised by Pozzo as the best of the tournament. Aston cunningly let the centre run, and Oscar Heisserer, the Alsatian inside-right, equalised.

In the second half, Piola settled matters. When Jordan and Diagne unwisely went upfield together, Biavati robbed Diagne and sent a long deep pass to Piola, who ran on to score. Next, Piola sent Colaussi down the left, a long crossfield ball found Biavati, the right-winger drew Mattler and flicked it to Piola, who headed it in.

The Swedes, managed by Joseph Nagy, a Hungarian, now annihilated the weary and inept Cubans by 8–0. Torre Keller, captain and inside-right, a survivor of the 1924 Olympic team and now aged thirty-five, made and scored a goal, while Gustav Wetterstroem, the 'bombardier of Nörrkoping', forerunner of the great Gunnar Nordahl, scored four, his flaxen hair flying.

At 5–0 the French journalist, Emmanuel Gambardella, shut his typewriter. 'Up to five goals,' he announced, 'is journalism. After that, it becomes statistics.'

At Bordeaux, where Brazil played the Czechs, there was carnage. The final toll was one broken leg—alas, the dazzling Nejedly's—one broken right arm, Planicka's, a bad stomach injury for Kostalek, lesser injuries for Peracio and Leonidas, and three expulsions, for Machados and Zeze of Brazil, and Riha, the Czech outside-right.

Soon after the start Zeze, Brazil's right-half, inexplicably and brutally kicked Nejedly, to be sent off by Hertzka, the Hungarian referee. Despite this, Brazil scored after half an hour through Leonidas. A minute from half-time, off went Riha and Machados for exchanging punches.

Fifteen minutes after the interval, Domingas Da Guia, so elegant yet so unpredictable, so opposed to what he called 'shock football' yet at times so violent, handled the ball and Nejedly, then still in one piece, scored the penalty. There were no goals in extra time, and Brazil's impertinent appeal against the result of the match was rejected.

The replay, a strange study in group psychology, was as proper and placid as the first match was violent. Georges Capdeville of France succeeded Hertzka as referee; the atmosphere might also have been helped by the fact that the Czechs chose six new players and the Brazilians nine.

So confident were the Brazilians of victory that the main party left for Marseilles, and the semi-final against Italy, before the game began! They were taken aback when Kopecky—a fine, attacking left-half, moved to inside-left to replace the irreplaceable Nejedly—scored. In the second half, however, Brazil got into their stride, played much exquisite football, and should have had many more than the two goals they scored. Leonidas, splendid again, equalised after an hour, beating Planicka's deputy, Burkert. What looked like a good goal by Senecky was not awarded when Walter, Brazil's keeper, seemed to pull the ball back from behind his goal line, and Roberto was thus able to volley the winner.

The Semi-Finals   Italy v. Brazil

Pozzo, before the game, visited the Brazilian headquarters to point out to them that they had booked every seat on the plane to Paris for the day after the match. 'What of it?' was the reply.

'Only that if you lose,' said Pozzo, 'you will have to go back to Bordeaux to play the third place match, while we go to Paris for the final.'

'But we shan't lose,' was the answer. 'We shall win in Marseilles.'

'Quite sure?' asked Pozzo.

'Quite sure.' Hubris to be punished by Nemesis.

Now, however, Brazil's self-assurance would undo them. Eight changes were made, the revenants including Zeze and Machados, the man sent off in Bordeaux, who would later, but only later, be punished.

It was a sad, bad day for the Olympian Domingas Da Guia, whose son, Ademir Da Guia, would himself play for Brazil some thirty years later. Piola, big and physical, was just the kind of player to unsettle and annoy him, while to make matters worse the fleet Colaussi streaked past him to score the first goal. For Domingas the game plainly reduced itself to a personal duel with Piola, and when, after fourteen minutes, Piola went past him again, he chopped him down. Piola made a histrionic meal of it; up came the cool captain, Meazza, to convert the penalty—an instant before his ripped shorts fell down.

That was the end of Brazil, whose two best chances went to and were missed by Peracio, standing in for Leonidas. Their one goal came, meaninglessly, from Romeo after eighty-seven minutes, at a time when the *azzurri* had relaxed. Brazil, incredibly, had 'rested' Leonidas and Tim.

Hungary v. Sweden

Sweden, christened 'the team of steel', now played Hungary at Colombes on the eightieth birthday of their monarch, Gustav v. It was of no help. Hungary, undeterred when Nyberg scored in a mere thirty-five seconds, majestically walked over them. By half-time Zsengeller had scored twice, Titkos once, and the Hungarians were so dominant that the second half was a formality. Sarosi headed a fourth, Zsengeller got the fifth; there could have been ten. 'An excellent trainmatch for the Hungarians', remarked Rudi Hiden, now keeping goal for the

Racing Club de Paris.

Three days before the Final, Sweden, without the veteran draught-splaying Keller, still held a 2–1 lead against Brazil at half-time in the third-place match at Bordeaux. In the second half Leonidas, appropriately captain for the day, scored twice, bringing his personal total to eight, the highest of the tournament. Patesko missed a penalty and Brazil won, 4–2.

The Final   Italy v. Hungary

On June 19, fifteen days after the opening match, Italy defended their Cup against Hungary at Colombes. Pozzo had chosen a pleasant retreat in St Germain-en-Laye, where all passed placidly; the team was composed and confident.

The Hungarians were at Vesinst. It was agreed that Sarosi himself had still to show his true form; but if he showed it in the Final that would be good enough. On the other hand, his one failing was a lack of devil, a distaste for physical contact, which was hardly a quality to bring success against the ever-robust Italians. Still, half a dozen of the Hungarians had World Cup experience from 1934, Zsengeller had been scoring freely, and the level of individual skill was as always exceptionally high. The players were however, inclined, to be static; nor had they the tremendous finishing power of their successors in the fifties. In the event, it was Italy's greater drive and commitment which would prevail.

Six minutes into the match, Serantoni cleared to the deep-lying Biavati, who raced almost the length of the field, employing his celebrated foot-over-the-ball feint, before finding Meazza, from whom the ball went swiftly on for Colaussi to dash in and score. There was a sweep and scope about the move which was beyond the powers of the Hungarians.

In less than a minute, however, Sarosi had touched Sas's cross to the unmarked Titkos, and it was 1–1.

But Meazza and Ferrari, Italy's inside-forwards, were still being given far too much leeway, and after fifteen minutes Meazza nonchalantly made the chance for Piola to restore Italy's lead. From this point, the more dynamic, modern Italians never lost their hold. Ten minutes from half-time the balding Ferrari, with an imperious gesture, pointed out the unmarked Colaussi to Meazza. Straight to the winger went the ball, and Colaussi sped past Polgar to get his second goal.

Twenty minutes into the second half, after a goalmouth mêlée, Sarosi unexpectedly reduced the lead, but Vincze, Locatelli and Sarosi himself were well mastered by the Italian defence, and only the left-winger Titkos gave any real trouble. Meazza and Ferrari quickly recovered their grip on midfield, Colaussi, the master of Polgar, was given plenty of the ball, and the Hungarian right flank tottered.

It was from the Italian right, however, that the last goal came, ten minutes from the end, Biavati interpassing with Piola and finally backheeling him a pass which the centre-forward smashed into goal.

Italy, most deservedly, had kept the Cup. At the end of the game Meazza wept; Monzeglio, the reluctant reserve, wept; Biavati put his head in his hands; Andreolo went round embracing everybody; and Pozzo stood uncaring while water poured from the trainer's bucket into his shoes.

There would be no more World Cups for a dozen years.

RESULTS: France 1938

First round

Switzerland 1, Germany 1 (HT 1/1, 1/1) after extra time
Switzerland 4, Germany 2 (HT 0/2) replay
Cuba 3, Romania 3 (HT 0/1, 3/3) after extra time
Cuba 2, Romania 1 (HT 0/1) replay
Hungary 6, Dutch East Indies 0 (HT 4/0)
France 3, Belgium 1 (HT 2/1)
Czechoslovakia 3, Holland 0 (HT 0/0, 0/0) after extra time
Brazil 6, Poland 5 (HT 3/1, 4/4) after extra time
Italy 2, Norway 1 (HT 1/0, 1/1) after extra time

Second round

Sweden 8, Cuba 0 (HT 4/0)
Hungary 2, Switzerland 0 (HT 1/0)
Italy 3, France 1 (HT 1/1)
Brazil 1, Czechoslovakia 1 (HT 1/1, 1/1) after extra time
Brazil 2, Czechoslovakia 1 (HT 0/1) replay

Semi-finals

Marseilles

Italy 2	**Brazil 1**
Olivieri; Foni, Rava; Serantoni, Andreolo, Locatelli; Biavati, Meazza (capt.), Piola, Ferrari, Colaussi.	Walter; Domingas Da Guia, Machados; Zeze, Martin (capt.), Alfonsinho; Lopez, Luisinho, Peracio, Romeo, Patesko.

SCORERS
Colaussi, Meazza (penalty) for Italy Romeo for Brazil
HT 2/0

Paris

Hungary 5	**Sweden 1**
Szabo; Koranyi, Biro; Szalay, Turai, Lazar; Sas, Zsengeller, Sarosi (capt.), Toldi, Titkos.	Abrahamson; Eriksson, Kjellgren; Almgren, Jacobsson, Svanstroem, Wetterstroem, Keller (capt.), Andersson, H., Jonasson, Nyberg.

SCORERS
Zsengeller (3), Titkos, Sarosi for Hungary Nyberg for Sweden
HT 3/1

Third place match

Bordeaux

Brazil 4	**Sweden 2**
Batatoes; Domingas Da Guia, Machados; Zeze, Brandao, Alfonsinho; Roberto, Romeo, Leonidas (capt.), Peracio, Patesko.	Abrahamson; Eriksson, Nilssen; Almgren, Linderholm, Svanstroem (capt.), Berssen, Andersson, H., Jonasson, Andersson, A., Nyberg.

SCORERS
Romeo, Leonidas (2), Peracio for Brazil Jonasson, Nyberg for Sweden
HT 1/2

Final

Paris

Italy 4	**Hungary 2**
Olivieri; Foni, Rava; Serantoni, Andreolo, Locatelli; Biavati, Meazza (capt.), Piola, Ferrari, Colaussi.	Szabo; Polgar, Biro; Szalay, Szucs, Lazar; Sas, Vincze, Sarosi (capt.), Zsengeller, Titkos.

SCORERS
Colaussi (2), Piola (2) for Italy Titkos, Sarosi for Hungary
HT 3/1

BRAZIL
1950

Background to Rio

The 1950 World Cup, now known officially as the Jules Rimet Trophy, was dubiously organised, ludicrously unbalanced, and produced one of the finest climaxes, as well as one of the greatest shocks, of any World Cup yet.

Hurdling the world war, it took place for the second time in South America, and for the second time there were defections and withdrawals. England at last competed.

Brazil had approached the competition with great ambitions, buoyant zeal and intensive effort—even if this was not quite intensive enough to complete in time the building of the immense three-tiered Maracanà Stadium by the banks of the little Maracanà river. This colossal edifice, with room for 200,000 spectators—the largest in the world—was still in the process of completion when the teams arrived. The very soldiers were called in, in a desperate attempt to finish it in time, but on the day of the Final itself, when 200,000 people did throng the Maracanà, its approaches still resembled a vast builder's yard.

Enthusiasm for the game in Brazil, already huge before a war in which they had been only tangentially concerned, was by now fanatical. For the poor, it was the way out of the dreadful slums of the *favelhas* which tumbled down the hills of Rio, of the remote hovels of a vast state-like Minas Gerais. Black players had long since transformed and dominated Brazilian football. Their extraordinary reflexes, at once balletic and gymnastic, their conception of the game, so radically new, so explosively effective, at one point in the tournament caused a Roman newspaper to cry: '*Come resistere?*'—How to resist?

The four British Associations had returned to FIFA in 1946, and the World Cup Committee had indulgently designated the British Championship a qualifying zone—for *two* teams. Scotland rewarded their courtesy by sullenly and indefensibly announcing that unless they won the British title they would not compete. All thus turned on their traditional meeting with England at Hampden Park in April. England won streakily with a goal by Chelsea's Roy Bentley. Bauld's shot hit the English bar, and the Scottish FA refused to change its mind. Billy Wright, the England captain, pleaded with the Scottish captain, George Young, to appeal, insisting that Scotland's presence in Brazil would make a great difference to England, but Young got nowhere.

Not that Scotland were the only team to withdraw. The Argentinians, having squabbled with the Brazilian Federation, repeated their peevish behaviour of 1938 and sourly pulled out of a tournament that this time took place on their doorstep. Czechoslovakia, too, who took a long time after the war to regain their powers, opted out in a flurry of spiteful criticism.

The case of France was rather more complex. They did not qualify, for Yugoslavia won their group, but when Turkey refused to come, after beating Syria 7–0 to gain a place, the French were invited. After all, the idea of the World Cup had been nurtured in Paris, where Jules Rimet had kept the trophy under his bed throughout the war; even if no less a pioneer than Henri Delaunay had resigned from the World Cup Committee in protest against the decision to play the tournament in pools rather than on the previous knock-out basis which had been intended.

Delaunay, as we shall see, did have a point.

France at first agreed to come, then sent an experimental team to Belgium which was whipped 4–1, lost at home to Scotland, and had second thoughts. These were exacerbated when they heard what their programme would be. Drawn in the same group as Uruguay and Bolivia, they would have to play one game at Porto Alegre, the next two thousand miles away at Recife. They sent a cable threatening to stay at home if the arrangements were not changed. The Brazilian Federation refused and, to their immense chagrin, France withdrew.

There is no doubt that the arrangement of the tournament greatly and grossly favoured Brazil, who played every one of their six matches but the second in Rio, while the other teams were obliged to traipse exhaustingly around the whole of this huge country. The idea seems to have escaped everybody that if there were groups, these should logically be centred on one place. Moreover, the muggy, humid, debilitating climate of Rio was certainly a handicap to visiting teams.

Since Portugal refused to take Scotland's place, the World Cup was left with a miserable complement of only thirteen teams; leaving the Uruguayans with merely feeble Bolivia to beat. It was extraordinary that another team could not have been moved into their pool from one of the two pools which had four; the more so as the groups had no geographical basis.

There were other, distinguished, absentees. Germany were still excluded from FIFA as a result of the war. Austria, beaten 3–0 by Sweden in the first round of the 1948 Olympiad, had limply decided that their team was too young; though it gave them the lie by beating Italy on Prater just before the competition started. By 1954, it would be too old.

Hungary, like Russia, was for the moment lurking behind the Iron Curtain.

The Contenders   Italy

Italy, the holders of the Cup, would compete even though the terrible disaster of the Superga air crash in May 1949 had largely destroyed their chances. That day the aeroplane carrying the brilliant Torino team, returning from a friendly in Lisbon on their way to a fifth consecutive Championship, crashed into the wall of a hillside monastery. Every player was killed, including eight of the current Italian national side. Among them was the splendid captain and inside-left Valentino Mazzola, whose son would be a star in the 1970 World Cup Final.

Pozzo had gone that very year, disappointed by the flight to *sistema*, the third back game, from his beloved *metodo* tactics, and disgusted by the galloping commercialisation of Italian football. In his place reigned Ferruccio Novo, the President of Torino; and, surprisingly, a Tuscan journalist, Aldo Bardelli. Bardelli, together with a number of the Italian players, refused to travel by air, and the protracted sea voyage played havoc with the condition of a team which had insufficient time to get fit again. Moreover, Bardelli and Novo quarrelled like cat and dog, and before the competition even began Bardelli had been relieved of his powers. There was talent in the team, but the auguries were bad.

Sweden

Italy played in the same group as Paraguay and Sweden. The Swedish team had been pillaged by Italian clubs after its fine Olympic victory in 1948, when four of the splendid forward-line had decamped. The team manager, an ebullient little Yorkshireman called George Raynor, had put together, with astonishing speed, a new side good enough to qualify for Brazil. A splendid guerrilla-general of a tactician—whose 1953 Swedish team, depleted again, was good enough to draw 2–2 with Hungary in Budapest mere weeks before they thrashed England at Wembley—Raynor was also much loved by his men. He had been a moderate outside-right with clubs like Rotherham and Aldershot, but the war had dramatically changed his career. Posted as a physical training instructor to the Staff College at Baghdad, he had organised an international football team with such rapid success that Stanley Rous, the progressive and internationally-minded Secretary of the English FA, had taken notice. Like good fairies, the FA whisked him in 1946 from reserve team trainer of Aldershot to the team managership of Sweden.

With his coaches' conventions—'a stewpot of brains'—his camps for 'tomorrow's men' and his devoted coaching of individual players, he made Sweden into a real power. Hans Jeppson, the imminent scourge of the Italians, was one of his protégés; Raynor had marked him early on as a potential international centre-forward and had spent hours in pressure-training on his kicking.

'Nacka' Skoglund, a Stockholmer, only just twenty years old, had emerged propitiously just in time for the World Cup. He joined AIK Stockholm from a Third Division club, playing splendidly on their tour of England; little, very blond, he was a delightful ball player with a very good left foot. Kalle Palmer, whose shooting, unexpectedly strong for one so slight, had toppled Eire in Dublin, complemented him well.

England

England's team manager, the first they had ever appointed on a full-time contract, was a very different figure. Walter Winterbottom, who took office in 1946, was a Lancashire man from Oldham; a tall, pleasant, pedagogic figure who had paid his way through Carnegie College of Physical Education by playing centre-half for Manchester United, and had reached high rank in the Royal Air Force during the war.

Fluent and dedicated, he combined with his managership the job of director of coaching, which he pursued with almost religious application, never disguising the significant fact that he considered it the more important of his tasks. Perhaps it was, for he and his followers ultimately changed the reactionary face of British football, but this was not really an attitude to go with winning World Cups. The hardened England professionals at first received Winterbottom with immense scepticism, insisting, as Stanley Matthews did in print, that an international player should be let alone to play his own game. In fact one of the chief charges against Winterbottom is precisely that he did *not* impose and apply sufficiently stringent tactics. But with all his virtues, he was never a players' man, could never bridge the gap left by his complete lack of experience of club management. Moreover, as a team manager he was responsible to a bumbling selection committee of club directors, and in a position paralleling that of a permanent civil servant who stays in office while governments fall. Sir Stanley Rous was unquestionably his mentor, and there was something a little hierarchical about the situation, a sort of officers-and-men, gentlemen-and-players, aspect which would change radically with the appointment of Alf Ramsey.

The England team he brought to Brazil was among the favourites, and was full of talent. There were Wright and Ramsey, Finney and Mortensen, Mannion and Matthews. Yes, Matthews; held in deep suspicion by the English selectors as too brilliant, too agelessly indestructible an outside-right to trust. He had been playing for England since 1934, was now thirty-five years old and as embarrassingly effective as ever. The marvellous swerve which, as he said, 'came out of him under pressure', was intact. Tom Finney, a wonderful two-footed winger in his own right, had provided the excuse for dropping him, but when Finney was chosen on the left and Matthews on the right there had been ten goals in Lisbon, four in Turin. Now grudgingly and belatedly, Matthews was recalled from the Football Association eleven's tour of North America, where they had played and beaten the USA World Cup eleven despite an exhausting train journey.

Bert Williams, the Wolverhampton goalkeeper, blond and resilient, was a splendid athlete who had ably succeeded the famous Frank Swift. Billy Wright, the fair-haired wing-half and captain, had a boyishly loyal personality that made him a perfect third man in the chain of command which devolved from Rous to Winterbottom. Ultimately winner of 105 international caps, he was not a great player but he was a very fine one, above all in defence, where he would eventually settle down as a centre-half despite his lack of height.

The inside-forwards, Stanley Mortensen and Wilf Mannion, were both possibly a little past their peak, but still players of exceptional quality. Mortensen, a north-easterner who had turned himself from a slow player into a thrillingly fast one and had survived an aeroplane crash during the war, was a fearless and prolific scorer and Matthews' partner at Blackpool. Mannion, from Middlesbrough, spanned the war with his career; a quick, inventive player who had been the best man on the field when Britain beat 'The Rest of Europe' team 6–1 in Glasgow three years earlier in the match which celebrated Britain's return to FIFA. At centre-half the big, young Laurie Hughes of Liverpool succeeded Franklin.

The other teams in the group were Spain, with fine wingers in Basora and Gainza; Chile, with George Robledo of Newcastle to lead them; and the United States.

Brazil

The new, saturnine, moustached coach of the Brazilian team, Flavio Costa, who was said to earn £1,000 a month, clearly meant there to be no repetition of 1938 and its vagaries. His team was cloistered for four months in a house just outside Rio with veranda and swimming pool, lavishly furnished from top to bottom with the gifts of Rio firms. Married men were forbidden to see their wives, bedtime was ten o'clock sharp and before it each player had to swallow a vitamin drink.

The Opening Games

The competition was given a spectacular start at the Maracanà, where the traffic jam was such that hundreds of motorists had to leave their cars and walk to the stadium. Many entrances were still not ready, others were blocked by the crowds, swarming over rubble and smashed scaffolding. When Brazil came on to the field in their white shirts with blue facings they were greeted by a twenty-one gun salute and a cacophony of fireworks let off by the crowd. Toy balloons floated into the air, Brazilian troops released 5,000 pigeons and a cascade of leaflets dropped from an aeroplane on to the pitch. The Mexicans, with a sharp sense either of self-preservation or of *comme il faut*, did not enter this maelstrom till fifteen minutes later.

The game itself was a dull one, in which Brazil scored four goals while scarcely forcing themselves at all. The powerful black Baltazar was Brazil's centre-forward for the moment, with the graceful, incisive Ademir and Jair on either side of him, and these three divided the goals, Ademir getting two.

In São Paulo, Sweden toppled Italy. The Italians were accomplices of their own defeat, for Novo picked an almost perversely unbalanced team. True, he was without the vivacious Benito ('Poison') Lorenzi, his best inside-forward, who was injured, but to replace him with a veteran left-half in Aldo Campatelli, a pre-war survivor playing out of position, was ludicrous.

Italy began well enough in front of an Italo-Brazilian crowd which was loudly behind them. Riccardo Carapellese, their clever outside-left and captain, gave them the lead after seven minutes, but by half-time Jeppson and Sune Andersson, the right-half, had scored, Jeppson got another midway through the second half. Muccinelli, the little Italian right-winger, replied and Carapellese hit the bar, but Italy were beaten. Their 'revenge' was oblique but comprehensive; eight of that Swedish side would join Italian clubs.

Now Sweden had only to draw with Paraguay at Curitiba, which they did. Italy, in São Paulo, beat Paraguay 2–0, but it was to no avail. Pool iii was Sweden's.

In Pool ii, England and Spain began with unexceptional victories. At the Maracanà England found breathing difficult but beat Chile 2–0, with goals from Mortensen in the first half and Mannion in the second. England omitted Matthews, playing Finney on the right and Jimmy Mullen, the tall, fast Wolves winger, a prodigy before the war, on the left. The attack was led by Roy Bentley, a Bristolian. He was perhaps a little too far ahead of his time for the team's good, for when playing for Chelsea he rejoiced in wandering and falling deep. England, used to a Dean or a Lawton—who had played his last international a couple of years before—were not quite geared to such subtleties.

Spain won 3–0 at Curitiba against the United States, who were captained from right-half by Eddie McIlvenny, a Scot who only eighteen months earlier had been given a free transfer by Wrexham, of the Football League's Third Division; and emigrated. Maca, the left-back, was a Belgian; Larry Gaetjens, the centre-forward, a Haitian who would disappear sadly and mysteriously in that sinister island some twenty years later.

Four of the 1948 Olympic team, which playing with a roving centre-half had lost 9–0 to Italy, were present. Now they had a good stopper in Colombo, and they astonished Spain when their clever inside-forward, John Souza, scored after seventeen minutes, a lead they held gallantly till the last ten minutes. Then Spain scored twice in two minutes through the dashing Basora, and the robust centre-forward, Zarra, so powerful in the air, made it 3–1.

Bill Jeffrey, the dedicated Scot who managed the American team, had every reason to feel proud of it. He had emigrated to the United States thirty years earlier, played for a railway works team and was then persuaded to join Penn State College as coach after playing against them. It was a temporary appointment which had lasted ever since. Combining his coaching with teaching in the machine shop, he had produced an unending series of successful teams; but none as remarkable as this World Cup side.

In Pool iv Uruguay had nothing to do but beat Bolivia, which they did 8–0 at Recife. Four goals were by Juan Schiaffino, a tall, pale, slender inside-left of great elusiveness and consummate strategic skill. Schiaffino and the right-wing pair, Alcide (Chico) Ghiggia and Julio Perez, had been members of the previous year's 'amateur' team which took part in the South American Championship, during yet another of Uruguay's endemic strikes. 'Amateur' Uruguay had lost 5–1 to Brazil, but did discover three stars. Perez was little behind Schiaffino in craft, while the hunched, thin, moustached, sunken-cheeked Ghiggia, a personification of the anti-athlete, had an acceleration, a control at speed and a right-foot shot that made him formidable.

England v. U.S.A.

For their ill-starred second match against the United States, the formality that turned out a fiasco, England travelled to Belo Horizonte. Though the little stadium, with its bumpy surface and inadequate changing facilities, was primitive—the great 100,000-stadium of today lay far in the future—England seemed otherwise to be in clover. The mountain air, by contrast with that of Rio, was invigorating, and the party stayed happily as guests of the Morro Velho gold mine, English-owned and employing 2,000 British workers. Mr Arthur Drewry, acting as sole selector, clearly had two possibilities: to regard the match as a practice run for the team which had beaten Chile, or to rest them and make use of his reserves. He chose the first alternative; and who could blame him? Subsequent criticism, the argument that he should have picked Matthews, was pure wisdom after the event. Even Bill Jeffrey admitted that the United States had no chance. Several of his players stayed up into the small hours the night before.

But for England the game would turn into the waking equivalent of an anxiety dream, in which it was impossible to do the one essential thing, the thing which should have been so farcically easy—score goals.

The day was heavy with cloud, through which the sun broke only fitfully. The England attack quickly set up camp in the American half, hit the post, shot over the bar, and all in all they seemed to be comfortably adjusting their sights. In the meantime the excellence of Borghi in goal and the resilience of the half-back line of McIlvenny, Colombo and Bahr, kept them at bay.

Then, eight minutes from half-time, the incredible happened. Bahr shot from the left, Williams seemed to have the ball covered, when in went Gaetjens with his head to deflect it out of his reach. Did he head it, or did it hit him? There were supporters of both views, but the question was irrelevant; the goal was valid. England, keeping the ball too close, shooting wide or not at all, scored none, while the clever distribution of John Souza saw to it that the defence could not relax. Once, from Ramsey's typically immaculate free kick, Mullen's header seemed to have crossed the line before it was kicked clear, but England—with Mortensen now at centre, Finney at inside-right—gained only a corner.

At the final whistle, newspapers burned on the terraces, a funeral pyre for England, and spectators rushed on to the pitch to carry the brave American team out shoulder-high.

The Pool Winners

England went back to Rio, to try their last throw against Spain. Reports had told them that the Spanish backs played square and were vulnerable to the through pass. Milburn, the perfect centre-forward to exploit this with his marvellous sprinting, was preferred to Bentley, Matthews was brought in on the right and Finney moved to the left. After fourteen minutes, Milburn headed Finney's centre past the otherwise unbeatable Spanish reserve goalkeeper Ramallets, but the goal was disallowed for offside by Italy's Signor Galeati. Newsreel photographs would show a Spanish defender putting Milburn onside, but as it was Zarra headed in Basora's centre for the winner, five minutes after half-time. So Spain won Pool III.

In Pool I there was a closer finish than had been expected. The Brazilians were pushed very hard by a Yugoslav team light years ahead of the 1930 World Cup side. Above all it possessed the essential for a W formation team, a magnificent 'quadrilateral' of wing-halves and inside-forwards: Zlatko Cjaicowski I and Djajic; Rajko Mitic and Stefan Bobek.

They had no trouble in mopping up the Swiss 3–0 in Belo Horizonte, Tomasevic scoring twice from centre; and the Mexicans 4–1 at Porto Alegre, where Cjaicowski's younger brother got two from left-wing. But these were long journeys they were making and, worse still, just before they were due to take the field in their decisive match against Brazil in Rio, Mitic cut his head on a girder.

It was decisive because Brazil, against all expectations, had slipped, dropping a point to Switzerland at São Paulo, which meant that a draw would see Yugoslavia through.

The Swiss, playing their recently adopted *verrou* formation, the fore-runner of *catenaccio*, had made only three changes from the team defeated by Yugoslavia, but it was enough to work wonders. Antenen, later a distinguished outside-right, moved from inside-right to centre; Bickel, the veteran skipper, to the right-wing, while in Jacky Fatton they had a fast, insidious left-winger. The Brazilians—faint echoes here of the 1938 semi-final—had picked something of a political team to please São Paulo, between which city and Rio their football was at that time polarised. The half-back line was completely changed to *paulistas*, of whom the strong, immaculate right-half Carlos Bauer would keep his place, Jair was hurt and Alfredo, a wing-half, played outside-right, with Maneca moving inside.

Against the rugged Swiss *verrou*, with the blond Neury a great barrier in the middle, it wasn't good enough. True, Alfredo put Brazil ahead, but Fatton met one of Bickel's strong, accurate crosses to equalise. Baltazar scored a spectacular goal to restore Brazil's advantage before half-time, but two minutes from the end, after the *verrou* had absorbed much punishment, Switzerland broke, for Tamini to make it 2–2.

For the Yugoslav match, Flavio Costa now chose the remarkable Zizinho-Ademir-Jair inside-forward trio, and chose Chico for the left-wing. Yugoslavia came out without Mitic, waited while the Mayor of Rio exhorted the teams, then turned straight round and went back to the dressing-rooms. They were pursued by Mervyn Griffiths of Wales, the referee, who ordered them back and refused to postpone the kick-off while Mitic was treated, his head cut on an exposed girder. So the unlucky Slavs began reluctantly and anxiously with ten men, and had lost a goal traumatically within three minutes, when Ademir received from Bauer and scored. When Rajko Mitic—team manager of their fine 1968 side—finally came on, wearing a huge white bandage, his subtle skills and clever probing, his fine understanding with Bobek, transformed his team, and by half-time Brazil looked a troubled side. Perhaps if Cjaicowski II had taken a marvellous chance to equalise, things might have been different, but he missed it. Within minutes Bauer had found Zizinho, who dribbled his sinuous, irresistible way through Yugoslavia's defence to make it 2–0.

The following day, Uruguay and Spain came through; these three and Sweden would make up the final pool.

The idea of having a final pool was a strange one which has never since been adopted. The trouble with a World Cup is that it is precisely that; a *cup* competition, greatly restricted in duration, in which luck and injuries have little time to level out, however you arrange things. Sometimes, as in the three pre-war World Cups, the three won by Brazil, and perhaps that won in 1966 by England, the strongest team prevails. But on other occasions, as in 1950 and again in 1954, there were dramatic upheavals.

Final Pool Matches   Brazil v. Sweden; Brazil v. Spain

Sweden were Brazil's first victims. George Raynor's plan was to seek an early goal—the goal he and Sweden would get in the 1958 World Cup Final—and 'We had two chances before they even moved.' But both were missed, and in the nineteenth minute a hopeful shot by Ademir beat Svensson, after which—the deluge.

Brazil now played the football of the future, an almost surrealist game, tactically unexceptional but technically superb, in which ball players of genius, while abrogating none of their own right to virtuosity and spectacle, found an exhilarating *modus vivendi*.

Before half-time, Ademir had scored his second goal, while Chico added the third. The second half was sheer exhibition: Ademir brought his total to four, Chico his to two, while Maneca's goal made seven. All Sweden could muster was a penalty by Sune Andersson, their right-half.

Spain were next on the chopping block, tired after their fine, close match against Uruguay. Brazil thrashed them, with Eizaguirre back in goal for splendid Ramallets, 6–1; 3–0 at half-time. Jair and Chico scored a couple each, Zizinho one, Parra an own goal, Ademir none at all.

That meant four points to Brazil, while Uruguay had with difficulty amassed three; a draw would thus give Brazil a Cup which seemed as good as theirs.

Uruguay v. Spain; Uruguay v. Sweden; Spain v. Sweden

On July 9, while Brazil were annihilating Sweden, Uruguay were just holding out in a dramatic match against Spain in São Paulo. It was a rough game, full of the Spanish temper, but kept under control and saved as an admirable match by the refereeing of Mervyn Griffiths.

Uruguay, whose swift, skilled forwards always troubled the rather heavy, third back Spanish defence, took the lead through Ghiggia. But with Igoa and Molowny a fine, foraging pair of inside-forwards in the best W formation manner, Basora setting Andrade problems on the wing, Spain were 2–1 ahead by half-time; both goals Basora's. Meanwhile, the two Gonzalvos and the gymnastic Ramallets were keeping Uruguay's attack at bay.

In the second half, the inspiring Varela drove the Uruguayans forward, just as he would against Brazil, and eighteen minutes from the end he himself thundered into the Spanish penalty area to equalise.

In their second game, once more at São Paulo, Uruguay were lucky to get the better of Sweden, who also held a 2–1 lead against them at half-time. The determining factor was probably the weariness of Skoglund, who made little contribution; nor were Sweden helped when a bad foul by Matthias Gonzales put Johnsson, their right-winger, off the field for an extended period.

Though the Uruguayans were both immeasurably fresher and technically much superior to the Swedes, they never dominated them. Kalle Palmer even gave his team the lead after five minutes for Ghiggia to equalise, but Sundqvist, the fast Swedish left-winger, like Ghiggia, would play for Roma—made it 2–1. Sweden, however, had shot their bolt, and two goals in the second half by Miguez, the Uruguayan centre-forward, gave them a bare 3–2 win.

For their last match, against Spain, Raynor switched his team's wingers, brought in Rydell for Skoglund, while Bror Mellberg, already standing in for Jeppson, moved to inside-right. The result, again in São Paulo, was a splendid 3–1 win over Spain.

Brazil v. Uruguay

If you are going to have a cup at all, you had better have a Cup Final. The odd thing was that in 1950, though no provision was made for one, the Brazil-Uruguay match which decided things was such a thriller, such a glorious climax, that no official Final could have done its job better. Indeed, people still talk about it, erroneously if understandably, as the Final.

Though Flavio Costa showed anything but over-confidence, the mood in Brazil before the decisive match with Uruguay was one of bounding euphoria. How could they lose? How, indeed, could they do anything but win? The intricate, galvanic combination of their inside-forward trio, Zizinho, Ademir and Jair, was devastating. One move, which Raynor had particularly admired, was especially unusual and effective. To vary the normal method of attack—short passes alternating with deeper, sharply-angled balls to the wings, sometimes over twenty yards—Ademir would pass back to the dominating Bauer. Bauer would wait, foot on the ball, while Zizinho in his relaxed, loping way would trot back like an obedient dog to take it from him.

'The Uruguayan team,' warned Costa presciently, 'has always disturbed the slumbers of Brazilian footballers. I'm afraid that my players will take the field on Sunday as though they already had the Championship shield sewn on their jerseys. It isn't an exhibition game. It is a match like any other, only harder than the others.'

Colonel Volpe of the Uruguayan delegation remained sturdily sanguine, reminding those who spoke to him that Uruguay had already beaten Brazil once that year.

Vittorio Pozzo, present this time not as a combatant but as a journalist, was staggered by the address made by the Governor of the state of Rio at the Maracanà, immediately before the game.

'You Brazilians, whom I consider victors of the tournament . . . you players who in less than a few hours will be acclaimed champions by millions of your compatriots . . . you who have no equals in the terrestrial hemisphere . . . you who are so superior to every other competitor . . . you whom I already salute as conquerors.' The Uruguayans, long before the eulogy had ended, were clearly fretting. Finally, the teams lined up; and Brazil attacked.

With most of the immense crowd roaring them forward, they beat against a Uruguayan defence in which, for the moment, the huge Varela played a wholly destructive part. If he was marvellously resilient, the little, black Andrade was no less stalwart, while Maspoli performed acrobatic prodigies in goal. Time and again, Zizinho, Ademir and Jair, that terrifying trio, worked their sinuous way through the blue walls of Uruguay's defence. Time and again, a last-ditch tackle by Andrade or Varela, an interception by the flying Maspoli, frustrated them. In the sixteenth minute there was a tremendous mêlée in the Uruguayan area, but Andrade strode into the middle of it and cleared. Seven minutes later Jair let fly a tremendous shot, only for Maspoli to leap across his goal and deflect it for a corner. There was another massed onslaught on the Uruguayan goal, this time thwarted at last by Varela, glad to kick upfield.

The respite was short. Soon Friaça was taking Brazil's third corner of the match and shooting when the ball came back to him out of the vortex, only for Maspoli to hurl himself among the lunging legs and turn it for another corner. Next minute Ademir, deadliest shot of the competition, was left alone in front of goal; the shot was powerful and well placed, but again Maspoli somehow reached it.

It was just about now that Uruguay, shaking themselves like a great dog, began at last to come into the game. Barbosa, the agile black Brazilian goalkeeper who had virtually been watching the game, now found himself in sudden, desperate movement as Ghiggia and Miguez broke to make a chance for Schiaffino, whose raking shot forced Barbosa to leap mightily.

Brazil retaliated at once, forcing another corner, at which Jair banged a shot against the post. Now Maspoli performed new heroics, saving from Ademir, diving wonderfully to a low shot by Zizinho.

The last seven minutes of the half saw a relaxing of the Brazilian pressure, a time out of war for Uruguay's defence. Three times their attack got away for a shot and there were substantial straws in the wind by half-time.

But they were forgotten two minutes after the restart when the Uruguayan citadel fell at last. Ademir and Zizinho, working the ball quickly and cleverly, drew Uruguay's defence left, switched it right, and there was Friaça, running in to shoot in full stride—and score.

The goal had come too late to demoralise Uruguay. They had held out long enough, ultimately launched sufficient attacks, to be quite sure the Brazilians were mortal. Their response to the blow was not to crumble but to hit back vigorously, and while the crowd was distracted by the grim sight of a corpse being taken away on a stretcher, the Uruguayan forwards set about Brazil's defence. After two raids had been beaten off, Schiaffino's typically precise through pass sent Perez away for a rocketing shot which Barbosa reached only with his fingertips. Now Varela had definitively committed himself to attack. Brazil's wingers, thus given more space, enjoyed it briefly, Andrade having to recover superbly to tackle the galloping Friaça. But Ademir, waving his arms urgently to encourage his colleagues, seemed to realise something was amiss.

After twenty minutes Uruguay struck again; and scored a goal which had long been in the wind. Varela trundled the ball into the Brazilian half before sending little Ghiggia flying down the right, where he was now the master of inadequately covered Bigode. The winger's centre reached a totally unmarked Schiaffino who, after four strides, let fly a shot Barbosa had no hope of saving.

Brazil kicked off; but the virtue, the *brio*, had gone out of them. It was Varela who bestrode the field, nonchalant and indomitable, masterfully breaking up and launching attacks, the old-school centre-half *par excellence*.

After thirty-four minutes of the half Ghiggia received a pass and found Perez, who shook off Jair, made ground, and returned the ball to Ghiggia.

Once more Brazil's left flank was turned. Ghiggia ran on to the ball, shot—and it was in the net again. Uruguay led, 2–1.

Moments later, by some trick of the sun, Maspoli's goal was bathed in light, as if to symbolise the victory. In the last minute even Augusto, Brazil's captain and right-back, was in the Uruguayan penalty area, but there was no breaching that defence. Mr Reader, the referee and consummate master of the occasion, blew his whistle; and the World Cup, after twenty years, had returned to Montevideo.

RESULTS: Brazil 1950

Pools I, II, III, IV

Brazil 4, Mexico 0 (HT 1/0)
Yugoslavia 3, Switzerland 0 (HT 3/0)
Yugoslavia 4, Mexico 1 (HT 2/0)
Brazil 2, Switzerland 2 (HT 2/1)
Brazil 2, Yugoslavia 0 (HT 1/0)
Switzerland 2, Mexico 1 (HT 2/0)

	P	W	D	L	GOALS F	A	Pts
Brazil	3	2	1	0	8	2	5
Yugoslavia	3	2	0	1	7	3	4
Switzerland	3	1	1	1	4	6	3
Mexico	3	0	0	3	2	10	0

Spain 3, United States 1 (HT 0/1)
England 2, Chile 0 (HT 1/0)
United States 1, England 0 (HT 1/0)
Spain 2, Chile 0 (HT 2/0)
Spain 1, England 0 (HT 0/0)
Chile 5, United States 2 (HT 2/0)

	P	W	D	L	GOALS F	A	Pts
Spain	3	3	0	0	6	1	6
England	3	1	0	2	2	2	2
Chile	3	1	0	2	5	6	2
United States	3	1	0	2	4	8	2

Sweden 3, Italy 2 (HT 2/1)
Sweden 2, Paraguay 2 (HT 2/1)
Italy 2, Paraguay 0 (HT 1/0)

	P	W	D	L	GOALS F	A	Pts
Sweden	2	1	1	0	5	4	3
Italy	2	1	0	1	4	3	2
Paraguay	2	0	1	1	2	4	1

Uruguay 8, Bolivia 0 (HT 4/0)

	P	W	D	L	GOALS F	A	Pts
Uruguay	1	1	0	0	8	0	2
Bolivia	1	0	0	1	0	8	0

Final pool matches

São Paulo

Uruguay 2	**Spain 2**
Maspoli; Gonzales, M.,	Ramallets; Alonzo,
Tejera; Gonzales, W.,	Gonzalvo II; Gonzalvo
Varela (capt.), Andrade;	III, Parra, Puchades;
Ghiggia, Perez, Miguez,	Basora, Igoa, Zarra,
Schiaffino, Vidal.	Molowny, Gainza.

Ghiggia, Varela for Uruguay
Basora (2) for Spain
HT 1/2

Rio

Brazil 7	**Sweden 1**
Barbosa; Augusto	Svensson; Samuelsson,
(capt.), Juvenal; Bauer,	Nilsson, E.; Andersson,
Danilo, Bigode;	Nordahl, K., Gard;
Maneca, Zizinho,	Sundqvist, Palmer,
Ademir, Jair, Chico.	Jeppson, Skoglund,
	Nilsson, S.

SCORERS
Ademir (4), Chico (2), Maneca for Brazil
Andersson (penalty) for Sweden
HT 3/0

São Paulo

Uruguay 3	**Sweden 2**
Paz; Gonzales, M.,	Svensson; Samuelsson,
Tejera; Gambetta,	Nilsson, E.; Andersson,
Varela (capt.), Andrade;	Johansson, Gard;
Ghiggia, Perez, Miguez,	Johnsson, Palmer,
Schiaffino, Vidal.	Mellberg, Skoglund,
	Sundqvist.

SCORERS
Ghiggia, Miguez (2) for Uruguay
Palmer, Sundqvist for Sweden
HT 1/2

Rio

Brazil 6	**Spain 1**
Barbosa; Augusto	Eizaguirre; Alonzo,
(capt.), Juvenal; Bauer,	Gonzalvo II; Gonzalvo
Danilo, Bigode; Friaça,	III, Parra, Puchades;
Zizinho, Ademir, Jair,	Basora, Igoa, Zarra,
Chico.	Panizo, Gainza.

SCORERS
Jair (2), Chico (2), Zizinho, Parra (own goal)
for Brazil
Igoa for Spain
HT 3/0

São Paulo

Sweden 3   **Spain 1**

Svensson; Samuelsson,   Eizaguirre; Asensi,
Nilsson, E., Andersson,   Alonzo; Silva, Parra,
Johansson, Gard;   Puchades; Basora,
Sundqvist, Mellberg,   Fernandez, Zarra,
Rydell, Palmer   Panizo, Juncosa.
Johnsson.

SCORERS
Johansson, Mellberg, Palmer for Sweden
Zarra for Spain
HT 2/0

Rio

Uruguay 2   **Brazil 1**

Maspoli; Gonzales, M.,   Barbosa; Augusto (capt.),
Tejera; Gambetta,   Juvenal; Bauer,
Varela (capt.), Andrade;   Danilo, Bigode; Friaça,
Ghiggia, Perez, Miguez,   Zizinho, Ademir, Jair,
Schiaffino, Moran.   Chico.

SCORERS
Schiaffino, Ghiggia for Uruguay
Friaça for Brazil
HT 0/0

Final positions

	P	W	D	L	GOALS F	A	Pts
Uruguay	3	2	1	0	7	5	5
Brazil	3	2	0	1	14	4	4
Sweden	3	1	0	2	6	11	2
Spain	3	0	1	2	4	11	1

SWITZERLAND
1954

Background to Switzerland

If the result of the 1950 World Cup was a shock, that of the 1954 World Cup was a cataclysm. Never had there been so hot, so inevitable, a favourite as Hungary; the team which had brought new dimensions and horizons to the game. For the past few years, since they had ended a long sojourn behind the Iron Curtain by coming out to win the 1952 Helsinki Olympic title, they had been, quite simply, unbeatable. They had squared the circle, solved football's equivalent of the riddle of the Sphinx: how to reconcile the traditional skills, the supreme technique, of Continental football with the strength and shooting power of the British.

Since Poland had scratched, the Hungarians had not even been obliged to win a match to qualify. They were grouped with the West Germans—now readmitted to the World Cup, still under the shrewd command of little Sepp Herberger—and the Turks.

The World Cup Committee, in its doubtful wisdom, had devised a new eliminating scheme whose complexity was rivalled only by its illogicality. Instead of putting a total of four countries in four groups and getting each group to play the others, it seeded two teams in each group and kept them apart, each being thus obliged to play only the two unseeded teams. Since equality on points became highly probable it was laid down, first, that teams level at full-time would play extra time, and second, that if at the end of the group two teams were still level, they would play-off. It was this tortuous, fatuous arrangement which produced the ultimate anomaly of Germany winning the Final against a Hungarian team that had previously beaten them 8–3.

Switzerland itself was a curious choice for the staging of a World Cup, and in the event the task was too great. Though the crowds were encouragingly large, thanks no doubt to Switzerland's accessibility, organisation was haphazard and the excesses of the Swiss police sometimes unpleasant.

The Contenders Germany

At the start, Germany were not much fancied. Their team had qualified with some ease against Norway and the Saar, and was built round players from Kaiserslautern. Above all there was the thirty-three-year-old captain and inside-forward, Fritz Walter, an admirable player, not quite presaging the extraordinary, more spectacular Netzer, but certainly a very skilled ball player and a fine, economical, strategist, with an excellent shot besides. Otmar Walter, his brother, played at centre-forward, while Horst Eckel, the versatile right-half, was another Kaiserslautern man.

Uruguay

Uruguay, the Cup holders, had another strong team, though now they were no longer an unknown quantity. There were a couple of splendid new wingers in Julio Abbadie, succeeding the frail Alcide Ghiggia, and Carlo Borges, while even the excellent Julio Perez had been surpassed and replaced, at inside-right, by Xavier Ambrois. The massive Varela was still there, fourteen years after his first cap, as were Andrade, Maspoli, Miguez and the incomparable Schiaffino.

The Uruguayans were seeded in Pool III with Austria, Scotland and the Czechs making up the number. The Czechs, who had qualified against Bulgaria and Romania, were still far from regaining their pre-war stature.

Austria

Austria—such seemed to be their fate in World Cups—were marginally over the crest. Three years before, they had had what was probably the best team in Europe, playing the old *metodo* game, pivoting in the classical way round a marvellous, attacking centre-half in Ernst Ocwirk, who was still their captain. Ocwirk, tall, muscular and dark, the possessor of a wonderfully strong and accurate left foot and impeccable technique, was ironically a supporter of the third back game. Now he had had his wish fulfilled; Austria had espoused it at last. Uruguay still hadn't, but Brazil had.

Scotland

Scotland, having finished second to England in a British championship which doubled as a World Cup qualifying group, this time deigned to compete. They also broke with custom by appointing Andrew Beattie, their former celebrated left-back and manager of Huddersfield Town, as team manager. Unfortunately, the players themselves were a poor lot. Lawrie Reilly, the lively Hibernian forward, was ill, and there was no obvious goalkeeper, the job going to Fred Martin of Aberdeen. Willie Fernie, the Celtic inside-right, was a player of undoubted technical gifts but most doubtful consistency; his club colleague, Neil Mochan, was a centre-forward who had returned to Scotland after failing in English football.

Tommy Docherty, the fair-haired, powerful Preston North End wing-half, was a footballer of bite and intelligence, deeply interested in foreign football, who would afterwards praise Schiaffino as the finest inside-forward he had ever met. But even in prospect the general impression was one of honest mediocrity.

England

England were grouped with Belgium and Switzerland, with Italy the other seeded team. Their selectors chose a ridiculous team in which two men—Peter Harris, outside-right, and Bedford Jezzard, centre-forward—were winning their first caps.

Matthews, now aged thirty-nine, and still good enough to shame the selectors with his untarnished excellence, had again been grudgingly recalled to the colours at the last moment. There was no successor at centre-half to Neil Franklin, after four uneasy years; if the backs had been defenestrated, Gil Merrick had been retained as goalkeeper.

Tom Finney was still about; Nat Lofthouse, the squat, strong Bolton centre-forward, with bags of courage and a fierce left foot in addition to his ability in the air, would lead the line. Ivor Broadis, a Londoner who had begun with Spurs and then made a name as the clever player-manager of Carlisle before joining Sunderland and other leading clubs, was at inside-forward; a neat prompter with a good shot. Once again the captain was Billy Wright, who would gain new fame in a new position.

Brazil, Yugoslavia and France

Brazil, with Pinheiro as a third back and Zeze Moreira as their sternly dedicated manager, came without their marvellous 1950 trio, Zizinho, Ademir and Jair. Of these only Zizinho was a possible choice, but he had been rigorously passed over in favour of less exotic players. One of these was the black Didi, master of the swerving free kick. Baltazar, another negro, was back again at centre-forward, and there was a formidable new outside-right in Julinho.

At full-back the two Santoses—stalwart, black Djalma and tall, strong, stylish Nilton—would play, while Bauer, a hero of 1950, would captain the team from wing-half. Yugoslavia and feeble Mexico would make up the pool, the fourth team being France.

The Yugoslavs, who had given Brazil such a run for their money in Rio, had taken full points in a qualifying group with Israel and Greece, but scored a mere four goals. They had developed a spectacular new goalkeeper called Vladimir Beara, who had once briefly studied ballet, and had all the associated attributes. Zlatko Cjaicowski was captain again, Mitic and Bobek resumed at inside-forward, while there was a resourceful new left-half in Boskov and a superb left-winger in the versatile Branko Zebec.

The French team had a talented half-back line in Penverne, Jonquet and Marcel, the young, emerging Raymond Kopa at outside-right, Jean Vincent on the left wing. They too had taken maximum qualifying points, against Eire and Luxembourg.

Italy

Italy arrived in some turmoil. All had gone right, now all had suddenly been going wrong.

Lajos Czeizler, an elderly, *rusé* Hungarian, had built his qualifying team on the so called *blocco viola*; that is on the Fiorentina defence. This had not pleased the Milanese fans, and Czeizler abandoned his previous attacking principles, recalling the vulpine, veteran Capello and making the slim Carlo Galli of Roma his centre-forward. Though Italian football had not yet succumbed to the dreadful dead hand of *catenaccio*, with its manic defensive posture, pressures were enormous, economics arcane.

Still, there was Benito 'Poison' Lorenzi, the Tuscan with the forked tongue, whose control, imagination and finishing power had been so valuable to Inter. There was the handsome, blond, olive-skinned, blue-eyed *jeune premier* Giampiero Boniperti of Juventus, whom the Agnelli—of Fiat—would later make into a millionaire and who, captaining club and country, would later become Juventus' very President. Giorgio Ghezzi, nicknamed 'Kamikhaze', was a brave and elastic goalkeeper; and surely Switzerland and Belgium formed no great obstacle?

Unfortunately Czeizler, despite his outward appearance of middle European aplomb and sophistication, simply lost control in Switzerland, picking ridiculous teams—or allowing them to be picked for him—and letting discipline go to the winds. By the time the team was ensconced in its picturesque *ritiro* outside Basel for the play-off, anarchy reigned.

Hungary

Puskas, Kocsis, Hidegkuti, Bozsik; these were the names, the men, around whom the extraordinary Hungarian team was built. Ferenc Puskas, nicknamed the 'Galloping Major' in England for his army rank, was the captain, the star of stars, a squat little Budapest urchin-figure, plastered hair parted down the middle, with superb control, supreme strategy, and above all a left-footed shot which was unrivalled in the world, dangerous from any distance up to thirty-five yards.

Sandor Kocsis—'Golden Head'—a smaller and more delicate player than Puskas, was just as formidable when the ball was in the air; another accomplishment in which foreign footballers could previously never match the British, with their Lawtons, Deans and Lofthouses.

Nandor Hidegkuti had perfected a quite new concept of centre-forward play. His secret was that he not only lay deep much of the time, allowing Kocsis and Puskas to work as a double spearhead and to ply them with clever passes; he was also deadly when he broke upfield, to make use of his own tremendous right-foot shot.

In midfield—a term which then still lay in the future—Hidegkuti had the vigorous assistance of the team's right-half, Josef Bozsik, a driving, attacking player, with strength, confidence and, of course, superb control; his side's chief dynamo.

On the wings there were excellent players, little behind these three, in Budai II on the right, and the fast and incisive Zoltan Czibor on the left.

Gyula Grosics, the goalkeeper, was a player of particular importance, not only because he was an excellent and supple performer beneath the bar, good with crosses, but because he was so ready to tear out of his penalty area to kick clear as an extra back.

Though nobody applied the term at the time, it can be seen with hind-sight that Hungary's tactics were an early version of 4–2–4. Zakarias, the left-half, was always tucked in beside his burly centre-half Lorant, leaving Bozsik to roam the area of midfield. The tendency of Hidegkuti to go up as well as back, however, was a major variant.

The Hungarian backs, Buzansky and Lantos, were big, muscular players who did not stand on ceremony. The tendency was to say that Hungary's attack carried its defence, but if the record were analysed the 'goals against' were relatively few.

Over this remarkable team presided the Deputy Minister of Sport, Gustav Sebes, and under him a coach, Gyula Mandi. Training was varied and inventive, and the players were encouraged to practise athletics, even mountaineering. Needless to say there was great emphasis on training with the ball—still, amazingly, a rare thing in bizarrely conservative Britain—and 'match situations' were re-created in practice.

It seemed as if, having harnessed finishing power to their new Sarosis, Orths, and Konrads, Hungary had produced a type of superfoot-baller, had found a way of preparation which was ideal. Yet when the smoke cleared, when Puskas and Kocsis decamped a couple of years later, it became perfectly clear that all we had been seeing was an illustration of Walter Winterbottom's dictum that every great team is built round a core of great players. While Kocsis and company were present, every man looked a giant, Sebes was a wizard, Mandi an inspired manager. When they went, the fabulous structure of Hungarian football proved to be nothing of the sort; the lean years began.

The Opening Matches

The Hungarians began by scoring seventeen goals in their first two games. Ultimately more significant was the fact that in the second, against West Germany, they lost Puskas, kicked by the big, blond German centre-half, Werner Liebrich. In retrospect, it was the kick that won the World Cup. Puskas would later vow it was deliberate. Observers felt that the tackle was at least harsh.

Hungary found no great difficulty in scoring nine goals against South Korea in Zurich. Kocsis and Puskas scored five between them and Lantos, the burly left-back, belted a free kick through the Korean wall.

West Germany, having easily beaten Turkey 4–1 in Berne, virtually threw away the Hungarian match in Basel. All the German forwards but Fritz Walter scored for Germany, the first goal going to Berni Klodt, for the moment their right-winger. In the wings lurked the brawny, dark-haired Helmut Rahn, belatedly recalled in the nick of time from Montevideo, where he had played superbly for his club, Rot Weiss Essen, when they beat Penarol—who had offered him a prodigious contract.

The team annihilated 8–3 by Hungary at Basel was not quite the scratch side some later called it. For one thing, it included Rahn himself, scorer of the third German goal; an augury to which few can have paid attention. For another, it introduced at centre-half Liebrich, who would regain his place in the quarter-final. But it cannot be pretended that Germany played flat out. Even with Puskas off the field for an hour with his injured ankle, it was a Hungarian picnic; especially for Kocsis, who scored four. The Germans then made seven changes of personnel and thrashed Turkey 7–1 in Zurich, with Morlock, the strongly-built inside-right, scoring three. Clearly their Hungarian experience had left no trauma.

England began with a curious game against Belgium in Basel; one awash with goals. The Belgians had eliminated Sweden, hopelessly denuded of their stars by Italian clubs, and had beaten Yugoslavia in Zagreb. They had two admirable centre-forwards in Anderlecht's great-hearted Jef Mermans, who now played on the right wing, and Rik Coppens, the well-sprung Beerschot leader, famous for the skill he showed with his back to the goal.

This game, like many others, was televised. Television would now become a potent reality in the World Cup; not always, as we shall see, for the better. The beginnings, in 1954, were modestly substantial; by

1970 the television audience for the Final had built up to a stupendous 800 million.

For the English television audience at least, the game was a disappointment, even though there was consolation in the splendour of Matthews, sinuously beating opponents, cleverly making openings, a complete forward and footballer whose suggestions were all too often spurned.

The English team, lamented *The Times*, were 'like those rare children of light who can pass through any experience protected by a sheath of impenetrable innocence'. The blond, versatile Pol Anoul shot Belgium into the lead from the irrepressible Coppens' pass after only five minutes. England responded with three goals. After twenty-five minutes an admirable through pass from Billy Wright sent Broadis through to equalise. Nat Lofthouse, with a spectacular diving header, gave them the lead and in the second half, after Taylor of Manchester United should have had a penalty, Broadis made it 3–1 with a deflected shot.

The match looked signed, sealed and delivered; but then the English defence, in which Luton's Sid Owen was a shaky centre-half and Merrick a porous goalkeeper, collapsed twice, allowing first Anoul and then Coppens to make it 3–3. Another remarkable burst by Matthews, finishing this time with the untypical crescendo of a fine shot, almost restored the lead, but Gernaey seized the ball under the crossbar.

So there was extra time, and a very quick goal for England; a dummy by Taylor, a square pass by Broadis, a strong, high shot by Lofthouse. The crowd, steadily pro-British throughout the series, seemed relieved; but then Jimmy Dickinson, the quiet, consistent Portsmouth left-half, headed Dries' long free kick into his own goal. 4–4. Billy Wright, significantly, spent the closing minutes at centre-half, with Owen limping on a wing with cramp. Wright would stay there for five distinguished years.

The previous day, a Scottish team showing plenty of fight had lost 1–0 to Austria in Zurich. The defence played strongly and well; the forwards might have had two goals: once when Ernst Happel flung Mochan to the ground in the penalty area—but the kick was given outside it—and once in the very last minute. Willie Ormond, the clever Hibernian left-winger, crossed the ball, Alan Brown backheeled, Neil Mochan shot through a crowd of players. The ball struck Happel, and as Schmied, Austria's goalkeeper, plunged, it hit his hand, rolled up his arm: he finally seized it just the right side of the line.

So the goal which Probst had coolly scored, taking a return pass from Alfred Koerner to beat Martin after thirty-three minutes, won the game.

What Scotland had lacked in finesse they had largely made up in spirit, but now came disaster. Andy Beattie resigned. He would go, he said, immediately after the second game, which was to take place in Basel against the champions, Uruguay. The implication was that the Scottish officials, having gone as far as appointing a team manager, could not bring themselves far enough to let him manage. The immediate consequences would be atrocious.

Uruguay had not begun well. In Berne, they had beaten the Czechs 2–0 on an unfamiliar, muddy pitch, presenting Abbadie, Borges and Ambrois in attack, and the powerful, fair-haired José Santamaria as stopper. So far, indeed, did he sometimes fall behind the rest of his defence that he virtually became a sweeper. The champions did not score till Miguez headed in Ambrois' centre twenty minutes from time. Schiaffino adding a second with a thundering free kick; one of those shots which belied the slenderness of his limbs.

In Basel, the Uruguayans simply cut the Scots to pieces; ridiculed them, toyed with them, humiliated them. The 'vulnerable' defence contained Scotland's plodding forwards without difficulty, while Scotland's own defenders, in the words of an English critic, 'stood around like Highland cattle'.

'They will die in the sun,' predicted Vittorio Pozzo before the kick-off—and, metaphorically at least, he was right. Schiaffino quite simply bestrode the field, his swerve and footwork baffling Scotland's defence, his passes splitting it time and again. To such delectable promptings Abbadie and Borges responded with glee, running the Scottish backs ragged. Obdulio Varela, huge-thighed and ubiquitous, made nonsense of the fact that, at thirty-nine, he was a few months older even than Stanley Matthews. Rodriguez Andrade, on the right flank now, distributed the ball immaculately and controlled it effortlessly. Again one was told that the defensive system 'left gaps', though a more obvious inference was that the system as a whole was flexible, and would open or close, oyster-like, according to the circumstances.

Not one of Uruguay's seven goals was headed. Borges and Miguez scored in the first half, while in the second Borges and Abbadie got a couple each, Miguez another. The last of all, ten minutes from time, saw Abbadie dribble round both Scottish backs and then Martin, the goalkeeper. With their glorious technique, their bewildering changes of pace—an ability they shared with the Hungarians—Uruguay had taken Scotland back to school. Most ironically, it was in Scotland itself that such football had been conceived.

Italy, meanwhile, were having vertiginous ups and downs. Their first game, held in Lausanne, was narrowly lost to Switzerland when it might have been won. The Swiss, who had drawn 3–3 with Uruguay a month before the tournament, had less of the play, but prevailed through enthusiasm, while the erratic refereeing of Brazil's Viana led to chaos. 'An English or Scottish referee,' wrote the doyen of French critics, Gabriel Hanot, 'would have given two or three penalties in the first half against the Swiss, and would have sent the two Italian backs Vincenzi and Giacomazzi off in the second.' Galli and Boniperti were dumped or obstructed time and time again without let or hindrance, till the Italians decided on lynch-law, Fatton being kicked in the stomach and Flueckiger in the back.

Twenty-four minutes into the second half, when Benito Lorenzi scored a goal which would have made it 2–1 for Italy but was given by Viana as offside, there was pandemonium.

The goal looked a perfectly good one to most people, and there were those who thought Viana's decision had been influenced by the way Lorenzi had been chiding him throughout the game. After a limpid movement, Galli drove Pandolfini's pass against a post, and Lorenzi finished the job; only for the goal to be denied.

One then, as the *Corriere della Sera* put it, 'witnessed one of those scenes which often occur on our grounds, the players swarming round the referee, some tearing their hair, some eating the grass in their desperation. Boniperti was the fiercest towards Viana, who in his turn vigorously shoved the *azzurri* away until the little storm had blown over.'

So, some twelve minutes from time, when Giacomazzi missed a pass by Jacky Fatton, Hugi was able to beat Ghezzi for the winner.

The Italians now made three changes and, on the familiar territory of Lugano, thrashed a wearied Belgian team 4–1, to force a play-off with Switzerland. The star of the Italian attack was the vivacious Lorenzi, switched to the centre from the right wing after thirty-five minutes. This time when he scored, in the second half, the goal was allowed, and he might have had several more, in a dazzling performance.

Switzerland, meanwhile, lost 2–0 to a far from exceptional English team on a boiling hot afternoon in Berne. England made a number of changes, the most significant of which was the moving of Billy Wright to centre-half, where he had a dominating game. Matthews and Lofthouse were unfit, so the Wolverhampton left-wing pair of Dennis Wilshaw and the veteran Jimmy Mullen, in his fifteenth year as a professional, played. Tommy Taylor, who would die so wretchedly at Munich four years later, led the attack, while Bill McGarry (Huddersfield) was successfully capped at right-half. Merrick, encouragingly but, as it proved, deceptively, had a much better game in goal.

The most distinguished features of the match were the goals scored by Wolves' left wing. Mullen, receiving Taylor's flick three minutes from half-time, went round Parlier, the goalkeeper, for the first. Midway through the second half, Dennis Wilshaw calmly and cleverly

evaded Eggimann, Bocquet and Neury, before beating Parlier, too. So
much, it seemed, for the Swiss *catenaccio*; Italy must surely win the play-off
in Basel.

But in their castéllar retreat the Italians were in a state of turmoil and
anarchy. 'Open acts of indiscipline' were spoken of, and when Czeizler
announced his team it was a weird one. Cappello was out, Galli was out
and Segato, the Fiorentina left-half, an essentially defensive player, was at
inside-left. The formation never began to get together. 'It was not a
defeat,' observed the *Corriere della Sera*, 'it was a disaster. . . . We left the
stadium in a state of authentic prostration, unable to look the Swiss in the
face.'

At half-time the Italians were but one goal behind—scored by Josef
Hugi after thirteen minutes. But a couple of minutes into the second half
the lively Ballaman headed in a corner he himself had forced, and Italy
cracked. Though Nesti did head a goal some twenty minutes later, the
Swiss were constantly on top, Hugi and Jacky Fatton adding goals in the
last five minutes. Switzerland were triumphantly through to the quarter-
finals against Austria.

Having squeezed through against Scotland, the Austrians had had no
trouble with the Czechs, whom they despatched 5–0 in Zurich; two for
Stojaspal, three to Probst, all but one in the first half.

The best of all these group games was unquestionably that drawn 1–1
by Brazil and Yugoslavia in the exquisite setting of Lausanne's Olympic
Stadium, with Lake Geneva lambently below and the misted Savoy Alps
above. The teams provided football of a purity worthy of the setting,
though it was a pity that the tournament's silly rules should automatically
oblige them to play extra time when there was no question of a deadlock
on points.

Yugoslavia were an impressive blend of youth and experience, their
1950 stars now being supported by such players as Bernard Vukas, the
wiry, blond centre-forward, and Milos Milutinovic, a fair-haired, skilful
outside-right. Zeze Moreira had justified the 'new order' in Brazilian
football on the grounds that 1950's was a fair-weather attack, capable of
scoring goals only when it did not matter; yet now his team played some
beguiling football.

At first, the supple Vladimir Beara had much to do in goal, but then
Yugoslavia, strong in their formidable 'quadrilateral', took hold of the
midfield and might have scored, were their finishing only better. The
Brazilians entertained with the wizardries of Didì and the tight, fast dribbling of Julinho, his face as impassive as an Aztec god's, his right foot
a mighty hammer.

Three minutes from half-time, Vukas and Mitic made an opening
for Branko Zebec which the left-winger exploited. From that point,
Brazil controlled the game. Didì hit a post, Julinho put in three deadly

shots and at last Didì, with a cannonade on the turn, got the equaliser. Neither team over-exerted itself in extra time.

The draw meant that France were eliminated. Narrowly defeated by Yugoslavia in their opening game, they had a most impoverished 3–2 win over Mexico, secured with a late penalty by Raymond Kopa, which prompted several enraged Mexicans to attack the referee.

The Quarter-Finals   Brazil v. Hungary (Battle of Berne)

The quarter-finals pitted Hungary against Brazil at Berne, in a match which was destined to become notorious; England against Uruguay in Basel; Germany against Yugoslavia, in Geneva; Austria against Switzerland, in Lausanne.

The Battle of Berne, as it has come to be known, has in retrospect been blamed chiefly on Brazil. Theirs were the first and greater excesses on the field, theirs the shameful, brutal invasion of the Hungarian dressing-room after the game. Yet there was provocation. The World Cup Disciplinary Committee would, Pilate-like, wash its hands of the horrid affair; Brazil and Hungary themselves would lamentably refuse to punish their players. Indeed, when Arthur Ellis, the game's one hero, later asked the expelled Josef Bozsik whether he had been suspended, Bozsik haughtily replied: 'In Hungary, we don't suspend Deputies.'

What remains a matter for contention is the exact part played in the fracas by the injured Ferenc Puskas, who watched the match from the touchline. At the end of the game, according to the *Corriere della Sera*, he 'struck the Brazilian centre-half Pinheiro in the face with a bottle as he was entering the dressing-rooms, causing a wound eight centimetres long.' The same report quoted Ernst Thommen, the Swiss President of the World Cup Committee, as saying that he had seen Puskas' attack on Pinheiro, that he had been present at the battle in the dressing-rooms which followed, and that he would be making a full report. Subsequently, however, doubt was cast on Puskas' alleged aggression; though there is no doubt that Pinheiro left the stadium heavily bandaged. Some accounts later made the assailant 'a spectator'; but which?

In the event, it was only the superb refereeing of Arthur Ellis that enabled the match to be completed at all; and even then he was obliged to send off three players. In England his refereeing was eulogised, in Brazil it was excoriated—but neutral critics agreed that it deserved the warmest praise. An Italian journalist called it 'magisterial', adding that if it was severe, then 'severity was legitimate and necessary'.

Without Puskas—at least *on* the field—Hungary moved Czibor to inside-left, and used the Toths on the wings. Brazil made three changes in attack, keeping only their formidable right-wing pair of Didì and Julinho. Within eight minutes, under pelting rain, they found themselves two goals down; the Hungarians had made their familiar galloping start.

Hidegkuti's was the first goal, coming after only three minutes. He drove the ball home after Castilho had blocked shots by Czibor and Kocsis, having his shorts ripped off him in the process. Then he was involved in the second goal, moving Toth II's pass on to Kocsis for the inside-right to drive in his shot leaving Brazil's defence bemused. At this point the Hungarians seemed altogether too quick in thought and pace for the Brazilians. But some of the virtue now went out of them, and Brazil's abundantly gifted, if tempestuous, team came more and more into the game. Their apologists later maintained that the burly Hungarian defenders maddened them with a series of commonplace but irritating fouls. At the same time, those who proceeded from here to discern weaknesses, possible vulnerabilities, in Hungary's team, were surely out of order; for how could they be properly assessed without Puskas? What was perfectly plain was that Brazil had not assimilated the third back method of defence; which, indeed, would be abandoned by 1958.

After seventeen minutes a move between Didì and Indio was brusquely ended when Buzansky felled Indio. Djalma Santos thumped in the penalty. By half-time the Brazilians were giving quite as good as they got, Julinho was marauding on the right wing; and Toth I, his Hungarian equivalent, was a limping passenger.

The second half was soon besmirched with sly fouls, deliberate obstructions which in turn bore fruit in another penalty. Pinheiro handled Czibor's pass to Kocsis, and this time it was the turn of Lantos to score from the spot with tremendous power.

Just as powerful, however, was the ferocious, right-footed shot with which the brilliant Julinho beat Grosics, after an amazing undulating dribble, to make it 2–3. Twenty-four minutes were left, the game was open, the moral climate abysmal. Six minutes more, and two great players, Bozsik and Nilton Santos, came squalidly to blows and were both sent off, Bozsik having reacted to Santos' harsh tackle. Twice Julinho got away again, once to shoot wide and then to give Didì a ball which he struck against the bar.

The Brazilians were now on top, but their very insistence left them open, Hungary breaking in the forty-fourth minute of the half for Czibor to dash down the right and cross, and Kocsis to head past Castilho. It must have been especially gratifying to Czibor, who at one point had been chased about the field by an incensed and threatening Djalma Santos.

There was still time for Humberto Tozzi, the young Brazilian inside-left, to kick Lorant and be expelled in his turn, though he fell weeping on his knees to plead with Arthur Ellis. Then the violent match was over, giving way to worse violence still in the dressing-rooms, where bottles and football boots were swung and Gustav Sebes had his cheek cut open. Perhaps it should be recorded that Castilho had tried to calm his colleagues, that Kocsis and Hidegkuti stayed steadfastly aloof—but these were small comforts. To the Battle of Bordeaux now had to be added the Battle of Berne.

Uruguay v. England

The game between Uruguay and England produced the same score but none of the same brutality. Though there were several injuries, mostly to Uruguayans, the match was a clean and memorable one, in which Matthews, for England, and Schiaffino, for Uruguay, were superb.

Though the cupholders were unquestionably the better, more gifted team, and won despite the fact that Varela, Abbadie and Andrade pulled muscles, they were much helped by Merrick's feeble goalkeeping. He should certainly have saved two of the goals; he might well have saved three, a fact particularly galling to an English defence inspired by Billy Wright to resist splendidly. In attack, Matthews was the driving force, again playing not merely on the wing but often in the middle, at inside-right or left.

Uruguay opened the score with a lovely goal, after only five minutes. The masterly Schiaffino sold the dummy to McGarry, who never dominated him, and unleashed Borges. The outside-left raced away, crossed a long diagonal ball to Abbadie and, with England's defence entranced, raced in to convert the return pass.

England rode the punch well and equalised eleven minutes later, when Matthews turned the defence with a clever ball behind Varela, Wilshaw ran on to it and gave Lofthouse a reverse pass to score. For twenty bright minutes England called the tune, but now one saw the flexibility of the Uruguayan methods; saw that the allegedly 'open' defence could be manned, when necessary, by seven or eight players. Lofthouse had a fine shot beaten out by Maspoli; Wilshaw shot just wide when a goal seemed sure. A sly shove was largely responsible.

Two minutes from the interval, Uruguay delivered a counter-punch— to the solar plexus. Varela shot from near the edge of the area, and Merrick allowed the ball to pass across him—and home. It was bad enough that England should go in at half-time a goal down when they could have been a goal up. It was still worse to fall a second goal behind almost immediately afterwards; and a dubious goal, at that. Varela picked the ball up for a free kick and was allowed, inexcusably, to drop kick it. Schiaffino ran through a bewildered English defence to score.

With three players limping, it was inevitable that Uruguay should find the second half difficult, but with Schiaffino now playing splendidly in Varela's position they kept the lead. After sixty-seven minutes Maspoli got his hand to a shot by Tom Finney, and the ball bounced into the net to make it 2–3. Matthews hit the post and had one shot punched by Maspoli for a corner, but the last word was Uruguay's.

With thirteen minutes left, Miguez found Ambrois, who scored with a shot which Merrick should have saved, just as he should have saved Schiaffino's. England were out; but at least, by comparison with the Scots, they had gone out with honour.

Austria v. Switzerland

At Lausanne that same Saturday, Austria and Switzerland produced one of the highest-scoring World Cup matches there has ever been; twelve goals, seven of them to Austria.

It was an astounding match in which the Swiss, roared on by their crowd, scored three in the first twenty minutes; only for the defiant Austrians to reply with three in three minutes, five in seven minutes, building a 5–4 lead by half-time—and missing a penalty into the bargain!

The strange score was partly to be accounted for by an uncharacteristically poor display by Roger Bocquet, the Swiss captain; behind which lurked a sad tale.

Bocquet, in fact, had been suffering for some time from a tumour. His doctor had earnestly advised him not to play, but Bocquet, perhaps his country's most celebrated player of the era, replied, 'Afterwards, I shall be going into hospital for an operation, and I don't know whether I shall survive.'

Play, therefore, he did, and the intense heat provided the worst possible conditions for his tumour. Several times Karl Rappan, the Swiss team manager, tried to persuade him to move from his vital position at centre-half, but on each occasion Bocquet told him, 'It's all right, it's all right!'

'We all felt,' said a Swiss Federation official years afterwards, 'that he was playing in a sort of trance, and didn't know what happened on the field.'

In due course, Bocquet had his operation, which was happily successful; though it left him with a fearful scar, and the need to wear dark glasses, in consequence.

Austria, who so comprehensively overturned the Swiss *catenaccio* which had mastered Italy, did it in a most un-Viennese manner: with sizzling long shots after runs by the Koerners down the wings. At 5–3 to Austria, Ballaman replied for the Swiss. 'All goals scored against Switzerland owing to the sun,' announced the official, unblushing Press *communiqué* at half-time, though it was true that Parlier, the Swiss 'keeper, had a touch of sunstroke. But even with the sun at their backs the Swiss could not recover. In the second half the forceful Theo Wagner ran through for his third goal and Austria's sixth. Though Hanappi put the dynamic Hugi's shot past his goalkeeper for Switzerland's fifth, Probst dribbled through for the most spectacular goal of all. 7–5. It had been a magnificent game for Ernst Ocwirk, and for two forwards who did not score: Stojaspal of Austria and the dark Roger Vonlanthen of Switzerland.

In Geneva the following day the West Germans sprang their first great surprise of the tournament. They beat Yugoslavia. The match proved that the Yugoslavs had the finesse, but not the finish, whereas the Germans had muscle, stamina, and immense determination. Moreover, after ten minutes they were presented with a goal.

Ivan Horvat, the tall Yugoslav centre-half, was possibly the best in the tournament; a Titan in this match, too. But running back with Schaefer towards a ball headed on by Morlock, he headed it in his turn, without observing that Beara had come off his line. 1–0 to Germany. Their second goal came four minutes from the end when Schaefer put through Rahn—offside, in the opinion of some critics—who ran on, on, on before beating an injured Vladimir Beara unable now to move. It was absurd, wrote an Italian critic, that a team like Germany should be in the semi-final when a team like Brazil was out, but this was irremediably what could happen in Cup competitions.

Germany would now play Austria, their victims in the third-place match of 1934, their companions in the World Cup of 1938. The Uruguayans, who had enraged their fellow hotel guests by perpetually and loudly playing a record which proclaimed their virtues, would meet Hungary. They promised there would be no violence; the Brazilians, they said, had lost their heads.

The Semi-Finals Hungary v. Uruguay

Uruguay kept their word at Lausanne in one of the classic matches of World Cup history. Either team might have won, for the game went into extra time. Moreover, it lacked a key player in each side, for if Puskas did not play for Hungary, Varela could not play for Uruguay. Each side, moreover, had to change its outside-right—Abbadie being forced to give way to Souto, while Budai replaced the injured Toth I, whose brother was succeeded by Palotas. This enabled Czibor, in turn, to go back to the left wing. Miguez, another absentee, was succeeded as Uruguay's centre-forward by Hohberg, though Schiaffino nominally played there. Hungary were favoured, but Uruguay had never yet been beaten in a World Cup.

The Uruguayans were slightly faster and more energetic than they had previously been; but after a quarter of an hour Hungary went ahead. Kocsis headed a pass by Hidegkuti to Czibor, and the left-winger volleyed the ball past Maspoli. Just after half-time, Hungary doubled their lead when Buzansky intercepted a poor clearance by Carballo, Varela's deputy. He sent Budai and Bozsik flying away, and when Budai crossed Hidegkuti flung himself at the ball to head it in.

Uruguay seemed beaten beyond hope, but their marvellous morale, not to mention their skill, brought them back into the game. Schiaffino began to work his spells, nicely supported by Juan Hohberg, a naturalised Argentinian who would manage their World Cup team of 1970. Lorant had to clear on the line, Schiaffino had a couple of near misses, and then at last, fifteen minutes from the end, Schiaffino gave Hohberg the chance to beat Grosics. Three minutes from the end Schiaffino and Hohberg did it again, Hohberg being so violently felicitated by his team mates that they knocked him out.

His goal necessitated extra time, and soon after it had started Schiaffino put him through yet again, this time for a shot which smacked the post.

Poor Uruguay; it was not to be their night. In the second extra period, the peerless Andrade was hurt in a tackle and, desperate to get back into the game, was still having treatment behind the goal when right in front of him Budai centred for Kocsis to soar and head past Maspoli.

Seven minutes from the end Kocsis headed another memorable goal, and Hungary had won 4–2. 'We beat the best team we have ever met,' said their manager, Gyula Mandi.

West Germany v. Austria

At Basel a crowd of 58,000 saw the Austrians fall to pieces like a burning house. They had been expected to win quite easily; their technique was far ahead of the Germans', and they had scored a cascade of goals against the Swiss. In the meantime, Sepp Herberger had worked hard at training Toni Turek, who he felt should have made Kohlmeyer's saves on the line superfluous. Austria, for their part, made the cardinal mistake of dropping Schmied and restoring the famous Walter Zeman—a goalkeeper previously omitted precisely because he had lost form.

It proved a disastrous error, for Zeman, once so polished and authoritative, played like a man who had lost his nerve, running about his area like a chicken with its head cut off, utterly confused by crosses. Two of the goals, indeed, came from centres, two more from corners; a damning commentary on Austria's defence in the air. The other two were from penalty kicks.

The Germans now showed that they were a great deal more than mere destroyers, a mincing machine for other people's talent. Their football was sweepingly effective, splendidly incisive, with Fritz Walter the supreme strategist, scorer of two penalties to boot, and Helmut Rahn as powerfully effective a right-winger, in his muscular way, as the exotic Julinho.

During the first half there was little sign of what awaited poor Austria in the second. For twenty minutes their team did pretty things, relaxed and elegant, but on the half-hour Max Morlock sent Fritz Walter away, and Hans Schaefer flicked in his well-judged centre. At half-time it was still 1–0.

In the third minute of the second half an equally exact corner kick by Fritz Walter was headed in by Morlock, and though four minutes later Germany gave Austria a chance, Turek dropping the ball for Probst to score, the die was cast. The German attack, with only Rahn keeping his position firmly, the others switching at speed, overran the Austrians. Fritz Walter scored the third and fifth goals from the spot, each time sending the unfortunate Zeman the wrong way, while his brother Otmar headed the other two—one from Fritz's corner, one from Schaefer's cross—after Fritz had sent him down the right. In turning from the old *metodo* to the third back game, Austria seemed to have gained no more defensive solidity than Brazil.

They consoled themselves a little by beating Uruguay 3–1 in the third-place match at Zurich, Ocwirk dominating the game, but it was scarcely one in which the Uruguayans gave their all.

The Final   West Germany v. Hungary

The great question before the Final was whether Puskas would play. He would, said the reports. He wouldn't. He was hoping to. There was no chance. There was a fifty-fifty chance; a specialist had said so. The ankle was better. It would never recover in time. The Germans had offered him special treatment; and been rejected.

In the event, however, Puskas *did* play; and it would prove a manifest mistake, a testimony to the captain's own powers of persuasion rather than the good sense of Sebes and Mandi.

Ciro Veratti, the Italian journalist, spoke to Sepp Herberger, the little German manager, and wrote of his 'formidable ascendancy' over his players, his power to make them give almost more than they possessed. There had been 30,000 Germans in Basel when they beat

Austria. There would be about the same number in Berne for the Final, so they would virtually be playing at home. Living now 'in a climate of exaltation', the Germans hoped to give the lie to everybody. If it happened, 'it would be the greatest upset of the World Championship. But we don't believe it, and we are making ready to hail as champions tomorrow that marvellous goal-scoring machine which is the great Hungarian team.'

Sunday was a rainy day; rain, indeed, drenched the players and most of the 60,000 crowd at the Wankdorf Stadium throughout the match. If Hungary were the favourites, Gustav Sebes had still warned that their 'greatest enemy is not so much physical fatigue as nervous tension. I had never suspected that the World Cup would be such a test of nerves.'

Restoring Puskas, they also dropped Budai, who had played so well against the Uruguayans but had never been *persona grata* with Puskas. Germany's team was that which beat Austria, with Posipal, centre-half of the Rest of Europe team, still at right-back, Liebrich as stopper.

Once again, Hungary made a devastating, potentially a demoralising, start. Within eight minutes they were two goals up, and there seemed every prospect of another Basel. In the sixth minute, after Germany had three times menaced the Hungarian goal, Hungary counter-attacked. Bozsik sent Kocsis through, his shot hit a German defender in the back, the ball ran to Puskas, and that formidable left foot drove it past Turek.

Within a couple of minutes Kohlmeyer, Germany's saviour against the Yugoslavs, had given Hungary their second goal with the complicity of Turek. His misjudged back pass, suddenly bewitched, sprang out of Turek's grasp and Czibor drove the ball in.

It was enough to unhinge most teams; but not Germany. Within three minutes, shaking off the effects of so depressing a goal, they had struck back. Hans Schaefer crossed, Rahn returned the ball to the centre and this time Bozsik erred, fractionally deflecting it into the path of Morlock. The inside-forward stretched out a telescopic leg, and jabbed it past Grosics.

It was becoming plain that for all the fury of their beginning, Hungary were not running smoothly. Puskas, clearly hampered by his ankle, was unwontedly heavy and slow, and now threw away a chance when he insisted on carrying on alone, losing the ball, when Czibor was free and better placed. Czibor, meanwhile, switched to the right, was obviously not at ease there, and things would go better when he moved to the left after half-time.

So, after sixteen minutes the Germans equalised. Taking the third of three successive corners, Fritz Walter curved an insidious ball which was missed both by his brother's head and by Grosics' hands. It thus reached Helmut Rahn, who drove it thunderously back into goal.

To this the Hungarians responded vigorously, Turek making the first of his many gallant saves from a header by Kocsis, then being saved by a post when beaten by Hidegkuti. Thus reprieved, the Germans attacked in their turn, and banged away at the Hungarian goal for a full three minutes. At half-time, the game was pulsatingly open.

The Hungarians began the second half with a new and furious assault on the German goal, and only Turek denied them. Twice he saved gloriously from Puskas—who on one occasion was alone in front of goal—once Kohlmeyer kicked Toth's shot off the line; once Kocsis' header from Toth's cross skidded off the bar.

The storm weathered, Germany returned to the attack; the Hungarians were now beginning to look weary. Yet twelve minutes from the end of a game so well refereed by Bill Ling, the fast, dark Czibor broke brilliantly away, Turek saved his shot, the ball reached Hidegkuti; and Hidegkuti missed. Five minutes later came the *coup de grâce*.

Leaving Bozsik behind, Hans Schaefer got away down the left wing and crossed. The ball flashed over a crowded, pullulating goalmouth, touched, perhaps, by Otmar Walter's head. For a moment Lantos seemed to have it, then it escaped him, reaching Rahn. The big outside-right controlled it, advanced with it, and seemed, for a moment of pregnant hiatus, to stop and deliberate. Then he drove it past Grosics with his left foot.

Frantically the Hungarians sought to equalise, and two minutes later it seemed they had. Toth, from the right, took Posipal out of the game with an exquisite through pass and Puskas, seeming to judge the moment perfectly, darted through the gap to beat Turek in his old, irresistible style. The Hungarians embraced; but the flag of Mervyn Griffiths, the Welsh linesman, was up. Puskas had been given offside, and to this day the decision is argued.

Hungary had one shot left in their locker. Suddenly Zoltan Czibor was away once more, to let fly a strong, precise shot which Turek elastically reached again to punch clear, while Czibor rolled on the ground in despair.

So, in the drenching rain, it was over, and Jules Rimet, the retiring President of FIFA, gave to Fritz Walter the Cup which had seemed destined for Puskas. In the dressing-rooms, Gustav Sebes spoke of bad luck, and slumped on a bench; Herberger spoke of seriousness and enthusiasm. His team, physically exceptional, morally resilient, tactically straightforward, had won a remarkable triumph.

Marred by accusations of doping when most of the team succumbed to jaundice; seemingly confirmed long afterwards when a dressing-room attendant remembered finding hidden syringes.

RESULTS: Switzerland 1954

Pool I

Yugoslavia 1, France 0 (HT 1/0)
Brazil 5, Mexico 0 (HT 4/0)
France 3, Mexico 2 (HT 1/0)
Brazil 1, Yugoslavia 1 (HT 0/1) after extra time

	P	W	D	L	F	A	Pts
					GOALS		
Brazil	2	1	1	0	**6**	**1**	3
Yugoslavia	2	1	1	0	**2**	**1**	3
France	2	1	0	1	**3**	**3**	2
Mexico	2	0	0	2	**2**	**8**	0

Pool II

Hungary 9, Korea 0 (HT 4/0)
Germany 4, Turkey 1 (HT 1/1)
Hungary 8, Germany 3 (HT 3/1)
Turkey 7, Korea 0 (HT 4/0)

	P	W	D	L	F	A	Pts
					GOALS		
Hungary	2	2	0	0	**17**	**3**	4
Germany	2	1	0	1	**7**	**9**	2
Turkey	2	1	0	1	**8**	**4**	2
Korea	2	0	0	2	**0**	**16**	0

Play off Germany 7, Turkey 2 (HT 3/1)

Pool III

Austria 1, Scotland 0 (HT 1/0)
Uruguay 2, Czechoslovakia 0 (HT 0/0)
Austria 5, Czechoslovakia 0 (HT 4/0)
Uruguay 7, Scotland 0 (HT 2/0)

	P	W	D	L	F	A	Pts
					GOALS		
Uruguay	2	2	0	0	**9**	**0**	4
Austria	2	2	0	0	**6**	**0**	4
Czechoslovakia	2	0	0	2	**0**	**7**	0
Scotland	2	0	0	2	**0**	**8**	0

Pool IV

England 4, Belgium 4 (HT 2/1)
England 2, Switzerland 0 (HT 1/0)
Switzerland 2, Italy 1 (HT 1/1)
Italy 4, Belgium 1 (HT 1/0)

	P	W	D	L	F	A	Pts
					GOALS		
England	2	1	1	0	**6**	**4**	3
Italy	0	1	**5**	**3**	2	2	1
Switzerland	2	1	0	1	**2**	**3**	2
Belgium	2	0	1	1	**5**	**8**	1

Play off Switzerland 4, Italy 1 (HT 1/0)

Quarter-finals

Geneva

Germany 2	**Yugoslavia 0**
Turek; Laband,	Beara; Stankovic,
Kohlmeyer; Eckel,	Crnkovic; Cjaicowski,
Liebrich, Mai; Rahn,	I., Horvat, Boskov;
Morlock, Walter,	Milutinovic, Mitic
O., Walter, F. (capt.),	(capt.), Vukas, Bobek,
Schaefer.	Zebec.

SCORERS
Horvat (own goal), Rahn for Germany
HT 1/0

Berne

Hungary 4	**Brazil 2**
Grosics; Buzansky,	Castilho; Santos, D.,
Lantos; Bozsik (capt.),	Santos, N.;
Lorant, Zakarias; Toth,	Brandaozinho,
M., Kocsis, Hidegkuti,	Pinheiro (capt.), Bauer;
Czibor, Toth, J.	Julinho, Didi, Indio,
	Tozzi, Maurinho.

SCORERS
Hidegkuti (2), Kocsis, Lantos (penalty) for
Hungary
Santos, D. (penalty), Julinho for Brazil
HT 2/1

Lausanne

Austria 7	**Switzerland 5**
Schmied; Hana-	Parlier; Neury, Kernen;
pi, Barschandt; Ocwirk	Eggimann, Bocquet
(capt.), Happel, Koller;	(capt.), Casali;
Koerner, R., Wagner,	Antenen, Vonlanthen,
Stojaspal, Probst,	Hugi, Ballaman,
Koerner, A.	Fatton.

SCORERS
Koerner, A. (2), Ocwirk, Wagner (3), Probst
for Austria
Ballaman (2), Hugi (2), Hanappi (own goal)
for Switzerland
HT 2/4

Basel

Uruguay 4	**England 2**
Maspoli; Santamaria,	Merrick; Staniforth,
Martinez; Andrade,	Byrne; McGarry,
Varela (capt.), Cruz;	Wright (capt.),
Abbadie, Ambrois,	Dickinson; Matthews,
Miguez, Schiaffino,	Broadis, Lofthouse,
Borges.	Wilshaw, Finney.

Borges, Varela, Schiaffino, Ambrois for
Uruguay
Lofthouse, Finney for England
HT 2/1

Semi-finals

Basel

Germany 6	**Austria 1**
Turek; Posipal,	Zeman; Hanappi,
Kohlmeyer; Eckel,	Schleger; Ocwirk
Liebrich, Mai; Rahn,	(capt.), Happel, Koller;
Morlock, Walter, O.,	Koerner, R., Wagner,
Walter, F. (capt.),	Stojaspal, Probst,
Schaefer.	Koerner, A.

SCORERS
Schaefer, Morlock, Walter, F. (2 penalties),
Walter, O. (2) for Germany
Probst for Austria
HT 1/0

Lausanne

Hungary 4	**Uruguay 2**
(after extra time)	
Grosics; Buzansky,	Maspoli; Santamaria,
Lantos; Boszik (capt.),	Martinez; Andrade
Lorant, Zakarias;	(capt.), Carballo, Cruz;
Budai, Kocsis, Palotas,	Souto, Ambrois,
Hidegkuti, Czibor.	Schiaffino, Hohberg,
	Borges.

SCORERS
Czibor, Hidegkuti, Kocsis (2) for Hungary
Hohberg (2) for Uruguay
HT 1/0

Third place match

Zurich

Austria 3	**Uruguay 1**
Schmied; Hanappi,	Maspoli; Santamaria,
Barschandt; Ocwirk	Martinez; Andrade
(capt.), Kollmann,	(capt.), Carballo, Cruz;
Koller; Koerner, R.,	Abbadie, Hohberg,
Wagner, Dienst,	Mendez, Schiaffino,
Stojaspal, Probst.	Borges.

SCORERS
Stojaspal (penalty), Cruz (own goal), Ocwirk
for Austria
Hohberg for Uruguay
HT 1/1

Final

Berne

Germany 3	**Hungary 2**
Turek; Posipal,	Grosics; Buzansky,
Kohlmeyer; Eckel,	Lantos; Bozsik, Lorant,
Liebrich, Mai; Rahn,	Zakarias; Czibor,
Morlock, Walter, O.,	Kocsis, Hidegkuti,
Walter, F., Schaefer.	Puskas, Toth, J.

SCORERS
Morlock, Rahn (2) for Germany
Puskas, Czibor for Hungary
HT 2/2

SWEDEN
1958

Background to Sweden

Played in Sweden, the 1958 World Cup was notable for the emergence of 4-2-4, the explosion of Pelé, the first victory by Brazil, the surprise of France and Fontaine. Though it was won by an immensely distinguished team it was not, overall, a distinguished competition.

The Contenders   Sweden

For the Swedish team, which ultimately and admirably became runners-up, it was a World Cup of nostalgia. At last the Swedish Federation had decided to allow overtly professional football and overtly professional footballers, a corollary of which was not only that such great players as Gunnar Gren returned to Sweden but also that others were recalled that summer from Italy. George Raynor, meanwhile, came back as team manager after the heartaches and the thousand natural shocks of management in Italy and to make his team happy.

One of the most beguiling features of the side was that it harked back not merely to 1950 and Sweden's last World Cup in Brazil, but even earlier—to the 1948 Olympic Games. From these, Gren and Liedholm were mighty survivors. Like the powerful and prolific centre-forward Gunnar Nordahl, they had left Sweden for Milan, making up the so-called Grenoli trio, with Nordahl in the middle, 'The Professor' Gren at inside-right, Nils Liedholm at inside-left. Liedholm, indeed, after a long and impressive spell at right-half, had just played splendidly at inside-left for the Milan team which had lost 3–2 to Real Madrid in the European Cup Final in Brussels.

The little, two-haired Nacka Skoglund was back, too, after eight splendid years with Internazionale of Milan. On the right wing, a more recent Italian 'export' was Kurt (Kurre) Hamrin, a sturdy little man, coolly insulated and taciturn, with superb powers of dribbling and acceleration and the ability and courage to strike through the middle as well as from the wing.

At centre-half was another Italo-Swede, Julli Gustavsson, a former policeman playing for Atalanta who had been at right-back for the Rest of Europe team which beat Great Britain in Belfast in 1955. Atalanta, indicted by the Italian Federation for alleged corruption, had a vital play-off game against Bari coming up, and at first were reluctant to let Gustavsson go. Eventually they compromised grudgingly, after a tense time when it seemed that he would be unable to play for Sweden in the semi-final, allowing him to go on provided that if he wished to take part in the Final he would pay the massive indemnity of 25,000 crowns! Gustavsson, who had a superbly dominating match against Russia in the quarter-finals, did play the Final.

Ironically, however, the Swedish Press and public had no initial confidence in their team's chances, despite home advantage and the return of the Italian brigade. But as the Swedish team made more and more progress, won one match after another, the patriotic euphoria of this traditionally neutral, peaceable, unchauvinist nation rose to an orgy of patriotism in the semi-final match against West Germany. It was a riveting and somewhat alarming study in national behaviour.

Russia

The Russians were competing for the first time in a World Cup, under the managership of the blond, Cagneyesque figure of Gabriel Katchaline assisted by the huge Mikhail Yakushin, who resembled some craggy hero of the revolutionary war and had taken Moscow Dynamo on its famous tour of Britain and Sweden in 1945. Thereafter the Russians, whose elegant, enterprising football had been excitingly successful, withdrew into splendid isolation till the Olympic tournament of 1952 in Helsinki, where they were put out 3–1 by Yugoslavia after an astonishing, oscillating 5–5 draw. They had just drawn a lively game against England in Moscow, and would now contest the same group in Gothenburg, together with Brazil and Austria.

They had gifted players in Simonian, the mobile little Armenian centre-forward; Lev Yachine, the superb goalkeeper who had succeeded and surpassed 'Tiger' Khomich in the Moscow Dynamo goal; Salnikov, a thoughtful inside-left; and Igor Netto. This blond left-half, captain of the side, who had helped it to win the Olympic title of 1956 in Melbourne, had hurt his left knee and was an uncertain starter; a blow to a Russian team which greatly depended on his lively, attacking play.

Northern Ireland, Wales and Scotland

Of the British teams, England were the most fancied, Northern Ireland the most intriguing. It was the first occasion on which all four had qualified for the Finals.

England's chances were severely affected by the disastrous Munich air crash the previous February, when the Manchester United team's Elizabethan, twin-engined aircraft failed to gain sufficient height on a snowy day and hit a building at the end of the runway. The team, which had just drawn a European Cup tie 3–3 in Belgrade, was cruelly afflicted. Among those who died instantly were the captain, England's resourceful left-back Roger Byrne, and Tommy Taylor, their excellent centre-forward, a fine player in the air and a vigorous one on the ground. Duncan Edwards, still only twenty-one years old, a superbly powerful player thought by many to be the finest left-half to have played for his country since the war, died pitifully in hospital after fighting for life with the help of a kidney machine. The experience profoundly disturbed the twenty-year-old Bobby Charlton, whose natural shyness became a persistent melancholy which would remain with him for the next decade. He had played for England on their pre-World Cup tour, done badly in Belgrade, when they lost 5–0 in intense heat to Yugoslavia, and would not play a single World Cup match. This represented a perverse decision by team manager and selectors but, as we shall see, it may have been better for Charlton, in the circumstances, that he did not play.

Northern Ireland had won their way to the finals against all expectation by eliminating Italy—and their cohorts of South Americans. Unlucky to lose 1–0 in Rome, when the tough but tiny Wilbur Cush played successfully at centre-half and Sergio Cervato slyly moved the ball to the right to make a gap through which he could score from a free kick, they finished the job in Belfast. The decisive game should have taken place in January, but Istvan Zsolt, the Hungarian referee and theatre director, was held up in the fog, the Italians refused to accept an Irish referee and what followed was the unfriendliest friendly which can ever have been seen in Belfast.

Juan Schiaffino, star of the previous two World Cups with Uruguay, now playing for Milan and—on tenuous qualification—for Italy, broke Wilbur Cush's shinpad with a kick; Chiapella, the Fiorentina right-half, jumped with both knees into McAdams' back after a challenge on the goalkeeper, and when the final whistle blew on a 2–2 draw the crowd invaded the field. Danny Blanchflower, the Irish captain, allocated each Italian player to an Irish one. Ferrario, the huge centre-half who had jumped feet first at two Irish forwards at a corner, knocked down a couple of invaders, then panicked and cowered on the ground, and the police badly beat up a fan who had come on merely in quest of an autograph. It was a brutal, sombre affair, but Ireland eventually won the real match 2–1 on their merits, with goals by McIlroy and the ill-used Cush. Alcide Ghiggia, another Uruguayan hero of the 1950 World Cup called up by Italy, was sent off, ironically for a trivial offence.

Having fought their way through so bravely to the finals, the Northern Ireland team them had to fight again—against pressure in Ulster to prevent their playing on Sundays, an unavoidable necessity in the World Cup. The Irish Football Association was torn, but eventually sanity prevailed over bigotry.

Northern Ireland's extraordinary improvement and success was the result of the inspired managership of Peter Doherty and the emergence of a nucleus of greatly talented players—notably Gregg, the Blanchflowers, Peacock, McParland, Cush, McIlroy and Bingham.

Doherty was fortunate in having two splendid lieutenants to implement his policies on the field. Danny Blanchflower, the right-half, and Jimmy McIlroy, the Burnley inside-forward, were two drily witty, technically gifted, tactically sophisticated footballers whose good influence permeated the rest of the team. Before the World Cup, in which Ireland were drawn in a group with the West German holders, the Czechs and the Argentinians, Blanchflower whimsically observed that their plan would be to equalise before the other side had scored.

Billy Bingham, the well-sprung little Sunderland and Luton outside-right, who would form such a fine right wing with Cush in the World Cup and later become team manager himself, attributed the team's success to Doherty's 'pep talks', his double centre-forward plan which largely made up for the lack of a sufficient centre-forward, the devoted rehearsal of free kicks, corners and throws-in, and the fact that the minimal changes Doherty made ensured that the team became 'more like a club side'.

This was true of the equally impressive Welsh. Initially Wales were lucky to be going to Sweden at all, for they had been eliminated by the Czechs. When the withdrawal of all Israel's opponents—on political grounds—left them with a free passage to Sweden, FIFA decreed that those countries which had taken second place in their group should be put in a hat, the team drawn out to meet Israel, home and away. Uruguay proudly refused, Wales came out of the hat, won 2–0 home and away, and went to Sweden, their chances improved by Juventus's release of the massive, formidable John Charles to play centre-forward. Charles, who had made his international debut as a seventeen-year-old centre-half, had just finished a wonderfully successful first season in Italy. The Welsh team manager was the lively Jimmy Murphy, who had efficiently taken over Manchester United when Matt Busby was badly hurt in the Munich crash, and there were other famous players in Jack Kelsey, a strong, calm, agile goalkeeper, and the classical inside-left, Ivor Allchurch.

Scotland had done well to eliminate Spain, but they had just been thrashed 4–0 by England at Hampden and would predictably finish bottom of a group which included Paraguay—Uruguay's unexpected conquerors—Yugoslavia and France.

Hungary

The Hungarians, moral victors and actual losers in 1954, were a parody of their great team of the early 1950s. Comes the Revolution; in this case, the Hungarian Revolution of 1956. Honved, the army team into which, willy nilly, the authorities had stuffed almost all their best footballers, was touring abroad; and the authorities were properly hoist with their own petard. The incomparable, irreplaceable inside-forwards, Kocsis and Puskas, exiled themselves and eventually, like Kubala before them, found gainful employment in Spanish football. The excellent winger, Zoltan Czibor, expatriated himself, too, and though Josef Bozsik and Nandor Hidegkuti duly went dutifully home, they were fading veterans by now.

Moreover, it was alleged that there had been a descent by police on the Hungarian players at Budapest airport to confiscate money which they were taking out of the country to buy goods. It may well have been true, for the players seemed very much down in the mouth. Gustav Sebes, who led them in the 1954 World Cup, remarked, 'I have never seen a Hungarian team in such a deplorable physical condition and nervous state.' The myth of Hungarian superiority, their supremacy in tactics, men and training, went to the winds, though the comfortable journalese soubriquet of Magic Magyars would be with us for a few wistful years to come.

France

The French arrived nineteen days before the competition started at Kopparberg under the inspiring and benevolent guidance of Monsieur Paul Nicolas, once an international himself, with their former splendid goalkeeper Alex Thépot among the selectors and Albert Batteux an excellent manager assisted by Jean Snella. No one thought France a serious candidate, which if anything helped them by removing pressure. They had not won a game that year, though the release of little Raymond Kopa by Real Madrid was sure to improve them. Banished to the wing at Real by the dominating Alfredo Di Stefano—who could not, even with Kubala's help, enable Spain to eliminate Scotland— Kopa flourished anew when back in the middle and on the conductor's podium. A superbly balanced player with exquisite control and a splendid eye for the through pass, his partnership with Just Fontaine would be one of the features of the tournament, bringing Fontaine a record thirteen goals.

Fontaine, born in Morocco, had come to Sweden quite reconciled to being a reserve, and even said, 'I'm centre-forward only till Kopa comes'. When René Bliard kicked the ground in training, hurt his ankle and went home—singing Fontaine's praises—his choice was assured. Dark, sturdily built, a fast and determined runner with excellent acceleration and a fine shot, Fontaine was also extremely intelligent in his responses to Kopa's splendid prompting.

West Germany

Since their victory in Berne little had gone right for the West Germans. Almost at once their team had been smitten with an epidemic of jaundice, which led to wide but unsubstantiated charges that they had been on drugs. No fewer than seven of the 1954 team had fallen by the wayside: Turek, Kohlmeyer, Liebrich, Mai, Otmar Walter and Morloch. But Fritz Walter was still there to be the chief strategist at the age of thirty-seven, and Hans Schaefer would resume his dialogue with Rahn on the wings. Rahn, the enormous right-winger, bombardier of the last World Cup Final, had been drinking heavily since then, but he was rehabilitated, morally and physically, in time to play admirably in Sweden. Moreover, there were two exciting additions to the team in the strong young left-half, Horst Szymaniak, and Uwe Seeler, a stalwart, highly mobile and combative centre-forward from Hamburg, who had been capped initially in 1954 at the age of eighteen and would become the very symbol of German football for years to follow.

Argentina

Argentina played in West Germany's group, but their team had been sadly plundered by the Italians. Only a year before, its young 'Angels with Dirty Faces', its *Trio de la Muerte* of Maschio, Angelillo and Sivori, had won it a spectacular South American title in Lima. In swooped the marauding Italian clubs to sign all of them, and the accomplished inside-left Ernesto Grillo for good measure.

It was only by rehabilitating the famous forty-year-old inside-left Angel Labruna of River Plate, that Argentina had managed to scrape through the qualifying rounds, in which they had the shame of losing to obscure Bolivia. Another celebrated veteran in the giant, perambulating centre-half, Nestor Rossi, was in the side, but the omens were poor.

Brazil

Not that Brazil had had an easy passage to Sweden, even if they were the favourites by the time they got there. Their last, all-important qualifying match—against Peru in Rio—had been won only by 1–0, thanks to one of Didì's celebrated *foglia secca* (falling leaf) free kicks; which by 1970's World Cup would be known as banana shots. Yet Didì was very nearly not brought to Sweden, and his place was in doubt until the opening game. First, he was criticised for being, at the age of thirty, too old! Second, he had married a white woman; third, he was supposedly not trying hard enough. 'It would be funny if they left me out,' he remarked with irony, 'after I had paid for their ticket.' He had the remote, brooding aspect of a great negro jazz musician.

Vicente Feola, a São Paulo man of Salernitan descent, brought to Sweden the best, most thoroughly organised Brazilian side ever to visit Europe. His right-hand man was the large and imperturbable doctor Hilton Gosling, who had covered hundreds of miles in Sweden before he found the ideal place for a training camp among the trees of Hind as outside Gothenburg. The Russians too, had taken up residence there, and sometimes, when they were not fishing, would come lumbering out of the woods like bears to watch the Brazilians joyfully train, with the cacophony of a male voice choir gone berserk.

The Brazilians not only had Gosling, whom the players treated as father or father-confessor, they also had, with memories of Berne in mind, their own psychologist, an amiable eclectic from São Paulo, grey-sweatered, often unshaven, whose precise methods were a little hard to comprehend. He did not, he said, believe in haranguing the players in groups, yet neither did he believe in talking to them individually, since this made their problem bigger. He believed in getting them to draw pictures of a man. The more cerebral players drew sophisticated pictures, the instinctive players drew virtual matchstick-men. The two made good wing partnerships. Forwards must project their aggression, defenders must contain it; a theory which must have taken heavy punishment if he chanced to see such defenders as the terrible Erhardt of West Germany.

Feola, meanwhile, shook his heavy head and said, 'How can he know the ambience?' He was also critical of his nineteen-year-old, blond centre-forward José Altafini, known then by the nickname of Mazzola for his resemblance to the old captain of Italy and father of Sandrino. Altafini had just been transferred for a large fee to Milan—the team, indeed, had played two impressive matches in Italy en route to Sweden. 'He's nineteen,' complained Feola. 'All the publicity about his transfer to Milan; how can it help but go to his head? He doesn't fit in with the team.'

Feola's preference and ultimate choice went to the Vasco da Gama centre-forward, Vavà, a sturdy, Aztec figure, while there were two other imponderables. The seventeen-year-old Pelé, already described as the finest player ever produced by Brazil, was injured, while Feola was reluctant to choose the forward the psychologist regarded as the most unsophisticated of all, the outside-right Garrincha.

Garrincha, 'the Little Bird', was all the more dangerous and unpredictable because he had been crippled since childhood; he was a footballer of superb natural gifts, astonishing speed and swerve, but utterly inconsistent. The safe and early choice was Flamengo's Joel—with another Flamengo winger in Zagalo on the left, and their club mate Dida at inside-right, beside Vavà.

The 4-2-4 system, adopted instead of the third back game which was foreign to them, solved the old Brazilian problem of pivotal covering in defence by simply putting the left-half alongside the centre-half; just as Hungary had done with Zakarias. Two players foraged and passed in midfield, while two wingers and two central strikers stayed in attack. If you had the extraordinary talent at your command that the Brazilians had, it was a marvellous system. If not, it would present as many difficulties as it solved, especially in midfield.

England

England, who were expected to qualify from Gothenburg with Brazil, had compounded the problems created by Munich with their odd choice. They brought only twenty players, though entitled to twenty-two (the Czechs brought only eighteen) and these twenty included neither Stanley Matthews nor Nat Lofthouse, both successes of the 1954 World Cup and both still in imposing form. Matthews, indeed, had run ragged the usually impeccable Brazilian left-back Nilton Santos at Wembley in 1956—at the age of forty-one—while Lofthouse had just scored both Bolton's goals in the Cup Final.

The loss of Edwards, Byrne and Taylor was thus exacerbated. Any hope of overcoming it was severely compromised by the fact that Fulham and Blackburn Rovers had just been engaged in a fierce, exhausting struggle to emerge from the Second Division which had left its mark on Johnny Haynes, the young Londoner whose superb cross-field and through passing made him the key man in attack, and the talented little right-winger, Blackburn's Bryan Douglas. Ronnie Clayton, Blackburn's captain and right-half, gained a place only in the group's play-off.

Group Matches

Worse still was to come, for in the opening game in Gothenburg's new Ullevi Stadium where the roof, with its wire suspensions, suggested a monster puppeteer, Tom Finney was hurt. It did not prevent his inspiring the English revival in the last half hour or equalising from a penalty six minutes from time when Douglas was tripped, but his loss was a dreadful blow. Beyond question he was the one forward of world class England possessed, and there was no one now to compensate for the staleness of Haynes and Douglas, the banal crudities of the huge centre-forward Derek Kevan, the patent inadequacy of his successor Alan A'Court—and Walter Winterbottom's astonishing reluctance to make changes.

It was Salnikov, not Haynes, who was the arch strategist of this interesting match, one in which Russia played much clever football, even without Netto. Voinov and Tsarev, the robust wing-halves, made up for his absence, Krishevski dominated the centre, and it was as well that England's cool new goalkeeper, Colin McDonald of Burnley, was the equal even of Yachine.

After thirteen minutes, however, he could only block a shot by the vivacious left-winger Ilyin, and Simonian, who usually lay deep, was there to score. England's short, square, unimaginative passing was making no progress against a Russian defence whose methods often transgressed the rules.

Ten minutes into the second half the second Russian goal arrived. The English defence, in these pre-overlapping days, stood bemused as Kessarev, the right-back, advanced, crossed beautifully; and Ivanov scored. It was Finney's mastery of Kessarev, however, which began to turn the tide. After sixty-five minutes Billy Wright, an indomitable centre-half and a fine captain, booted a free kick high into the goal-mouth. Kevan's fair head rose above the defence, even above Yachine, and headed down into goal.

Brazil, meanwhile, had had no trouble with ponderous Austria at Boras' little ground, Mazzola scoring twice, and Nilton Santos strolling through from left-back to get the third. Their critics, however, were dissatisfied, in particularly accusing Dida, who had done some good running off the ball, of lack of courage. Dida promptly disappeared from the side.

Elsewhere there were various alarms and excursions, though Sweden had opened the ball, unscathed, on the afternoon of June 8 with a 3–0 win in Stockholm over indifferent Mexico. Two of their goals were scored by a tall, talented young centre-forward, Agne Simonsson, while thirty-six-year-old Liedholm, at right-half for the moment, got the other from a penalty.

In Group I, the astonishing Northern Irish beat Czechoslovakia by Cush's solitary goal at Halmstad, while the holders, West Germany, showed up Argentina's deficiencies at Malmö, defeating them 3–1. Poor Fritz Walter, who would end the tournament in bed nursing his injuries, was horribly fouled by Rossi towards the end; a foul which many thought deserved to be punished with expulsion.

Not even a goal scored by Argentina's slim and dangerous little outside-right Corbatta in two minutes, cutting past the muscular Juskowiak, could give them the impetus they needed. The Germans were superior in teamwork and stamina, the Argentinians too much inclined to play off the cuff. So Rahn, half an hour after the goal, equalised with a sudden ferocious left-footer from the inside-left position when served by Walter, and five minutes from half-time Seeler, giving and receiving from Schaefer, lunged forward to make it 2–1. Even an injury to Eckel which had him limping on the left wing for most of the second half could not tip the balance, and ten minutes from the end Rahn bent his shot past the veteran Carrizo with the outside of the foot. 3–1.

The Irish used the young Derek Dougan at centre-forward. The first choice, Billy Simpson of Rangers, had pulled a muscle after a mere five minutes' training in Sweden. Dougan had an awkward first half, but when Billy Bingham was pushed into the middle in the second he made good use of his fine acceleration. Harry Gregg allayed all fears with his performance in goal, Bertie Peacock had an exceptional game at left-half and Wilbur Cush headed the only goal from the rugged Peter McParland's centre. The lack of Jackie Blanchflower had a seriously negative effect on the team, obliging his brother to play a far more defensive game alongside their makeshift centre-half, the full-back Willie Cunningham, but the defence held out well under vigorous pressure in the closing phases.

France got away to a spectacular beginning, annihilating the Paraguayans 7–3 at Nörrkoping, five of their goals coming in the second half; a rampant Fontaine got three. Paraguay actually scored first through Amarilla, and were level, 2–2, at half-time. Thereafter the superb combination of the French inside-forwards, Kopa, Fontaine and the incisive Roger Piantoni, was simply too much for them.

Scotland, at Vasteras, did a great deal better against Yugoslavia than had feeble England in Belgrade, holding them to a 1–1 draw in a strangely schizophrenic match.

Yugoslavia, far superior in technique, began the game as if they were going to treat Scotland as they had England. With the blond, elegant Milos Milutinovic in splendid form at centre-forward and abetted by a new star, the dark little gipsy inside-left Dragoslav Sekularac, and the admirable Boskov at wing-half, they assailed the Scottish goal. At first, wrote one commentator, the Scots seemed like juniors getting a lesson. The right-winger Petakovic gave Tommy Younger, the big, blond Scots goalkeeper, no hope; from Milutinovic's pass Eric Caldow kicked off the line; Younger made a fine save, and somehow no more goals resulted.

In the second half Scotland's immense determination and robust challenge ground down the more fragile Slavs. Petakovic had scarcely hit a post when Turnbull crossed, Beara—in goal—and Krstic confused one another, and Murray headed the equaliser. Though Veselinovic also hit the post, Yugoslavia had lost their command.

In Group I Wales held Hungary to a draw at Sandviken. In Gothenburg, England would now play Brazil for the first time in a World Cup. Bill Nicholson, Tottenham Hotspur coach, having watched the Brazilians, evolved a defensive scheme whereby Don Howe, the tall, cool West Bromwich right-back, would play as a second centre-half beside Billy Wright; Eddie Clamp, the big, dark Wolves half-back, as an attacking full-back; while another Wolves man, the studious Bill Slater, would play 'tight' on Didì.

With Pelé and Garrincha still missing from Brazil's attack, though Vavà now lined up beside Mazzola, the scheme worked remarkably well, Brazil dominated the first half, Didì and the attacking right-half, the bald Dino, dominating midfield, but Vavà hit the bar, Clamp kicked off the line, and Colin McDonald made two spectacular saves from headers by Mazzola.

In the second half, the pattern changed and England might even have won. If some had cast doubt on the English penalty against Russia, claiming that the foul took place outside the box, then England were most unfortunate not to get one when Bellini hauled Kevan down as he thundered after one of Haynes's rare through passes. But by and large, however, the England attack was as grey as it had been against Russia.

In Boras, goals by Ilyin and Valentin Ivanov gave Russia a 2–0 win over Austria and put England's qualification in doubt.

The Irish, paying for bad intelligence on the Argentinian team, lost 3–1 to it at Halmstad. The sheer skill of the Argentinians overcame an Irish team which lacked bite in the middle, Coyle's unexpected replacement of Dougan bringing no improvement. This above all was a game in which Danny Blanchflower's subtle talents, his always imaginative use of the ball, were needed not in defence but in midfield, where Rossi and the splendid veteran Labruna dominated.

West Germany at Hälsingborg brought Hans Schaefer in from the wing to inside-left, and it was his controversial goal, scored on the hour, which turned a game they seemed to be losing to the lively Czechs. Two goals down, they made it 1–2 when Schaefer charged the Czech goalkeeper Dolejsi over his line with the ball, and the goal was surprisingly allowed to stand. Helmut Rahn—again—equalised.

An unexpected result was the defeat of France 3–2 by Yugoslavia at Vasteras, despite two more goals for the prolific Just Fontaine. A lack of authority in defence, despite the composed presence at centre-half of the accomplished Bob Jonquet, an inability to get the best out of two excellent wingers in Wisnieski and Jean Vincent, a penalty refused when Fontaine was fouled; all these played a part in France's defeat. So did the opportunism of Veselinovic, who got two of the Yugoslav goals. The winner came three minutes from time when France were besieging Beara's goal. Then Yugoslavia broke away, Roger Marche—France's bald, experienced left-back—erred, and Veselinovic scored his second.

Scotland, seemingly weary after their display against the Yugoslavs, went down 3–2 to Paraguay at Norrkoping where Silvio Parodi, an inside-forward with experience of Italian football, was the dominant player and Bobby Evans an excellent centre-half. Indeed, not one of the British teams won their match in this round, for Wales played very poorly in Stockholm, to be held 1–1 by Mexico. 'Every time you knocked one of them down, he cried,' complained the Manchester United forward Colin Webster, never the most gentle of players, but Kelsey was impressed by their ball control and fitness.

Sweden made heavy weather of winning their evening game in the same stadium against Hungary, a match notable for the tremendous right-footed shooting of Hungary's Lajos Tichy and the deadly finishing of Sweden's Kurre Hamrin.

The concluding round of matches brought, above all, the annihilation of Argentina by Czechoslovakia at Hälsingborg, a humiliation which may now be seen as the bleak turning point in Argentinian football. What was especially strange was that the Argentinians should be made to look so slow and obsolete by the Czechs, so often criticised—as they would be even in the 1962 World Cup—for one-pace football.

The Czechs, who confirmed the burly Popluhar at centre-half in his second World Cup match, simply overwhelmed the Argentinians. Borovicka, who had missed the German game—there were tales of a bitter quarrel in the dressing-room during the Irish match—returned to blend perfectly with the powerful Molnar, while Hovorka was a strong and effective outside-right, making two goals and scoring the last two. Another two went to Zikan, the outside-left, and Argentina's only reply came from a penalty by the inevitable Corbatta. With the exception of him, Menendez and Varacka—who, commentators were quick to point out, was of Czech origin—the team looked slow and unfit.

When the Argentinians arrived at Buenos Aires airport initial disbelief had turned to fury and they were pelted with rubbish. The wound went deep. In future, Argentinian football would shed its old traditions of spectacle and artistry and become more destructive than the most negative.

In Malmö, with thousands of their supporters in attendance, West Germany were held to an exciting 2–2 draw by Northern Ireland, for whom Harry Gregg, superb in goal, and Peter McParland, a deadly opportunist, surpassed themselves.

In Gothenburg, Brazil at last let slip the astonishing Pelé and the inimitable Garrincha, routing the Soviets in the process. Though the score was 2–0 it might easily have been doubled or even trebled.

Pelé had been an international for almost a year, a striking inside-forward who came from a poor black family at Tres Coracoes in the heart of the great state of Minas Gerais. As a boy he had been coached by the old Brazilian international forward, de Brito, who brought him to the Santos club where his progress had been phenomenal. Five feet eight inches tall, weighing some ten and a half stone, superbly muscled, he was at this stage a goal-scorer *par excellence*, gymnastically agile and resilient, a tantalising juggler of the ball, a fine right-footed shot with the ability to climb and head like a Lawton. Above all, his temperament was extraordinary, his coolness in the thick of the battle, the most tense and dramatic situations, uncanny.

His face, which would become so familiar throughout the world over the next decade, never lost its innocence, its boyish appeal. He was no saint; in years to come his policy under provocation was much more the Old Testament one of an eye for an eye than the New Testament's turning the other cheek, but somehow the image remained untarnished, the pristine appeal untouched.

Garrincha came into the team by popular request of the players themselves. A deputation led by Nilton Santos went to Feola and asked for his inclusion. Feola gave way. From the opening minutes, Garrincha's incomparable swerve and acceleration left his opponent Kuznetsov helpless. First he beat him to the wide, shot, and hit the left-hand post. Next, Pelé hit the right-hand post. Finally, after three minutes, Didì emerged calmly and magisterially from a group of Russian opponents, and with an exquisite pass found Vavà who dashed through to score.

Didì had now found his ideal complement in the Santos right-half Zito, who had replaced Dino. Stronger in defence, much less inclined to carry the ball, an adroit passer who could strike for goal when necessary, Zito would emerge as the best half-back in the tournament.

It was extraordinary that Russia's bemused defence should hold out till thirteen minutes from time when Vavà, after an exchange of passes with Pelé, got the second. At one late, memorable instant, Garrincha had and held the ball against five encircling Russians. Genius had overwhelmed mere effort.

At Boras, in a match played on a lower plane, England laboured to a draw with the ponderous Austrians, who were twice ahead. The British sailor who ironically blew the Last Post when a histrionic Austrian went down might well have been blowing it for England. Haynes, at his best, must have made more of Kevan's dominance of the ageing Happel, Austria's stopper. He himself scored England's first goal after fifty-six minutes and made the second for Kevan. Austria's goals both came from impressive, uncharacteristic long shots, by Koller and Koerner.

In Group ii France duly beat Scotland, but they found it hard. Each team changed its goalkeeper. Bill Brown, of Dundee and later of Spurs, won the admiration of Kopa and Fontaine with his agility; Abbes replaced Remetter for France. Kopa volleyed home Fontaine's cross—a brief reciprocation—but Scotland struck back forcefully. Abbes had to make a fine save from Murray; then, when the Hearts forward was fouled—by Jonquet and the talented right-half Armand Penverne—John Hewie, Charlton Athletic's South African, wastefully hit the penalty against a post.

It was as well for France that in the very last seconds of the half Fontaine, served by Jonquet, should sprint away to make it 2–0. In the second half, when they were much less good, Baird emulated him and the final score was a narrow 2–1.

At Eskilstuna a hero tottered, Vladimir Beara having one of his worst games in goal for Yugoslavia against Paraguay. The score was 3–3, and all three Paraguayan goals could be blamed on the unhappy Beara. Three times the Paraguayans, inspired again by Parodi, equalised against a Yugoslav team which had dropped the graceful Milutinovic; but the Slavs went through.

Play-Offs for Quarter-Finals

Goal average counting for nothing, three of the British teams now entered play-offs—and two got through. It was, most unforeseeably, England who failed, losing 1–0 to Russia in Gothenburg. Almost perversely, having stubbornly refused to make changes, they now, still disdaining Charlton, capped two new forwards: Peter Brabook, the Chelsea right-winger, and Peter Broadbent, the industrious young Wolves inside-right.

In the tepid Ullevi—tepid till Sweden arrived there—England did not deserve to lose, though Haynes, apparently untouchable, had another grim game. Brabook twice hit a post; Ilyin hit one after sixty-eight minutes, and scored. Sadly for the otherwise faultless McDonald, it was his careless throw which put Russia away.

Decimated Ireland, faced by a Czech team which had swamped Argentina, patched up their team at Malmö and won, as Peter Doherty promised they would.

Norman Uprichard replaced Gregg in goal, and Jackie Scott was capped for the first time in place of the injured Tommy Casey. Uprichard was hurt, Peacock was hurt, Czechoslovakia took the lead, the game went into extra time; and still Ireland won.

Zikan gave the Czechs the lead after nineteen minutes, but on the stroke of half-time the irresistible McParland equalised after Cush had had two shots blocked. Nine minutes into extra time he volleyed home Danny Blanchflower's free kick. Bubernik of Czechoslovakia was sent off. Ireland qualified.

So did Wales, eliminating Hungary at Stockholm; a match in which an opponent was also sent off—Sipos, for brutally kicking Hewitt; also in extra time.

Neither British team survived the quarter-final, though Wales, even without the mighty John Charles, gave Brazil immense trouble in Gothenburg. Perhaps Charles would have exploited the early centre with which Webster, his deputy, did nothing.

Thereafter, it was the iron Welsh defence against the Brazilian attack which found the going harder and harder. Mazzola was back again for Vavà, Garrincha was most cleverly played by Mel Hopkins, Dave Bowen was an inspiring captain, Stuart Williams and Derek Sullivan a muscular right flank. Behind them, Jack Kelsey held everything. 'Chewing gum,' he modestly explained afterwards. 'Always use it. Put some on my hands. Rub it well in.'

Pelé has often said that the goal with which he cut the Gordian knot after sixty-six minutes was the most important he ever scored. It was also one of the luckiest, for Kelsey had the shot covered before it struck the foot of the impeccable Williams and was deflected past him. There was a pile-up, a very pyramid of yellow-shirted Brazilian bodies in the goalmouth.

The weary and depleted Irish team, all the wearier for an ill-planned coach journey, did their best against France but blew up. The two hundred and ten-mile drive to Nörrkoping the previous day was bad enough preparation; the absence of Gregg and Peacock (with torn ligaments) and the need to play the damaged Casey still a greater handicap. There was just one early moment in which the team might have scored and thus found the morale, the magic energy, they had before. In one of their set-piece throw-ins, Blanchflower threw the ball to Bingham's head and the little winger flicked it on for McIlroy, but he, clear through, squared it instead of shooting. That was that. With McParland on this occasion lost in the middle, Wisnieski scored just before half-time and Ireland collapsed. In the second half Fontaine, twice more, and Piantoni added goals.

The Quarter-Finals

Sweden found a weary Russian team stiff opponents in the first half at

Stockholm, where the public's incredulity still kept the crowd down to less than 32,000. In the second half Kurt Hamrin embarked on a one-man siege of the Russian goal. Twice he almost headed in; eventually, after his own run and cross, the ball bobbled loose and head it in he did. He made the second goal for Simonsson from the left-hand goal line two and a half minutes from time.

Jasseron, an experienced French coach, observed of the Swedes that they were a good enough team provided they were not outpaced. Raynor knew it; Brazil would capitalise on it.

At Malmö Helmut Rahn yet again won the match for Germany, racing away from the vulnerable Crnkovic to score after twelve minutes, Krivocuka, Beara's equally unhappy replacement, failing to narrow the angle. It was a match blemished by the ruthlessness of Juskowiak and Erhardt, who was lucky indeed not to give away a penalty when, nine minutes from the end, he not only brought down Milutinovic—restored and iridescent—but held his leg for good measure.

The Semi-Finals   Sweden v. West Germany

The semi-finals pitted Sweden against West Germany in Gothenburg and Brazil against France in Stockholm. The Gothenburg match provided an extraordinary study in national behaviour, as the Swedes' unfettered chauvinism put even the Germans' in the shade, and very nearly resulted in the game not being played at all.

In the first place, the Swedes outraged all the canons of hospitality by bringing their own cheerleaders right on to the pitch before the match, to incite the crowd. The German cheerleaders, meanwhile, were confined to the running-track.

In the stand, an embittered row was going on between Dr Pecos Bauwens, the Olympian President of the German Football Association, whose own chauvinistic pronouncements after the 1954 World Cup had caused concern in West Germany, and Swedish officials. The Swedes would not provide seats for some of the West German supporters. Dr Bauwens threatened that if they were not forthcoming he would withdraw his team from the match. They were provided.

The game itself was a fascinating one, even though blemished by fouls and at least one major refereeing error. With the tremendous Swedish choruses of *Heja, heja, heja!* thundering over the stadium, the home team dictated the early play. Erhardt had chosen the wrong studs and slipped about parlously on the greasy ground, while Herkenrath looked an uncertain goalkeeper. Nevertheless, it was Germany who broke away for a sensational goal.

Seeler, always busy and thoughtful, went to the left to catch a ball rolling out of play and centred, and Hans Schaefer despatched it past Svensson with a ferocious twenty-five-yard volley.

Sweden's equaliser, after Liedholm and Gren had gradually brought them back into the game, should never have stood. Liedholm blatantly brought the ball under control with his hand before running on with an approving wave from the referee, and Skoglund ultimately scored from a sharp angle. There were only five minutes between the goals.

It was Hamrin, already tormenting Juskowiak, who turned the game early in the second half, though in a somewhat unusual way. In the third minute Herkenrath had to plunge at his feet. In the twelfth he fouled Juskowiak, who was foolish enough to kick him. Hamrin made the most of it, rolling about in apparent agony, though when Juskowiak was sent off, his recovery was quick.

Parling, the large, blond Swedish left-half known as the Iron Stove, was just as worthy to be sent off for a dreadful foul on Fritz Walter sixteen minutes from the end. Walter was carried off for a couple of minutes, and spent the next day in bed. So Sweden, now virtually playing against nine men, finished the job.

Nine minutes from time, when Hamrin's shot was blocked, Gunnar Gren let fly immediately for the top left-hand corner, for one of his rare goals. Finally, Hamrin scored a goal of rare skill and impertinence, first stopping with the ball and walking it towards the right touchline like a man bemused, then coming to galvanic life, dancing past three men and beating Herkenrath. The slowest team in the tournament had reached the Final.

Brazil v. France

So did Brazil, though the promised feast against France never materialised. It would have been fascinating to see how the deep central thrust of Fontaine and Piantoni, fed by Kopa, would have fared against Brazil's uncertain central defence. For thirty-seven minutes, indeed, the marvellous little Kopa caused all sorts of trouble. Didì, Garrincha and Pelé made Vavà a devastating goal in the second minute, but Fontaine had equalised within nine. Then Bob Jonquet was hurt and left the middle, Didì scored within two minutes, and in the second half the fabulous Pelé ran riot with three more goals, Piantoni scoring a late, meaningless second for France.

The Final   Sweden v. Brazil

So Sweden would play Brazil, and the Brazilians worried about the effect an atmosphere as torrid as Gothenburg's might have on their emotional players. The World Cup Committee set their minds at rest by sternly forbidding the Swedes to bring cheerleaders on to the pitch again. Thus deprived of example and instruction, the crowd at Rasunda was astonishingly quiet.

As an *hors d'oeuvre* Kopa and Fontaine played ducks and drakes at Gothenburg with a weakened Germany—in which the young, blond Karl-Heinz Schnellinger made his second appearance of the series, at right-half. Kopa, the son of a Polish miner and a Frenchwoman, who might never have turned professional footballer were it not for a boy-hood mining accident, was irresistible. Svengali to Fontaine's Trilby, he helped him to four splendid goals and got a penalty himself. France took the third-place match 6–3.

Thus to Stockholm, and a day heavy with rain. George Raynor cheerfully forecast that if the Brazilians went a goal down they would 'panic all over the show'. They did go an early goal down; and stayed serene.

Feola made a bold change in defence, suddenly withdrawing his right-back de Sordi to give the powerful black Djalma Santos, a veteran of 1954, his first game in the competition. The two Santoses snuffed out Hamrin and Skoglund with the nonchalance of men extinguishing a candle.

Yet Sweden had a goal in four minutes, a goal worked out by Gren and Liedholm with such facility that many seemed sure to follow. Gren gave Liedholm the ball, Liedholm picked his way precisely past two Brazilian defenders in the penalty box and beat the poised Gilmar with a low, strong shot into the right-hand corner. It was the first time in the tournament that Brazil had been in arrears.

Six minutes later they were level, thanks to the pantherine Garrincha. Receiving from Zito on the right wing, he took the ball up to Parling and Axbom, caught them both off balance with a miraculous swerve and acceleration down the line and cut the ball back hard and fast. In tore Vavà to score.

The game grew wonderfully vivid. Pelé crashed a shot against the post, tireless Zagalo headed out from almost beneath the Brazilian bar. After thirty-two minutes, however, Garrincha again left the Swedish left flank standing, and Vavà again drove in his pass.

Sweden were losing the battle in midfield and were impotent on the wings. Their last hopes died ten minutes after half-time, when Pelé scored a marvellously impertinent goal. Catching a high ball in the thick of the penalty box on his thigh, he hooked it over his head, whirled round and volleyed mightily past Svensson.

Now Zito and Didì were switching play at will, now Djalma Santos was racing up from full-back, now Pelé and Vavà were probing, interpassing. With thirteen minutes left Zagalo went past Boerjesson, then Bergmark, and shot the fourth, and knelt in tears of joy.

Next, with the overjoyed Brazilian fans keeping up a shout of *Samba, samba!*, Liedholm sent Agne Simonsson through the middle, possibly offside, for Sweden's second goal—only for Pelé to reply with Brazil's fifth. Zagalo's was the centre, and Pelé rose to it with majestic elevation and power.

The World Cup was Brazil's at long last, and who could not rejoice with them as they ran, like ecstatic children, round the pitch, holding first their own flag, then the Swedes'? There was no doubt this time that the best, immeasurably the finest, team had won.

RESULTS: Sweden 1958

Pool I

Germany 3, Argentina 1 (HT 2/1)
Ireland 1, Czechoslovakia 0 (HT 1/0)
Germany 2, Czechoslovakia 2 (HT 1/0)
Argentina 3, Ireland 1 (HT 1/1)
Germany 2, Ireland 2 (HT 1/1)
Czechoslovakia 6, Argentina 1 (HT 3/1)

	P	W	D	L	GOALS F	A	Pts
Germany	3	1	2	0	7	5	4
Czechoslovakia	3	1	1	1	8	4	3
Ireland	3	1	1	1	4	5	3
Argentina	3	1	0	2	5	10	2

Pool II

France 7, Paraguay 3 (HT 2/2)
Yugoslavia 1, Scotland 1 (HT 1/0)
Yugoslavia 3, France 2 (HT 1/1)
Paraguay 3, Scotland 2 (HT 2/1)
France 2, Scotland 1 (HT 2/0)
Yugoslavia 3, Paraguay 3 (HT 2/1)

	P	W	D	L	GOALS F	A	Pts
France	3	2	0	1	11	7	4
Yugoslavia	3	1	2	0	7	6	4
Paraguay	3	1	1	1	9	12	3
Scotland	3	0	1	2	4	6	1

Pool III

Sweden 3, Mexico 0 (HT 1/0)
Hungary 1, Wales 1 (HT 1/1)
Wales 1, Mexico 1 (HT 1/1)
Sweden 2, Hungary 1 (HT 1/0)
Sweden 0, Wales 0 (HT 0/0)
Hungary 4, Mexico 0 (HT 1/0)

	P	W	D	L	GOALS F	A	Pts
Sweden	3	2	1	0	5	1	5
Hungary	3	1	1	1	6	3	3
Wales	3	0	3	0	2	2	3
Mexico	3	0	1	2	1	8	1

Play off Wales 2, Hungary 1 (HT 0/1)

Pool IV

England 2, Russia 2 (HT 0/1)
Brazil 3, Austria 0 (HT 1/0)
England 0, Brazil 0 (HT 0/0)
Russia 2, Austria 0 (HT 1/0)
Brazil 2, Russia 0 (HT 1/0)
England 2, Austria 2 (HT 0/1)

	P	W	D	L	GOALS F	A	Pts
Brazil	3	2	1	0	5	0	5
England	3	0	3	0	4	4	3
Russia	3	1	1	1	4	4	3
Austria	3	0	1	2	2	7	1

Play off Russia 1, England 0 (HT 0/0)

Quarter-finals

Norrköping

France 4	**Ireland 0**
Abbes; Kaebel, Lerond;	Gregg; Keith,
Penverne, Jonquet,	McMichael;
Marcel; Wisnieski,	Blanchflower,
Fontaine, Kopa,	Cunningham, Cush;
Piantoni, Vincent.	Bingham, Casey,
	Scott, McIlroy,
	McParland.

SCORERS
Wisnieski, Fontaine (2), Piantoni for France
HT 1/0

Malmö

West Germany 1	**Yugoslavia 0**
Herkenrath;	Krivocuka; Sijakovic,
Stollenwerk, Juskowiak;	Crnkovic; Krstic,
Eckel, Erhardt,	Zebec, Boskov;
Szymaniak; Rahn,	Petakovic, Veselinovic,
Walter, Seeler, Schmidt,	Milutinovic,
Schaefer.	Ognjanovic, Rajkov.

SCORER
Rahn for West Germany
HT 1/0

Stockholm

Sweden 2	**Russia 0**
Svensson; Bergmark,	Yachine; Kessarev,
Axbom; Boerjesson,	Kuznetsov; Voinov,
Gustavsson, Parling;	Krijevski, Tsarev;
Hamrin, Gren,	Ivanov, A., Ivanov, V.,
Simonsson, Liedholm,	Simonian, Salnikov,
Skoglund.	Ilyin.

SCORERS
Hamrin, Simonsson for Sweden
HT 0/0

Gothenburg

Brazil 1	Wales 0
Gilmar; De Sordi,	Kelsey; Williams,
Santos, N.; Zito, Bellini,	Hopkins; Sullivan,
Orlando; Garrincha,	Charles, M., Bowen;
Didì, Mazzola, Pelé,	Medwin, Hewitt,
Zagalo.	Webster, Allchurch,
	Jones.

SCORER
Pelé for Brazil
HT 0/0

Semi-finals

Stockholm

Brazil 5	France 2
Gilmar; De Sordi,	Abbes; Kaelbel,
Santos, N.; Zito, Bellini,	Lerond; Penverne,
Orlando; Garrincha,	Jonquet, Marcel;
Didì, Vavà, Pelé,	Wisnieski, Fontaine,
Zagalo.	Kopa, Piantoni,
	Vincent.

SCORERS
Vavà, Didì, Pelé (3) for Brazil
Fontaine, Piantoni for France
HT 2/1

Gothenburg

Sweden 3	West Germany 1
Svensson; Bergmark,	Herkenrath;
Axbom; Boerjesson,	Stollenwerk,
Gustavsson, Parling;	Juskowiak; Eckel,
Hamrin, Gren,	Erhardt, Szymaniak;
Simonsson, Liedholm,	Rahn, Walter, Seeler,
Skoglund.	Schaefer, Cieslarczyk.

SCORERS
Skoglund, Gren, Hamrin for Sweden
Schaefer for Germany
HT 1/1

Third place match

Gothenburg

France 6	West Germany 3
Abbes; Kaelbel,	Kwiatowski;
Lerond; Penverne,	Stollenwerk, Erhardt;
Lafont, Marcel;	Schnellinger, Wewers,
Wisnieski, Douis,	Szymaniak; Rahn,
Kopa, Fontaine,	Sturm, Kelbassa,
Vincent.	Schaefer, Cieslarczyk.

SCORERS
Fontaine (4), Kopa (penalty), Douis for France
Cieslarezyk, Rahn, Schaefer for Germany
HT 3/1

Final

Stockholm

Brazil 5	Sweden 2
Gilmar; Santos, D.,	Svensson; Bergmark,
Santos, N.; Zito,	Axbom; Boerjesson,
Bellini, Orlando;	Gustavsson, Parling;
Garrincha, Didì,	Hamrin, Gren,
Vavà, Pelé, Zagalo.	Simonsson, Liedholm,
	Skoglund.

SCORERS
Vavà (2), Pelé (2), Zagalo for Brazil
Liedholm, Simonsson for Sweden
HT 2/1

CHILE
1962

Background to Chile

Brazil retained the 1962 World Cup, held in Chile, showing in the process that they were very much more than a one-man—or one-demigod—team; or rather that if one hero succumbed, another sprang up to take his place. It was the World Cup of Garrincha, the World Cup of 4-3-3. That long, thin, impoverished Chile should put it on at all was remarkable. Earthquakes had devastated the country at the time they were pleading their case, and Carlos Dittborn, the President of the Chilean Football Federation, coined the magnificent *non sequitur*, 'We must have the World Cup *because* we have nothing.'

They got it, quickly building one superb new stadium in Santiago in the snowy lee of a still more superb mountain and another, small but exquisite, on the coast at Viña del Mar, where pelicans sat on the rocks and the sea wrack blew in over the pitch. A third group would play in seedy, broken-down Rancagua in the stadium of the Braden Copper Company, and a fourth thousands of miles to the north, at Arica, near the Peruvian border.

Criticisms of the country, of the organisation, were often unfair. If there was corruption over tickets, at least an official was hauled off to gaol. When there were similar stories, four years later, in England, the dirt was swept quickly under the carpet. If there were tales of over-charging for accommodation, then the police quickly made indictments. The two Italian journalists who indicted Chile as a backward country, and thereby exposed their own team to the calvary of the Battle of Santiago, were not even justified in their criticism. It was a country at once squalid and sophisticated, backward yet subtle, but for the visitor, Chile left more congenial memories than either Sweden or Mexico.

Brazil, playing on South American soil, were inevitably the favourites, though illness had obliged Vicente Feola, that rumbling, Buddha-figure, to stand down as manager in favour of Aymore Moreira, brother of 1954's Zeze. Aymore was a white-haired, patient, courteous man who, with Hilton Gosling beside him, had again ensured a climate in which the Brazilians could express their overflowing gifts in peace and with effect. They would play in the Viña del Mar group with the Czechs, Spaniards and Mexicans.

The Contenders

The Viña group: Brazil, Czechoslovakia, Spain and Mexico

In the four years since they had won the World Cup, the component pieces of the Brazilian team had sprung apart, then strangely and steadily come together again. Two players had gone to Madrid, with sharply varying fortunes; and had come back. Vavà, the centre-forward who scored twice in the Final was transferred to Atletico Madrid, did well for a few seasons, then returned to play in Brazil; in time to displace Pelé's precocious teenaged colleague at Santos, Coutinho, with whom he had worked many a spectacular one-two.

Didì, the great orchestrator in Sweden, and already a star in Switzerland, had joined Real Madrid, but had come home, in time to win back his place from the confident young Cinesinho.

Zito, his midfield colleague, challenged by Zequinha, had edged in front of him at the eleventh hour, while an injury precluded any chance of Pepe supplanting Zagalo on the left wing; history repeating itself. Garrincha, that extraordinary child of nature from Pau Grande, was there again.

There were changes, however, in the central defence. Mauro, a reserve in 1958, took over at centre-half and captain from Bellini. The little black Zozimo, who had toured Europe with Brazil in 1957, succeeded Orlando, who had been playing in Argentina.

The Santoses, though veterans now—Nilton was thirty-six—were irreplaceable at back; the grey-jerseyed Gilmar was as calmly efficient as ever in goal. And of course there was Pelé, as wonderfully gymnastic, as astonishingly inventive, as brave, strong, inimitable and explosive as ever. At twenty-one there was little doubt that he was now the best footballer in the world.

At Viña—or rather, just outside it at Quilpue, where Pelé rejoiced to play daringly in goal—Aymore Moreira confessed his fears of Czechoslovakia. 'The Czechs play a very athletic game, hard and vigorous, which will certainly give us trouble. And then I know that they are also good technicians!' They were known to be a gifted team though a slow one but, as one acute French journalist wrote, their very slowness, their very pessimism, were turned to advantage.

Slowness—when players were at the same time such fine ball-players—meant precision; a packed defence, a sparsely-manned attack, with large areas of space to play in. Pessimism meant lack of pressure, plus a desire to show everybody they had been undervalued. Teamwork was guaranteed by the fact that most of the side played for the Dukla Prague (Army) club; and there was an outstanding left-half in Josef Masopust, a calm, deft player who used the ball cunningly and could score goals, too. In the centre of the defence, Pluskal and the massive, bald Popluhar, both World Cup centre-halves in their time, were no mean barrier, while behind them played the bald, elastic goal-keeper Wilhelm Schroiff, whose contribution would, until the Final, be so great.

Spain were managed by Helenio Herrera, the Internazionale

manager, who had previously flanked Giannini Ferrari as coach to the Italian side. Controversy over the drugging of Inter players, and Herrera's public delight when Juventus were knocked out of the European Cup, had led to his resignation. Spain—where he had worked for many successful years—now appointed him.

It was a surprising development, which led predictably to a conflict of egos between Herrera and Alfredo di Stefano. Pulling a muscle just before leaving Spain, di Stefano announced he would be coming merely 'as a tourist'. His cheerful father arrived from Buenos Aires with a 'magic' liniment which he urged him to use, but the prevailing view was that no liniment would heal the breach between di Stefano and Herrera.

Still, there was Luis Suarez, a fine, creative inside-forward, once with Herrera at Barcelona and now with him again at Inter. There was the leggy Peiró of Atletico Madrid. There was Martinez from Paraguay, and Puskas from Hungary. The talent was there, if not the team.

The remaining country was Mexico, two of whose players had tried on their arrival in Viña to attack an Australian journalist who had written that they would be there only to live the gay life.

In retrospect, there are good reasons for calling this Zagalo's World Cup as much as Garrincha's. 'One could never sufficiently stress the key role played by Zagalo in the Brazilian victory,' wrote the French journalist Jean-Philippe Réthacker. 'An active and courageous footballer, very perceptive in his passing and positional play, precise and varied in his technique, Zagalo was certainly, with the Czech Masopust, the most intelligent player of the 1962 World Cup.'

Seriousness was the keynote of his game and his personality. In hot, gay Rio, he was the player who spent his evenings quietly with his fiancée, his Sunday mornings in church. Strength of lung and strength of will would transform him into an international star, capable now of labouring in midfield, now of bursting forward to deliver a short, deadly accurate cross, who had never been more important to Brazil than at this moment.

The Rancagua group:
England, Hungary, Bulgaria and Argentina

England had Walter Winterbottom in charge, for what would be his fourth and last World Cup. He had just been out-voted for the Football Association's Secretaryship, in which he was expected to succeed his mentor, Sir Stanley Rous, now President of FIFA. He was assisted as coach by the English Footballer of the Year, Burnley's Jimmy Adamson, a tall, lean, humorous Geordie, captain and future manager of his club, who would subsequently turn down Walter Winterbottom's job.

Yet although they had scouted the ground this time, had got the retreat that everybody wanted, there was still something vaguely amateurish and haphazard about the English preparation. What other team, for instance, would include in its practice matches a middle-aged Australian millionaire businessman?

The 1958 side had largely evaporated, with one major exception; the attack was still built round Fulham's inside-left Johnny Haynes, who was now the captain. 'Why is everything with England number 10?' a Yugoslav coach would demand rhetorically, as his team's aeroplane finally flew out of Santiago. 'Number 10 takes the corners! Number 10 takes the throw-ins! So what do we do? We put a man on number 10! Goodbye, England!'

It was exactly what the Hungarians would do in the first match at Rancagua, when Rakosi dogged Haynes' every move. And indeed, the nemesis of making one man so important was precisely that if he failed, so did the team. Haynes had failed in Gothenburg; he would fail, alas, again in Chile. But since he was captain, the failure would if anything be more costly. A most gifted player with a superb left foot, brisk control and high strategic flair, Chile saw him at his least amenable. There was a thin-skinned petulance about him which seemed to permeate the team, and led to strained relations with the Press. On the other hand, it was not Haynes' fault that the over-hierarchical atmosphere of the England team was so marked that players still tended to give less for England than they gave for their clubs; and they still travelled without a doctor, an omission which might have had fatal results for Peter Swan, the reserve centre-half, in Viña del Mar.

Bryan Douglas, the skilful little Blackburn outside-right, who had scored an important goal in the vital qualifying match against Portugal, also survived from Sweden. As for Bobby Charlton, the blameless cause of such controversy in 1958, he had developed in these years from a goal-scoring inside-forward into an outside-left of classical gifts, marvellous acceleration, a willowy swerve, a prodigious shot not only in his right foot but now in his left.

Then there was Jimmy Greaves, quintessentially Cockney, a 'boy-wonder' still more remarkable than Charlton; an East Ender who at the age of seventeen had walked straight into the Chelsea First Division team on the opening day of the season at Tottenham to embark on a dazzling series of goals. His turn of speed was extraordinary, his confidence more remarkable still, his left foot a hammer, his instinct for being in the right place near goal almost psychic. The previous year he had gone briefly and reluctantly to A.C. Milan, hated the atmosphere and the disciplines, and obliged them to transfer him home; but to Tottenham, not to Chelsea. He was one of the most exciting talents England had thrown up since the war; yet now, when the chips were truly down, he would be as disappointing as Haynes.

Another East Londoner had just won a place in the team—Bobby Moore, capped for the first time in Peru *en route* to Chile. England had played extremely well, winning 4–0 on a ground where, three years earlier, they had lost 4–1, and the twenty-one-year-old Moore, tall, blond, quite imperturbable, had had a fine game at right-half. This imperturbability was evident even when he was a West Ham United youth player, running up a record number of youth caps for England. Haste seemed anathema to him; even in the tightest goal-line situations he would remain calm and relaxed.

Encouraged by Ron Greenwood, West Ham's manager, a disciple of Winterbottom, he had worked hard at his football, developing from a centre-half of great poise but unexceptional talents into a defensive wing-half who read the game superbly, covering and tackling faultlessly, using the long ball well. If he had weaknesses, they lay in strange, transient lapses in concentration and a vulnerability to small, quick-turning forwards who would play close up on him.

He well deserved his place, and would have an excellent World Cup, but the choice of the equally bold, equally large, straightforward Ron Flowers as the other wing-half meant that England lacked the ball-playing half-back they needed in a 4–2–4 formation. Bobby Robson, who had developed since 1958 into a thoughtful half-back, had dropped out in Lima through injury, and would otherwise have been a more sensible choice in the circumstances.

In goal was yet another Londoner, the cheerful, robust, fearless Ron Springett of Sheffield Wednesday. He was Fulham-born, resilient on the line, but vulnerable to shots from afar, as his colleagues knew. There was a worrying doubt about his vision.

At full-back there was a resilient pair in the calm, pipe-smoking Jim Armfield and the tough ebullient Ray Wilson, while at last there was a choice between two tall and powerful centre-halves, Tottenham's Maurice Norman and Sheffield Wednesday's Peter Swan. For centre-forward there was the brave, blond Shropshire miner, Gerry Hitchens, who unlike Greaves had stayed happily that season in Milan, scoring freely for Inter. He arrived in Chile, to the admiration of his colleagues, dressed to kill.

Hungary, Bulgaria and Argentina were the other teams in the Rancagua group, where England were favoured. Their own critics, however, feared they might again distil the familiar, bitter-sweet essence of mediocrity for which they were known in World Cups; and the opening game would bear out this pessimism.

Hungary, though they had just lost to Italy B, were in better plight than in 1958. They had beaten England two years before in Budapest, thanks to the prowess of Florian Albert, a fluent young centre-forward whose skills evoked the earlier Hidegkuti, and who combined beautifully with the lean Gorocs while Tichy was still there to fire his rightfooted shells. Gyula Grosics alone survived from the great team of the 1950s. There was a tall, supple, blond, linking right-half in Erno Solymosi, a formidable double pillar in defence in Sipos and Meszoly, and an insidious right-winger in dark little Karoliy Sandor who played, like Kurt Hamrin, with his socks around his ankles.

The Argentinians had a new young manager in Juan Carlos Lorenzo, but were still playing with the traditional roving centre-half; this time the fair-haired Sacchi. He, with the strong, blond, attacking left-back, Silvio Marzolini, would give the team much of its propulsion. José Sanfilippo, their free-scoring inside-left, had tried to drop out after a period of poor form. Lorenzo had him medically and psychiatrically examined, got highly positive reports—and picked him.

The Bulgarians, built around the CDNA (Sofia) Army team, had beaten France in a play-off, yet seemed to have little to offer apart from the clever left wing of the experienced Ivan Kolev and the young Yakimov. Kolev, with his speed and ball skills, had now moved to the flank.

The Santiago group:
Italy, Chile, West Germany and Switzerland

Italy, playing in Santiago, had arrived in their customary state of chaos, warned by Herrera that it was always a bad thing to fall into the group which included the host country. At once flamboyant and dictatorial, hooded and extrovert, a coiner of slogans and of money, a ruthless manipulator and a superb preparer of players, Herrera had become the best paid, most controversial manager in the world, though the World Cup would elude him.

By now, *catenaccio* had Italian football in its clammy grip, and bright young players who began with all the traditional joy in ball play and invention soon had it bred out of them when they reached the stony reality of Serie A, the First Division.

To qualify, Italy had to negotiate the low hurdle of Israel; yet at one point in the game in Tel Aviv they found themselves two down. They recovered to win 4–2, thanks partly to the accomplished left-footed finishing of the Veronese, Mario Corso of Inter. By the time the World Cup was due, however, Corso was dropped from the chosen twenty-two. It chanced that shortly before the party flew off he played a leading part in Inter's victory at San Siro over the Czech World Cup team.

Chilean hostility to the Italians had been aroused by the old policy of *oriundi*. José Altafini, lately Italy's chief goal-scorer, had in 1958's World Cup played centre-forward for Brazil. Humberto Maschio and the immensely talented little inside-left, Omar Sivori of the rolled-down socks, limpid control and deadly left foot, would have played for Argentina in the 1958 World Cup had Italian clubs not swooped on them in 1957. No policy could be more perfectly calculated to offend the South Americans in general, and the Argentinians, playing only ninety kilometres away in Rancagua, in particular.

As though this, and the presence of Italian club scouts hanging round the South American training camps, were not enough, two Italian journalists sent home disparaging articles about Chile which raised local hostility to a crescendo. One had, at all events, to sympathise with the poor Italian (or putatively Italian) footballers, who would be obliged so painfully to bear the brunt of what had been written.

If there were *oriundi* in the team, there was also an authentic Italian star in Gianni Rivera, one of the most precocious and gifted footballers produced since Meazza. He was still only eighteen, yet already he had been capped against Belgium in their last international, won in Brussels. Already he had had two seasons as strategist of the Milan attack. He was a dark, grave, faunlike figure who, playing in the Olympic football team at the age of sixteen, had already been talking like a man of thirty. His technique was flawless; despite a fragile physique, he struck a ball beautifully, and his passing was wonderfully imaginative.

West Germany were also in this group, bringing with them such doughty warriors as Uwe Seeler, Horst Szymaniak, Hans Schaefer and Karl-Heinz Schnellinger. They had qualified without hardship against Greece and Northern Ireland and, under the cunning leadership of Sepp Herberger in his last World Cup, had the tactical expertise, the physical hardness, to worry anyone.

Switzerland, the fourth team in the group, had accounted for Sweden in a play-off in Berlin, but were little fancied.

Of the Chileans themselves not a great deal was known, though they had lately thrashed and drawn with Hungary, and lost narrowly to Russia in Santiago. They were under the sophisticated managership of Fernando Riera, a debonair, good-looking man who had played football in France, they used a 4-2-4 formation, and were bound to be galvanised by an impassioned crowd.

The Arica group: Uruguay, Russia, Yugoslavia, Colombia

Finally, in Group I, up in remote Arica, there were three giants and a probable pygmy. The giants were Uruguay, twice Cup winners;

Russia, who had beaten them during their splendid November tour of South America; and Yugoslavia. The pygmy was Colombia, who had come down from high altitudes after unexpectedly putting out Peru. There were Yachine, Sekularac, Gonçalves.

The Opening Games

In their opening game, Chile showed they would need to be reckoned with by beating Switzerland 3–1 in Santiago before a delighted 65,000 crowd. The *mis-en-scène* was glorious—bright sun, a soaring, snowy mountain. The President of Chile spoke, Sir Stanley Rous spoke and the President of the Chilean Federation spoke. After this came what seemed a brisk anticlimax when, in only seven minutes, a banal error by the Chilean defence allowed Wuthrich to score from over twenty-five yards. The Swiss *verrou* was working wonderfully.

Chile, with the tall, strong left-half Eladio Rojas and the energetic inside-right Toro giving them power in midfield, took half an hour to get into their stride. Their equaliser came at the most delicately telling moment—a minute before half-time, Leonel Sanchez, the rapid outside-left and son of a professional boxer—there would be reason to remember this—converting Landa's centre.

In the first ten minutes of the second half, Chile grasped their psychological advantage, overrunning the Swiss defence. Ramirez gave them the lead. Leonel Sanchez, tackling Grobety, beating man after man, then shooting home from the twenty-five yards, got the third.

In the same group the following day, Italy and West Germany walked round and round one another like two cautious boxers, under a suitably leaden sky. There were no goals. Italy played, as expected, with the tough Torino half-back Ferrini as 'false' outside-right; a decision which, in those still relatively innocent days, had roused much displeasure in their Press. Salvadore was sweeper; the inside forwards were Rivera, Altafini and Sivori. Germany, too, played *catenaccio*, with Schnellinger as sweeper. The two stoppers, Erhardt, a forbidding force in Sweden, and Willy Schulz, tackled implacably, and Seeler once struck the bar, but there was little variation of pace. Italy, matching greater power with greater skill, held their own, till the game degenerated into a kind of tank battle; a few of their movements were beautifully conceived and carried out. Their morale seemed to equal their skill, their possibilities seemed great; but for the Chilean match, they would make six silly changes, and their hopes would go out of the window.

In Rancagua, Argentina began by beating Bulgaria 1–0 through Facundo's early goal in a harsh, dull game, while Hungary beat England 2–1 the day after. The Argentinians, far from backward in physical contact, themselves cut an impressive figure when similarly treated. The gesture of hurt incomprehension, the slow, concertina-crumpling to the ground, the final, corpse-like prostration, would have touched a heart of stone.

England's prosaic attack found Hungary's packed defence an insoluble puzzle. No English player could match the splendidly supple Albert and Solymosi, and it was a glorious individual goal by Albert which won the game, eighteen minutes from time. One of Tichy's long-range cannon balls had given Hungary the lead on the quarter-hour, and shown up Springett's costly weakness; Ron Flowers had equalised on the hour from a penalty given away by Meszoly's hand-ling. So England went dispiritedly up the hill to Coya. 'You *want* us to lose,' Haynes reproached a journalist.

In Viña's little jewel of a seaside stadium, Brazil were given a surprisingly hard time by a brave Mexican team which lost four or five good chances to score. Brazil, aware that several of their team were bearing the burden of the years, had already pulled Zagalo deeper, in a 4–3–3 formation, and Zagalo it was, from the brilliant Pelé's cross, who headed the first goal.

Pelé, in splendid form, scored the other goal against Mexico—both came in the second half—after beating four defenders and then Carbajal, with a prodigious shot.

The Czechs then beat Spain 1–0 with a goal scored by their righ-twinger Stibranyi ten minutes from time; a brisk piece of opportunism when the injured Reija failed either to control a ball or to reach Santamaria (Uruguay's 1954 stopper) with his pass. That the Czechs were by then in a position to win was thanks to the way their defence, especially the impressive Schroiff, had withstood Spain's early pressure. Finally the ponderous Martinez had vented his frustration by kicking Schroiff in the stomach; which simply moved the stronger Czechs to punish their opponents with a series of mighty tackles. Schroiff contin-ued, undaunted, to perform small miracles, and at last Spain exposed themselves to the counter-thrust which brought Stibranyi's goal. Czechoslovakia, with Masopust and the tall, lean, jog-trotting Kvasniak so skilful in midfield, had announced their candidature.

In far-off Arica, strange things were happening. Little Colombia, opening the ball, took the lead against Uruguay from a penalty and succumbed, 2–1, only a quarter of an hour from the finish. It took a characteristically clever run by little, dark Cubilla, the Uruguayan outside-right, and a thumping shot by Sasia to beat Sanchez, Colombia's fine goalkeeper, after half-time.

The next day a Russian team, including such heroes of 1958 as Yachine, Voronin, Ivanov, Netto and two lively wingers from Torpedo in Metreveli and Meshki, beat Yugoslavia 2–0 in a grim game. The

Yugoslavs committed themselves furiously to the conflict, Mujic going so far as to break Dubinski's leg and to be sent home by his team in consequence. For all this, it was a fine, technically pleasing match; the only one in which the celebrated Yachine would justify his immense reputation.

Ponedelnik, Russia's muscular new centre-forward, was involved in both goals. After fifty-three minutes he struck a thundering free kick against the bar, and Ivanov beat Soskic, Yugoslavia's fine goalkeeper, to the rebound. Four minutes from the end Ponedelnik himself scored the second. He would later complain that his team's atmosphere was too cold, too impersonal; that at one crucial stage he and his roommate had lain awake, side by side in their beds, far into the night, unable to speak a word to one another.

In the second round of matches Germany, in Santiago, beat Switzerland 2–1 in a tedious game which was spoiled when Szymaniak's brutal tackle broke a leg of the Swiss forward, Norbert Eschmann, after fourteen minutes. In the circumstances, the Swiss did well to hold the score to 2–1 and to have the last word, the last goal, themselves, when Schneiter scored fifteen minutes from the end.

The game was played in the deep shadow of what had gone on the day before in Chile's ghastly game against Italy; a game which produced two expulsions, a broken nose and a welter of violence. The ground, as we have seen, had been abundantly prepared by those two inflammatory articles, while the question of the *oriundi*, the recent accusations of drug-taking among Italian clubs, had made things worse.

For the Italian players, as their own correspondents wrote, were far too easily provoked by the Chileans, who were from the first busily spitting in their faces. The referee himself, tall Ken Aston, was accused by the Italians of being 'hostile and provocative'. He in turn, limping through the rest of the World Cup, *hors de combat* with a damaged Achilles tendon, insisted that the match was 'uncontrollable'. What is beyond dispute is that from this day Aston's career in refereeing went from strength to strength; to membership of FIFA's Referees' Committee, to the surveillance of World Cup referees in 1966 and 1970.

Certainly he was ill-served by his linesmen who, when Leonel Sanchez, behind his back, broke Maschio's nose with a left hook that was televised around the world, elected to behave like the three wise monkeys. Thus Sanchez stayed on the field while Ferrini, for hacking down Landa in the seventh minute, and David, for a retaliatory kick at Sanchez's head, went off. Reduced to nine men, Italy still resisted till fifteen minutes from time, when Ramirez headed in Leonel Sanchez's free kick, Toro adding the second, in the last minute. It had been altogether a dreadful day for football.

The group concluded with a 2–0 win by a much more sophisticated, economical German team over Chile, and an easy but meaningless 3–0 victory by Italy against Switzerland. So Chile and Germany passed into the quarter finals.

In Rancagua, England found form at last, beating Argentina by a clear 3–1; their first World Cup victory since 1954 outside the qualifying competition.

Much was achieved with the replacement of the disappointing Hitchens at centre-forward by Middlesbrough's Alan Peacock, a tall, straight-backed, guardsman-like figure even to the short haircut, who won many balls in the air despite ill usage from Navarro. Though it was his first international, he showed great aplomb, provoking the first goal after seventeen minutes. When Charlton, in ebullient form, centred from the left, Peacock skilfully headed the ball on, Navarro desperately handled, and Flowers scored his second penalty of the series.

Argentina were clever but unincisive, but served by Sacchi and the adventurous Marzolini; but Moore and Flowers tackled briskly, Jimmy Armfield was impeccable, Bryan Douglas far more lively than he had been against Hungary. Charlton, with a crisp, low, right-footed shot, made it 2–0 before half-time.

Then Hungary, in remarkable form, whipped Bulgaria 6–1, with a goal by Albert in the first minute and four goals by the twelfth. Albert and the greyhound Gorocs worked their fluent one-twos, their clever changes of pace, as easily as they had done in the 1960 Olympiad. Deprived of Iliev and Diev, Bulgaria could do little but let the wave wash over them. Hungary's was an iridescent performance, Solymosi, Albert and Gorocs bestriding the field as in the good old days of Bozsik, Hidegkuti and Puskas. Albert scored three; the result was 6–1.

In the final game, Lajos Baroti, the shrewd Hungarian coach, told his team not to exert themselves; a point was sufficient, and it was what they got, drawing 0–0 with Argentina. Albert and Sandor were rested. Gorocs, alas, tore a muscle in the eighteenth minute, while Meszoly, the blond stopper, played so majestically that the watching England players clapped him off the field.

England themselves, next day, gave a wretchedly mediocre performance against Bulgaria, drawing 0–0 in their turn, and lucky indeed to survive when Kolev beat Armfield on the line, to expose their goal with a cross nobody converted. England, second in the group, now had the daunting task of playing Brazil in Viña del Mar; while Hungary were much favoured to beat the Czechs in Rancagua.

Brazil had cataclysmically lost Pelé, victim of a torn thigh muscle, in their 0–0 draw with Czechoslovakia. After twenty-five minutes, taking a pass by Garrincha, he shot powerfully from twenty-five yards against the foot of the post; then hobbled off the field and out of the 1962 World Cup.

Brazil, with Pelé useless on the wing, drew all but Vavà and Garrincha back in defence; the Czechs gladly settled for a stalemate. No longer threatened by Brazil's explosive change of pace, they went their precise, skilful, somewhat monotonous way to a draw.

Brazil now pulled out of the hat the twenty-four-year-old Amarildo, Botafogo's inside-left; no Pelé, certainly, but a lithe, quick enterprising player with a nose for a goal, a cheerful and emotional child of nature, brown-skinned, curly-haired, effervescent. Succeeding Pelé was clearly less of a burden than an adventure.

The final qualifying match, against Spain, proved a tough one. A goal by Peirò in the last minute had given Spain meagre victory against surprising Mexico, so well coached by the Argentinian, Scopelli. Carbajal, in his fourth World Cup, had kept an impeccable goal, and now Spain needed at least a draw, probably a win, to qualify. Herrera gambled by dropping his two famous forwards, del Sol and Suarez, his goalkeeper Carmelo, and his centre-half Santamaria. Now Puskas would lead an attack which had three Atletico Madrid players, and the flying Paco Gento at outside-left. This was the game, one had heard, in which Didì planned his revenge on di Stefano for the humiliations of Madrid; but di Stefano was still not playing. Greatest all-round forward of his generation, inexhaustibly versatile, he never took part in the finals of a World Cup.

The 'new' Spain played with immense commitment and no little flair. Indeed, the match was possibly the best of the whole tournament, and it took the sudden, soaring flight of Garrincha to save and win it for Brazil.

Herrera, high priest of *catenaccio* with Inter, now used it with Spain, Rodri playing sweeper, the other defenders marking man to man. For an hour these tactics, given force and bite by the team's intense commitment, had Brazil at full stretch, and in the thirty-fourth minute a short, swift dribble by Puskas, a clever pass, made a goal for the energetic Adelardo.

For thirty-eight minutes, Spain deservedly kept their lead, their drive and *brio* several times taking them close to another goal; once especially, through Peirò. Then Amarildo, rising splendidly to the occasion and the opportunity, converted Zagalo's centre to equalise. Again Spain almost scored, this time through Verges, but with four minutes left Garrincha got electrically away, crossed, and Amarildo darted in to head the winner. It was a very near thing; and a manifest injustice to Spain.

The last game of the group produced the strangest result, Mexico defeating Czechoslovakia 3–1 and giving one of the best performances in their long but mediocre history in the World Cup. It meant that in the quarter-finals Czechoslovakia would play Hungary at Rancagua, while England came to Viña to meet Brazil.

Back in Arica, and Group 1, Russia, who had walloped the Uruguayans 5–0 in Moscow the previous month, now found that Uruguay in and Uruguay out of World Cups were two different teams; their 2–1 win was achieved only after eighty-nine minutes, and was extremely lucky. Reduced to ten men for an hour by an injury to Eliseo Alvarez, Uruguay pulled back their fine winger, Domingo Perez, and had the best of the argument, equalising Mamikin's goal through Sasia after fifty-four minutes, and hitting the post three times. Their 4-2-4, with Nestor Gonçalves deploying his unhurried skills in midfield, would surely have prevailed at full strength.

Not that Russia had covered themselves with glory in their second game. Colombia, astonishingly, had held them to a 4–4 draw which *L'Équipe*'s annual described as 'one of the greatest surprises of modern football'. Russia, after all, were 3–0 up after eleven minutes, and if Acero reduced it to 3–1, that was still the score at half-time, while Ponedelnik brought it to 4–1, early in the second half.

It was then, after sixty-eight minutes, that something very strange happened. Lev Yachine, of all people, gave a goal away straight from a corner. Suddenly the options were open. The little black insideforward, Klinger, began tearing holes in the strapping Russian defence, the whole team ran like furies, Rada scored a third goal, Klinger equalised. Though Yachine did make a couple of fine saves, *L'Équipe*'s annual solemnly, and prematurely, recorded that the match 'certainly marked an historic date, the end of the greatest modern goalkeeper, if not of all time: Lev Yachine.'

Yugoslavia, meanwhile, were winning their key match against Uruguay 3–1, with Sekularac in such transcendent form, working such wonders of control and construction that the very Uruguayans bore him off on their shoulders at the end! His henchmen were the powerfully made, thrusting double spearhead, Galic and Jerkovic, scorers of the second and third goals. The first came through Josip Skoblar, a young left-winger later to make a great name in Marseilles, from the penalty spot, equalising Cabrera's goal.

Beating a now exhausted Colombia 5–0 in their third match, Jerkovic scoring three, Yugoslavia finished second in the group. Their quarter-final opponents, for the third consecutive World Cup, would be . . . West Germany.

The Quarter-Finals   Brazil v. England

At Viña, Brazil—and Garrincha—accounted for England. Perhaps because he was no longer rivalled and obscured by Pelé, Garrincha continued in a vein of luminous virtuosity which would persist into the semi-final. Wilson did what he could with him; but it was inevitably little. To the panther swerve and acceleration, the deadly goal-line cross, which one had seen in Sweden, Garrincha had now added a thumping shot in either foot and remarkable power in the air. The first Brazilian goal, after thirty-one minutes, came when he, at five foot seven, utterly outjumped Maurice Norman at six foot two, to head in a corner kick. That it was no fluke, no mere aberration by Norman, was shown when he did just the same against Chile.

A much worse error by Ron Flowers would have put Brazil 2–0 up, were it not for a marvellous save by Springett. Flowers, retrieving a ball on the right, bemusedly turned and pushed it straight across his own goal area. Amarildo was in like a ferret; only for Springett, still quicker, to dive and block at his feet. It was a save too easily forgotten afterwards when attempts were made to turn Springett into a scapegoat.

Within five minutes of the second half, Garrincha decided the game. After fifty-four minutes, his fulminating, swerving free kick bounced off Springett's broad chest for Vavà to score as easily as Hitchens; then his diabolical swerving long shot utterly deceived the goalkeeper and curled in by the right-hand post. Brazil had won their place in the semi-finals.

Yugoslavia v. Germany

Yugoslavia flew down to Santiago to play Germany. Milovan Ciric, the Yugoslav manager, a large, bald, consistently amiable man, deplored his lack of wingers and smilingly promised that his team would know how to cope with Germany's physical challenge.

Third time proved lucky; for at last Germany were conquered, at last their sheer, forbidding muscularity did not subdue Yugoslavia's greater finesse. The Germans played *catenaccio* again, the Yugoslavs 4-2-4. It was a spirited and splendid game, perhaps decided by its tactics. For the Germans, playing so tightly and cautiously, gave Radakovic, the little Yugoslav right-half, a scope and space that finally proved fatal.

Germany favoured the long pass, Yugoslavia the short. In an absorbing half Germany initially forced the game, Seeler hitting a post, but then until the half-hour it was the Yugoslavs who dominated, making but not taking chances. The second half, though still exciting, was less distinguished, both teams appearing tired. Schnellinger, curiously anticipating Germany's 'total football' of a decade later, often left his post as sweeper to join in attacks, a dangerously effective stratagem which several times almost brought a goal. As for the Yugoslavs, they now had Radakovic, who had collided with Seeler, playing with a bandaged head, and somewhat diminished in consequence.

Extra time seemed certain, a German win the more likely, when at last, after eighty-six vibrant minutes, Galic pulled the ball back to Radakovic whose shot, from fifteen yards, flew under the bar to beat the able Fahrian.

Chile v. Russia

In Arica, Chile astonished and uplifted their supporters by defeating Russia, with Yachine once more betraying strange deficiencies. He should have saved both Chilean goals, each a long shot. Leonel Sanchez got the first after ten minutes from a twenty-five-yard free kick, a searing cross shot from the left. Eladio Rojas, the attacking half-back, scored the winner eighteen minutes later; two minutes after Chislenko had equalised from fully thirty-five yards. For all its formidable power, how so long a shot beat a goalkeeper as great as Yachine remains a mystery.

The Chileans, for the occasion, pulled Toro deeper, turning their 4-2-4 into a virtual 4-3-3, though at times Toro broke sharply and effectively from the back. It was not one of Chile's best days; if anything, the frenzied support of the 17,000-strong crowd, the knowledge that the whole country hung breathlessly on the result, inhibited more than it inspired them. Nevertheless, they were through.

Czechoslovakia v. Hungary

So, in the strangest fashion, were Czechoslovakia, outplayed at Rancagua by a Hungarian team which beat a tattoo on their goalposts, but could not beat the incredible Schroiff; as brilliant that day as Yachine was fallible. Scherer, in the thirteenth minute, surprised Grosics with a cross shot in one of Czechoslovakia's pitifully rare breakaways. It was enough, however, to put his team in the semi-final, for on the one occasion when Hungary, and Tichy, seemed to have scored, Russia's Latychev, the veteran referee, gave it obscurely offside.

The Semi-Finals   Brazil v. Chile

The Brazilians were so much superior to the Chileans that it was hardly a match. Garrincha, fiery and uncontrollable, seemed determined to win the game on his own. After only nine minutes, he pivoted on the ball in an inside-left position to beat Escutti with a killing twenty-yard left-foot shot. After thirty-two, he performed another of his trampoline jumps to head in a corner by Zagalo.

Chile, to their credit, were not supine. Ten minutes later Toro, right-footed, smashed a mighty free kick past Gilmar from the edge of the area to bring them back into the game; only for Vavà, a mere two minutes into the second half, to restore the margin, heading in Garrincha's dropping corner.

Once more the Chileans got up off the ground, inspired by the gifted Toro, the determined Rojas, the quick, slight, mobile right-back Eyzaguirre, fighting back into the game with a penalty by Leonel Sanchez for hands by Zozimo. But just as the match seemed alive again the indefatigable Zagalo moved up the left wing, spun past his man with princely ease and delivered a short centre which Vavà headed in.

The closing minutes were displeasing. Garrincha, kicked by Rojas and tired of being kicked, kicked back and was sent off. As he made his way round the field towards the dressing-rooms, to a cacophony of whistling, a bottle struck him and cut open his head. Soon afterwards Landa, the Chilean centre-forward, followed him. He was suspended. Garrincha, surprisingly, was pardoned.

Czechoslovakia v. Yugoslavia

In Viña del Mar, a mere, miserable 5,000 supporters stood under the pines, cypresses and willows to see Czechoslovakia beat the book again, this time defeating Yugoslavia. The Slavs, as Ciric had feared, were indeed weak on the wings, and could not breach the Czechs' packed defence in the centre. Tactically, Czechoslovakia were a credit to their manager, the silver-haired, silver-toothed, Austrian-born Vytlacil; surviving the first half, they got the goals they needed in the second.

Kadraba gave them a fortuituous lead three minutes after half-time, but when Jerkovic equalised in the sixty-ninth minute, a Yugoslav win again seemed probable. Instead, Schroiff defied them as superbly as he had defied the Hungarians, Scherer scored ten minutes from time in a breakaway, and a silly handling offence by Markovic allowed the same tall player to make it 3–1 from a penalty. The Final would reunite Brazil and Czechoslovakia.

The Final   Brazil v. Czechoslovakia

Needless to say, Brazil were favourites to beat the Czechs; but for that matter so had Hungary and Yugoslavia been in the quarter- and semi-finals. The Yugoslavs, in the third-place match, went through the irrelevant motions in Santiago and lost to a much more committed Chile with a last-minute goal by Eladio Rojas; the commanding Soskic would have saved it had the shot not been deflected. Sekularac, however, was splendid.

Perhaps Czechoslovakia *would* have brought off their greatest surprise of all had not the one crucial constant in their previous success been missing. Something snapped—Schroiff lost his form. Like a bomber pilot who has made one raid too many, an infantryman who cracks after too many campaigns, he would fall to pieces in the Final.

The game began with a shock; the shock of a Czech goal which, with no Pelé, with Schroiff in form, might have worked wonders. After sixteen minutes a superb combination between Scherer and Masopust split Brazil's defence asunder. Scherer, deep on the right, held the ball and judged his diagonal pass as exquisitely as clever Masopust judged his run. Through the gap he went, calm and implacable, to strike the ball past Gilmar with his left foot. For the second successive World Cup Final, Brazil had conceded the first goal.

For the second time, too, they fought back, though it would take them till after half-time to get ahead. The equaliser took no time at all; and it was Amarildo's. Beating the sturdy Pluskal, he advanced on Schroiff almost along the left goal line. What would he do? Shoot for the near post or the far; or not shoot at all, pull the ball back? It was a fearful dilemma, and Schroiff's answer was wrong. Guarding the near post, he gave Amarildo enough room for an extraordinary shot, the ball flying in at the far corner, striking the side netting.

In the second half the Czechs appeared to be holding their own, at their own *adagio* pace. Kadraba had a good shot, Jelinek another; Brazil seemed to have gone into their shell. Suddenly, after sixty-nine minutes, they struck, and again Amarildo was the decisive figure, a wonderfully effective replacement for Pelé. Boxed in on the left-hand goal line, he beat his man with a sudden galvanic turn from left to right, centred across the exposed goal with his right foot—and there was Zito, to head into the empty net.

It was over and done with, and Schroiff might have been spared the small calvary of the third goal thirteen minutes from the end. Djalma Santos, reaching casually, massively backwards to a ball bouncing on his touchline, booted it with his left foot high, high up into the sun. It fell upon the dazzled Schroiff like unmerited retribution. He held up his hands to it, dropped it, and the impassive Vavà kicked it in.

Comes the hour, comes the man. In losing Pelé, Brazil had found Amarildo, and their elderly, distinguished team had kept the Cup.

RESULTS: Chile 1962

Group I

Uruguay 2, Colombia 1 (HT 0/1)
Russia 2, Yugoslavia 0 (HT 0/0)
Yugoslavia 3, Uruguay 1 (HT 2/1)
Russia 4, Colombia 4 (HT 3/1)
Russia 2, Uruguay 1 (HT 1/0)
Yugoslavia 5, Colombia 0 (HT 2/0)

	P	W	D	L	GOALS F	A	Pts
Russia	3	2	1	0	**8**	**5**	5
Yugoslavia	3	2	0	1	**8**	**3**	4
Uruguay	3	1	0	2	**4**	**6**	2
Colombia	3	0	1	2	**5**	**11**	1

Group II

Chile 3, Switzerland 1 (HT 1/1)
Germany 0, Italy 0 (HT 0/0)
Chile 2, Italy 0 (HT 0/0)
Germany 2, Switzerland 1 (HT 1/0)
Germany 2, Chile 0 (HT 1/0)
Italy 3, Switzerland 0 (HT 1/0)

	P	W	D	L	GOALS F	A	Pts
Germany	3	2	1	0	**4**	**1**	5
Chile	3	2	0	1	**5**	**3**	4
Italy	3	1	1	1	**3**	**2**	3
Switzerland	3	0	0	3	**2**	**8**	0

Group III

Brazil 2, Mexico 0 (HT 0/0)
Czechoslovakia 1, Spain 0 (HT 0/0)
Brazil 0, Czechoslovakia 0 (HT 0/0)
Spain 1, Mexico 0 (HT 0/0)
Brazil 2, Spain 1 (HT 0/1)
Mexico 3, Czechoslovakia 1 (HT 2/1)

	P	W	D	L	GOALS F	A	Pts
Brazil	3	2	1	0	**4**	**1**	5
Czechoslovakia	3	1	1	1	**2**	**3**	3
Mexico	3	1	0	2	**3**	**4**	2
Spain	3	1	0	2	**2**	**3**	2

Group IV

Argentina 1, Bulgaria 0 (HT 1/0)
Hungary 2, England 1 (HT 1/0)
England 3, Argentina 1 (HT 2/0)
Hungary 6, Bulgaria 1 (HT 4/0)
Argentina 0, Hungary 0 (HT 0/0)
England 0, Bulgaria 0 (HT 0/0)

	P	W	D	L	GOALS F	A	Pts
Hungary	3	2	1	0	**8**	**2**	5
England	3	1	1	1	**4**	**3**	3
Argentina	3	1	1	1	**2**	**3**	3
Bulgaria	3	0	1	2	**1**	**7**	1

Quarter-finals

Santiago

Yugoslavia 1	**West Germany 0**
Soskic; Durkovic, Jusufi;	Fahrian; Novak,
Radakovic, Markovic,	Schnellinger; Schulz,
Popovic; Kovacevic,	Erhardt, Giesemann;
Sekularac, Jerkovic,	Haller, Szymaniak,
Galic, Skoblar.	Seeler, Brulls, Schaefer.

SCORER
Radakovic for Yugoslavia
HT 0/0

Viña del Mar

Brazil 3	**England 1**
Gilmar; Santos, D.,	Springett; Armfield,
Mauro, Zozimo, Santos,	Wilson; Moore,
N.; Zito, Didì,	Norman, Flowers;
Garrincha, Vavà	Douglas, Greaves,
Amarildo, Zagalo.	Hitchens, Haynes,
	Charlton.

SCORERS
Garrincha (2), Vavà for Brazil
Hitchens for England
HT 1/1

Chile 2	**Russia 1**
Escutti; Eyzaguirre,	Yachine; Tchokelli,
Contreras, Sanchez, R.,	Ostrovski; Voronin,
Navarro; Toro, Rojas;	Maslenkin, Netto;
Ramirez, Landa, Tobar,	Chislenko, Ivanov,
Sanchez, L.	Ponedelnik, Mamikin,
	Meshki.

SCORERS
Sanchez, L., Rojas for Chile
Chislenko for Russia
HT 2/1

Czechoslovakia 1	**Hungary 0**
Schroiff; Lala, Novak;	Grosios; Matrai,
Pluskal, Popluhar,	Sarosi; Solymosi,
Masopust; Pospichal,	Meszoly, Sipos;
Scherer, Kvasniak,	Sandor, Rakosi,
Kadraba, Jelinek.	Albert, Tichy, Fenyvesi.

SCORER
Scherer for Czechoslovakia
HT 1/0

Semi-finals

Santiago

Brazil 4	**Chile 2**
Gilmar; Santos, D.,	Escutti; Eyzaguirre,
Mauro, Zozimo, Santos,	Contreras, Sanchez,
N.; Zito, Didì,	R., Rodriguez; Toro,
Garrincha, Vavà,	Rojas; Ramirez,
Amarildo, Zagalo.	Landa, Tobar,
	Sanchez, L.

SCORERS
Garrincha (2), Vavà (2) for Brazil
Toro, Sanchez, L. (penalty) for Chile
HT 2/1

Czechoslovakia 3	**Yugoslavia 1**
Schroiff; Lala, Novak;	Soskic; Durkovic,
Pluskal, Popluhar,	Jusufi; Radakovic,
Masopust; Pospichal,	Markovic, Popovic;
Scherer, Kvasniak,	Sujakovic, Sekularac,
Kadraba, Jelinek.	Jerkovic, Galic,
	Skoblar.

SCORERS
Kadraba, Scherer (2) for Czechoslovakia
Jerkovic for Yugoslavia
HT 0/0

Third place match

Santiago

Chile 1	**Yugoslavia 0**
Godoy; Eyzaguirre,	Soskic; Durkovic,
Cruz, Sanchez, R.,	Svinjarevic;
Rodriguez; Toro, Rojas;	Radakovic, Markovic,
Ramirez, Campos,	Popovic; Kovacevic,
Tobar, Sanchez, L.	Sekularac, Jerkovic,
	Galic, Skoblar.

SCORER
Rojas for Chile
HT 0/0

Final

Santiago

Brazil 3	**Czechoslovakia 1**
Gilmar; Santos, D.,	Schroiff; Tichy, Novak;
Mauro, Zozimo,	Pluskal, Popluhar,
Santos, N.; Zito, Didì,	Masopust; Pospichal,
Garrincha, Vavà,	Scherer. Kvasniak,
Amarildo, Zagalo.	Kadraba, Jelinek.

SCORERS
Amarildo, Zito, Vavà for Brazil
Masopust for Czechoslovakia
HT 1/1

ENGLAND
1966

Background to 1966

The 1966 World Cup was the first for thirty-two years to be won by the home side. To this extent England's achievement was an unusual one, and indeed their form in the exciting, pleasing semi-final and Final made up for much of the tedium which had gone before.

It was a passionate and controversial World Cup; controversy persisting long after the dramatic Final was lost and won, thanks to the shot by Geoff Hurst of England which struck the underside of the bar and came down—or did not come down—behind the line. It was a World Cup distinguished by the enigmatic presence, and final triumph, of Alf Ramsey, the collapse of the Brazilians, the astonishing prowess of the North Koreans, the turbulence of the Argentinians, the absolute superiority of the Europeans over the South Americans—who cried conspiracy and threatened mass withdrawal, in consequence. It was a World Cup in which, for the second consecutive occasion, the fabled Pelé was laid low by injury, though this time in displeasing circumstances; in which Hurst scored the first hat-trick in a World Cup Final, and extra time was needed for the first time since 1934.

Whatever else may be said about the tournament's quality, the merits of England's win, there is no doubt that the Final was a glorious climax, the best there had been since 1954, and a great deal better than the one-sided Brazilian exhibition of 1970. Again, though England may not at any time have matched the technique and artistry of the Brazilian teams which won the two previous competitions, though they may have struggled all the way to the semi-final putting effort above creativity, hard work above joy in playing, the team had its undoubted stars. The commanding Bobby Moore, captain and left-half, was properly voted best player of the tournament, and this was followed by the immensely popular Bobby Charlton's election as European Footballer of the Year. Then there was Gordon Banks, whose splendid displays excelled even those of the veteran Lev Yachine—playing in his last World Cup—not to mention Geoff Hurst and the indefatigable Alan Ball, the two true heroes of the World Cup Final.

Alf Ramsey

We have met Ramsey, in this World Cup saga, before; as England's right-back in Brazil, when the United States so saucily and painfully twisted the lion's tail. As though this were not trauma enough, he had also played in the team which was beaten 6–3 at Wembley by Hungary in November 1953.

Born to a poor family in Dagenham, the London 'overspill' town, in 1920, his early ambition was to become a successful grocer. As a footballer, he was a curiously late developer. Southampton discovered him during his Army service when he was an inside-forward, but eventually converted him to full-back where his strength, vision of play and somewhat deliberative approach put him more at his ease. By December 1948, he was good enough to play for England against Switzerland, but only as a second choice. In the summer of 1949 his career took a crucial turn when Arthur Rowe signed him for Tottenham Hotspur in a deal involving the Welsh international left-winger Ernie Jones, and which, overall, valued Ramsey at the surprisingly low figure of £21,000. It must have been the best bargain Tottenham ever made.

For Ramsey fitted instantly into the new, push-and-run, quick, wall-passing tactics devised by Rowe. Though he was not the captain of the team, his nickname at Spurs, 'The General', shows clearly enough who was in command. His moral influence over the side was immense. He may have lacked pace, but his positional sense was admirable, his tackling strong, and above all he made consistently fine use of the ball. It was long before the days of the overlapping full-back, but Ramsey was what one might call a constructive full-back, whose thoughtful, scientific play set the tone for the whole ebullient team. He was also a dab hand at penalty kicks, with one of which he would temporarily save England's unbeaten home record, in October 1953 against FIFA at Wembley. When Hungary destroyed it a few weeks later, Ramsey again, to some degree, had the last word; or at least the last goal—from the penalty spot.

His approach to the game, his unfailingly thoughtful play, made it probable he would succeed as a manager, and so he did, taking Ipswich Town, a small East Anglian club which had entered the Football League only in 1937, from the Third Division to the Championship of the First, an extraordinary feat, achieved with a team of obscure and rehabilitated players.

When, after the 1962 World Cup, it was decided to appoint a full-time team manager with no other interests—Walter Winterbottom, disappointed in his ambitions for the Football Association secretaryship, had resigned—Ramsey was not the first choice. Indeed, he was probably no better than the third; Jimmy Adamson, the dedicated Burnley player who had coached the 1962 team, being first. He turned the job down.

Ramsey, who must have known he had got all he was ever likely to get out of his Ipswich side, poised on the verge of rapid disintegration, accepted the job, but on the specific understanding that he and he alone picked the team, that the Selection Committee which had for so many years theoretically held sway over the team manager would disappear. Ramsey never pretended to have much time for selectors and their ilk.

Ramsey built his success and his managerial reputation on the fact of being a player's man, and there is no doubt that it was his strength during the years which led to his success in 1966. Winterbottom, by contrast, had been, for all his virtues and his charm—a quality which scarcely distinguished Ramsey—an 'Establishment' man. He had been Sir Stanley Rous' choice, Sir Stanley's *protégé*, a theorist and an idealist whose chief concern, by his own admission, was the development of coaching. The players, who gave him a hard time when he first took over, came to like and accept him, but for all his own career in professional football, he did not move on their level, live in their world, talk in their terms. Ramsey did. Indeed, he seemed uncomfortable in any other world, afflicted by a feeling of social and cultural inadequacy reflected in a suspicion of the unfamiliar, a deep mistrust of the Press, a lurking xenophobia. But however tense and taut he might be with the world at large, Ramsey with his players was generally relaxed, friendly, avuncular, even humorous, cheerfully joining in their training games, never losing his authority but never wielding it in the paternalist manner of a Vittorio Pozzo.

The Contenders   England

Ramsey's first international fixture, against France, was held in Paris in the Nations Cup early in 1963, and was a disaster; England were thrashed 5–2, though goalkeeping errors made the defeat look worse than it should have been. Having taken stock, Ramsey then quickly rebuilt the side, and by the European tour of the summer of 1963 it was a very good one; well balanced, incisive, well 'motivated'. Ramsey had also made it his business to do something which Winterbottom had not done over his sixteen years; he appointed a team doctor. As we have seen, it was only when Peter Swan, given dangerously mistaken treatment, almost died in Viña del Mar during the 1962 World Cup, that the FA woke up to the need for a regular medical adviser.

They were especially fortunate in the man they chose, a gifted Harley Street consultant called Dr Alan Bass, Arsenal's team doctor, a native of Leeds, who carried his knowledge lightly, got on splendidly with the enigmatic Ramsey and his trainer, Harold Shepherdson, and just as well with all the players.

On that 1963 tour, Ramsey's relations with the Press were for once as good as they were with the players. He conceived and patiently explained successful tactics, in which wingers were of the essence; vital in their role of getting round the back of a packed defence and pulling the ball back into the goalmouth.

Gradually, as we shall see, he abandoned this tactical conception in favour of a 4–3–3 system, modulating at times into a 4-4-2, which eschewed orthodox wingers, putting its emphasis on hard work and hard running.

That his strategic grasp was less than impeccable was shown the following summer, when he took England to play in an international tournament organised by Brazil. England lost the opening match in Rio against Brazil 5–1, and did not win either of their two subsequent games in the competition, against Argentina and Portugal. Before the Brazilian match, moreover, Ramsey had a taste of the gamesmanship he was likely to meet in major international football. The Brazilians, having fixed the kick-off time, blithely arrived over an hour late, while the English players sat and fretted in their dressing-room. Shades of Pozzo's foresight before the 1938 World Cup Final. Ramsey would see that nothing like this happened again.

The 1964 tour was also significant for his collision with Bobby Moore. The tour, ill-planned, began with a meaningless game against the United States in New York, followed by the long haul down to Rio and inadequate time to prepare. In New York, certain English players broke curfew, but more serious was the stand made by several, Moore among them, against a training session organised on the tour by Ramsey. The 'revolution' quickly petered out, but had its strange, though not uncharacteristic, sequel in Ramsey's refusal to confirm Moore as England's captain till the very eve of the subsequent match against Northern Ireland in Belfast the following October.

Ramsey has a long memory, and it was some while before he and Moore achieved a reconciliation. Indeed, before the 1966 World Cup there seemed a real possibility that Moore would be replaced by the infinitely less commanding, but considerably more aggressive, Norman Hunter of Leeds United. It was perhaps not entirely fortuitous that during the pre-World Cup tour Moore's closest companion should be another East Londoner, another player never truly *persona grata* with Ramsey, Tottenham's Jimmy Greaves.

Players like Greaves, whose immense natural talent allowed them to do in a flash what other players could not achieve with endless effort, clearly worried Ramsey. Greaves, a goal-scoring prodigy in his teens, manifestly worried him. Ramsey was not at bottom without his own particular humour, but Greaves's irreverence was not something he could easily accept or understand. Indeed, his first real fracas with the Press had come a year before, on tour in Gothenburg, when he omitted Greaves from the team, said there were no injured players, then was incensed when newspapers reported that Greaves had been dropped. It was, however, equally characteristic of the man that he should in due course cool down and have the generosity to apologise.

Greaves, on the summer tour, looked fit and sharp again after long months fighting the effects of jaundice. He scored four splendid goals in Norway but did much less well in Denmark, where on a dreadful pitch England won crudely, 2–0.

Since Ramsey's accession, and since the 1962 World Cup, the team had been greatly modified. Gordon Banks, making his debut in May 1963 at home to Brazil, and letting in, to Ramsey's displeasure, a wildly swerving free kick by Pepe, had confirmed himself as the best goalkeeper since Bert Williams; perhaps since Frank Swift.

A Sheffield man who played for Leicester City, he combined physical strength and courage with astounding agility. His high cheekbones, his narrow eyes, gave his face an almost Red Indian, rather than a Yorkshire, look. He was modest, quiet and diligent. Ramsey, he said, on the day before the World Cup Final, had convinced him that 'my mind's got not to wander'. Nor did it.

To partner the still excellent Ray Wilson at full-back Ramsey had chosen George Cohen, an immensely amiable Londoner who had played all his professional football with Fulham, a strong, fast, endlessly determined player with a penchant for overlapping and a bottomless good humour.

At right-half there was . . . Nobby Stiles, the players' player, *bête noire* of the purists, a tiny, toothless, urban, gesticulating figure, perenially in the bad books of referees and opponents, forever urging on, castigating, his own defenders, a player with no obvious physical or technical gifts, a poor passer of the ball, but a formidable marker and an extraordinary competitor. By the end of this World Cup he would be the player whom most of the footballing world loved to hate, yet his was the satisfaction of nullifying Eusebio, the tournament's leading scorer and, till then, most dangerous forward.

The attack was clearly more of a problem than the defence. Bobby Charlton had been transformed, by Ramsey and by Manchester United, from a flowing, accelerating left-winger with a terrific shot in either foot into the general of the team, the role that he preferred. 'You're active all the time, you're in the game,' he declared. He exercised this role, however, in a very different manner from Johnny Haynes. A naturally more gifted player in terms of technique—though Haynes's ball control was often undervalued—he had none of Haynes's vision of play, eye for an opening, great strategic sense. His long, powerful crossfield passes were usually cause for a delighted roar at Wembley, but often they were merely lateral and spectacular, making no real impact. Yet his sinuous ability to beat a man with a lovely swerve could set problems to a defence which then found itself obliged to commit another defender, while his glorious shooting when he did come forward was a harbinger of goals.

His brother Jack, of Leeds United, had become the regular centre-half. A veteran by now, his spectacular improvement had much to do with the new spirit at Leeds inculcated by its manager, Don Revie. Charlton, a tall, tough, laconic man from a miner's family, with a miner's robust attitudes, could scarcely have been more of a contrast to his gentler brother, whom he so admired. As children, it appeared, they had never been close. There was none of Bobby's Prince Myshkin-like quality about Jack who, immeasurably less gifted, relied on strength, experience and intelligence.

Geoff Hurst had been something of a marginal choice for the party. When a journalist in Oslo expressed surprise that the brilliant young Chelsea forward Peter Osgood had not been chosen, Hurst replied, with uncharacteristic bitterness, 'Instead of me, I suppose'. Like Bobby Moore, he owed much to the coaching and percipience of West Ham's manager, Ron Greenwood. He was superbly built, tall, with immensely muscular thighs, a fine jumper, shot and header, but he had originally been no more than a moderate wing-half, and Greenwood had countermanded a decision to sell him to a Second Division team. The son of an Oldham Athletic half-back, Hurst had moved early to Essex, for whom he had played cricket. He was marvellously philosophical about the harsh treatment he often got from opponents, superbly unselfish and intelligent in his movement 'off' the ball, especially to the left wing.

Martin Peters was a third West Ham player in the party, a quiet, almost withdrawn, Londoner whom Ramsey had described as 'ten years ahead of his time', technically exceptional, a right-half by preference and position, who had just 'made' the England team in time the previous May. Ramsey had chosen him against Yugoslavia at Wembley and he had done well; many had felt his choice long overdue. Now he would blossom in a new role as a midfield player exploiting his flair for the unexpected, Panglossian appearance in the penalty area.

The little, red-haired, twenty-one-year-old Alan Ball, Blackpool's inside-forward, was quintessentially the kind of player Alf Ramsey wanted. He had first capped him on his twentieth birthday the previous year against Yugoslavia in Belgrade. The son of a former professional inside-forward, whom physically he closely resembled and who had been the Svengali of his career, Ball was a passionate enthusiast. Some felt he was neither fish nor fowl, that he lacked the subtlety of a great midfield player, the power and acceleration of a great goal-scorer; but in the Final none would play better or contribute more than he.

Roger Hunt, the Liverpool inside-forward, was another Ramsey player *par excellence*, fair-haired, sturdily built, as quiet as Martin Peters but much less talented, a doer of good by stealth, but essentially a workhorse.

England were drawn in Group I, which would play all its matches but one at Wembley; Uruguay and France were scheduled to play at the White City, a gesture towards the owners, who had allowed it to be used as World Cup headquarters. The fourth team in the group was Mexico, and England's passage to the quarter-finals seemed pretty secure. It was unfortunate that a Football Association booklet on the competition should give the impression that should England win the group they would play the quarter-final at Wembley but the semi-final at Everton. In fact, no such decision had been taken, as FIFA's own rules made clear. Nor, as some supposed, had it been decided that the winners of Group I would, if they cleared the quarter-finals, automatically play the semi-finals at Wembley. Instead, it was left to the World Cup committee to choose the respective venues, and it was not without considerable discussion and disagreement that it did so.

Indeed, given the nature of the discussion, it is especially ironical that certain European and South American journalists, pursuing what one might perhaps call the Conspiracy Theory of football, should darkly have blamed Sir Stanley Rous for loading the dice in favour of England.

Nothing could have been further from the truth. What in fact happened was that a strong group urged that England play their semi-final at Wembley, on purely—or pragmatically—economic grounds. This group argued that if England played at Wembley, it would be in front of a 90,000 crowd, whereas if Russia and West Germany played there, probably the crowd would be no bigger than 50,000. At Liverpool, the crowd would probably be a 'capacity' one, whoever played there. Rous argued strongly against this, but was finally persuaded to accept the majority's view.

Brazil

Brazil were in the Liverpool-Manchester Group III, though all their matches would be on Everton's ground. Once again the 'draw' had been a somewhat premeditated affair, the admirable Dr Hilton Gosling having long since picked out the pleasant Lymm for his team's headquarters. Vicente Feola was back again as team manager. In the event the selection would display a reverence for the past bordering on gerontophilia, but in prospect Brazil seemed well equipped to defend their title and even to win it a third consecutive time. Amazingly, they had not only stayed faithful to most of the old guard of 1962, they had even recalled Bellini and Orlando, their two centre-backs of 1958.

Of Garrincha Dr Gosling said, 'He has recovered (from injuries in a motor accident) but not completely. The problem with Garrincha is this; he can't play as often as he used to play, his recovery is quite slow now.' It was a point Brazil's selectors would wantonly ignore.

An ageing Djalma Santos and a fading Zito were also among the elect, while a third survivor of 1958, the thirty-four-year-old Dino, who had gone home from Italy to São Paulo promising to retire, was now in such splendid form with Corinthians that he seemed likely to win a place. In fact he did not even get into the final party. Lima, a powerful but straightforward half-back, did, while the gifted but inconsistent Gerson, a member of the 1960 Olympic team, was the designated successor to Didì.

But when all was said and done there was always Pelé, the sublime *deus ex machina*, throbbing with power and energy, capable of resolving and transforming any game in a flash. He, too, had had his problems with injuries, but at twenty-five he was at the peak of his career.

Hungary

Portugal and Hungary were in the same strong group. The Hungarian team manager had promised that his side would abandon 4-2-4 and play with Matrai as a sweeper, because otherwise 'we'd have no chance against Brazil and Portugal'. The Hungarians had won their qualifying group well, without losing a match. They still had the immaculate, Hidegkuti-like Florian Albert for centre-forward, and could afford the indulgence of playing Ferenc Bene, a huge success in the 1964 Olympic tournament, small and clever and fleet, on the right wing. As we shall see, however, their tactics were rather more than mere *catenaccio*.

Portugal

Portugal had staggered through the last phases of *their* group, losing in Romania, but in Eusebio they had one of the game's few authentic stars, a very great striking inside-forward with a staggering right foot, flowing control, wonderful acceleration. Born in Lourenço Marques, Mozambique, he had at the age of nineteen established himself in the Benfica team in 1961 in a world club championship match in Montevideo, having previously electrified Paris in a friendly tournament. His face had a pristine innocence and beauty in respose, his movements were graceful yet enormously powerful. If Europe had found a rival to Pelé in spectacle and efficiency, then this was unquestionably he.

There were several other stars from a Benfica team which had played superbly in the European Cup over the past five years, winning it twice and twice losing narrowly in the Final. Eusebio himself, after his thunderous shooting had resolved the 1962 Final against Real

Madrid in Amsterdam, had been symbolically presented by Ferenc
Puskas—scorer of three that night—with his jersey. José Augusto,
formerly the team's fast and clever outside-right, would now play in
midfield as a subtly creative inside-left, little Simoes would appear with
great effect both on the left flank and on the right, while the immensely
tall Torres would be a menace in the air.

Alas, two superb defenders had dropped out; and this would finally
prove decisive. Costa Pereira, a tall, calm goalkeeper, and Germano, a
mighty, resilient centre-half, had been the very props of the Benfica
defence and there was no replacing them.

The Groups

In England's group, Uruguay, who would be met in the curtainraiser,
were clearly the toughest nut to crack. They were managed by the
elderly, dedicated, courteous Ondino Viera, a man rich in experience
of South American football. They brought such stars of the 1962 team
as the dazzling inside-forward Pedro Rocha in midfield, and Ladislao
Mazurkiewiecz in goal, but to Viera's chagrin he could get hold of
none of the Uruguayans playing in Argentina—Silveira, Pavoni,
Matosas, Sasia, Cubilla.

In the Birmingham-Sheffield group there were Argentina, Spain,
Switzerland and West Germany. Luis Suarez, the Internazionale (Milan)
inside-forward, the first £200,000 transfer of all and a World Cup player
of 1962, had given England to win. His own country had qualified most
laboriously with a play-off in Paris against little Eire, won only 1–0 by a
goal from Ufarte, the Atletico Madrid right-winger, who had played
almost all his football in Brazil with Flamengo of Rio.

Argentina, who had progressively hardened their hearts since 1958
and had won Brazil's International Tournament of 1964, which
included England and Portugal, with ruthless defensive methods, had
had a palace revolution, Juan Carlos Lorenzo, their 1962 manager,
replacing Zubeldia. They had unexpectedly recalled Luis Artime,
centre-forward, and Ermindo Onega, inside-left, two players who had
till quite recently been playing in the River Plate reserves, for all their
celebrated understanding. Artime, known as *El Hermoso*, 'The Handsome', would go on scoring goals all over South America for the next
six years. As the perambulating half-back in a team hanging somewhere between *catenaccio* and *metodo* there was the tall, strong, unhurried
Antonio Rattin; a proper successor to Luisito Monti in more senses
than one.

The Swiss had been fortunate to edge ahead of Northern Ireland,
baulked by a frustrating draw in Albania, while the West Germans had
come in at the expense of Sweden. The return of the ever-resilient Uwe

Seeler, amazingly recovered from an operation to fit an artificial Achilles tendon, had enabled them to win the vital match in Stockholm.

In midfield there was abundant young talent: Helmut Haller, now with Bologna in Italy, Wolfgang Overath and his splendid left foot, and a tall, dark, immensely elegant young attacking right-half called Franz Beckenbauer from Bayern Munich, who was said to be better than either.

The Italians, who played in the north-eastern Group IV with Russia, Chile and . . . North Korea, came with a bevy of impressive recent victories behind them. In charge of them was the tiny, spectacled Edmondo Fabbri, who had vacillated between the kind of large-souled, attacking tactics which thrashed Poland 6–1 in Rome and the wretched *catenaccio*-ridden negativity which brought about a 1–0 defeat in Scotland. The return, in Naples, was won against a much depleted Scottish side, several of whose stars were kept at home by their English clubs for reasons more or less convincing. Jock Stein, the forceful and able Celtic manager who had been in charge, resigned in disgust.

When the draw was announced, after Italy's 3–0 win over Scotland, qualification for the quarter-finals seemed inevitable; even if, by a malign concatenation, Chile had to be met again. Then things began to go wrong. There was a disappointing 0–0 draw with France, in which Inter's turbulent midfield player Mario Corso not only played badly but previously insulted the assistant manager, Ferruccio Valcareggi, who elected not to hear the worst of his epithets. Poor Mora, meanwhile, after scoring a fine goal against the Scots and confirming himself as one of Italy's few natural wingers, had broken his leg.

Inter were angry enough when Corso was dropped from the team leaving Gianni Rivera unchallenged in midfield. They were incensed when Fabbri also left out their captain and sweeper, the superbly combative and resilient Armando Picchi, whose presence would be so badly missed. Fabbri also surprised the critics by omitting Giuliano Sarti, his most experienced goalkeeper, and the heavy-scoring Luigi Riva of Cagliari.

The Russians had made their customary pre-World Cup tour of South America. They still had the incomparable Lev Yachine, not to mention a fine winger in Chislenko and a forceful midfield half-back in Voinov. The charge against them, however, was the old one of lack of flair.

Chile no longer had their midfield pair of Toro and Rojas, both of whom had gone abroad, and failed, while North Korea—what could be expected of *them*? They had had to beat only Australia to qualify, since the rest of the Afro-Asian block had walked out in a huff because they were allowed only one representative. The two necessary games had taken place on neutral territory, at Pnom-Penh in Cambodia. Australia, who seemed to have enough experience to win comfortably, were thrashed 6–1, then beaten 3–1, by a team of little men who moved sweetly and finished splendidly. Sir Stanley Rous, who was present, warned everyone prepared to listen that this was not a team to be taken lightly, but scepticism remained.

Little, after all, was known about the North Koreans. Their contacts with football beyond their own remote confines were small, and beyond the range of Communist countries sympathetic to Russia—rather than China—nil. A couple of games in eastern Europe on the way to the World Cup was simply not enough. Had they deserted their sombre, rather than splendid, isolation as soon as they had beaten Australia, who knows how much more they might have done; though they would, it is true, have lost their aura of inscrutability, the charisma of the unknown.

The Opening Matches The First Round

The opening match of the tournament, held at Wembley, was a dreadful one; the most arid of goalless draws between England and Uruguay. The Uruguayan tactics had been predictable from the beginning; *catenaccio* defence and minimal ambitions. In the circumstances, Ramsey's own tactics and team selection were curiously obtuse. Connelly *did* play instead of Peters, but far from guaranteeing the attacking game Viera had expected it simply meant that England, with only one winger, Bobby Charlton out of form, and neither Hunt nor Greaves making much impression on Uruguay's solid, contemptuously resourceful defence, had little chance of a goal.

Brazil's beginning, at Everton, was better; they beat Bulgaria 2–0, thanks to two fulminating goals from free kicks, one in the first half by a splendid Pelé, one in the second by Garrincha.

At Old Trafford their rivals, Portugal and Hungary, played, and an injury to Szentmihalyi, Hungary's goalkeeper, only a few seconds after the kick-off, tipped the balance. José Augusto's first goal soon followed, Szentmihalyi missing a corner, and all Hungary's clever, furious attacks came to naught. Playing with a novel formation, three midfield men breaking splendidly to support Bene and Farkas up front, they twice hit the bar. At last Bene equalised, after sixty-one minutes, but six minutes later, with Szentmihalyi again at fault, Augusto made it 2–1. Torres got the third goal from an 'impossible' angle with almost the last kick, giving Portugal a 3–1 win which ridiculed the actual play.

In Sheffield the Swiss collapsed 5–0 before the West Germans, Beckenbauer gliding through for a couple of fluent goals. At the last

moment Switzerland had dropped two of their best players. Leimgru-
ber and Kobi Kuhn, for breaking curfew. The punishment seemed
rather severe, both for team and players.

At Villa Park, Argentina, who had lost 3–0 in Italy on the way to
England, beat Spain 2–1 in a disappointing game, twice cruelly hacking down Suarez, early on. Artime, sharply exploiting Onega's clever
suggestions, scored both goals for Argentina, while Pirri, in his first
international, replied with a curious, looping header for Spain.
Argentina had the blond Silvio Marzolini again as one of their two
overlapping full-backs, Roberto Perfumo as a composed and elegant
sweeper.

At Middlesbrough the North Koreans, who would be taken to the
hearts of the Ayresome Park crowd, referred to lovingly as 'us', for all
their exotic remoteness, began badly. Russia, physically much too
powerful, brushed their over-cautious team aside, 3–0, Malafeev and
Banichevski, the big strikers, getting the goals. There still seemed no
reason to believe that the Koreans could do anything.

Italy, at Sunderland, laboriously beat Chile 2–0 with an early goal and
a late goal. Something strange had happened to them since their string of
'friendly' victories; the cynical would whisper afterwards of the effects of
strict drug control. The players seemed tense, reflecting the tension of
little Fabbri, which seemed unassuaged by the fact that the Italian Federation had extended his contract to 1970.

The French, meanwhile, ensconced at Welwyn Garden City, began
badly with a draw against Mexico, whose goal was scored by the alert
Enrique Borja. The bone of contention was Lucien Muller, an experienced midfield player now with Barcelona, who had been brought from
Spain but would not play a match.

Succumbing 2–1 to Uruguay at White City, the French thus lost all
chance of qualifying; they could hardly hope to beat England.

Hungary v. Brazil

The second round of matches brought a glorious game between Hungary
and Brazil at Everton, worthy of standing with the best the World Cup
has ever produced. It was exciting, dramatic, full of fine goals and delightful football, played at extraordinary speed. It also represented the first
defeat of Brazil in a World Cup since 1954.

Pelé, let it be said at once, could not play, his place being taken by young
Tostao. Gerson replaced Denilson, essentially a half-back, in midfield,
while the veterans Djalma Santos and Garrincha were most unwisely
committed to their second match in a few days. The Hungarians made
several changes, including Gelei for Szentmihalyi in goal.

It was Albert, however, who dominated the field, left to wander at will by the Brazilians, orchestrating Hungary's flowing attacks, now running beautifully with the ball, now passing cleverly, always willing and able to beat his man, consummately versatile. At the end of the remarkable match, when he stood by the tunnel in the rain taking a pull from a bottle of water, the Everton crowd were chanting, 'Al-*bert*, Al-*bert!*' paying a great performance the tribute it deserved.

After only three minutes, little Bene was wriggling in from the right, infiltrating Brazil's ponderous defence, and striking his shot from the narrowest of angles past Gilmar. From that moment, Hungary had the bit between their teeth. Their defence was excellent, the prematurely grey Matrai sweeping diligently behind the muscular Sipos and Meszoly, with Sipos always ready to go forward. The attack, marvellously fast and fluid, struck now from this angle, now from that, as midfield players and even defenders dashed into the open spaces left by the clever two front runners.

Brazil were reprieved when, after fifteen minutes, Lima's free kick rebounded to Tostao, who whipped it smartly home, but the half-time score of 1–1 was illusory. Hungary finally regained a lead they would not lose with an exhilarating goal by Farkas. Albert's clever run and pass exposed the Brazilian defence again, sending Bene flying down the right. Bene pulled back a fast, low cross which Farkas met with a ferocious right-footed volley on the near post, a goal which left the crowd first breathless, then exultant. Ten minutes later a penalty by Meszoli, conceded by an overplayed Brazilian defence, fouling Bene, knocked the last nail in the Brazilian coffin.

Portugal v. Brazil and Italy v. Russia

Pelé came back for the final throw against Portugal, but he was obviously not fit, and the match was lost and won long before a brutal, inexplicable double foul by Morais put him out of the game. In the panic after the match with Hungary, Brazil made seven changes, ejecting the veterans Gilmar, Bellini, Djalma Santos and Garrincha, yet restoring the veteran Orlando for his first World Cup match since 1958. Manga, a tall, agile goalkeeper nicknamed 'Frankenstein' for his bizarre appearance, replaced Gilmar, and crossed himself anxiously as he emerged from the tunnel; all nerves, despite his excellence on a tour of Europe the previous year.

After fourteen minutes he had given away a goal, feebly punching out Eusebio's centre for Simoes, who had begun the move, to head in. After twenty-five minutes, another goal: Coluna, Portugal's splendid black captain and left-half, a beautiful striker of the ball, sent over a free kick which Torres nodded back from the far post. Eusebio headed in again.

The game was in Portugal's pockets, and there was no excuse, not even that of cynical necessity, for Morais to chop down Pelé. Later, Pelé would say that it was only when he saw the incident on film that he realised how bad it was. He would swear, then, never to play in a World Cup again. The indulgent, flaccid English referee, George McCabe, allowed Morais to stay on the field, so that now Portugal were virtually playing against ten men. Silva, Brazil's new centre-forward, had also been hurt, while even at full strength they had been quite unable to curb a rampant Eusebio, whose speed and flexibility were a dreadful torment to their defenders.

The second half was curiously barren of goals until, after sixty-four minutes, Rildo, the young, attacking left-back, gave Brazil false hope with an enterprising run and goal. Five minutes from time, Eusebio appropriately ended such illusions when, after a right-wing corner, he thrashed the ball back into goal.

Brazil were out, and with both Hungary and Portugal defeating Bulgaria, these two passed into the quarter-finals.

England's group went on its weary way. Calderon, Mexico's goal-keeper, knelt in prayer beneath his crossbar before the kick-off of another tiresome game, against England, ruined by a Mexican team which kept nine or even ten men in defence. At last, with the crowd chanting, 'We want goals!'—it was a crowd immeasurably more vocal than in Winterbottom's reign—Bobby Charlton obliged them. Seven minutes from half-time, from well outside the area and at a sharp angle, he struck a memorable right-footed cross shot past Calderon. In the second half, his excellent pass sent Greaves through, for Hunt to put in the rebound, but though Peters had been added to the midfield and Terry Paine tried at outside-right, the team was still creaking. Stiles, whatever his inspirational function, gave nothing in creativity, and seemed in these games, when goals had to be scored, no more than a testimony to Ramsey's penchant for counter-attacking football and at least one 'hard man'.

A crisis was reached in the subsequent game against France, again won 2–0, laboriously, against a French team which played most of the match with the injured Herbin at centre-forward. The English players complained afterwards that opponents spat at them. Be that as it may, Stiles' foul on Jacky Simon late in the game seemed a gross one. Two officials of the Football Association insisted that Ramsey withdraw him from the team. Ramsey, loyal to his players and his somewhat contentious ideology, said that if Stiles went, so would he. Stiles, inevitably, remained.

This, however, was the only match after which Ramsey reproached his team. Once back at the Hendon Hall Hotel, their headquarters, he castigated them for sins of presumption, though exempting the hard-working Roger Hunt, who had scored both goals. To the onlooker, England's performance had seemed, if anything, rather better than in the previous two games. The match was significant for an injury to Greaves which allowed him to be gently discarded, and Ramsey's last attempt to play with an orthodox winger, Ian Callaghan of Liverpool. It must also have convinced him of the value of the absent Ball.

If Calderon had prayed, Carbajal, after Mexico's 0–0 draw with Uruguay, kissed both goalposts. It was the thirty-seven-year-old 'keeper's final match, in his fifth World Cup; and a most satisfactory one for his country. This time it was the Uruguayans, cynical and negative, masters of the 'tactical' foul, who shut up shop, knowing that a draw would take them into the quarter-final.

More cynical and provocative still were their Argentinian neighbours, in a deplorable, goalless match against West Germany at Villa Park. This time the Germans could not frolic as they did against the Swiss, Beckenbauer being much too concerned with countering the clever, inventive Onega. Albrecht, who had outrageously rugbytackled Haller, was sent off after sixty-five minutes for another bad foul, on Weber, but still the Germans played it close to the chest; though Perfumo, acrobatic and resilient, cleared from beneath his own bar.

These two now proceeded to qualify, Argentina beating the Swiss 2–0 with goals by Artime and Onega, Germany defeating Spain 2–1 at Birmingham in a very tight match. A powerful shot from an astonishing angle by the hefty Emmerich, their left-winger, gave them the lead, but Fuste equalised, and Seeler won the match only six minutes from time.

Meanwhile the travails of Italy continued—and multiplied. Fabbri, in an evident state of alarm, put out a curiously unbalanced, hitherto untried, team against Russia at Sunderland, dropping Gianni Rivera and both wingers, choosing Giacomo Bulgarelli of Bologna, despite a knee injury.

With the vastly tall Giacinto Facchetti of Inter, essentially an overlapping full-back, helpless against clever Chislenko, Russia's outside-right, the Italians never found a rhythm, never made adequate chances for their chief bombardier, the slender but incisive Sandrino Mazzola, son of Valentino. A goal by Chislenko in the second half settled the match. Some critics remarked on the officiousness of the referee, a tiny, bald, dark West German called Herr Kreitlein, of whom more would be heard.

Italy v. North Korea and Russia v. Chile

So to the ultimate Italian trauma: Middlesbrough, and the match with North Korea. Finding confidence, the little Koreans had come out of their shells against Chile and, to the delight of the friendly Middlesbrough crowd, gained a draw which could have been something better. Speed, in Fabbri's view and that of others, was the North Koreans' only real weapon; it was generally agreed that quick, flexible men were required to counteract it. Fabbri, however, surprisingly chose for his defence two slow players in Janich and Guarneri. Worse still, he called up again the manifestly unfit Bulgarelli, who was out of the game in half an hour after attempting to foul an opponent and definitively injuring his knee.

The Koreans played with splendid spirit and refreshing sportsmanship: the kind of 'professional' foul to which the World Cup exposed them clearly filled these straightforward little men with pained surprise. After forty-two minutes their inside-left, Pak Doo Ik, tackled Rivera—who was back in the team—advanced, and beat Albertosi with a searing cross shot. There were no more goals, and for many months the mocking cry of 'Ko-re-a!' would echo over Italian stadiums when Fabbri or any of his World Cup men appeared. He himself in a volley of accusation and counter-accusation, would lose his job.

Russia, beating Chile 2–1 at Sunderland with a couple of goals by a new left-winger, Porkujan, maintained a one hundred per cent record, and passed into the quarter-finals, against Hungary, on the same ground.

The Quarter-Finals   England v. Argentina

In this round, run again on a knock-out pattern, the most brilliant and exciting match was unquestionably that between Portugal and North Korea at Everton, while it would be hard to decide which was the more turbulent—Wembley's England v. Argentina, or Sheffield's West Germany v. Uruguay.

The Wembley match, or fiasco, would reverberate for years to come, would polarise European and South American football, evoking almost paranoic reactions from the River Plate. The Brazilians were already away, arriving by train at Euston with the faces of condemned men, muttering, not without justice, of the inadequacies of English referees. Now Argentinian cynicism and provocation met the authoritarianism of Herr Kreitlein; and all was chaos.

Scarcely had the game begun than the Argentinians embarked on a maddening series of deliberate fouls so that England—who had left out Greaves and brought in Hurst for his first game—found every attack choked at birth. Herr Kreitlein rushed hither and thither, an exacerbating rather than a calming influence, inscribing names in his notebook with the zeal of a schoolboy collecting engine numbers. Where Herr Kreitlein's tiny form perambulated, there generally followed the much larger form of Rattin, looming above him like a tree in the cork forest he was supposed to own, arguing, protesting, provoking. When he was booked, ironically, it was for a trivial foul on Bobby Charlton, but his whole attitude was one incompatible with the proper running of the game.

At the same time his large, loping figure was at the centre of Argentina's elaborate web of short passes, of the occasional attacks which once caused Banks, unsighted, to dive vigorously to a sudden shot by Mas.

Nine minutes from half-time, however, objecting to the 'booking' of a colleague, Rattin was sent off; and refused to go. The incident itself may, in isolation, have been unexceptional, but cumulatively things had gone too far. Herr Kreitlein, bald head gleaming in the sunlight, had had enough. He said the day after that though he understood no Spanish, the look on Rattin's face was enough.

For ten long minutes there were arguments, petitions, appeals. Albrecht at one point seemed to beckon his whole team off. The tall, de Gaulle-ish figure of Ken Aston, victim of Santiago and now chief of the World Cup referees, appeared by the touchline to intercede. And at last, slowly and with huge reluctance, Rattin went, making the long, long circuit of the pitch, accompanied by his trainer, exchanging insults with the crowd, pausing now and then to watch as the game went on, like some reluctant phantom.

The ten Argentinians held out astonishingly well, harshly exposing England's bankruptcy in midfield, where there was no one with Onega's subtlety. Hurst, playing his first competitive match since Copenhagen, found the going quite exhausting at first, but his was the first really dangerous English shot of the match, a reward for his power and perseverance. Four minutes after the interval, Wilson, receiving from Moore, dropped a centre over the defence. Hurst seemed almost surprised when it bobbled beneath his feet on the far post, but he recovered in time to strike an immensely strong shot. Roma, with a jackknife dive of fabulous agility, got a hand to it, and turned it round the post.

Argentina, when they did break, were dangerously effective, with Artime and Mas so quick on the turn, the full-backs so keen to overlap, Onega so inventive. Thirteen minutes from the end, however, Wilson found Peters, whose high cross curled in from the left was met by Hurst, this time at the near post, with a prodigious jump, a header glanced beautifully into the right-hand corner. Mas, having cuffed a small boy who ran on to felicitate Hurst, was nearly through to score from the kick-off, but England were in the semi-final.

Ramsey, with justice, said he hoped England's semi-final opponents would not 'act as animals'. The words would haunt him.

Uruguay v. West Germany

Meanwhile, at Hillsborough, Sheffield, two Uruguayans were sent off and West Germany won, 4–0. Neither side was blameless; much went on which escaped notice at the time. Uruguay, beginning well, should have scored early on, but instead fell behind, Haller flukily diverting a shot by Held past Mazurkiewicz. The flashpoint came when Uruguay believed Schnellinger to have handled on the line. When Emmerich painfully kicked Troche, the Uruguayan captain, Troche kicked him back in the stomach, and was sent off, slapping Seeler's face on the way for good measure.

To those who accused the Germans in general, and Haller in particular, of 'acting', it might be pointed out that when Haller at one point collapsed and writhed, it was because a Uruguayan had seized his testicles, and that night he was oozing blood.

Troche had gone five minutes after half-time. Five minutes later, Jim Finney, the English referee, expelled Silva, the Uruguayan inside-forward, for chopping down Haller.

The nine surviving Uruguayans resisted with the determination for which their football is famous, but it could not last. With Beckenbauer able now to go fluently forward as he had not done since the Swiss match, the writing was on the wall; even if it was twenty minutes from time before Beckenbauer brought off a one-two with Seeler, casually dribbled round Mazurkiewicz, and scored. Seeler and Haller added two more.

Russia v. Hungary and Portugal v. North Korea

Hungary, after their excellence against Brazil, now blew up, losing, as they so often have done, to the Russians' greater physical power. Albert was consigned to the obsessive care of Voronin, who forsook, for the occasion, his usual constructive game to take part in the man-to-man marking. Sabo—ironically himself Hungarian by origin—outshone Albert as a general, splendidly abetted by Chislenko, who had begun the World Cup so well, and would finish so depressingly. He it was who exploited yet another in the series of Hungarian goalkeeping errors which had followed the going of Grosics, Gelei dropping an easy ball after only six minutes.

Porkujan, two minutes after the interval, made it 2–0, at a corner Gelei did not catch, little Bene replied, and hope revived; only for the energetic Rakosi, ten minutes from time, to miss the equaliser. A marvellous save by Yachine from Sipos' thumping free kick; and the Russian steamroller rolled on.

At Everton, the beginning of Portugal v. North Korea was sensational; a goal in a minute, followed by a second and a third; and all for North Korea. Their opening was extraordinary, a thunderclap of dazzling, attacking football, Pak Seung Jin driving home after a cutting right-wing move.

Portugal had some twenty minutes to ride the punch, but could not do so, Li Dong-Woon scoring a second, Yang Sung Kook, the outsideleft, a third. The Portuguese team, conquerors of Brazil, seemed now quite *bouleversés*. It would take genius to revive them; and Eusebio provided it, running, shooting and fighting with indomitable flair, long legs threshing past the little Korean defenders.

After twenty-eight minutes Simoes put him through for his first goal. Three minutes from half-time a Korean brought Torres tumbling like a forest giant. Eusebio belted in the penalty, then urgently picked up the ball and galloped back to the centre-spot, to be intercepted and upbraided by an obscurely outraged Korean.

Eusebio would, in the event, have the best of the argument. Fifteen minutes from half-time, he sprinted through again to equalise, then, after another of his exhilarating left-wing runs, in which he negotiated tackles with electric ease, he was hacked down—and scored another penalty. At a corner kick Augusto got the fifth, and the Koreans, too generous and ingenuous to sit on their lead, were out. Alas, they would sink back into their strange isolation, leaving us with memories of their courage, their talent, their generosity.

The Semi-Finals   Germany v. Russia and England v. Portugal

The semi-finals pitted West Germany against Russia at Everton; England against Portugal at Wembley. The first match, played a day earlier, was a wretched parody of football; the second, if it fell short of the glories of Hungary v. Brazil, a tribute to the game.

The Germans and the Russians produced a sour, ill-tempered, impoverished match, refereed without illumination by the handsome, obtrusive Sicilian, Concetto Lo Bello. Sabo, stupidly trying to foul Beckenbauer and laming himself in the process set the tone, and it was only the majestic goal-keeping, the immaculate sportsmanship, of Yachine that gave the game any distinction. It was especially ironic that afterwards he should be blamed by Morozow, the team manager, for conceding a goal, when he had kept Russia afloat for so long.

A minute from half-time Russia found themselves in still worse plight. A powerful tackle by Schnellinger robbed Chislenko, and hurt him in the process. The left-back ran on to send a perfect crossfield ball to the blond Haller, who ran on to it and scored. Russia then ill-advisedly brought the hobbling Chislenko straight back on to the field.

He at once lost the ball to Held and, in his pain and frustration, kicked him. Lo Bello instantly sent him off; and then there were nine.

These nine the Germans treated with extraordinary respect and caution. They scored only once more, with a remarkable left-footed shot, curling from outside the box around the Russian wall and in at the far post, by Beckenbauer. But with Voronin and Khusainov fighting bravely and skilfully the Russians actually managed a goal of their own. A couple of minutes from the end Tilkowski, always vulnerable in the air, dropped a left-wing cross under pressure, and Porkujan put the ball in. It was a meagre victory.

England won much more handsomely, though the score was the same, in a game which they should have won with ease, but nearly allowed to slip away from them, a game in which Eusebio, the tournament's leading scorer, was simply blotted from sight by the tenacious Stiles, who also found time to exhort, upbraid and castigate his own defence.

Bobby Charlton had much his best game of the World Cup, perhaps the best he ever played for England, his distribution for once being quite the equal of his fine running and shooting. When, after half an hour, Ray Wilson cleverly sent through Hunt, and Pereira could only block the shot, Charlton coolly drove it back into the net. At half-time, with Ball running like a Zatopek—or a Zagalo—the score 1–0 remained, and England had missed a dangerous number of chances.

For a quarter of an hour after the break, Portugal's gifted forwards pressed, only to find a defence in which the tall, blond Moore and Jackie Charlton, the faultless Banks, the galvanic Stiles, defied them, too compact to be breached.

So England regained ascendancy, and eleven minutes from the end they at last scored again. Hurst forcefully shook off Carlos' challenge, went to the right-hand goal line, pulled the ball back, and Bobby Charlton's right foot struck a fulminating goal.

Portugal again revived, driven on by the muscular, tireless Coluna. In another three minutes, Simoes had curled the ball over from the right, Torres rose to it above the defence and headed over Banks, Jackie Charlton punched it out, Eusebio scored still another penalty.

Now Portugal assailed the English goal, and only Stiles' fine covering tackle thwarted Simoes, after which Stiles turned on his defence with a wealth of outraged gesture. Bobby Charlton let fly a left-footed shot which Pereira smothered but again could not hold, and Banks had to tip over a raking, right-footed shot by Coluna. Then it was time; England had reached the Final.

The Final   England v. Germany

They had reached the Final without Greaves, and the question now was whether he would return. To Greaves himself, it was one of absolute importance; this was the match on which he had set his heart. Hurst, who had replaced him, was obviously playing far too well to be dropped; if anyone went it would plainly be Roger Hunt, diligent but mediocre, a selfless and intelligent runner, a more than adequate finisher, but never a forward of true international class.

The Germans had two problems: goalkeeper and outside-left. They were not satisfied with Tilkowski's performances, above all when it came to dealing with high crosses, and he had injured his shoulder against Russia. Helmut Schoen, their team manager, would have liked to replace him with the fair-haired Bayern Munich goalkeeper Sepp Maier; but Maier was himself injured.

Then there was the question of Lothar Emmerich, the Bundesliga's most prolific scorer, a tall, strong player with a ferocious left foot who had got that important goal against the Swiss, but was not renowned for his audacity. The temptation was to drop him; the fear was that should Germany then lose, fury would break about Schoen's head. He chose Emmerich.

Ramsey, following a strangulated Press conference on the Bank of England grounds at Roehampton at which, after agonised reflection, he reaffirmed that England would win the World Cup, chose Hunt.

So, after a meaningless third-place match in which Portugal, with yet another penalty by Eusebio, beat Russia 2–1, the lines of battle were drawn.

History spoke firmly in England's favour. After sixty-five years they had yet to lose to Germany, whom they had been beating regularly since a team of amateurs overplayed them 12–0 at Tottenham in 1901. The Germans, now esconced at Welwyn Garden City, were all too cognisant of the fact. To beard the lion in his den was no joking matter. Perhaps if the match had been played elsewhere, Schoen would have been more enterprising than to sacrifice Beckenbauer to the ungrateful task of 'policing' Bobby Charlton. The Germans would in fact again play a flexible version of *catenaccio*, with the robust Willy Schulz as sweeper, Weber at centre-back, Haller and Overath in midfield, Seeler, Emmerich and the rapid Held up front.

Ramsey had hoped to exploit the relative slowness of Schnellinger by getting Ball to draw him into the middle. In fact this slowness would be much more fully and logically exploited out on the wing, where Ball would show an unsuspected talent for beating his man, then leaving him standing.

England, however, made a bad beginning. After only thirteen inconclusive minutes Ray Wilson, most uncharacteristically, headed Held's left-wing cross straight to the feet of Haller on the far post. Haller crisply controlled the ball and drove it low and wide across Banks into the left-hand corner. The banners waved in triumph.

It took England, morale as high as ever, only six minutes to equalise. Tilkowski had already looked unhappy on crosses, had already needed treatment after a collision in the air with Hurst. Handsome and anxious, he fretted on his goal-line; alas, certainly no Turek.

Now, when Overath fouled Bobby Moore, the English captain took the German defence unawares with a quick, long, accurate free kick from the left. Hurst, timing his run immaculately, ran in from the right to glide the ball with his head past Tilkowski, who exchanged recriminations with his colleagues.

The match was open again—in both senses of the word, for though Beckenbauer's fluent excursions into midfield to link up with Overath were inevitably limited, the Germans were certainly not committed to mere defence. With Held running forcefully on the left, Seeler finding space on the right, Haller lurking slightly behind the strikers, they were flexible and dangerous, a different team from the grim company that beat the Russians.

Tilkowski's weakness showed again when he could only palm out Hurst's gentle header, and Ball whipped it across an empty, tempting goal. Germany soon struck back, twice. Held, strongly tackled on the goal line by Jackie Charlton, took the corner himself. It was weakly headed out, Overath drove it back again, Banks blocked, Emmerich, still nearer, shot again, and again Banks saved. His mind was indeed not wandering.

Three minutes from half-time Hunt's preference to Greaves was put severely in question. When Wilson brought off yet another of his over-laps and well-judged crosses, Hurst outjumped the German defence and glided the ball to Hunt on the left-hand post. Greaves would surely have put the chance away, but Hunt's left foot was his 'swinger'. Tilkowski raised his arms like a man in prayer, and his prayer was answered as the ball struck him and bounced loose. There was time for a shot by Seeler, a tip-over by Banks, then a pleasing, inconclusive half was at an end.

The second half began with a heavy shower, and two intricate, fine pieces of control on the right by Ball who, in the first half, had been tire-lessly pulling Schnellinger across the whole face of the forward-line. Then came a period of stalemate, phoney war, in which no chances were made. Each defence had the measure of its opposing attack, and if Bobby Charlton still ran gracefully, there was a gaping space on England's left wing unless Wilson filled it.

Only twelve and a half minutes remained when England broke the deadlock. Ball thumped into Tilkowski, bundling him over the goalline for a left-wing corner which he then took. The ball ran loose to Hurst, who shot, Weber lunged in to block and the ball rose tantalisingly into the air as though on a jet of water in a shooting gallery. It was Peters who shot—and scored.

After the hugging, the congratulations, Stiles and Wilson turned to the touchline, eyebrows questioningly raised, fingers upstretched, as if they had some premonition of what was in store.

With four minutes left England spurned a handsome chance to finish the job. With Germany now desperately committed to seeking the equaliser they broke away, a superb through pass by Ball cutting the defence to shreds and putting Hunt quite clear. On his right he had not only Bobby Charlton but Geoff Hurst, while in front of Tilkowski there was only Schulz; a *three* to one situation which should automatically have produced a goal. But for the second time in the match Hunt blundered, making his pass to Charlton too soon, before Schulz was fully drawn; too shallow and too square. This haste communicated itself to Charlton, who sliced wildly at the ball and hit it wide.

For this England paid heavily. There was less than a minute left when Held and Jackie Charlton jumped for a header. Many thought Held had backed into Charlton. Herr Dienst, the Swiss referee, was of the view that Charlton had fouled Held. He gave a free kick on the left, just outside the penalty area, which at last allowed the hesitant Emmerich to justify his choice. His strong, left-footed shot hit Schnellinger in the back, was sent across the goal-mouth by Held, and there was driven home past the lunging Wilson and the plunging Banks by another defender, Weber. There would now be extra time.

Exhausted by the drama, the tension of it all, as much as by the running, the players sprawled about the grass. Ramsey, in his bright blue tracksuit, marched onto the field and told the England team that they had won the World Cup once; now they must win it again. 'Look at them!' he said, indicating the weary Germans. 'They're finished!'

Alan Ball was anything but finished. Within ninety seconds he was tearing down the right wing yet again, a miracle of perpetual motion, far too much for heavy Schnellinger, letting go a shot which Tilkowski turned over the bar.

England had the wind in their sails. Jackie Charlton came up and passed to his brother, whose blistering left-footed shot Tilkowski—a new goalkeeper, now—turned full stretch on to the post. After a hundred minutes, however, a long, excellent pass to the right wing by Stiles found Ball again. Ball would later write that he thought, 'Oh, no! I can't get that one! I'm finished!' He had already, he said, 'died twice', but once more he found the energy to leave Schnellinger standing, then centre on the run.

This time, Geoff Hurst met the ball on the near post with a furious right-footed shot. Tilkowski had no chance with it; it tore past him, hit the underside of the bar and bounced down. Roger Hunt stood with arms joyfully raised, not troubling to apply the *coup de grâce* which, in retrospect, would have avoided so much controversy. Clearly he was sure the ball had crossed the line.

Herr Dienst was not. Besieged by protesting German players, he marched to the right-hand touchline to consult his Russian linesman, Bakhramov. He, a tall, silver-haired, distinguished figure, reminiscent of a chess-player or a violinist rather than a referee, quickly ended the poignant hiatus, jerking his flag with the utmost emphasis towards the centre spot. For the English crowd, the England players, it was a moment of ecstatic catharsis. The goal stood; the World Cup was clearly theirs.

Once more the Germans threw their men into unbridled attack; once more their defence broke down in consequence. It was in the last seconds that Moore's long pass, capping an immaculate performance, sent Hurst through, and this time there would be no erring. As joyful small boys dashed on to the pitch, anticipating the goal, the final whistle, he carried on alone, blew out his cheeks, and beat Tilkowski with a terrible left-footer. He was the first man to score three in a World Cup Final; and the Cup itself had at last come to the country where football began.

RESULTS: England 1966

Group I

England 0, Uruguay 0 (HT 0/0)
France 1, Mexico 1 (HT 0/0)
Uruguay 2, France 1 (HT 2/1)
England 2, Mexico 0 (HT 1/0)
Uruguay 0, Mexico 0 (HT 0/0)
England 2, France 0 (HT 1/0)

	P	W	D	L	GOALS F	A	Pts
England	3	2	1	0	**4**	**0**	5
Uruguay	3	1	2	0	**2**	**1**	4
Mexico	3	0	2	1	**1**	**3**	2
France	3	0	1	2	**2**	**5**	1

Group II

West Germany 5, Switzerland 0 (HT 3/0)
Argentina 2, Spain 1 (HT 0/0)
Spain 2, Switzerland 1 (HT 0/1)
Argentina 0, West Germany 0 (HT 0/0)
Argentina 2, Switzerland 0 (HT 0/0)
West Germany 2, Spain 1 (HT 1/1)

	P	W	D	L	GOALS F	A	Pts
West Germany	3	2	1	0	**7**	**1**	5
Argentina	3	2	1	0	**4**	**1**	5
Spain	3	1	0	2	**4**	**5**	2
Switzerland	3	0	0	3	**1**	**9**	0

Group III

Brazil 2, Bulgaria 0 (HT 1/0)
Portugal 3, Hungary 1 (HT 1/0)
Hungary 3, Brazil 1 (HT 1/1)
Portugal 3, Bulgaria 0 (HT 2/0)
Portugal 3, Brazil 1 (HT 2/0)
Hungary 3, Bulgaria 1 (HT 2/1)

	P	W	D	L	GOALS F	A	Pts
Portugal	3	3	0	0	**9**	**2**	6
Hungary	3	2	0	1	**7**	**5**	4
Brazil	3	1	0	2	**4**	**6**	2
Bulgaria	3	0	0	3	**1**	**8**	0

Group IV

Russia 3, North Korea 0 (HT 2/0)
Italy 2, Chile 0 (HT 1/0)
Chile 1, North Korea 1 (HT 1/0)
Russia 1, Italy 0 (HT 0/0)
North Korea 1, Italy 0 (HT 1/0)
Russia 2, Chile 1 (HT 1/1)

	P	W	D	L	GOALS F	A	Pts
Russia	3	3	0	0	**6**	**1**	6
North Korea	3	1	1	1	**2**	**4**	3
Italy	3	1	0	2	**2**	**2**	2
Chile	3	0	1	2	**2**	**5**	1

Quarter-finals

Wembley

England 1 — **Argentina 0**

Banks; Cohen, Wilson, Stiles, Charlton, J., Moore; Ball, Hurst, Charlton, R., Hunt, Peters.

Roma; Ferreiro, Perfumo, Albrecht, Marzolini; Gonzalez, Rattin, Onega; Solari, Artime, Mas.

SCORER
Hurst for England
HT 0/0

Sheffield

West Germany 4 — **Uruguay 0**

Tilkowski; Hottges, Weber, Schulz, Schnellinger; Beckenbauer, Haller, Overath; Seeler, Held, Emmerich.

Mazurkiewicz; Troche, Ubinas, Gonçalves, Manicera, Caetano; Salva, Rocha; Silva, Cortes, Perez.

SCORERS
Held, Beckenbauer, Seeler, Haller for West Germany
HT 1/0

Everton

Portugal 5 — **North Korea 3**

José Pereira; Morais, Baptista, Vicente, Hilario; Graça, Coluna; José Augusto, Eusebio, Torres, Simoes.

Li Chan Myung; Rim Yung Sum, Shin Yung Kyoo, Ha Jung Won, O Yoon Kyung; Pak Seung Jin, Jon Seung Hwi; Han Bong Jin, Pak Doo Ik, Li Dong Woon, Yang Sung Kook.

SCORERS
Eusebio (4) (2 penalties), José Augusto for Portugal
Pak Seung Jin, Yang Sung Kook, Li Dong Woon for North Korea
HT 2/3

Sunderland

Russia 2	**Hungary 1**
Yachine; Ponomarev,	Gelei; Matrai,
Chesternijev, Voronin,	Kaposzta, Meszoly,
Danilov; Sabo,	Sipos, Szepesi; Nagy,
Khusainov; Chislenko,	Albert, Rakosi; Bene,
Banichevski, Malafeev,	Farkas.
Porkujan.	

SCORERS
Chislenko, Porkujan for Russia
Bene for Hungary
HT 1/0

Semi-finals

Everton

West Germany 2	**Russia 1**
Tilkowski; Hottges,	Yachine; Ponomarev,
Weber, Schulz,	Chesternijev, Voronin,
Schnellinger;	Danilov; Sabo,
Beckenbauer, Haller,	Khusainov; Chislenko,
Overath; Seeler, Held,	Banichevski, Malafeev,
Emmerich.	Porkujan.

SCORERS
Haller, Beckenbauer for Germany
Porkujan for Russia
HT 1/0

Wembley

England 2	**Portugal 1**
Banks; Cohen, Wilson;	José Pereira; Festa,
Stiles, Charlton, J.,	Baptista, José Carlos,
Moore; Ball, Hurst,	Hilario; Graça,
Charlton, R., Hunt,	Coluna, José Augusto;
Peters.	Eusebio, Torres,
	Simoes.

SCORERS
Charlton, R. (2) for England
Eusebio (penalty) for Portugal
HT 1/0

Third place match

Wembley

Portugal 2	**Russia 1**
José Pereira; Festa,	Yachine; Ponomarev,
Baptista, José Carlos,	Khurtsilava, Korneev,
Hilario; Graça, Coluna,	Danilov; Voronin,
José Augusto; Eusebio,	Sichinava; Metreveli,
Torres, Simoes.	Malafeev, Banichevski,
	Serebrianikov.

SCORERS
Eusebio (pénalty), Torres for Portugal
Malafeev for Russia
HT 1/1

Final

Wembley

England 4	**West Germany 2**
(after extra time)	
Banks; Cohen, Wilson;	Tilkowski; Hottges,
Stiles, Charlton, J.,	Schulz, Weber,
Moore; Ball, Hurst,	Schnellinger; Haller,
Hunt, Charlton, R.,	Beckenbauer, Overath;
Peters.	Seeler, Held,
	Emmerich.

SCORERS
Hurst (3), Peters for England
Haller, Weber for Germany
HT 1/1

MEXICO
1970

The Challenge of Mexico

The 1970 World Cup, played, inexplicably and inexcusably, in Mexico, was gloriously won by Brazil. For all the appalling problems of heat and altitude, all the preceding threat of violent, negative play, they triumphed with a panache, elegance and enterprise which raised new hope for attacking football. It was especially suitable that in the Final they should thrash an Italian team which stood for all that was most cautious and destructive in the contemporary game.

The decision to make it Mexico, rather than Argentina, had been taken by FIFA at their Congress in Tokyo during the 1964 Olympic Games, thus following the dubious example of the Olympic Committee which had decided to hold the Games in Mexico City in 1968. What may euphemistically be described as lobbying by the interested parties was particularly fierce. Several delegations, including that of the Football Association, whose Secretary had personal experience of conditions in Mexico City, opposed the choice of Mexico. What possibly swayed the final choice was the inconsistency of Argentina's support for the World Cup, and their tenuous economic situation.

The displeasing machinations in Tokyo—one delegate admitted that his fare had been paid by an aspirant World Cup host—the whisperings in hotel corners and corridors, prompted Sir Stanley Rous to cry 'Enough!' Mexico, as it was, prevailed by fifty-six votes to thirty-two, with seven abstentions, but he, and others, wanted no more of such gerrymandering.

The intense heat of the Mexican summer—rising to well over ninety degrees—and the breathing difficulties experienced at heights of over seven thousand feet, in Puebla, Toluca, Mexico City and the rest, were problems enough. To make matters worse, the World Cup Committee entered a lamentable agreement with international television to begin their Sunday matches—including the Final—at twelve noon. In almost every one of the chosen venues noon is an hour at which it is inadvisable even to walk about. To attempt to play football, and World Cup football at that, was both ludicrous and potentially dangerous. It was particularly difficult for teams from northern Europe; the holders, England, would find themselves melting in the torrid ninety-eight degrees of Guadalajara, when up against Brazil, and finally succumbing in the still stickier heat of Leon.

In retrospect, the decision to play in Mexico, and to play frequently at noon, looks as shameful as it did in prospect. The World Cup of 1970 ultimately succeeded in spite of the abominable conditions, and one hopes, though without any great confidence, that the lesson has been learned.

Acclimatisation

One inevitable effect, just as in the case of the 1968 Olympiad, was a huge increase in the cost of preparation. Though medical opinions varied sharply on the best means of acclimatisation and the optimum period of adaptation, there was no doubt that such a period was essential. The Olympic soccer tournament of 1968, in which Mexico's team of young League players was well beaten by France and Japan, showed that teams from sea level could settle down quite happily after three weeks or so. The Final, after all, had been between Hungary and Bulgaria.

The Contenders   Brazil

Brazil's preparation, heavily and generously underwritten by the President of their Sports Confederation, Joâo Havelange, was a protracted one, extending over some three months. Their prospects, however, were seriously compromised by a sudden change of horses in mid-stream when, in March 1970, João Saldanha, the team manager, was replaced by Zagalo. It was a situation heavy with irony, for Zagalo, Brazil's left-winger in the victories of 1958 and 1962, had been a protégé of Saldanha when he was managing Botafogo.

With his intelligence, enthusiasm, and vigour, Saldanha gave the national side new direction and allure. It did not look terribly impressive when it scraped through 2–1 in the Maracanà against England in June 1969, with late goals by Tostao and Jairzinho, but the following August, with Tostao scoring abundantly, it swept through its qualifying group against Colombia, Paraguay and Venezuela, uniting the vast country behind it.

Saldanha, intellectual and revolutionary, dialectician and, we were to understand, master of unarmed combat, departed for Europe trailing clouds of glory, saw seven international games, locked horns with the dour Alf Ramsey in a television interview; and returned to Brazil a changed man. Something had happened; something at once radical and puzzling. Now Saldanha's policies, always unexpected and spectacular, became frenetic and bizarre. In November 1969, without an international match being played for four months, he suddenly dropped four defenders, including both goalkeepers, and called up five new men.

There was instant outrage and protest, compounded the following February, when Toninho and Scala were, on medical grounds, sent back from training camp to their clubs by Dr Toledo, the Brazilians' medical adviser, only to be pronounced perfectly fit by their own infuriated clubs. On March 4, Brazil played at Porto Alegre, and lost to Argentina, who had already been eliminated from the World Cup by Peru. Four days later, Saldanha committed the ultimate and unforgivable crime: he contemplated dropping Pelé, with whom he had for some time been embroiled in a struggle for power. The heavens opened, Saldanha disappeared, Zagalo took over.

Thorough, calm, reputedly and invariably 'lucky' in all that he did, Zagalo made certain small but vital changes. The most important of them was using Rivelino, a powerfully built inside-left with a magnificent left foot, the equal of the celebrated Gerson's, as a nominal left-winger. This, at one blow, solved the problem of incorporating both these splendid talents in the team and also relieved Rivelino of the necessity to play flat out for ninety minutes. His previous appearances had been distinguished but insufficient, falling away after one dazzling half.

Zagalo's famous luck was confirmed by the recovery of Tostao from a severe eye injury. Suffered in training, when a ball hit him, all unaware, and detached the retina, it had necessitated two operations in Houston, Texas. Since his brief appearance in the 1966 World Cup, Tostao had developed into a player of glorious technical skill, great subtlety and considerable courage. Certainly the lack and loss of him had clipped the wings of Saldanha's Brazil; but now he was back.

Back, too, though less significantly, came the little Fluminense goalkeeper, Felix, first called up and then jettisoned by João Saldanha. Felix would play every game in Mexico, but his performances, his vulnerability to the high cross, would, *mutatis mutandis*, recall the old, cruel Harry Truman joke; that indeed, 'anybody' could be President; 'any' goalkeeper could win a World Cup medal. A far cry, this, from the immaculate, imperturbable Gilmar.

Brazil were assigned to the same qualifying group as England, Guadalajara, together with Romania and Czechoslovakia. They arrived there with an evident, shrewd policy of 'beads for the natives'. Clearly they knew their Mexicans. Distributing flags, smiles and pennants, full of protestations of good will, admiration and affection for the local populace, they had done a thorough job of seduction by the time they took off for their training redoubt at Guanajuato. On their return, they ran their training camp, outside Guadalajara at the Suites de Caribe, like a fortress, even obliging journalists to obtain and produce a separate identity card from that required and issued by the World Cup Committee. It did not matter. Good will had been shown and reciprocated. It would cost England dear.

England

It was clear at the time, and is still clearer now, that the confrontation between Ramsey and the Mexicans, ultimately so disastrous for his team, should have been mediated. Indeed, it was quite clear on England's exploratory tour in 1969. It was Sir Alf's hope and ambition, frequently and fervently expressed, that England in 1969 would make friends, and create the climate they required for success in 1970. In these circumstances, his own performance was sometimes a little surprising.

After the goalless draw between Mexico and England in the Azteca Stadium in May 1969, he gave a short Press conference outside the dressing-rooms, and was asked if he had anything to say to the Mexican Press. 'Yes,' he replied. 'There was a band playing outside our hotel till five o'clock this morning. We were promised a motor cycle escort to the stadium. It never arrived. When our players went out to inspect the pitch, they were abused and jeered by the crowd. I would have thought the Mexican public would have been delighted to welcome England. Then, when the game began, they could cheer their own team as much as they liked. But'—a happy, hasty, afterthought— 'we are delighted to be in Mexico, and the Mexican people are a wonderful people.'

In Guadalajara a few days later, after an England XI had thrashed a Mexican XI 4–0, there were further solecisms. When the game was over, the Governor of the state of Jalisco made a presentation to Ramsey, and was then escorted into what were then, before the building of the World Cup stadium, the underground dressing-rooms. After them scuttled a flock of Mexican journalists, who re-emerged almost instantly, chivvied by an irate Sir Alf, very much like the moneychangers being driven from the temple. '*You've* got no right in here!'

Whatever Ramsey's many solid qualities, diplomacy was scarcely one of them, and in the difficult circumstances it was of the essence. Instead, apparent xenophobia was compounded by his well-known aversion to the Press; one which had by now been widely reciprocated. It was no use explaining to Mexican journalists that they were being treated no more brusquely, no more indifferently, than their English counterparts. The Mexican capacity for self-hatred, wounded feelings, is large; the seed fell upon ground already dangerously fertile.

England, indeed, had clearly become the team the Mexicans loved to hate: 'a team of thieves and drunks', as one local newspaper amiably put it. There had been Ramsey's indifference to the Press, Bobby Moore's absurd persecution in Colombia, and the arrival of Jeff Astle, most nervous of air travellers, at Mexico City airport in a state of some disarray.

Moore's astonishing, impregnable calm, that icy self-possession which had made him such a force in the England defence, had never been so impressively manifest as it was in his Colombian tribulations. While the England team were staying at the Tequendama hotel in Bogotà, he and Bobby Charlton visited the Green Fire jewellery shop inside the hotel. While they were afterwards sitting just outside it, they were approached, and asked to explain the alleged disappearance of a bracelet. Both were naturally astonished, unaware of the well-established Colombian pastime of thus accusing visiting celebrities. Indeed, when the news of Bobby Moore's subsequent arrest and detention broke upon the world, a rash of similar cases was exposed, their victims ranging from singers to bullfighters.

England, despite the eight thousand-foot altitude, won easily against Colombia in Bogotà—as did their second eleven, on the same night— then travelled for two similar matches in Quito, Ecuador (nine thousand feet), both of which they also won, Moore behaving throughout with his customary poised detachment. On arriving once more in Bogotà, on the way back to Mexico City, he was arrested by the Colombian police and put under house arrest in the care of the President of the Millonarios Football Club.

Accusations were made against him by the proprietor of the jewellery shop, the shopgirl, and a mysterious 'witness', whose background would turn out to be, at the least, equivocal, and who would ultimately disappear. Following diplomatic intervention, Moore was 'bailed' to play in the World Cup, played superbly, and was persecuted for a few months more with threats of further charges before the case died a belated, murky death. Plainly it was a fabrication from the start (its perpetrators were charged for conspiracy in 1972), but this cannot detract from the extraordinary qualities of resilience shown by Moore, whose 1970 performances outstripped even those of 1966.

England's hopes of keeping the World Cup seemed quite substantial, for all the oppressive conditions. Though Cohen and Wilson, the full-backs, Nobby Stiles, Hunt and Jackie Charlton had dropped out of the 1966 side (Stiles and Charlton remaining in the 1970 party) morale was excellent. New stars had been discovered. A most useful aid, slow sodium, had been adopted. Of the old brigade, Bobby Moore, Gordon Banks and Geoff Hurst seemed better than ever. Terry Cooper, a small, strong, immensely mobile left-back who had begun with Leeds as a left-winger, was the perfect man for an overlap, full of pace, control and enterprise. Alan Mullery, a cheerful Londoner, had efficiently succeeded Stiles. He was a solid, all-round player who, though scarcely an artist, was technically better endowed than his predecessor, even if he lacked Stiles' galvanising qualities. Both he and Manchester City's lean inside-right, Colin Bell, had excelled on the 1969 Latin American tour.

Francis Lee, the blond, stockily-built Manchester City striker, had come into the team at outside-right in 1968 and shown a heartening response to the great occasion. An explosive runner with a strong shot, especially happy when operating on the right flank, he was a most useful ally for the muscular, self-sacrificing Hurst, whose positional play now equalled his admirable finishing.

Perhaps the team had no great flair; it had gone out to Yugoslavia in the violent semi-final of the 1968 European Championship, had continued to exalt effort over talent. Nevertheless, it was respected and feared.

Some World Cup countries perhaps took caution too far—England among them. The English players arrived in Mexico early in May, the best part of a month before their first game. The West Germans, who would ultimately beat them, arrived weeks later.

Germany

West Germany, playing in the group at Leon—a small, hot, rather squalid city north-west of Guadalajara—were moderately fancied. They could again call on the gracefully inventive Franz Beckenbauer and Wolfgang Overath in midfield, not to mention the resilient Uwe Seeler, playing his fourth World Cup. Moreover, there was a new and formidable threat in the person of Gerd Muller, the young Bayern Munich centre-forward. Short, dark-haired, with heavy, powerful thighs, Muller was a finisher *par excellence*, deadly in the box, a splendid volleyer.

How, then, could he be reconciled with that other fine centre-forward, the veteran Seeler? Helmut Schoen, though violently and vociferously criticised by his lieutenant of 1966, little Dettmar Cramer, resolved the question masterfully. First, Pozzo-like, he set Seeler and Muller to share a hotel room. Secondly, he decided to play Seeler in midfield; an inspired choice.

West Germany had strong rivals in Peru, whose ebullient, inventive, highly adventurous team had put out dour Argentina. Skilfully managed by Didì, the old Brazilian general of 1958 and 1962, the Peruvians scorned negative methods—even in their last, decisive qualifying game in Buenos Aires, when they had daringly used two wingers in a 4-2-4 formation, forced a draw, and come through. Though star players had been suspended for violence perpetrated in that eliminating series, there was talent to burn: the black, effervescent, twenty-year-old Teofilo Cubillas at inside-forward; the powerful, adventurous

Chumpitaz, with his mighty right foot; the experienced black striker, Gallardo.

Italy

The Italians, drawn in the high altitude Puebla-Toluca group with Israel, Uruguay and Sweden, were placing almost messianic hopes in Luigi Riva. Long before they flew off to Mexico, it was clear to any visitor that the country was burdening the Cagliari forward with a responsibility and a mission he could scarcely hope to discharge.

Of Riva's great, goal-scoring talent, of his control, acceleration, his mighty left foot, his courage, there was no doubt. Yet his very fame and presence were enough to confirm Italy in their dreadfully sterile addiction to *catenaccio* tactics; enough to lull them into a belief that if ten men stayed in defence and Riva was upfield, it was sufficient to guarantee goals. On top of this, and the North Korean complex which exacerbated it, there was the contretemps of Rivera and Mazzola, which threatened to split the team asunder before ever a ball was kicked.

We are familiar by now with both players. Gianni Rivera, as poised, elegant and economical as ever, captain and orchestrator of Milan, was now a ripe twenty-six, playing in his third World Cup, chosen as European Footballer of the Year. Sandrino Mazzola, who had made his name as a scoring centre-forward or striker, had in 1968, when Rivera was injured, used the Nations Cup final against Yugoslavia, in Rome, to affirm himself as a superb midfield player. Finals, indeed, seemed to bring out the best in him, for he played heroically well in Mexico City.

If the Italians were haunted by nightmares of North Korea, at least the North Koreans were not there to trouble them in person. After their mysterious and remarkable presence in England, they had characteristically withdrawn from the 1970 World Cup, refusing to play qualifying games against Israel. The Israelis, in consequence, were able to win in an immensely far-flung group, including South Korea and the ultimate runners-up, Australia. Their team had already played, and played well, in Mexico in the 1968 Olympics, and had an excellent inside-left in Mordecai Spiegler, an Israeli of Russian birth.

This time, there was both an African and an Asian entrant, for the Afro-Asians had had their way, the groups had been separated and a displeasingly anomalous situation thus created. De-zoning alone could at once content the Afro-Asians and see to it that Europe had a proper representation. As it was, Morocco and Israel qualified, while such teams as Scotland, Yugoslavia and Spain did not.

Belgium

Group I, in Mexico City, had the Mexicans themselves, the mathematical and solid Russians, El Salvador—whose elimination of
Honduras had provoked a short and bloody war—and Belgium,
greatly favoured. Discovering a fine midfield player in Odilon
Polleunis, reaffirming the talents of Paul Van Himst, 'motivated' by a
forceful coach in Raymond Goethals, they had surprisingly put out
both Yugoslavia and Spain, though they had flagged towards the
close. Alas, they would disappoint everybody with their wretched performances in Mexico.

The Opening Games

The tournament opened with a ploddingly dull midday game between
Mexico and Russia at the immense, vertiginous Azteca Stadium. No
goals were scored, little drama was distilled. Mexico did not choose their
admirable striker, Enrique Borja, who had been enmeshed in the coils of
their tangled football politics, transferred from Universidad to America
and mysteriously kept on the sidelines. Russia, with their big captain,
Albert Chesternijev, sweeping up in his diligent, crouching bird dog's
manner, obviously suffered from the great heat, and showed scant initiative. The most passionate moment was evoked by the appearance of the
Union Jack in the parade before the game; it was fervently and ferociously whistled.

If the Mexico-Russia game was notable for anything, it was for the
fussy, officious refereeing of West Germany's Herr Tschenscher. Strong in
what to many of us seemed the equivocal experience of the Olympic
tournament, the FIFA Referees' Committee had once more put its trust in
the flourishing of coloured cards, and in Draconian instructions to its
officials. Herr Tschenscher, all too keenly conscious of the occasion,
'booked' a succession of largely inoffensive Russians, dealt much more
leniently with the Mexicans, and was partly responsible for the tedium of
the occasion, which was to a certain extent redeemed by a fine save in
each half by the Russian goalkeeper, Kavazashvili. Mexico certainly felt
the unlucky loss of their midfield player, Onofre, who had broken a leg in
training only a few days previously.

That Herr Tschenscher's interpretation of the new refereeing dispen-
sations was largely personal was shown the following Tuesday, when
England opened their series against Romania in Guadalajara. Mocanu,
the Romanian left-back, committed at least three brutal, crippling fouls,
swinging knee-high kicks which lamed two English players, yet was so
indulgently treated by M. Loraux, the Belgian referee, that he did not
even have his name taken.

England, winning with a goal smartly and powerfully taken by Geoff Hurst's left foot in the second half, certainly deserved their victory. The star of the afternoon was unquestionably Terry Cooper, who exploited Romania's defensive tactics to overlap, on both flanks, with high spirit and effectiveness.

Meanwhile, the Brazilians had begun more impressively with their 4–1 victory over the Czechs, featuring the prodigies of Pelé, Jairzinho, Gerson and Rivelino. As so often in the past, the Brazilian defence had not looked remotely equal to the attack, yet it had not mattered. Perhaps it would have done had the Czechs been less prodigal with their chances. 'They played basketball football,' said Ball scornfully. 'As soon as the Brazilians got the ball, they all ran back, seven of them. The midfield was wide open.'

Petras, the stalwart, blond Czech centre-forward, swept easily past Brito to give his side the lead, and might in that opening period have had at least one other goal. One of Rivelino's swerving, fulminating, celebrated free kicks brought an immediate equaliser, and just after half-time Pelé got the second. He immaculately caught a long, high pass from Gerson's superb left foot on his chest, before volleying in.

The tall Kvasniak, a star of the 1962 World Cup Final, who had come on as a slow substitute, missed a palpable chance to equalise, after a corner, and the error was punished at once, Jairzinho breaking away to score from what might have been an offside position. There could be no doubts, however, about his and Brazil's last goal. Running with marvellous control and power, shaking off three defenders and an attempted foul, he cut in to drive the ball home with his strong right foot.

Didì, their black master spirit, and strategist of two World Cups, meanwhile took his gifted Peruvians into action. The omens and the beginning could scarcely have been more depressing. A minute's silence was observed in Leon for the appalling Peruvian earthquake. No doubt the psychological reaction had something to do with the fact that the Peruvians quickly went two goals down to Bulgaria, who cleverly exploited a couple of free kicks. But then, bringing on substitutes, in Campos to tighten the defence and the coloured Hugo Sotil to enliven the attack, Peru hit back. The elusive dribbling of Cubillas, the powerful breaks from the back four of Hector Chumpitaz, the running of Sotil and Gallardo, turned the tide. Gallardo, once an unsuccessful Milan player, later with Cagliari, answered Bonev's goal quickly with a cross shot. In the second half, Chumpitaz's mighty right foot scored from a free kick for Peru, by way of revenge, and Cubillas ran on to the impressive Mifflin's pass to get the winner.

The following day, on the same ground, the untrumpeted Moroccans gave West Germany an appalling fright. Who would have expected these minnows to come out and attack furiously for the opening twenty minutes? Not the puzzled Germans, whose *catenaccio*, Schulz, sweeping up again, was overcome when Hottges headed weakly back to his blond goalkeeper, Sepp Maier, and the ball fell as a gift before Houmane, who scored.

For the first but by no means the last time in this tournament, Grabowski came on as substitute, with telling effect. This was, indeed, the first World Cup in which substitutes had been allowed—two for each side, at any juncture of the game, the formality and fiction of being able to replace only an injured man having been abandoned. Ironically, as we shall see, the Germans would later be hoist with their own petard. Meanwhile, Helmut Schoen made his first good use of Grabowski, a fair haired right-winger of pace, initiative and subtle control, who replaced Helmut Haller and created the winning goal.

Not until eleven minutes after half-time did the anxious Germans equalise, and Schoen must have been particularly pleased that it should come from the co-operation of Seeler and Muller, the old warhorse driving home Muller's pass. Twelve minutes from the end, Grabowski got away on one of his characteristic runs, Loehr, the other winger, headed against the bar and Muller, forever in the imminent, deadly breach, scored the first of his ten World Cup goals.

The second game in Group I saw Belgium's talented team make a good enough start, easily defeating, 3–0, an El Salvador side which clearly had no real business to be there; indeed, would not have been, had Mexico's status as hosts not exempted them even from their customary facile passage to the finals. Wilfried Van Moer, the sturdy and dynamic little Standard Liège midfield player, scored two of the goals, Raul Lambert, the powerful Bruges striker, the other. With Van Himst and another fine opportunist in Devrindt also in the attack, goals seemed potentially abundant. In fact, this was the merest flash in the pan.

The Puebla-Toluca Group II produced a couple of deadly dull games. Uruguay made very heavy weather of winning 2–0 against a determined Israeli team. Worst of all, their splendid midfield inside-forward, the lithe, dark Pedro Rocha, hurt himself so badly after twelve minutes that he would take no further part in the competition.

The Italians, in all their three opening games, played in a lather of foreboding, as if defeat would result in execution. In the first match, against Sweden at Toluca, they scored through Domenghini after eleven minutes, with a shot that might have been saved, then sat on their lead. Domenghini's was the only goal Italy would get in their group matches.

The remaining games, against Uruguay and Israel, were both of them grim and goalless. Not unexpectedly, the exaltation of Riva had inhibited the functioning of the team; for what star footballer, used to earning his 40 million lire a year, takes kindly to being reduced to a kind of water carrier?

Uruguay were lucky to join Italy in the quarter-finals, for they lost 1–0 to the Swedes in the final game, Grahn heading the only goal. Previously, they had been held to a draw by the determined Israelis, who had surpassed themselves in their results and their competent displays.

Meeting of Champions   Brazil v. England

The meeting of England, the holders, with Brazil, for former holders, was without doubt the *pièce de résistance* of the qualifying rounds. The conditions would certainly favour Brazil, but news that Gerson, with an injured thigh, would probably miss the game, threw it open.

On the previous afternoon, Romania beat the disappointing Czechs 2–1, though Petras, with a fine, glancing header, got his customary early goal. Petras ran powerfully and dangerously on either flank, but the Romanians came back into the game, equalised through Neagu after half-time, and won through a penalty by the blond, talented Florea Dumitrache.

As in 1958, England had elected to stay at an hotel in the middle of town, and now it would cost them still dearer. The previous year, on their arrival from Mexico City on their tour, to them the Guadalajara Hilton, with its swimming pool, its sham-colonial style, had seemed a quiet haven. What no one had been percipient enough to realise was that it would be flooded with supporters, and within easy access of the malevolent.

Day by day, as the rows of half-naked bodies formed around the swimming pool, the England players in their blue tracksuits looked like wistful trusties out on parole, denied the benefits of sun and still water. Considerably worse was to befall them on the eve of the Brazilian match.

From quite early in the evening, the advance guard of the besieging army began to arrive; on foot, in cars, on motor cycles, shouting, honking and chanting. The chant was largely for '*BRA-sil, BRA-sil!*' though its intention was fundamentally hostile to England. Round and round the hotel drove the cars and motor cycles, honking obscenely and provocatively, while the crowd in front of the hotel steadily grew.

There was to be no remission. As the night wore on, so the noise increased—now an obvious, malign attempt to disturb the English players' slumbers. It succeeded and many of the English team were forced to add the effects of a broken night to the already formidable hazards of the next day's game.

Ramsey made only one change for the match. Mullery would again look after Pelé; Brian Labone, the strong Everton defender, would play stopper. At right-back, however, Keith Newton, who had been one of those kicked by Mocanu, was replaced by Tommy Wright of Everton. 'He can beat you,' Ramsey warned Wright of Paulo Cesar, who played on Brazil's left wing; and he did. He was picked to replace Gerson, to advance from deep positions and give help in midfield to Rivelino and the young right-half Clodoaldo, a player who would not come fully into his own till later on.

'It's when they get to the eighteen-yard box,' said Bobby Charlton of the Brazilians, 'if you *let* them get to the eighteen-yard box.' He himself had shown greater fire and efficiency against Romania than he had for a long time—the unquestioned prince of midfield, where only a year before he had been threatened by the excellence of Colin Bell. Though Bell would substitute him in both this match and against the West Germans, he would never show the form he had shown the previous year, when he played so hearteningly well, with such stamina and versatility.

Many have seen the England versus Brazil game as the 'real' Final, England as the 'real' runners-up, and there is no doubt that they gave Brazil a far more courageous and substantial fight than craven Italy. Yet the absence of Gerson cannot be discounted, while if England missed a couple of fine chances, then only Gordon Banks could have made the miraculous save from Pelé's header that came in the tenth minute of the game.

The groundwork was done by Jairzinho, confirming fears that Cooper would not be able to hold him, nor be able to attack as he had done against largely wingless Romania. Brushing past the left-back with all the strength and acceleration of his predecessors, Garrincha and Julinho, Jairzinho dashed to the line and centred perfectly. Pelé headed the ball down hard, on the bounce, inside the left-hand post, and was already shouting, 'Goal!' when Banks, with incredible, gymnastic agility, somehow launched himself across his goal from the opposite post, to flail the ball, one-handed, over the bar.

With the dry, blazing heat reaching ninety-eight degrees, it was extraordinary, even with their slow sodium tablets, that England resisted as they did. No English player lost less than ten pounds in weight, and their doctor pointed out that an American Army manual forbade even training to be done when the thermometer exceeded eighty-five degrees. The World Cup Committee had prostituted their tournament and sacrificed its players to the demands of European television.

England threw away a couple of good opportunities in each half. In the first, Geoff Hurst, clear through the Brazilian defence, made the elementary mistake of presuming himself in an offside position, hesitating, and at length shooting hastily and feebly. Francis Lee, when a right-wing cross by Tommy Wright put the goal at his mercy, contrived to head straight at Felix.

The goalkeeper again betrayed his fallibility with high centres, but England's long inimicality to orthodox wingers meant that he was not often under pressure. It was only late in the game that Ramsey at last sent on the tall Jeff Astle, whose greatest strength was in the air, while Charlton gave way to Bell. Astle, though he would miss horribly, at once set the Brazilians problems; but by this time England were a goal down.

It came after fourteen minutes of the second half, and Tostao was its motivating force. His splendid dribbling on the left took him past three English defenders; though he certainly pushed off Bobby Moore, who played throughout with superb aplomb. Finally, he passed to Pelé in the goalmouth, and Pelé, without ado, laid the ball off beautifully to his right, for Jairzinho to dart in and score.

A cross headed down by Astle gave Alan Ball a chance which he squandered; Astle himself contrived to shoot over the bar when a panicky defender headed the ball straight to his feet, and another shot by Ball clipped the bar. Brazil, however, held out. It had been a magnificent, enthralling display of football, admirably referred by the obscure Israeli referee, Abraham Klein; an inspired appointment. In the English defence, Alan Mullery had played Pelé as cleanly and resourcefully as he had a year before in Rio. Next morning, Ball sat disconsolate by the swimming pool: 'How could Jeff miss that chance?'

Towards the Finals

In Group I, the Russians suddenly cut loose against a surprisingly feeble Belgium, thrashing them 4–1. Two of the goals went to the Dynamo Kiev striker, Bychevetz, and the Russian midfield functioned sweetly with another Kiev player, the elegant Muntijan, in incisive form.

Mexico then disposed of El Salvador 4–0, though they owed their first goal to an abominable refereeing error; one which presaged the decision which would win them their match against Belgium. El Salvador in fact began well, Rodriguez, in the ninth minute, hitting the post, then Calderon with successive shots. A couple of minutes from half-time, however, Hussain Kandil, the Egyptian referee, gave El Salvador a free kick. It was promptly taken by Perez of Mexico, who pushed to it Padilla. The latter centred, Valdivia scored, and Kandil gave a goal. In vain did the El Salvador players argue, weep and lie on the ground; the goal, disgracefully, stood. Mexico went on to score three more against a demoralised side.

So to Belgium, a crowd of 112,000 in the immense Azteca, and another gravely dubious goal. This time it was the only one of the game; a penalty, given after fifteen minutes. Jeck cleared the ball, Valdivia, rushing onward after the event, fell over his leg. Señor Coerezza, of Argentina, gave a penalty kick. Despite two minutes of Belgian protests, Pena took it and scored, and Mexico narrowly survived the remainder of the game. 'The penalty,' said Goethals, Belgium's manager, 'was the worst I have ever seen, nor have I ever experienced such a hostile, biased crowd.' So Mexico attained the quarter-finals for the first time in their long World Cup career.

Russia beat El Salvador 2–0 in the ante-penultimate game.

In Leon, Peru, with a couple of goals from the exciting Cubillas, disposed of Morocco 3–0, while the West Germans thrashed a flaccid Bulgaria 5–2, Gerd Muller scoring three, one from the penalty spot. The blond Karl-Heinz Schnellinger, playing, like Seeler, in his fourth World Cup, took over from Willie Schulz as sweeper.

It was plain that Brazil would win Group III, probable that England would accompany them. The Brazilians put out a diminished team against Romania, lacking both Rivelino and Gerson, pushing Piazza into midfield, and winning only by 3–2. Pelé got a couple of crisp goals, Jairzinho the other when Paulo Cesar—again emphasising what Brazil could do and wingless England could not—went to the by-line and pulled the ball back. The Romanians, after a poor start, played brightly, Dumitrache once more casting doubt on Brazil's central defence with his first-half goal, Dembrowski heading a second near the end. Felix again looked vulnerable, but Brazil were hardly extended.

England, next day, looked quite abysmal. Drafting in a bevy of reserves, they struggled pitifully to find rhythm against the Czech team who, as Keith Newton ruefully observed, never stopped running, and ridiculed their previous form. Allan Clarke, far from a success, scored the only goal of the match early in the second half, from a penalty so dubious that even the French referee, M. Machin, gave a mysterious explanation. When Kuna tackled Bell he appeared to fall on the ball and handle it, yet Machin said afterwards he had given the penalty for tripping. With Jackie Charlton sadly at sea in defence, Astle easily mastered in the air and ineffectual on the ground (the Czech defence was not Brazil's), the English display was embarrassing. Indeed, the enterprising Czech right-back, Dobias; almost equalised with a shot which deceived Banks but hit the bar. As against that, Ball hit the bar, for England.

The Quarter-Finals Italy v. Mexico

The quarter-finals drew West Germany against England in Leon, Brazil against Peru in Guadalajara, Italy against Mexico on the heights of Toluca, Uruguay against Russia in Mexico City, where the rejoicing at the home team's success had reached frightening proportions. Santiago, eight years before, was almost docile by comparison, as the mobs gave vent to their fearful joy.

It would not last long. Freed at last from the Korean complex, Italy and Riva came out of their shell; their extravagantly talented players, for once allowed to express themselves, swept the weak Mexican team aside.

Though Riva scored two goals, it was Gianni Rivera's day. Valcareggi's compromise was to play Mazzola for the first half, Rivera in the second, and it was with Rivera's arrival that Italy took charge of the game. At half-time, the score was 1–1, Gonzalez giving the Mexicans a false dawn with a goal in twelve minutes, which was equalised when Domenghini's shot was deflected home. In the second period, Rivera ruled the field.

Exchanging passes with the clever little Picchio De Sisti, Rivera crossed to Riva, who burst past two defenders, then beat Calderon from a sharp angle. Next his shot, then Domenghini's, were blocked, but Rivera drove the second rebound home. Finally, Rivera's immaculate pass sent Riva through for the fourth. There would be no more rowdy rejoicings in Mexico City.

Uruguay v. Russia

The Azteca Stadium confirmed its recent reputation for dubious goals when Uruguay defeated Russia 1–0 in the last seconds of extra time. As little, dark Cubilla, the serpentine Uruguayan right-winger, pulled the ball back, it seemed quite clearly to have crossed the goal-line. But neither the referee nor his linesman thought so, and when Esparrago scored the goal stood. So the Russian team, purportedly fed up that promises to pay them a large bonus had not been kept, went out of the Cup. Their attack had again lacked flair and punch, but disappointment may have had something to do with that.

As for the Uruguayans, their achievement in reaching the semi-finals without Rocha had to be saluted. Apart from the experienced Cubilla, who had not long since returned from playing in Buenos Aires for River Plate, their stars were in defence; Ancheta, the big, dark, young centre-half, splendid on the ground and in the air, and of course the famous Mazurkiewiecz, keeping a superb goal in his third World Cup.

Brazil v. Peru

In Guadalajara, Brazil, still the darlings of the crowd, accounted for Peru in a spectacular and effervescent game, a game in which both sides delighted in attack and scorned caution. That Peru's defence was very far from the equal of their shining attack had been plain in their concluding group game with West Germany. Again, the persisting importance of wingers was shown as the Germans, despite their *catenaccio* formation, used Libuda—then Grabowski—and Loehr wide on the flanks, to pour out a cornucopia of centres. Gerd Muller, seldom troubling to move out of the middle, as his future opponent Brian Labone remarked, made superb use of them, scoring three times; once with a magnificent header. Indeed, despite his lack of height, or perhaps because of its lulling effect on opposing defences, he was surprisingly dangerous in the air. Curiously enough, he also missed a very good chance, when the score was still 0–0, and the subtle Beckenbauer lobbed a free kick above the wall to find him unguarded. Peru scored just before half-time, and had the better of the second half, when the height and heat seemed to have sapped the Germans and given the Peruvians the advantage their native conditions implied. But there were no more goals, and a dull 1–1 draw between Bulgaria and Morocco completed the group.

Now, against Brazil, Peru played with dash and spirit but ultimately with little hope. Brazil had Gerson back again; and Rivelino, with his thumping left foot and his bandit's moustache. Both left feet, indeed, thumped to excellent purpose, with Rivelino often working alongside Gerson in midfield. Peru brought back their black winger, Baylon, of whom so much had initially been expected, but though Brazil had to use the young Marco Antonio in place of the injured Everaldo, Baylon got little change out of him. On Brazil's right wing the muscular Jairzinho was ill, and even though he scored Brazil's fourth from Tostao's insidious pass, was not the force he had been in the group matches.

Brazil went ahead after eleven minutes with a goal which emphasised their quick thinking and equally swift reflexes. When Campos, trying to breast the ball down, slipped, Tostao instantly found Rivelino, whose deadly left foot struck again. The ball beat Rubiños, to go in off the post. Hard on the heels of that Tostao, now moving with all his old provocative sleight of foot, feinted right to unbalance an opponent, then beat Rubiños with his left.

Peru, inevitably depressed, were allowed to come back into the game on the half-hour, with the complicity of Felix, who totally misjudged Gallardo's long spinning cross from the left.

It didn't matter. Just after the interval, Pelé's long shot was deflected home by Tostao. Again Peru reacted, Sotil, who had replaced Baylon as he did in their first match, having a shot which Brito could not clear, Subillas driving in from twenty yards. Then came Brazil's fourth, from Jairzinho.

West Germany v. England

At Leon, it may with hindsight be said that England lost the match at the moment when Gordon Banks inexplicably fell sick. 'The world's best goalkeeper!' his colleagues had jokingly been calling him throughout the tour, but it was no more than the truth. On the Saturday, however, he was taken ill, and on the Sunday morning, on the large green lawn of the English team's hotel in Leon, he was to be seen hobbling, white and manifestly sick, on the arm of the England team doctor, Neil Phillips. There was plainly no hope of his playing and so it might be said, a little callously, that his place went to Peter Bonetti and the match to West Germany.

That it was by no means so simple as this is shown by the controversy which has surrounded the game ever since; not the kind of controversy evoked by Hurst's goal in the two teams' previous World Cup meeting, but by the question of tactics, the question of Ramsey, the question of Bonetti's fallibility. Was it an oversimplification, too easy an escape for Ramsey, to say that if Banks had played England would have won—or had his mistaken tactics, his ill-handled substitutions, been fundamentally responsible?

What is quite beyond doubt or argument is that England, forty minutes from the end, were leading 2–0, and that they finally lost, in extra time, 3–2.

The match, in prospect, had several fascinating attributes. In the first place, it included the teams which had contested the 1966 Final. In the second, West Germany had at long last broken their protracted run of defeats against England; a run which had begun in 1901 with the visit of the first German team to play in England. Admittedly, the crucial victory had more extrinsic than intrinsic significance, for West Germany's 1–0 win against England in Hanover in May 1968 was a trivial one. The England team was below strength, the standard low, the occasion tedious. Nevertheless, after sixty-seven years, a win was a win.

The West Germans, however, looked strong favourites. After their dull beginning against Morocco they had swept aside Bulgarians and Peruvians in a flurry of goals, Wolfgang Overath, with his splendid, long, 'quarter-back's' left-footed passes, combining with Seeler and the matchless Beckenbauer in midfield, to make the bullets for the formidable Muller to fire. The wingers, all three of them, had been fast and dangerous, ideas had been many. By contrast, England had scored only a couple of goals, and though admittedly below full strength had looked dreadful against the Czechs. Their 4-4-2 plan, described by the Manchester City manager and former England left-half, Joe Mercer, as 'cruelty to centre-forwards', had been neither effective nor entertaining. Later, the handsome, multilingual Romanian World Cup captain, Mircea Lucescu, an anglophile and an admirer of British football, would complain that England had come to Mexico with the too narrow ambition of keeping the World Cup rather than of playing good football.

Among England's senior players there had been a rumble or two; some would have preferred a more active policy against the Brazilians. But Ramsey, putting Lee back into the team alongside Hurst, was unshakeably committed to 4-4-2, and it was only to be hoped that the full-backs' overlap would compensate for the lack of wingers, that Martin Peters would at last rediscover his 1966 form in midfield and around the goal area, and that Bobby Charlton would do something special in his record-making 106th appearance.

Bonetti, Banks' replacement, was no tyro. A vastly agile, slim, spectacular keeper, he had made his debut just before the 1966 World Cup, and in his sporadic games for England had always shown a fine response to the occasion. But he had never played in so important a match before, and he had not taken part in a competitive game for a month.

Yet for an hour England played quite splendidly, showing strength, pace and invention, together with a finishing power quite absent in their previous games. The two goals came, but they were not enough.

The first was scored after half an hour; a goal transcendently Mullery's from start to finish, in conception and execution. First giving and taking passes with Lee, he hit a splendid crossfield ball out to Newton on the right. As the full-back made ground, Mullery raced diagonally towards the far post, getting there, meteoric and unexpected, exactly with Newton's centre, which he drove past Maier.

Five minutes after the interval Geoff Hurst, tirelessly unselfish, set Newton off again. Once more the run finished with an excellent cross, and this time it was Martin Peters, in his best 1966 manner, who popped up, to score.

It was just after this that Schoen took off Libuda and put on Grabowski; and the game changed. In a nutshell, Grabowski was fresh and full of running, Cooper exhausted by the killing heat and unaccustomed altitude. From being one of England's most effective players, he now degenerated into one of their most vulnerable; and was not substituted. It was the second German substitution, for Willi

Schulz had come on instead of Hottges at half-time to take over the marking of Hurst, who had been rather too much for Fichtel.

Grabowski's pace and enterprise gave the Germans new heart, and it is significant, given the subsequent theory that all went awry when Charlton departed, thus allowing Beckenbauer to come forward, that Beckenbauer scored his vital goal *before* Charlton was replaced. It came when he advanced, picked up a rebound, and sent a low, right-footed, unexceptional shot towards the left-hand corner. Bonetti went down too late, the ball ran under his dive, and the score was 2–1.

Now Bell came on for Charlton, who had been showing certain signs of wear; though hardly as obviously as Cooper. On, too, subsequently and quite inexplicably, came the hard-tackling, quintessentially destructive Norman Hunter of Leeds in place of Peters. Thus, almost at a stroke, the English midfield had been radically altered. Moreover, the obvious inference that Hunter had been brought on to stiffen the defence was proved wrong when he began to run wild and free; even, at one moment, taking a corner.

England were far from recumbent. Ball unleashed Bell, to whose low, near-post centre Hurst—who had had far too few of them—stooped in his most effective manner. The ball flew across the goal, beating Maier, but passed just outside the far post.

So Germany, with an extraordinary headed goal by Uwe Seeler, were able to equalise. A weary Labone cleared out of the goalmouth straight to Schnellinger, who lobbed back again. The English defence had not moved up quickly enough to put Seeler offside, and the stocky little forward, leaping mightily with his back to goal, managed to send the ball in a remarkable, tantalising parabola over the head of Bonetti, who was off his line and in limbo.

Thus there was extra time, and the initiative was now palpably Germany's. England's last chance went when Lee wriggled past Schnellinger on the right-hand goal-line, delivered one of the few perfect, pulled-back crosses which England produced in the series, and Hurst drove it in. The goal was disallowed for no evident reason; neither English player could have been offside, and Lee had certainly not fouled Schnellinger. So Muller, with a thundering volley, knocked the last nail into England's coffin. Inevitably, the goal derived from Grabowski's mastery of Cooper. Beating him again, he crossed, Loehr headed the ball back from the left, and once more Bonetti was out of the picture.

It was a splendid recovery by West Germany, a harsh blow to England, whose exhausted players sprawled in the sunshine on the lawn of their hotel like the casualties of a war. The burden placed on their overlapping full-backs in such cruel conditions had finally worn them out; and yet it had been such a close thing.

The Semi-Finals   Brazil v. Uruguay

The semi-finals pitted those old foes, Uruguay and Brazil, against each other at Guadalajara, and Italy against West Germany in Mexico City. The Uruguayans were highly displeased to be playing on what was by now Brazil's home from home ground. They maintained, not without some logic, that the game should take place in Mexico City, arrived late in Guadalajara, and snubbed the Governor's reception.

Nonetheless, with poor Felix's complicity they took the lead. Little, dark Cubilla advanced with the ball along the right-hand goalline, to be confronted by Piazza. He shot from the 'impossible' angle and the ball, against all probability, bounced past Felix into the goal.

Uruguay held their lead till late in the first half, when Clodoaldo ran in on the blind side to score a fine equaliser. The sturdy, twenty-year-old right-half was now expressing the full range of his exceptional talent; a self-expression which would bear strange—and bitter—fruit in the Final.

Pelé, Clodoaldo's idol and mentor at Santos, was again in glorious form and, as in the opening match, came close to scoring a spectacular goal. Having observed Mazurkiewiecz's habit of kicking the ball out, short, to his defenders, he once whirled to intercept one of these clearances, volleyed superbly, and brought from the goalkeeper an equally superb save.

The first half was marred by a great deal of violent play by the Uruguayans; Zagalo, indeed, had feared the consequences of Uruguay scoring first, then tried to shut up shop. Though Jairzinho had too much speed and power for Mujica, Ancheta and the veteran Matosas covered well, the Uruguayan defence survived the free-kicks they ruthlessly and recklessly gave away, and it was only in injury time that Clodoaldo raced on to Tostao's fine pass to make it 1–1.

Brazil, in the second half, took hold of the game, and Uruguay's resistance became still more cynical and physical. Repeating their quarter-final ploy, they substituted Maneiro with Esparrago. This time, however, the quick sequel was a goal to Brazil. Tostao, that inspired artificer, was again behind it, serving Jairzinho under full, imposing sail. Mujica had neither the pace nor the force to hold the winger, who raced in to drive the ball past Mazurkiewiecz. Uruguay, to their credit, retaliated, and Felix now came into his own when he saved from Cubilla. Then Pelé cunningly drew the defence before rolling the ball aside to let Rivelino do proper and spectacular execution. By way of a last, bravura flourish, Pelé, fiendishly inventive, confronted Mazurkiewiecz on a through ball, ran to one side, *away* from the ball, drawing the keeper after him, then shot fractionally wide of the unguarded goal.

Italy v. West Germany

In Mexico City, meanwhile, a thrilling, fluctuating but scarcely classic match was taking place between Italy and West Germany. This time, Germany's fortune would rebound on them; and so would Schoen's penchant for substitution.

Playing for the first time in the Azteca, and doubtless weary after their quarter-final, Germany were slow into their stride; it was Italy, through the persistent Boninsegna, who scored the only goal of the first half. Boring his way through in the eighth minute, he twice had lucky rebounds from the German defence, and finally drove the ball past Maier, left-footed, from the edge of the box.

At half-time, Italy duly took off Mazzola to bring on Rivera, but the switch was less relevant than the fact that they fell back cautiously and characteristically to defend their lead. This allowed the Germans, who had generally been making little progress, to occupy the midfield and surge forward. It is always unwise to allow space to such players as Beckenbauer and Overath, and the initiative passed to Germany; indeed, their supremacy steadily turned into a bombardment. Seeler, when the sweeper Cera allowed a ball to run past him, Grabowski, who for once played a full match, and Overath all missed very good chances. Libuda succeeded Loehr early in the second half, and twenty minutes later Schoen gambled doubly by using up his second substitute and making it Held, an attacker, for the full-back, Patzke.

It seemed, at first, another inspired alteration, for the blond Held, a star of the 1966 Final, produced just the running and finishing on the left that Germany needed. He had a tremendous drive kicked off the line, Seeler's fine header provoked a splendid save from Albertosi, and the match was in its third, breathless minute of injury time when Germany at last equalised. Grabowski crossed from the left, and the blond sweeper, Karl-Heinz Schnellinger, materialised in the goalmouth, to bang the ball home.

Now came extra time. Italy now brought on Poletti for Rosato, but the most significant sight was that of Franz Beckenbauer with his arm strapped to his side. He had been brutally chopped down, not for the first time in the game, while in full, spectacular flight towards the Italian goal, accelerating with that sudden, irresistible power and grace which are so much his own. Technically, it was not a penalty, for the foul took place, by cunning intent, a few yards outside the box. Morally, it was a hundred times a penalty. As it was, Germany did nothing with the free kick, and crime emphatically paid, for the game was won and lost in that moment. Italian critics would later blame Schoen for his tactics and substitutions, but the turning point was unquestionably the foul on Beckenbauer.

Extra time began well enough for Germany. Only five minutes had gone when Poletti clumsily and anxiously ran the ball away from Albertosi and almost over his own goal-line, for Muller to do, inevitably and typically, the rest.

Now the goals came thick and fast; as though it were indeed basketball. Tarcisio Burgnich, switched to centre-half, took a leaf out of Schnellinger's book by appearing in the goalmouth to score after Rivera's free kick on the left. Then Riva sharply pivoted to beat Schnellinger and drive home a low, left-footed cross shot from outside the box. So the first period ended with Italy again in the lead against a Germany now without a sweeper, and with Beckenbauer crippled.

Germany, and especially Seeler, were nevertheless far from done for. Once more, and at the same end, Seeler had a header saved by Albertosi. This time, however, when the corner came over, he met it on the far, left-hand post, nodded it across goal, and Muller flung himself to head the equaliser; his tenth goal of a tournament in which he would finish the leading scorer.

Six minutes of the second extra period had gone when Boninsegna got away on the left, went to the line, pulled the ball accurately back and little Rivera thumped it past Maier for the winner.

The Final   Brazil v. Italy

So Brazil would play Italy in the Final; a meeting of two countries each of which had won the World Cup twice, even if the *azzurri*'s last victory lay thirty-two years in the past. Meanwhile there was the empty ceremony of the third-place match, in which West Germany were lucky to beat Uruguay 1–0. Wolfgang Overath, with his phenomenal left foot, was the star of an otherwise indifferent afternoon, and it was appropriate that he, and it, should score the only goal.

Brazil were so strongly favoured to win the Final that it was almost a burden for them. True—despite the indications of that strange semi-final—Italy had a strong, *catenaccio* defence. True, Burgnich and Facchetti, the Inter full-backs, were veterans of innumerable hard international matches for both club and country, even if the giant Facchetti was hardly the overlapping force he had been, and might find himself in trouble against Jairzinho. (Indeed he did; but not, as we shall see, quite as was expected.)

What was perfectly plain was that the Italians could hope to win only by playing as the Dr Jekyll of the quarter- and semi-finals, rather than as the destructive Mr Hyde of the eliminators. There was talent enough in midfield and up front. Riva had recovered his goal-scoring flair, Boninsegna was in splendidly incisive form, and how many teams in the world could afford the luxury of choosing between two such marvellous inside-forwards as Mazzola and Rivera?

The Brazilian defence was there to be attacked; even if Peru, the only team which had so far done so, had too porous a defence of their own to succeed. Felix's deficiencies were manifest. Carlos Alberto, the captain and right-back, was a great force when he was coming forward, but very much less impressive when he was against a winger who would take him on. Brito and Piazza could well be troubled by the thrust of Boninsegna and Riva, backed up by the sinuous dribbling of Mazzola or the winged passes of Rivera. As against that, Italy could scarcely expect to have again the advantage of such inept and permissive refereeing as one had seen from Señor Yamasaki, of Mexico and once of Peru, in the semi-final.

No one put the realities of the situation more succinctly than Francis Lee, who observed in Guadalajara: 'Against the Brazilians, you've got to push up and play. If you let them come at you, you're asking for trouble.'

Italy did let the Brazilians come at them, and trouble was inevitably what they got. For the game at large, however, the World Cup Final was a marvellous affirmation of what could still be done with attacking football, a splendid reassurance that cynicism, caution and negativity had not, after all, gained a stranglehold on football. The Brazilians won by playing beautifully, imaginatively and adventurously.

Pelé, who had sworn, after 1966, that he would never play in a future World Cup, and had changed his mind, would soon announce his retirement from all international football; but in this final he excelled himself. One might also call this match his apotheosis, such was his skill, audacity and sheer effectiveness. He scored a magnificent goal, he created two, evoking and fulfilling, in his second World Cup Final, all the immense promise of his first, twelve years before.

Italy's tactics were not only drearily negative but also strangely ineffectual; even in defence. They quickly switched Burgnich to centre-back, but never began to get to grips with Gerson, or with Carlos Alberto. Gerson, bewilderingly, was allowed infinite space and time in midfield, which he used with grateful and devastating mastery. Jairzinho, drawing Facchetti cunningly into the middle—Italy's man-to-man marking was inflexible—thus gave Carlos Alberto equal scope and leisure to advance down the empty right wing, for Italy were not playing with a left-winger.

After eighteen minutes Brazil took the lead. Rivelino crossed a long, high, unexceptional centre from the left; Pelé, being an exceptional player, got up above the Italian defence with a spectacular jump, and headed in as powerfully as he had done in Stockholm.

Though Mazzola was running and dribbling superbly, the very soul of Italy's resistance, and Boninsegna was responding vigorously to his clever passes, Italy's tactics made it seem most unlikely they could save the game. They needed a gift; and suddenly, seven minutes from half-time, they got it. Clodoaldo, intoxicated, perhaps, by his newfound freedom of expression, stupidly back-heeled the ball deep in his own half, at once putting Boninsegna clear through and the rest of his defence on the wrong foot. As Boninsegna swept in from the right of the goal, Felix dashed out, in futile desperation, was passed in his turn, and Boninsegna put the ball into the unguarded net.

That was the moment at which Italy might well, had they only had the character and courage, have turned the game. Pelé, visiting Rome a couple of years later, expressed his astonishment and relief that they had not pressed home their psychological advantage against a Brazilian team momentarily demoralised. But they did not. In the second half Brazil, despite Mazzola's continued excellence, steadily regained the advantage, until, after sixty-six minutes, Gerson, the artificer turned bombardier, pivoted to hit a tremendous low, left-footed cross shot from outside the penalty box, to make it 2–1.

That was the end of Italy. Five minutes later, Gerson took a free kick, Pelé touched it skillfully to Jairzinho, and he, pelting into the goalmouth, ran the ball in on the left-hand post. Italy brought on Juliano for Bertini; then, six absurd minutes from the end, Rivera for . . . Boninsegna, surely the most mindless substitution of the tournament.

With so little time left, it was clearly all but impossible to save the game. Equally clearly, Valcareggi had been caught in a cleft stick over the Rivera-Mazzola duality. On this occasion it was quite unthinkable to take off Mazzola at the interval, so splendidly was he playing; at the same time, the non-appearance of Rivera would certainly inspire more sound and fury. Valcareggi's 'solution' was to put Rivera on in place of Boninsegna, the one Italian forward who, given the ineffectuality of Riva, seemed capable of scoring goals. So Brazil, three minutes from time, scored a fourth goal, in the way they had so often threatened. Jairzinho found Pelé, who laid the ball off immaculately to his right for Carlos Alberto to thunder on to it, and drive it past Albertosi.

The Brazilian jubilation afterwards was as spectacular and memorable as anything one had seen on the field: a joyful, dancing invasion of fans milling around their victorious players, pulling off their bright yellow shirts and hoisting them, bare to the waist, on to their shoulders. In this exuberance, this unconfined delight, one seemed to see a reflection of the way Brazil had played; and played was, indeed, the word. For all their dedication, all their passion, they and their country had somehow managed to remain aware that football was, after all, a game; something to be enjoyed.

So the Jules Rimet Trophy, won by them for the third time, went permanently to Brazil, who had shown that enterprise, fantasy, attacking play were still compatible with success; provided you had the talent. There could be no comparison with England's brave but ultimately sterile victory of 1966, a victory which had led only to myths of 'athletic football', 'work rate', the elevation of the labourer above the artist. It would take a couple of years for the new lesson to sink home in Europe, but sink it finally would.

Overall, despite the abominable conditions, the 1970 World Cup had been a marvellous triumph of the positive over the negative, the creative over the destructive. The Final itself took on the dimensions almost of an allegory.

RESULTS: Mexico 1970

Group I

Mexico 0, Russia 0 (HT 0/0)
Belgium 3, El Salvador 0 (HT 1/0)
Russia 4, Belgium 1 (HT 1/0)
Mexico 4, El Salvador 0 (HT 1/0)
Russia 2, El Salvador 0 (HT 0/0)
Mexico 1, Belgium 0 (HT 1/0)

| | | | GOALS | | | |
	P	W	D	L	F	A	Pts
Russia	3	2	1	0	6	1	5
Mexico	3	2	1	0	5	0	5
Belgium	3	1	0	2	4	5	2
El Salvador	3	0	0	3	0	9	0

Group II

Uruguay 2, Israel 0 (HT 1/0)
Italy 1, Sweden 0 (HT 1/0)
Uruguay 0, Italy 0 (HT 0/0)
Sweden 1, Israel 1 (HT 0/0)
Sweden 1, Uruguay 0 (HT 0/0)
Italy 0, Israel 0 (HT 0/0)

| | | | GOALS | | | |
	P	W	D	L	F	A	Pts
Italy	3	1	2	0	1	0	4
Uruguay	3	1	1	1	2	1	3
Sweden	3	1	1	1	2	2	3
Israel	3	0	2	1	1	3	2

Group III

England 1, Romania 0 (HT 0/0)
Brazil 4, Czechoslovakia 1 (HT 1/1)
Romania 2, Czechoslovakia 1 (HT 0/1)
Brazil 1, England 0 (HT 0/0)
Brazil 3, Romania 2 (HT 2/1)
England 1, Czechoslovakia 0 (HT 0/0)

| | | | GOALS | | | |
	P	W	D	L	F	A	Pts
Brazil	3	3	0	0	8	3	6
England	3	2	0	1	2	1	4
Romania	3	1	0	2	4	5	2
Czechoslovakia	3	0	0	3	2	7	0

Group IV

Peru 3, Bulgaria 2 (HT 0/1)
West Germany 2, Morocco 1 (HT 0/1)
Peru 3, Morocco 0 (HT 0/0)
West Germany 5, Bulgaria 2 (HT 2/1)
West Germany 3, Peru 1 (HT 3/1)
Morocco 1, Bulgaria 1 (HT 1/0)

| | | | GOALS | | | |
	P	W	D	L	F	A	Pts
West Germany	3	3	0	0	10	4	6
Peru	3	2	0	1	7	5	4
Bulgaria	3	0	1	2	5	9	1
Morocco	3	0	1	2	2	6	1

Quarter-finals

Leon

West Germany 3	**England 2**
(after extra time)	
Maier; Schnellinger,	Bonetti; Newton;
Vogts, Hottges (Schulz);	Cooper; Mullery,
Beckenbauer, Overath,	Labone, Moore; Lee,
Seeler; Libuda	Ball, Hurst, Charlton
(Grabowski), Muller,	(Bell), Peters (Hunter).
Loehr.	

SCORERS
Beckenbauer, Seeler, Muller for West Germany
Mullery, Peters for England
HT 0/1

Guadalajara

Brazil 4	**Peru 2**
Felix; Carlos Alberto,	Rubiños; Campos,
Brito, Piazza, Marco	Fernandez,
Antonio; Clodoaldo,	Chumpitaz, Fuentes;
Gerson (Paulo Cesar);	Mifflin, Challe; Baylon
Jairzinho (Roberto),	(Sotil), Perico Leon
Tostao, Pelé, Rivelino.	(Eladio Reyes),
	Cubillas, Gallardo.

SCORERS
Rivelino, Tostao (2), Jairzinho for Brazil
Gallardo, Cubillas for Peru
HT 2/1

Toluca

Italy 4 | **Mexico 1**

Albertosi; Burgnich, Cera, Rosato, Facchetti; Bertini, Mazzola (Rivera), De Sisti; Domenghini (Gori), Boninsegna, Riva.

Calderon; Vantolra, Pena, Guzman, Perez; Gonzalez (Borja), Pulido, Munguia (Diaz); Valdivia, Fragoso, Padilla.

SCORERS
Domenghini, Riva (2), Rivera for Italy
Gonzalez for Mexico
HT 1/1

Mexico City

Uruguay 1 | **Russia 0**
(after extra time)

Mazurkiewicz; Ubinas, Ancheta, Matosas, Mujica; Maneiro, Cortes, Montero Castillo; Cubilla, Fontes (Gomez), Morales (Esparrago).

Kavazashvili; Dzodzuashvili, Afonin, Khurtsilava (Logofet), Chesternijev; Muntijan, Asatiani (Kiselev), Kaplichni; Evriuzhkinzin, Bychevetz, Khmelnitzki.

SCORER
Esparrago for Uruguay
HT 0/0

Semi-finals

Mexico City

Italy 4 | **West Germany 3**
(after extra time)

Albertosi; Cera, Burgnich, Rosato (Poletti), Facchetti; Domenghini, Mazzola (Rivera), De Sisti; Boninsegna, Riva.

Maier; Schnellinger; Vogts, Schulz, Beckenbauer, Patzke (Held); Seeler, Overath; Grabowski, Muller, Loehr (Libuda).

SCORERS
Boninsegna, Burgnich, Riva, Rivera for Italy
Schnellinger, Muller (2) for West Germany
HT 1/0

Guadalajara

Brazil 3 | **Uruguay 1**

Felix; Carlos Alberto, Brito, Piazza, Everaldo; Clodoaldo, Gerson; Jairzinho, Tostao, Pelé, Rivelino.

Mazurkiewicz; Ubinas, Ancheta, Matosas, Mujica; Montero Castillo, Cortes, Fontes; Cubilla, Maneiro (Esparrago), Morales.

SCORERS
Clodoaldo, Jairzinho, Rivelino for Brazil
Cubilla for Uruguay
HT 1/1

Third place match

Mexico City

West Germany 1 | **Uruguay 0**

Wolter; Schnellinger (Lorenz); Patzke, Fichtel, Weber, Vogts; Seeler, Overath; Libuda (Loehr), Muller, Held.

Mazurkiewicz; Ubinas, Ancheta, Matosas, Mujica; Montero Castillo, Cortes, Fontes (Sandoval); Cubilla, Maneiro (Esparrago), Morales.

SCORER
Overath for West Germany
HT 1/0

Final

Mexico City

Brazil 4 | **Italy 1**

Felix; Carlos Alberto, Brito, Piazza, Everaldo; Clodoaldo, Gerson; Jairzinho, Tostao, Pelé, Rivelino.

Albertosi; Cera; Burgnich, Bertini (Juliano), Rosato, Facchetti; Domenghini, Mazzola, De Sisti; Boninsegna (Rivera), Riva.

SCORERS
Pelé, Gerson, Jairzinho, Carlos Alberto for Brazil
Boninsegna for Italy
HT 1/1

WEST GERMANY
1974

Introduction to West Germany

After twenty years, West Germany regained the World Cup and history further repeated itself in that they lost a game dramatically on the way. Dazzling in 1972, when they won the European Nations Cup with glorious panache, the West Germany of 1974 had passed their peak with the loss of Gunter Netzer. A sparkling star in Brussels, blond hair flying as he made his thrilling runs, huge boots distributing great, sweeping passes, curling diabolic free kicks, he had since gone to Madrid and lost his form.

Poland were the surprise. Having first—surprisingly—eliminated England, despite the loss of the brilliant Lubanski from their attack they grew in stature in the intervening months, and in the tournament itself. By the end of it, Lato, Deyna and Gadocha were recognised as three of the finest players in the world, and many thought that had their match against West Germany in Frankfurt been played in decent conditions, they would have reached the Final. As it was, they took a richly merited third place. These three teams showed, triumphantly, that attacking football still lived, still worked, could still prevail.

The Contenders

Ironically, it was the Brazilians, always in the past the banner bearers of adventurous football, who now lived precariously on their defence, to take a fourth place which flattered them. Predictably, Zagalo was bitterly blamed, just as he'd been eulogised in 1970, yet to an outsider it seemed once more essentially a question of personnel.

For a start, there was no Pelé; or rather, there was Pelé, but a Pelé who criticised, shook people's hands, and advanced the cause of Pepsi Cola, adamantly loyal to his decision not to play in another World Cup. All might have been well had not the loss of Pelé been compounded by that of three other splendid players. Tostao, whose recovery from a damaged retina to play in the 1970 World Cup had been a small miracle, was hurt again, and this time no miracle supervened. Gerson, of the sublime left foot, the forty-yard passes, the tremendous shots, was injured too and was to be found only on the periphery of the competition, smoking of course, wryly critical. As if this was not enough, on the very eve of the competition, the dynamic young Clodoaldo, who had grown and grown throughout the 1970 tournament, broke down on the preliminary tour of Switzerland and had to be withdrawn. João Saldanha, fearsome critic of Zagalo, blamed him for this, as well, saying that *he*, when manager, had been aware of Clodoaldo's fragility, and had behaved accordingly. Such criticism seemed unfair, but Saldanha and the rest were on firmer ground when they blamed Zagalo—who after all was ultimately responsible—for the Brazilians' harsh defensive methods, methods which reached their peak, or their nadir, in the match in Dortmund against Holland.

It was the first World Cup England had entered and failed to reach the Finals. In retrospect, to be eliminated by so fine a side as Poland seems no disgrace, but this is *a posteriori* reasoning. I doubt if England could have made so dazzling a contribution as Poland to the tournament, yet it should be remembered that the Poland which beat England and the Poland which took their place were two very different propositions.

Had Poland not eliminated England, it seems doubtful that they would have taken wing. That they did so at all after losing Lubanski in the first match against England, in Katowice, was extraordinary for Lubanski had been recognised till then as their one player of undoubted world class. Yet with a more adventurous, flexible manager than Sir Alf Ramsey, eventually and somewhat clumsily dismissed the following April, England might have prevailed. He had badly misread the first Polish game. After promising to field an attacking team, he inexplicably left out his best front-running forward, Southampton's graceful Mike Channon, played a 4–4–2 formation which gave the initiative to Poland, and would not bring Channon on even when the Poles scored their second goal.

The following September, the Poles had their revenge on Wales in a bloodthirsty match in which old Cardiff scores were paid off, and things might have been a little different had the Welsh not had a perfectly valid-looking goal by Wyn Davies disallowed.

So England, who had lamentably failed to beat Wales at Wembley, had to beat Poland to survive. A misleading 7–0 win against an uncommitted Austrian team raised false hopes. In the event, England pressed for most of the evening but hadn't the wit to make many clear chances. The game was drawn 1–1, England were out; and so, after his one splendid success and eight years of anticlimax, was Ramsey.

Total Football

This World Cup was the World Cup of Total Football; both finalists were famous for it. For a couple of years, the more sophisticated European critics had been saying that Total Football was the new reality, as persuasive and historically irresistible a phenomenon as, in turn, the W formation, 4-2-4 and 4-3-3.

The term itself was confusing and imprecise. What it meant, and means, was the kind of football played by the West German team which won the Nations Cup, and the Ajax team which had won the European Cup three times in a row, and would assuredly have made it four or five times had not Cruyff, the outstanding Dutch player, insisted on a transfer to Barcelona in the autumn of 1973. If one was briefly to describe it, one might call it *Dynamic Catenaccio*.

Catenaccio itself had been borrowed by the Italians from the Swiss and turned into something deeply negative, however effective. On the brink of the World Cup, the Italians themselves were among the favourites. Their *catenaccio* defence with its resolutely negative sweeper and with Dino Zoff an astonishing goalkeeper, unbeaten for almost 1,100 minutes, had given them a long, impressive and unbeaten run; and there was Riva to snap up goals, Rivera and Mazzola to construct them.

But the new football made the *libero*, or sweeper, no longer a defensive figure; he was a man who used his deep role as a kind of springboard or, if you wish, a secluded lair whence he could foray upfield. If any one player invented the new role of the new sweeper, it was unquestionably Franz Beckenbauer, who had persuaded first his club, Bayern Munich, then Helmut Schoen, manager of West Germany, to let him implement it. How wonderfully it had worked in the 1972 Nations Cup. Giacinto Facchetti of Inter had inspired Beckenbauer with his attacking full-back play. If a full-back could do it, thought Beckenbauer, then why not a central defender? So the attacking sweeper was born!

The implicit theory of Total Football was that anyone could do anything: forwards become defenders, defenders become forwards. In fact—ideally—there is no such thing as either; there are merely footballers, totally versatile, totally interchangeable. Ajax, under the Romanian coach, Stefan Kovacs, and West Germany had approached this aim, though an aim it remained. Holland's chances of encompassing it had plainly been limited by the loss of two key Ajax men—the powerful centre-half, Barry Hulshoff, always ready for a run upfield, and the vigorous left-side midfield player, Gerry Muhren. In the latter's place would play a footballer who, for all his talents, seemed the very embodiment of the older school; Wim Van Hanegem of Feyenoord, powerful and tall, a lovely striker of the ball with his left foot whether at goal or in passing, hard in the tackle, a fine creative forward, but unhurried, sometimes to the point of appearing static. In the event, he would emerge as one of the outstanding players of the World Cup.

The Groups Holland

Holland had qualified with extreme difficulty, held both at home and away by their traditional rivals, Belgium, to a goalless draw. Their players seemed mercenary and unintegrated; Ajax men just did not get on with Feyenoord men. Despite the excellence of both these clubs, each a European Cup winner, Holland had failed to reach the Nations Cup finals, and had not qualified for the World Cup Finals since 1938. In addition, their players seemed thoroughly mercenary, for ever agitating for more money, until at one point the forceful Rinus Michels, now manager of Barcelona, had apparently said that those not satisfied with the terms could stay behind.

Nevertheless, the Dutch players had obtained the promise of a king's ransom, and even then had threatened up to the last moments to strike. For all that, their performance had improved immensely and a fine 4–1 win over Argentina in May caused many, myself among them, to favour them. In terms of talent—Cruyff, Van Hanegem, the irrepressible Johan Neeskens, the dashing full-backs Suurbier and Krol—there was none to surpass them. Only in goal did there seem a lacuna, and this surprisingly, would be made good.

When the 34-year-old veteran Jan Jongbloed was called to the colours, he assumed he would be going to Germany merely as a reserve. But with the costly Van Beveren injured and Schrijvers, the second choice, in turn getting hurt, Jongbloed got his chance. Once again, Rinus Michels was proved wonderfully shrewd, for Jongbloed was just the goalkeeper Holland needed.

The lack of Hulshoff turned their defence into an alarmingly flimsy affair, with Aarie Haan, another highly gifted midfield player, pulled into defence as a putative sweeper, though if anything more of a centre-back, ever eager to go forward. In these circumstances, Holland brought Rijsbergen, the blond young Feyenoord stopper, into the back four, relied heavily and dangerously on offside, and were lucky to have in Jongbloed an adventurous keeper in the traditions of Grosics, ever ready to dash out of his area and save the day when the offside trap broke down.

Scotland

If England were not present, Scotland were, for the first time since 1954. They had qualified thanks to an inspired evening at Hampden against Czechoslovakia the previous September, when their little manager Willie Ormond, himself once Scotland's left-winger, had brought Coventry's clever Tommy Hutchinson into the team for his first cap at outside-left and the long legged Hutchinson had taken wing. Goals headed by the big, controversially rugged, Manchester United centre-half Jim Holton, and the young Leeds centre-forward Joe Jordan, had wiped out a soft, potentially demoralising goal by Nehoda, to give Scotland victory and put them through. The Czechs paid very dearly for having lost a point to Denmark.

Billy Bremner, the galvanic little Leeds right-half and captain, a player whose temperament did not belie his red hair, had played superbly that night but he was now thirty-two, had an infinite number of hard matches under his belt and had been very much in the wars on Scotland's ill-fated tour before the competition. Deputed to conduct the team's commercial negotiations, a job he never did for Leeds, he had been involved in a series of squabbles and was concerned with Celtic's wayward celebrated winger Jimmy Johnstone, who had drifted out to sea in a boat at Largs after the win against Czechoslovakia, in an incident in Oslo.

Both turned up late in the bar of the Panorama Hotel—not so much a hotel as a mere students' complex—and were eventually ordered to their rooms by Ormond. It was not the first nor the worst such incident that season. Some of the Scottish officials wanted to pack both men home, but Ormond pleaded successfully for them; and Bremner rewarded him by becoming one of the outstanding figures of the World Cup, winning the praise of Pelé himself.

Scotland had fallen in the same tough group as Brazil and Yugoslavia, skilfully managed by Miljan Miljanic but disappointing in their recent 2–2 draw at home to England. The team that day had tired and Dragan Dzajic, its left-winger and most celebrated star, had still to regain full form after more than a year in the Army. Nevertheless, with inside-forwards such as the sturdy little pair of Karasi and Acimovic, backed by the muscular Oblak and the dashes of the tall Bogicevic from defence, the Yugoslavs looked formidable, and they had an exceptional goalkeeper in Maric.

The Outsiders

The fourth team was Zaire, with Australia and Haiti, the remotest outsiders of the competition. Like Morocco, their predecessors as winners of the African group, they were coached by the tall Yugoslav Vidinic, himself once his country's goalkeeper. They had fine individualists, had done well in Africa, but it was already clear from their performance in the recent African Nations Cup and from a mediocre tour of Europe that little was to be expected from them.

The Haitians, who figured in the Munich group with Italy, Argentina and Poland, were lucky to be there at all. Benefiting enormously as it was from being able to stage the whole of their CONCACAF qualifying competition, they had benefited in a still more particular way in their match with Trinidad when no fewer than four goals were disallowed to the visitors by the subsequently suspended El Salvadorian referee, Enriquez.

Argentina

For Argentina, still more than for West Germany, whom they had impressively beaten the previous season, the World Cup had not come at the right time. On that European tour, Argentina had played some splendid football in their most classical style, and had shocked the Germans by defeating them in Munich itself. But since then Omar Sivori, as volatile a manager as he was a player, had been dismissed. His successor was the much milder, amiable, red-headed Cap, nicknamed *el Polaco* for his Polish origin—less explosive, but also less inspiring.

Talent was not lacking. The thick-thighed, heavily moustached Ayala, hair hanging almost to his waist, had had a fine season with Atletico Madrid, and established himself as one of the most dangerous forwards in Europe, much faster than the traditional Argentinian attacker, possessed of fabulous control at speed and great incisiveness. But Miguel Brindisi, the midfield inside-right and supposed star of the team, whom Peron had given a medal for staying at home despite the blandishments of foreign clubs, had been a disappointment.

Fortunately there was time to call up Carlos Babington, Brindisi's fairhaired partner in the Huracan midfield. Surprisingly omitted from the original party, Babington—who had nearly joined Stoke on the basis of his English ancestry—was so pleased that he slept in his international shirt. He was to play stupendously against the Italians.

For the first time, the competition had adopted a new debatable formula, abolishing the system of quarter- and semi-finals. Now, the first- and second-placed teams in the four original qualifying groups would enter two final pools of four teams each, whose winners would contest the Final, while the second in each group would play what again transpired to be the dull and quite meaningless Third Place Match.

In the event, the plan worked better than one might have expected. This time it would not lead to any increase of defensive football in the second stage.

Opening Stages

The chief criticism of the way the World Cup was organised lay rather in its preliminary phases. Failure to de-zone the qualifying competition allowed teams from the weaker areas a relatively easy passage, and the decision to make one South American and one European group winner play-off for a place in the finals was bitterly unfair to both. Eventually, it was Russia and Chile who were obliged to meet, and they met only once, drawing 0–0 in Moscow.

At this, the Russians suddenly developed an attack of principle, refusing on political grounds to play the return in the national stadium at Santiago, where left-wing prisoners had been shot. Their protest would have looked better had it been made before the initial match. FIFA sent a committee of inquiry to Chile and would have been prepared to have the match elsewhere in Chile, but the Russians refused and there was no alternative but to rule them out.

The tournament began with its customary anticlimax: a goalless draw in Frankfurt between Brazil and Yugoslavia. But at least there were no violent incidents. Nor would there be throughout the tournament. Forewarned by the brutal terrorist murders of the Israeli athletes at the Olympic Games, West German security this time was of a military thoroughness with tanks on the tarmac of the airports, endless searches of the passengers and armed police around and within the stadia.

Yugoslavia had the better of the argument in Frankfurt. Free kicks by the inevitable Rivelino and a newcomer, the blond, attacking left-back Francisco Marinho, proper successor to Nilton Santos, were Brazil's chief threat. Acimovic, when Oblak pulled the ball back from the goal line, and Katalinski, with a muscular header, very nearly scored for the Slavs. What was sharply apparent was Brazil's lack of a centre-forward, a Tostao, a Vavà. Jairzinho, forced to play there, would clearly have been happier on the wing.

And so we were off, with the competition starting in earnest the next day. In Berlin, where the Chilean left-wingers demonstrated on the terraces, West Germany made terribly hard work of beating Chile. A tremendous long shot by Paul Breitner, their long-legged, woolly-haired full-back, that paradox, a rich Bavarian Maoist, won them the day against a clever, compact team. Figueroa and Quintano were like rocks in the middle, Caszely—most disputably sent off—and Reinoso fiery in attack. The German defence, especially Schwarzenbeck, looked oddly vulnerable at times. It was an unimpressive start and Wolfgang Overath, recalled to play in his third World Cup, hardly looked a fit substitute for Netzer.

In Hamburg the East Germans were scarcely more impressive, finding Australia a tough nut to crack. Australia's team, made up almost entirely of immigrants, well coached by the Yugoslav Rale Rasic, would prove far the best of the three outsiders.

Not that the Haitians began badly; they surpassed themselves against Italy in Munich, where Sanon, their centre-forward, soon after half-time, made monkeys of the Italian defenders and became the first man to beat Zoff in the Italy goal for 1,147 minutes of international football. Painfully the Italians pulled themselves together to win the match 3–1, but the happy Haitians were the heroes of the day and next morning in the sunshine they strolled about the Munich zoo beaming their satisfaction, none more than their fine goalkeeper, Francillon. Alas, there were clouds on the horizon.

Scarcely had the Haitians ceased rejoicing than a thunderbolt struck them. A dope test on Ernst Jean-Joseph, their red-haired, mulatto centre-half had proved positive. Jean-Joseph protested that he had to take pills for his asthma. The team's French doctor, with ruthless impartiality, told a Press conference that this was nonsense—that Jean-Joseph was not intelligent enough to know what he was doing.

For a day or two the melancholy Jean-Joseph was to be found hanging wretchedly around the lobby of the Penta Hotel. Then Haitian officials dragged him, tearful, out of the Grunwald Sports School where the team was staying, beat him, shoved him into a car and kept him incommunicado in a room at the Sheraton Hotel, flying him back to Haiti the next morning.

The terrified Jean-Joseph made several telephone calls to a sympathetic Polish Press hostess. The plump and humane Herr Kurt Renner, attaché to the Haitian team, was unable to sleep all night and told the whole grim story to the Press. Significantly, the World Cup Organising Committee was incensed not with the Haitians but with these two, removing Herr Renner from his post, threatening to dismiss the hostess. Small wonder that Haiti should in the meantime be thrashed by Poland, then comfortably beaten by Argentina.

Argentina needed those points and the four goals they scored to qualify. They, too, had had a troubled time in camp: a player accused of assaulting a chambermaid, journalists sharply critical of the officials. They had lost their opening match, in Stuttgart, to Poland, partly thanks to a couple of sad errors by the otherwise good goalkeeper, Carnevali, and to a bizarre defensive formation. Perfumo played as sweeper behind a line of three backs, risky enough in itself and positively suicidal given the vulnerability of Perfumo, who needed Bargas playing bang in front of him, rather than in an indeterminate role in midfield.

Had the tall, nineteen-year-old centre-forward, Kempes, scored when admirably sent through by Brindisi in the opening minutes, all might have been different. But he missed, Poland scored twice in the seventh minute, and the die was cast. First Gadocha, Poland's devastatingly fast and incisive left-winger, took a corner. Carnevali dropped it, Lato put it in. Then Lato utterly split Argentina's square defence with a through pass and Poland's latest ace in the hole, the 22-year-old Szarmach, ran on to score.

In the second half Argentina took off Brindisi, ill at ease as a striker, and introduced a player who at once transformed them and who was to become one of the toasts of the tournament: René Houseman, a tiny winger, brave, serpentine and fast; socks worn scornfully round his ankles. Heredia scored after fifty-five minutes but when Carnevali's careless throw went straight to Lato, who tore through to score, that was clearly that, though Babington did score, after hitting the post of an open goal.

Next, on the same ground, Argentina and Italy; a match that was a nightmare and a humiliation for the Italians in everything but the score. Quite what possessed Valcareggi, the Italian manager, to assume that Houseman, of all people, was going to play in midfield, and to set his own creative inside-forward, Fabio Capello, to mark him, heaven knows.

At all events Capello, turned by this error into a full-back, was run ragged by Houseman, who scored a lovely goal from a pass by Babington, who bestrode the field, calmly impeccable. Too late Valcareggi understood what was happening, pushed Capello upfield and set the ruthless Benetti to mark Houseman, who ran him ragged as well, unintimidated by his brutal tackling. Alas for Argentina, moral victors on the day, Italy equalised when Perfumo turned Benetti's cross past his own goalkeeper, but it had been inspiriting to see Argentina, in both matches, throw off the over-compensatory chains of defensive football and play as they can and should.

Italy now had to play the Poles and draw with them to survive. Changes were made. Rivera had been played out of the game with contemptuous facility by the cool, experienced Telch. He was dropped, claiming he had been made scapegoat. Mazzola, the best and bravest Italian forward, stayed. Riva, as inept as Rivera, went too. If he had been a disappointment in his first World Cup, he had been a disaster in his second; and who would score goals for Italy if not he?

Poland

Poland won 2–1, again in Stuttgart, but though Italy might have had a penalty, they were in fact overwhelmed. Fine crosses by Kasperczak, a splendid foil to Deyna in midfield, gave spectacular goals first to Szarmach with a header then to Deyna himself with a superb volley. Capello's late goal for Italy was no consolation. The Italians donned their customary sackcloth and ashes, swore to play with dynamic rather than static sweepers, to make their players run harder in training and, as always, did nothing, the wish substituting for the deed.

West Germany

In Group I, the West Germans' wheels still would not go round. They made very heavy weather of beating the brave Australians at Hamburg, where the crowd exchanged insults with Beckenbauer and Australia might have scored twice. Rasic, with justice, said he thought little of the German defence. In West Berlin, the resourceful Chileans, though without Caszely, whose goals had taken them to the Finals, held East Germany to a draw.

So in Hamburg, on June 22, the summit encounter took place: the first meeting ever between the two Germanies. Security was all enveloping; guns to be seen everywhere, a helicopter circling the ground. Had there not been a threat that a SAM rocket would be launched at it?

None was; the only, cataclysmic, surprise came in the shape of the result, and the goal by Jurgen Sparwasser eight minutes from time. Reversing their policy of the first two matches, East Germany abandoned attack for their more accustomed counter-attack, with Bransch a resourceful sweeper, Sparwasser moving from midfield into a twoman attack with the young Hoffmann.

Twice in the first half West Germany might have scored when Gerd Muller, that astonishing opportunist, twisted past Weise, once making a chance for Grabowski, once hitting the post. But Kreische of East Germany missed a sitter. Lauck too had a chance and though West Germany dominated second-half play, it was East Germany who scored. Hamann sent Sparwasser down the right; the dark, powerful Magdeburg forward thrust his way past Vogts, shot past Maier, and the game was won.

In retrospect, there is no doubt that it was a blessing in disguise for West Germany. Defeat meant that they played in an easier group, avoiding Holland, and caused them to remodel their team, bringing the driving Rainer Bonhof of Munchengladbach into midfield.

Meanwhile, poor Helmut Schoen became the butt of a sour and disappointed public. Schoen, one heard, was no manager, an opinion quite happily advanced with another: that Beckenbauer was running the team. Certainly there had been dissidence. The West Germany players, like the Dutch, had made intransigent demands before the tournaments, so much so that their Federation had threatened to pack them off home and play the reserves in their place.

Holland

The Dutch, meanwhile, were enchanting everybody, not only with their play but with the free-and-easy atmosphere of their training camp at Hiltrup, where wives and girl friends were allowed for one sunlit, cheerful day.

In their first match, at Hanover, they easily dispatched the Uruguayans, who were astonishingly poor, having little to offer but ruthlessness. Even this was ineffectual: they failed to kick the tormentingly elusive Cruyff, they had Montero Castillo sent off for punching Rensenbrink in the stomach, though Forlan was a much more serious offender.

Yet the Swedes, who had beaten Austria in a play-off to qualify, surprised the Dutch by holding them 0–0 in their next game. With nothing to lose, Sweden approached the tournament in a spirit at once relaxed, generous and determined. In Sandberg and the tall, slender Ralf Edstroem, they had a fine pair of forwards who had scored thirty-two goals between them for Atvidaberg the season before they left Sweden for pastures new, and in Nordqvist a resilient veteran at centre-half. In goal the blond Ronnie Hellstroem excelled himself, so much so as to regret the unexceptional contract he had signed with the Bundesliga's Kaiserslautern before the tournament.

The draw with Sweden illustrated Holland's lack of a finisher to exploit the amazing virtuosity of Cruyff and the fact that his old colleague and rival of Ajax days, Piet Keizer, was now over the hill as a left-winger. The lively Rensenbrink displaced him in their third match, against Bulgaria, who simply had no answer to the galvanic Cruyff, whirling past them at will, his pace, his passing and his finishing alike irresistible. Neeskens, breaking frequently and furiously into attack, scored twice from penalties.

Early Matches

For Scotland it was a World Cup of anticlimax; unbeaten alone among the sixteen teams, they yet failed to qualify for the second round.

Much of this was their own fault. Bravely though they played against Brazil, resourcefully against Yugoslavia, they were absurdly cautious in their first match against the chopping block, Zaire, against whom they needed an avalanche of goals. They got only two. 'Let's face it,' said their centre-half, Jim Holton, 'we underestimated them. For fifteen minutes I wondered what the hell was going on, where the devil had this lot come from, playing stuff like that.' At last Scotland got hold of the game, Lorimer's mighty right foot shot a spectacular goal from Jordan's header, Jordan headed another from Bremner's free kick. But in the last twenty minutes, Scotland unwisely relaxed, troubled by the heat, a mistake which would cost them qualification.

Bremner himself never stopped in the next game, at Frankfurt, against Brazil. For the first twenty minutes, Brazil played probably their best football of the tournament, football for which Scotland's defence did not seem tactically briefed. But Bremner was able, with his example and his encouragement, to revive the Scots, who finished the better team and three times might have scored in the second half through Bremner and his club mates, Jordan and Lorimer.

This left Scotland on three points, Brazil on two, but since Brazil were bound to beat Zaire, who had crashed 9–0 to Yugoslavia, Scotland knew they had to beat the Slavs. Alas, they hadn't the attack to do so. Indeed, lack of commitment to attack was their undoing. Not enough was risked, while in the midfield, Kenny Dalglish, of Celtic, greatly disappointing, survived when he should have been replaced.

Permissive refereeing by a Turk did not help Scotland in the heat of Frankfurt, and they fell a goal behind when Dzajic, on the right, cleverly spun past his man and centred, for Karasi to head past the resilient David Harvey. Scotland vigorously fought back, a corkscrew run by Hutchinson, who had belatedly substituted for Dalglish, brought the equaliser for Joe Jordan, but it was not enough. Brazil beat Zaire 3–0, the third and deciding goal by Valdomiro rolling under the goalkeeper's body; and the Scots were out, though with considerable credit.

The Surviving Groups

The two surviving groups were composed, respectively, of Holland, Brazil, Argentina and East Germany, and West Germany, Poland, Yugoslavia and Sweden.

It was quickly clear that the East Germans had shot their bolt. In Hanover they lost their opening match against Brazil to a second-half goal by Rivelino, inevitably from a free kick. Jairzinho stood on the end of the East German 'wall' and ducked as Rivelino's shot swerved wickedly in.

Argentina, alas, had to play Holland without Babington, who had mindlessly handled the ball deliberately not once but twice in the Italian game. He thus acquired three cautions and was rendered ineligible. Any chance Argentina might have had of containing the brilliant Dutch was lost. They were simply overrun; a dreadful foul by Perfumo on Neeskens was the measure of his and his team's frustration. Heavy rain in the second half was the saviour of Argentina, who would probably have lost still more heavily than 4–0. The electric Cruyff scored two of the goals himself, and made a headed goal for Johnny Rep.

In their next game—again at Gelsenkirchen—Cruyff found himself diligently marked by Weise, but Rensenbrink made a left-footed goal for Neeskens after nine minutes, scored a second himself, and Holland now faced Brazil, the holders, in the decisive match.

The Brazilians had beaten Argentina 2–1 in an all-South-American match at Hanover, the first time these famous rivals had ever met in the World Cup. Their decisive match, at Dortmund, was a sorry affair, redeemed by Holland's two marvellous winning goals in the second half. The Brazilian defence kicked, chopped and hacked from the first; and it must be said that the Dutch, thus provoked, returned the treatment with interest. Twice Brazil should have scored when the Dutch offside trap broke down, but first Paulo Cesar, then Jairzinho, missed palpable chances.

In the first half, Neeskens was knocked cold by Mario Marinho. In the second, he was scythed down by Luis Pereira, who was sent off by the unimpressive West German referee, Herr Tschenscher. Pereira could have no complaints, yet he had undeniably been one of the best defenders in the tournament; a tall, strong, mobile Negro of impressive authority.

Holland's goals redeemed the game, marvellous in their lightning simplicity. First Neeskens dashed down the middle, found Cruyff on the right and lobbed the swift, immaculate return over Leao's head, then Cruyff superbly volleyed home Krol's left-wing centre. Holland were in the Final.

The West Germans made heavier weather of it; and weather, indeed, was at the root of their victory over Poland. The weather was bad, though not as bad, in their exciting match against Sweden in Dusseldorf when Edstroem—a gorgeous volley—and Sandberg scored splendid goals, but West Germany's power, Bonhof rampant, eventually wore down the Swedish defence.

In their opening game West Germany, in Dusseldorf, had resumed their long World Cup dialogue with Yugoslavia. Dzajic, it was said, was displeased with Miljanic's defensive tactics. West Germany dominated play. Another of Paul Breitner's fulminating drives gave them the lead, after thirty-eight minutes and Muller scored the second after the blond, 22-year-old Uli Hoeness, at last showing his true ability, had got to the line and crossed. Franz Beckenbauer, at last, was in majestic form.

The Poles also won their first two games, but with little to spare. They were very lucky to get the better of Sweden, who overplayed them in the opening stages, shrewdly prompted by Grahn and Larsson in midfield, when Tapper and Grahn missed easy chances. In the second half, Tapper also missed a penalty, though Tomaszewski probably moved before the kick. So it was that Lato in the first half got the only goal; a cross by Gadocha, goal maker now rather than scorer, a header by Szarmach, another by Lato.

Then Poland beat Yugoslavia in Frankfurt, but might not have done so had Karasi not lost his head and felled Szarmach, who had been shoving him. Deyna opened the score from the penalty spot, Karasi atoned by whirling through the Polish defence to equalise, but the Lato-Gadocha combination again brought victory—Gadocha's corner, Lato's near-post header. Yugoslavia, though were without Dzajic.

Thus the decisive game was that between the Poles and West Germans in Frankfurt. A rainstorm made the pitch unplayable, but the Germans drew off the water as best they could, postponed the start and played. They won thanks to their superior strength. Yet only a staggering double save by Maier in the first half from—inevitably—first Lato, then Gadocha kept the German goal intact. In the second half, Tomaszewski saved another penalty, from Hoeness. The winning goal came when Hoeness's shot was deflected to 'The Bomber', Gerd Muller, who does not miss such chances.

The Final   West Germany v. Holland

So the Final, very properly as it seemed, would be between West Germany and Holland. West Germany had home advantage, Holland had the more imagination. It was hard not to polarise the contest into one of personalities; Beckenbauer against Cruyff, unquestionably the game's greatest players now Pelé had gone.

So far, Cruyff had plainly surpassed Beckenbauer on the field. Though he himself denied that he was particularly fast, insisting that it was a matter of *when* he accelerated, what fascinated the observer was not only his originality, but his amazing speed of thought and execution. Muller might be the goal-scoring machine *par excellence*, still deadly, despite those who felt he had passed his peak, but Cruyff was immensely more versatile, capable of roaming the field like his idol, Di Stefano, now goal maker, now scorer, slim, long legged, almost gawky, yet superbly elegant in motion.

Who would mark him? Udo Lattek, Bayern's manager, said, 'I know that Bonhof will kill Cruyff.' The general view, however, was that he would be marked (as he was) by Berti Vogts, the tenacious blond fullback, who had once, long ago, played him out of the game in a youth tournament.

What seemed clear to some of us was that the Dutch would need to score a minimum of three goals since their inadequate defence seemed almost certain to concede a couple. Could they get them? The answer to that seemed implicit in another question: could the Germans stop Cruyff?

On the previous day, Poland won a deadly dull Third Place Match against Brazil, jeered by a justifiably disappointed crowd; Lato, predictably, was the scorer. Ademir Da Guia, the blond mulatto, son of Domingas Da Guia who had played in the 1938 tournament, at last got a World Cup game and strolled shrewdly about before he was substituted, personifying a Brazilian school which was now hopelessly outmoded, as Deyna's immensely quicker, more effective, performance in the Polish midfield showed.

No World Cup Final has had such a sensational beginning as this: a penalty awarded, a goal scored, virtually before a German player had touched the ball. Holland kicked off and played almost insolent possession football, to the incensed whistling of the crowd, then suddenly and convulsively broke away. Cruyff, who had dropped behind the forward line, began a long, almost breathtakingly ambitious run, swerved round Vogts as though he wasn't there, raced on into the penalty area and there was tripped by the desperate leg of Hoeness. Penalty.

Neeskens, of course, took it, banging his right-footed shot between Maier and the right-hand post as Maier moved to the left.

It was a vibrantly dramatic moment and one which seemed so sure to decide the match, whatever one may now say with hindsight, that the Dutch were tempted to relax, moved to play cat and mouse with an opponent which, for historical reasons, they longed to humiliate. For twenty-five minutes the Dutch did as they pleased against a stunned German team, rolling the ball about, making pretty patterns, but creating no real opportunities. Dangerous indulgence against a host team; and so it was that West Germany got off the hook—with another penalty.

Young Holzenbein, a left-winger who, like Bonhof, had come into the team only with the second stage, took chief credit for the goal. Taking a neat pass from Overath, he set off up the wing, Breitner running inside him, scorned the easy option, cut into the penalty area, beat his man and was tripped by Jansen. Breitner, full of confidence, scored from the penalty and the tide had turned.

West Germany now exultantly carried the fight to Holland; even Vogts left Cruyff, whom he was now playing so effectively, to put in a searing shot, which Jongbloed saved one-handed. Then Hoeness, devastating in his long controlled runs and sudden bursts, had beaten Suurbier and rolled the ball past Jongbloed for the excellent Rijsbergen to kick out of the goalmouth. Beckenbauer's was the next attempt, a cunning lob from a free kick, which Jongbloed clawed over the bar.

Yet the decisive moment surely came when Holland broke away and caught the West German defence hopelessly undermanned, so much so that Cruyff and Rep together descended on Beckenbauer. Cruyff did everything he should, drawing his famous rival, then giving the ball sweetly to Rep. But Rep hadn't the skill to score; Maier saved boldly at his feet and, were we to know it, Holland had lost the Cup.

After forty-three minutes, the Dutch defence wilted again and Gerd Muller scored his sixty-eighth goal for West Germany; the most important of them all.

Grabowski began the movement with a pass up the right to Bonhof, whose speed and power took him past Haan on the outside. Hulshoff would no doubt have stopped him, but Hulshoff wasn't there and when the ball came over, Muller contrived to drag it back into his path with one foot and sweep it past Jongbloed with the other.

In the second half Holland had to substitute Rensenbrink, whose pulled muscle had made him doubtful initially and had clearly handicapped him and his team. Van de Kerkhof, the tall young forward who replaced him, would almost give Holland the equaliser when his long, straightforward cross from the left looped over all the German defence, and was ferociously met on the volley by Neeskens on the far post. Somehow Maier managed to block it.

Rijsbergen, too, hurt in a tackle by Muller in the first half, had to go off, giving way to De Jong, little Jansen dropping into the back four to look after Muller. When he brought down Holzenbein for the second time in the game, there might have been another penalty, while film has seemed to show that Muller was not offside when he ran through the Dutch defence to beat Jongbloed. For all that, Jack Taylor, the English referee, made a fine fist of the match and was very brave to give that first-minute penalty while Holland themselves scarcely deserved to lose more heavily.

So West Germany won the Cup in one of the most enigmatic of all Finals. Was Holland's penalty a poisoned gift? Would they have done better without it? Was Rensenbrink's injury decisive? All one could say with certainty was that it had been an immeasurably more dramatic Final than 1970's and that if West Germany had taken the Cup then Holland, surely, had been the most attractive and talented of all losers.

There may have been some significance in the fact that their inside-left, Wim Van Hanagem, the slowest man in the team, was that day palpably the best.

RESULTS: West Germany 1974

Group I

West Germany 1, Chile 0 (HT 0/0)
East Germany 2, Australia 0 (HT 0/0)
West Germany 3, Australia 0 (HT 2/0)
East Germany 1, Chile 1 (HT 0/0)
East Germany 1, West Germany 0 (HT 1/0)
Chile 0, Australia 0 (HT 0/0)

	P	W	D	L	GOALS F	A	Pts
East Germany	3	2	1	0	4	1	5
West Germany	3	2	0	1	4	1	4
Chile	3	0	2	1	1	2	1
Australia	3	0	1	2	0	5	1

Group II

Brazil 0, Yugoslavia 0 (HT 0/0)
Scotland 2, Zaire 0 (HT 2/0)
Brazil 0, Scotland 0 (HT 0/0)
Yugoslavia 9, Zaire 0 (HT 6/0)
Scotland 1, Yugoslavia 1 (HT 0/0)
Brazil 3, Zaire 0 (HT 1/0)

	P	W	D	L	GOALS F	A	Pts
Yugoslavia	3	1	2	0	10	1	4
Brazil	3	1	2	0	3	0	4
Scotland	3	1	2	0	3	1	4
Zaire	3	0	0	3	0	14	0

Group III

Holland 2, Uruguay 0 (HT 1/0)
Sweden 0, Bulgaria 0 (HT 0/0)
Holland 0, Sweden 0 (HT 0/0)
Bulgaria 1, Uruguay 1 (HT 0/0)
Holland 4, Bulgaria 1 (HT 2/0)
Sweden 3, Uruguay 0 (HT 0/0)

	P	W	D	L	GOALS F	A	Pts
Holland	3	2	1	0	6	1	5
Sweden	3	1	2	0	3	0	4
Bulgaria	3	0	2	1	2	5	2
Uruguay	3	0	1	2	1	6	1

Group IV

Italy 3, Haiti 1 (HT 0/0)
Poland 3, Argentina 2 (HT 2/0)
Italy 1, Argentina 1 (HT 1/1)
Poland 7, Haiti 0 (HT 5/0)
Argentina 4, Haiti 1 (HT 2/0)
Poland 2, Italy 1 (HT 2/0)

	P	W	D	L	GOALS F	A	Pts
Poland	3	3	0	0	12	3	6
Argentina	3	1	1	1	7	5	3
Italy	3	1	1	1	5	4	3
Haiti	3	0	0	3	2	14	0

Group A

Brazil 1, East Germany 0 (HT 0/0)
Holland 4, Argentina 0 (HT 2/0)
Holland 2, East Germany 0 (HT 1/0)
Brazil 2, Argentina 1 (HT 1/1)
Holland 2, Brazil 0 (HT 0/0)
Argentina 1, East Germany 1 (HT 1/1)

	P	W	D	L	GOALS F	A	Pts
Holland	3	3	0	0	8	0	6
Brazil	3	2	0	1	3	3	4
East Germany	3	0	1	2	1	4	1
Argentina	3	0	1	2	2	7	1

Group B

Poland 1, Sweden 0 (HT 1/0)
West Germany 2, Yugoslavia 0 (HT 1/0)
Poland 2, Yugoslavia 1 (HT 1/1)
West Germany 4, Sweden 2 (HT 0/1)
Sweden 2, Yugoslavia 1 (HT 0/0)
West Germany 1, Poland 0 (HT 0/0)

	P	W	D	L	GOALS F	A	Pts
West Germany	3	3	0	0	7	2	6
Poland	3	2	0	1	3	2	4
Sweden	3	1	0	2	4	6	2
Yugoslavia	3	0	0	3	2	6	0

Third place match

Munich

Poland 1 | **Brazil 0**

Tomaszewski; Szymanowski, Gorgon, Zmuda, Musial; Kasperczak (Cmikiewicz), Deyna, Masczyk; Lato, Szarmach (Kapka), Gadocha.

Leao; Ze Maria, Alfredo, Marinho, M., Marinho, F.; Paulo Cesar Carpeggiani, Rivelino, Ademir da, Guia (Mirandinha); Valdomiro, Jairzinho, Dirceu.

SCORER
Lato for Poland
HT 0/0

Final

Munich

West Germany 2 | **Holland 1**

Maier; Beckenbauer; Vogts, Schwarzenbeck, Breitner; Bonhof, Hoeness, Overath; Grabowski, Muller, Holzenbein.

Jongbloed; Suurbier, Rijsbergen, (De Jong), Haan, Krol; Jansen, Neeskens, Van Hanegem; Rep, Cruyff, Rensenbrink (Van de Kerkhof, R.).

SCORERS
Breitner (penalty), Muller for West Germany
Neeskens (penalty) for Holland
HT 2/1

ARGENTINA
1978

Fears About Argentina

The 1978 World Cup, though altogether less disastrous in actuality than it was in prospect, nevertheless left behind it a sour taste and a welter of controversy. Ecstasy and euphoria greeted Argentina's triumph within Argentina itself. Elsewhere, there was less elation. As the defeated Dutch bitterly said, it's unlikely that Argentina's team could have won the tournament anywhere but at home. Giovanni Trapattoni, manager of Turin's Juventus club, who attended the tournament, went even further. He believed that elsewhere Argentina would not even have survived the first round.

There were good reasons for such scepticism, good reasons for disappointment in a tournament whose level did not remotely approach that of 1974, whose Final was an ill-tempered, abominably refereed game, and whose whole course was marred and scarred by questionable refereeing.

Such feelings were given special pungency by the nature of Argentina's regime: a military dictatorship, its junta led by General Jorge Videla. For more than a year before the World Cup matches began, great opposition was expressed, above all in Western Europe and particularly by the Amnesty International organisation, to the holding of the Cup in Argentina. Since the junta took power in 1976, thousands of people had disappeared, thousands had been murdered and tortured. The moral aspect aside, there was the question of whether the safety of players could be guaranteed. West Germany in 1974, with the threat of the Arab terrorists, had been bad enough. In Argentina the threat came from within. There were serious doubts, moreover about whether stadia and communications would be ready in time. The previous, Peronist, Government had dragged its feet. The military junta had set up a new body, the Ente Autarquico Mundial, to speed proceedings but its task was monumental. Moreover its chief, General Omar Actis, had been assassinated en route to his first Press conference.

There were rumours that the competition would be reallocated to Holland and Belgium, rumours that the Dutch would withdraw—as Johan Cruyff had already withdrawn—if it were not. Meanwhile, even the Argentinian Minister of Economics objected to the colossal cost of the affair; it was expected to lose some $750 million.

A further fear concerned the behaviour of Argentine players and crowds. In the late 1960s, Argentinian club and international teams had been notorious for their violence. Argentinian crowds were well known for their intimidatory effect on referees. True, the new Argentine team manager, the tall, lean, fair, chain-smoking Cesar Luis Menotti, nicknamed El Flaco (the Thin One), had promised a new era. If a team could kick its way to the World Cup, he'd said, then he would pick such a team, but it was no longer possible. Such methods were obsolete. The emphasis must be on skill. Fine, if not fighting, words, but had they real substance? In June 1977, England and Scotland played Argentina within a week of each other in the notoriously vertiginous Boca Stadium, and each game threw up an ugly incident. Trevor Cherry of England was punched in the mouth by Argentina's Daniel Bertoni; the Uruguayan referee, Ramon Barreto, sent *both* of them off. The following week, Pernia, the Argentine back, knocked Willie Johnston of Scotland down with a cruel punch to the kidneys. Again, the referee sent off both players.

The Contenders   Argentina

Menotti, the Argentinian manager, had great problems in building a team. The end of the World Cup had seen a great exodus abroad, notably to Spanish clubs. Brindisi, Carnevali, Wolff, Babington, Kempes, Heredia and others were in Europe now. Menotti said boldly that he'd recall no more than three players: Kempes, Piazza, the Saint-Etienne centre-half, and Wolff. Kempes had matured into the most dangerous goal scorer in Spain, with Valencia. Wolff was now playing in defence—where Argentina looked weakest—with Real Madrid. Piazza had actually been released by Saint-Etienne and was back in Buenos Aires when his wife and child were hurt in a car accident, and he returned to France. Wolff was lost because Menotti insisted he be in Buenos Aires by the beginning of April. Real Madrid could not possibly release him then.

So, without Kempes, his team—which had played a long, indifferent series in the Boca Stadium the previous year—laboured on convincingly through a number of friendlies.

Holland

If Argentina would be missing many stars, the two greatest stars of all would not be there, either. Johan Cruyff of Holland, inspiration of the 1974 team, best and most versatile centre-forward in the world, had stood firmly by his decision not to take part, despite huge offers, endless pleading and pressure. Alas for Holland, Cruyff was not the only absentee of renown; indeed, he had seemed to set a fashion. For varying reasons, Van Beveren, the country's best goalkeeper, Ruud Geels, the excellent Ajax centre-forward and Wim Van Hanegem—as late as May 1978—dropped out, while the splendid attacking leftback Hovenkamp was hurt. It was thus a much-diminished Dutch team which flew to Argentina, even if such distinguished survivors as Rep, Rensenbrink, Haan and Neeskens were present. The new manager was Ernst Happel—an Austrian, once in charge of Rotterdam's Feyenoord, but now the most part-time of international managers, since he had charge of Belgium's Bruges.

West Germany

West Germany would be without Franz Beckenbauer, a loss which would prove irreparable. In April 1977 he suddenly, and shockingly, accepted a $2,500,000 offer to join the Cosmos of New York.

Schoen had already lost several other of his 1974 players. The tournament was scarcely over when the prolific Gerd Muller, the wily Jurgen Grabowski and the inventive Wolfgang Overath announced that they would play no more international football. They had had enough of its strains, its tension and its travelling. They wanted, they said, to spend more time with their families.

Yet the 1976 West German team seemed perfectly capable of winning the World Cup again, and the 1977 team won comfortably at Boca against Argentina. The pre-World-Cup season started cheerfully enough, with a fine win against Italy in West Berlin. Manny Kaltz, the Hamburg defender, was no Beckenbauer in skill and poise, but he had done well at sweeper and was, some said, at least a better defensive player than Beckenbauer. With the New Year, however, results fell away. The 'new' system of playing the acrobatic Schalke 04 centre-forward, Klaus Fischer, between two wide wingers was no longer so successful.

Scotland

From Britain, Scotland alone as in 1974 would make the trip, under the euphoric managership of Ally MacLeod. England, after a disastrous three years of management by Don Revie, which came to a squalid if lucrative end when he decamped to Arabia, were eliminated by the Italians. Northern Ireland found Holland too much for them. Wales went out to Scotland—controversially. The Czechs, winners of the 1976 Nations Cup with a glittering pair of performances—though they beat West Germany in the Final only on penalties—were also victims of the Scots as indeed they had been in 1974.

Wales had a justified grievance. Playing Scotland in a World Cup eliminator at Liverpool, where their home game had been switched, they were well in contention. Then a high ball came into the Welsh penalty box, a hand went up and touched it, the French referee,

M. Wurz, blew immediately for a penalty, and Scotland scored. The hand, however, had belonged to Joe Jordan, Scotland's centre-forward. Scotland went on to win the game.

Of Scotland's talent, there was no doubt. They had more outstanding players, certainly, than any of the other British teams. There was some doubt, however, both about the experience and the detachment of their manager, who had left Aberdeen to take over Willie Ormond's team little over a year before, and of the team's ability to turn its talent into results.

After qualifying for the World Cup by beating Wales at Liverpool, the euphoria of the Scots was infinite and continued to be so, even if their geographical sense was not always impeccable. WE'RE ON OUR WAY TO RIO! cried the headline of a Scottish daily newspaper, next morning. Wild plans were conceived by fans desperate to get beyond Rio, to Argentina; one even contemplated hiring a submarine. Others worked their way across the subcontinent, though ultimately the following was counted in hundreds rather than thousands.

The Scots had an abundance of fine midfield players at a time when most other countries looked for them desperately; Rioch, Masson, Hartford, Gemmill, Macari, Souness. They were severely weakened, though, by the news that Danny McGrain, the Celtic right-back, who had missed the game against Wales with a chronic foot injury, had no chance of recovering in time for the World Cup finals. McGrain, perhaps the best right-back in football, a player of power, authority, mobility and drive, by turns a stout defender and an extra forward, was without an equal.

To his unavoidable loss was added the quite avoidable loss of Andy Gray, the excellent young Aston Villa centre-forward, inexplicably left out of the final forty players, let alone the final, permitted, twenty-two, by an increasingly unpredictable MacLeod. His reasons made little sense, the less so as he preferred to Gray, in excellent form, the obscure Joe Harper, who had played for him at Aberdeen. Moreover, MacLeod decided to take to Argentina the injured Gordon McQueen, though it was all but certain that the big centre-half would be unable to play.

As the competition grew nearer, so MacLeod's statements and postures grew more extreme. 'I'm a winner!' he cried, promising great things, evidently borne along by the exultant optimism of the fans. The Scottish newspapers did nothing to restrain him; their nickname of 'supporters with typewriters', conferred on them by an English colleague, seemed amply earned.

If MacLeod was over-sanguine, he was also remarkably commercial. How much money he made in the year leading up to the World Cup is unknown, but he bought himself a public house for an estimated

£70,000. (MacLeod himself said that in fact it was rented, and its cost was exaggerated). Around the Scottish camp hung such an aura of materialism, of wheeling and dealing, that it was astonishing to read a Scottish FA report, three months after the World Cup, which blamed MacLeod for not having made clear to his players how much they stood to earn.

Brazil

Brazil, too, were under a new manager, the 39-year-old Army captain, Claudio Coutinho, an elegant polyglot who had come into football by the roundabout route of physical training. He was an enthusiast of the Cooper Test system of assessing athletes—the emphasis was on endurance—and had been physical 'preparer' of the 1974 World Cup team, manager of the 1976 Olympic soccer team. Charming, good looking, cosmopolitan, he took over from the São Paulo veteran, Osvaldo Brandao. Coutinho at once restored the wayward overlapping full-back Francisco Marinho to the team, which showed instant improvement, successfully completed the qualifying group against Colombia and Paraguay, then himself ran into the familiar torrent of criticism.

In his case he was blamed for trying to impose on the players the concept of 'polyvalence', which, he explained, was simply another way of saying Total Football. But by early 1978, when the team was in training camp outside Rio, Coutinho's approach seemed quite another one. Now the emphasis was on fitness and what he conceived to be 'European' hardness. Touch players such as the gifted young centre-forward, Reinaldo, were encouraged to chase back and challenge. Defenders were exhorted to stop their opponents by hook or by crook.

Italy

Enzo Bearzot, the new Italian manager at first appointed jointly with the veteran Fulvio Bernardini, had pulled his team together. A large, dark man of almost Red Indian looks, and an international half-back, he was a passionate moralist who hated much of what Italian football had become and was anxious to wean it away from negativity. This would take time, because almost every major club played with a static sweeper and attacked on the break, but Total Football was for Bearzot 'the true aim'.

The nearer the competition drew, the less impressive Italy seemed, though several new young players emerged—Cabrini, the attacking left-back, for instance—on the eve of the competition. Paolo Rossi, whose valuation by Lanerossi Vicenza at £3,000,000 in May, led to the resignation of the President of the Italian League in protest, was a centre-forward of outstanding talents. Small but marvellously adroit, he was unable, however, to win a place in the team before it left for Argentina.

Italy's task had been made no easier by some politicking which had gone badly astray. Initially, before the draw for the finals was made in Buenos Aires in January, Italy had expected to be seeded, with all the consequent advantages. Strong objection to this was made, however, by the West Germany FIFA delegate Hermann Neuberger, with the result that Holland—the 1974 finalists—were seeded instead. Italy then urged that they be placed in the Buenos Aires group, a privilege granted to them. Bizarre classification, however, which rated feeble Mexico on the same level as Hungary, Spain and Peru led to a lopsided grouping. In the second pool, the West German holders and the Poles were faced merely by Mexico and Tunisia, the African entrants, while Group I was composed, formidably, of Argentina, Italy, Hungary and France. The French, who possessed one of the best players in Europe in the 21-year-old Michel Platini, a midfield player from Nancy with a superb touch and a remarkable flair for scoring from free kicks, were known to be a gifted side.

The Preliminaries

Under the impetus of EAM, Argentina made up for the slack years of Peronism and licked their stadia into shape, though there were problems till the last—just as there had been, after all, in Montevideo when the World Cup began. At the rebuilt, imposingly modern River Plate Stadium, seawater was used to sprinkle the grass, which withered and died in the sun. A new field was hastily laid. Rich and green it looked, but the bounce was often capricious. At seaside Mar del Plata, where the Brazilians were reluctantly to play, concerned about the cold weather, heavy rain had made the pitch a fiasco in which divots were kicked up in dozens.

A few weeks before the tournament was due to start, a bomb was found, despite the heavy security, in the Press Centre in Buenos Aires. It exploded as it was being taken away, killing one policeman and wounding another. Many footballers, among them Paolo Rossi and West Germany's goalkeeper, Sepp Maier, signed an Amnesty International petition protesting about the torture and treatment of political prisoners, but it was easy for Argentina's military government, controlling almost all sources of information, to represent to them that their country was the victim of a conspiracy of vilification.

It is true that the Amnesty International campaign told only part of the story. Though there was no denying that dreadful outrages had been committed by the military regime, they had taken over a country in a state of virtual civil war in which normal life in the great cities had become almost impossible and kidnapping and assassination were rife. The attitude of the ordinary bourgeois citizen in Buenos Aires during the World Cup seemed to be one of relief that he could now live and work without fear—though the solemn parade of the mothers each Thursday afternoon in the Plaza de Mayo, where the Presidential palace stands, was a bleak reminder of what lay beneath the surface of 'normal' life.

Early Games

Thus the World Cup did not go to the Low Countries, nor to Brazil, which had made it plain that it would be ready to accept it. Instead, it opened on June 1 in the River Plate Stadium with one more of those stupefyingly boring curtain-raisers, this time between West Germany and Poland.

It had surely become plain enough that such preludes, pulling two teams from the pack and placing such pressure on them, were selfdefeating. It would grow equally clear that the clumsy new formula, initiated in 1974, whereby the first stage of four qualifying groups led not to quarter-finals but to two more league groups whose winners contested the Final, was disastrous.

For this first game, Helmut Schoen surprisingly and suddenly abandoned his policy of two wingers and a centre-forward, instead fielding only two strikers in the Schalke men, Abramczik and Fischer.

There seemed some consolation in the lively form of Hansi Muller, a tall 20-year-old from Stuttgart, more midfield fish than upfield fowl, but he was *persona non grata* to some of the senior professionals.

Though neither team deserved to win a depressingly cautious match, which was ultimately and deservedly whistled by the River Plate crowd, there might have been a Polish victory but for a couple of alert saves by Sepp Maier. The lack of Gadocha—and of their old spirit of adventure—was plain in Poland's team, but in Adam Nawalka, a 20-year-old right-half from Wisla Cracow they clearly had a new player of great energy and potential in midfield. It was characteristic of Gmoch's costive approach that the clever 22-year-old Zbigniew Boniek should come on only as a late substitute for the veteran Lubanski—who had missed the 1974 World Cup Finals with an injured knee but had found his way back into the team after moving to Belgium. Boniek would, in the event, emerge as one of the outstanding young players of the tournament, balanced, adroit, insidious and a good finisher into the bargain.

Schoen did not stick long to his 4-4-2 formation. Protests from his

players led him for the next game, against Mexico in Cordoba, to switch
to yet another new strategy, a two-centre-forward attack. It was about this
time that the old familiar pattern of West German participation in World
Cups asserted itself, as his senior coaches were to be heard pungently
criticising him for his vacillation. There was dissatisfaction, too, among
the players with the lonely, boring life they led in training camp at Asco-
chinga outside Cordoba, though things there were enlivened by the controversial visit of the Nazi war hero, Colonel Hans-Ulrich Rudel. As a
wartime fighter pilot, Rudel was said to have destroyed a thousand Russian tanks. Later, he had organised Peron's air force. An unrepentant
Nazi, he had been banned from addressing any political meetings in
Bavaria.

Group I   Argentina v. Hungary

The following evening, Argentina opened their programme in Group I
with a torrid match against Hungary. At Wembley Stadium ten days earlier, the elderly Hungarian manager, Lajos Baroti, had stood in the evening sunshine as his players trained and told me of his fears about the
tournament. Everything, he'd said, even the air, was in favour of
Argentina. He was afraid that the referees might well give them a couple
of penalties: 'The success of Argentina is financially so important to the
tournament.'

The Hungarians had surprisingly eliminated their old foes Russia
and then put out Bolivia in two final qualifying games. Much was
expected of the 22-year-old Andras Toroscik, a small, blond centre-
forward with delightful ball control, superb balance and an ability to
pick his way through penalty areas to score remarkable goals. The tall,
lean Tibor Nyilasi, who had played with him since they were youth
internationals, was an attacking midfielder of great talent, dangerous
in the air.

When Argentina took the field, it was to a snowstorm of torn-up paper,
swirling in the floodlights. The River Plate Stadium, its terraces set well
back from the field with a track between, was a much less intimidating
one than Boca's, but referees, as we would quickly see, were still alarmingly susceptible.

With so much bad faith on both sides, it would have required an
immeasurably stronger referee than the feeble Portuguese, Garrido, to
have brought the game smoothly into harbour. The Hungarians, who
had been rough at Wembley against England, were harsher still here,
pursuing a policy of ruthless challenge and quick counter-attack which
seemed for some time as if it might pay. It was in fact a game which
began with great promise but degenerated long before the end into sheer
beastliness.

Hungary took the lead after only twelve minutes when Zombori completed a clever move with a shot which Fillol, the Argentine goal-keeper, couldn't hold, Csapo driving in the loose ball. It was not till the second half, when the busy little Osvaldo Ardiles, so soon to come to Tottenham, moved from right to left in midfield that Argentina took a grip on the game, even though Leopoldo Luque had equalised within three minutes after Gujdar couldn't hold Mario Kempes's thundering left-footed shot.

Two things were impressively evident about Argentina: first that Cesar Menotti, undaunted by the looming shadow of Juan Carlos Lorenzo, his ruthless predecessor, really had persuaded his team to attack, second, that they now had the pace which in previous years Argentinian teams so plainly lacked. Lorenzo, manager now of Boca Juniors, was reduced to a mere benign commentator. The strength of the Argentine attack, mean-while, was the electric combination of the two big strikers, Luque, a right-footed player, and the left-footed Kempes. These two made space for one another, played off each other and in general showed a pace and power which was often splendidly exciting. Once Gujdar had to dive perilously at Luque's feet, but in the end he was beaten by Bertoni after he had brought Luque down in a fulminating Argentine attack, seven minutes from the end.

Toroscik, performing small miracles of skill against defenders who fouled him almost every time he tried to beat them, had had his name taken by Garrido in the first half merely for hurling the ball away in petulance when denied a throw-in. Given what had gone before, and would come after, it was rather like indicting and jailing a *mafioso* for income-tax evasion. When Gallego, however, yet again fouled Toroscik, something snapped. Toroscik kicked him to the ground, and off he went. A few minutes later he was followed by Nyilasi, guilty of a spiteful foul on the largely innocent left-back, Tarantini.

Italy v. France

What brought the Italians to life, ironically, was the goal headed against them in thirty-eight seconds at Mar del Plata by the French centre-for-ward Lacombe. It forced them out of their customary defensive crouch and made them attack. There was also the question of piqued pride. 'We wanted to show them we weren't the imbeciles they took us for,' said Dino Zoff, the veteran goalkeeper. 'We came here with no hope,' admitted Roberto Bettega, who had a splendid game. 'Some of the Press had writ-ten us off as tourists.'

Paolo Rossi played and scored a pin-table goal in Italy's 2–1 success. His excellent form in training games against local sides had moved

Bearzot finally to include him in preference to the bigger Torino striker, Francesco Graziani, who had had a lean season. Marco Tardelli, marking Platini—sometimes too aggressively—seemed a regenerated player. He owed this, he would later say, above all to the 'tranquillity' of the Hindu Club, where Italy (like France) had set up training camp. Wisely Bearzot banned all Italian newspapers from the camp and the players were gradually able to disperse the miasma of pessimism and criticism surrounding them on their arrival.

There was a new sweeper in the young Juventus player Gaetano Scirea, the 35-year-old Giacinto Facchetti having finally been forced out of the team by a bang in the ribs from the notorious Romeo Benetti during a League game between Inter and Juventus. This, too, would be a help for Scirea, uneasy in his previous appearances, would now take wing and make a much more adventurous contribution to the team than the static Facchetti could even have done.

Platini left the churned-up field of Mar del Plata complaining that he had had no decent support in midfield, where he missed the powerful, combative Bathanay. Things in the French camp had been tense, with the players painting out the Adidas stripes on their boots because they wanted more money. This distressed their idealistic manager Michel Hidalgo, already unnerved by an attempt to kidnap him shortly before the team left France.

France v. Argentina

In their next match, however, the French surpassed themselves. Their opponents were Argentina, again in the River Plate Stadium, and now they restored both Dominique Bathenay and Dominique Rocheteau, the Saint-Etienne men. Bathenay had been suffering from injury; Rocheteau, an elegant sinuous outside-right, had only lately recovered from it. Marius Trésor, the splendid black sweeper from Guadaloupe, had been injured too and was estimated by French critics to be at no more than seventy per cent of full efficiency. For all that he was one of the most impressive, dominant defenders of the World Cup.

That Argentina eventually beat France 2–1 was largely the fruit of two abominable decisions by the referee, M. Jean Dubach of Switzerland; a penalty given (and that is the right word) to Argentina, a penalty refused to France. The French, with Bathenay now giving Platini the muscular support he needed, played much delicate, delightful football in the first half. Argentina, whose rhythm would be destroyed when Luque dislocated his elbow, relied heavily on Kempes, who hit the post with a tremendous left-footed drive after beating Trésor in the forty-second minute. The game was in injury time when another majestic burst by Kempes, always wonderfully ready to run at and commit a defence, ended with Luque dashing through, Tresor fall-ing as he challenged him and landing on the ball with his hand. M. Dubach, well behind the play, blew his whistle, then astonishingly ran to consult his Canadian linesman, who had been even farther from the incident. This done he pointed for a penalty which Daniel Passarella, the Argentine centre-back and captain, drove left-footed into goal.

It was a monstrous decision, which looks no better in retrospect now that Winsemann, the Canadian linesman, has revealed what Dubach asked. 'Inside or outside?' he enquired in German. If he needed to ask that, then his eyesight was scarcely sufficient for a foot-ball referee. The only point at issue was whether or not the handling was intentional.

Though the goal had come so cruelly, and at so delicate a moment, the French fought back well. They equalised seventeen minutes into the sec-ond half after a splendid run and cross from the right by Battiston found the Argentine defence adrift. When Lacombe's attempt came back from the bar, Platini scored easily. Didier Six, who had a mixed game indeed, should have put France in the lead after twenty-seven minutes after a glorious run and pass by Platini, but he shot wide with Fillol alone to beat. Thus Argentina were allowed to win the game with a goal quite out of the blue by Luque, a tremendous right-footed shot from outside the box as the defence momentarily stood off. Eleven minutes from time, Platini put Six through again, but when he was manifestly pulled down, M. Dubach did nothing. France were out, but with honour.

Argentina v. Italy

Now Argentina met Italy, again by night. Both teams had already quali-fied. It was a question of which would win the group and thus stay in Buenos Aires, a consummation devoutly to be wished, it seemed, by Argentina. The second-placed team would have to play in Rosario.

Bearzot at first decided to use several reserves, but Paolo Rossi and oth-ers who would have been left out protested. Rossi said that he felt per-fectly fit; if there was any reason for excluding him, he would like to be told. So it was the full Italian team which met an Argentine side now without Luque.

It was in this game that Menotti made his one tactical error. He decided to play Kempes as an orthodox centre-forward between two wingers. Before the tournament began, there had been sustained dis-cussion in the Argentine Press about how Kempes should be used: should he play as a striker or just behind the front three of Bertoni, Luque and Houseman? This was the role he had often filled in Spain for Valencia, the one in which he would eventually play here. Now he was a fish out of water, denied the invaluable support of the injured

Luque in the middle, denied the room and space he would find by dropping farther back.

This time there would be no nonsense about the referreeing. The choice had fallen on the little Israeli, Abraham Klein, who made it clear from the first that he would not be influenced or frightened.

Though their pattern of play had been disjointed, Argentina still might have scored twice in the first half, were it not for glorious saves by Zoff from Kempes and Passarella—always ready to go up into attack. Gradually the Argentine fire was extinguished by Italy's tight, man-to-man defence and after sixty-seven minutes Bettega scored the only goal of the game. Rossi, with a fine determined burst on the left, began the move, winning the ball and crossing it. He then moved on into the middle to play an elegant one-two with Bettega, who ran on easily to shoot past Fillol. Italy would play in Buenos Aires, Argentina in Rosario. Later, disappointed Italian players said it was a pity it had not worked out the other way.

Group II

In Group II, the West Germans and Poles qualified, as everyone expected, but they were given a surprisingly hard time of it by an admirable Tunisian side. Opening the new stadium at Rosario, Tunisia, their midfield cleverly organised by Dhiab, seemed inferior to Mexico at first, fell behind to a penalty kick, but dominated the second half with their superior speed and stamina to win 3–1.

Poland were next, again at Rosario, and Tunisia gave them a hectic run for their money. They set Khaled Dasmi, rude but efficacious, to dog the steps of Deyna and were helped by the fact that the Poles again did not bring Boniek on till the closing stages. It was an unfortunate mistake by Amar Jebali which enabled Lato to score the game's only goal three minutes from half-time. Thereafter Tunisia were on top and surprised the critics by their technical superiority—to all but Lubanski. They deserved to equalise.

With West Germany they drew 0–0, and might have won. The left-footed Dhiab, slight but adroit, looked better than any of the West German midfielders, Flohe and Bonhof included. Dieter Muller and Klaus Fischer were easily snuffed out up front. The German team, according to *La Nacion* of Buenos Aires, was fragile and without imagination. But it had qualified to play in Pool A, the Buenos Aires group.

Group IV

In the Cordoba-Mendoza group, Peru astonished, Scotland succumbed and the Dutch made few friends. Iran, who had already lost at home to Wales before the competition began, had done well to knock out the Australians, but looked an uninspired, untalented lot in Argentina where they failed to win a game. Holland beat them quite comfortably, all three goals going to Rob Rensenbrink, two from the penalty spot, though an Argentine critic said the Dutch team resembled a superb machine which lacked the man who invented it. That man, clearly enough, was Johan Cruyff.

Scotland, the players restless at their hotel in Alta Cracia, maligned by the local Press as fervent drinkers, came out to play Peru at Cordoba absurdly unprepared. Quite simply, Ally MacLeod had failed to do his homework; otherwise Scotland could scarcely have given Teofilo Cubillas the untramelled freedom of midfield.

Cubillas, a black player of great virtuosity, had been one of the revelations of 1970, a rapid striker. Now, at twenty-nine, after experience in Portugal, he was back in Lima and had dropped into midfield. Peru's form in 1978 had been so poor that MacLeod had plainly decided they were not worth taking seriously; indeed, his whole approach by now seemed to be the old, hubristic British one of 'let them worry about *us*'.

Scotland's Departure

Surprisingly, he decided to persevere in midfield with Don Masson and Bruce Rioch, each a half-back rather than an inside-forward, despite the fact that both had been in such poor form, so disaffected, that Derby County had put them on the transfer list. True neither had played badly against England at Hampden, where Asa Hartford had been ebullient in midfield, but to leave out the tall, adroit Graeme Souness after he had run into such splendid form with Liverpool, playing such a large part in their conquest of the European Cup, seemed absurd. Not till the last game, against Holland, did he come into the side and then his impact was immediate. After the Peruvian débâcle, Martin Buchan, played out of position at left-back since Donachie was suspended, complained that he had not known Munante was so fast. It had long been an open secret throughout Latin America.

Ironically Scotland began quite well and scored a good goal after fourteen minutes. Dalglish and Hartford gave Rioch the chance of a shot, Quiroga, the eccentric Peruvian goalkeeper, who would cross the half-way line when the spirit moved him, couldn't hold the ball; Joe Jordan put it in.

Gradually, however, the virtue began to ebb out of Scotland. Cubillas, pacing his game beautifully, showing great skill both on the ball and in his use of it, was growing more and more apparent. Two minutes before half-time—a traumatising moment—he was involved in a quick, clever exchange of passes which let Cueto through to equalise.

Scotland's chance to win the game, and perhaps acquit themselves adequately in the tournament, arose and was thrown away after seventeen minutes of the second half. Diaz brought down Rioch and Masson took the penalty. He had scored coolly against Wales; surely he must do so now. But his shot was a poor one and Quiroga, who almost certainly moved before the ball was kicked, turned it round the left-hand post.

That was the end of Scotland, who had no answer to Cubillas. Two splendidly-struck right-footed goals in the seventy-second and seventy-ninth minutes cooked their goose. For the first, he was left unmarked. For the second, he thumped a swerving free kick high into the left-hand corner, after himself starting the move which led to it with a superb long crossfield pass—the kind which once was accounted a British speciality. Afterwards he remarked modestly that he didn't know why everybody had been writing him off as too old; after all, he was only 29.

Still worse was to follow for Scotland. Willie Johnston, the little 31-year-old outside-left, in tremendous form against Peru, was one of two players singled out for a dope test; and the test proved positive. He had taken two Fencamfamin pills. Shades of poor Jean-Joseph of Haiti (by now in Chicago with Gadocha) in 1974. Johnston at first protested that he had taken them for his hay fever, but it soon transpired that it was something that he'd often done in club games. 'Pep pills?' said a sceptical Glaswegian fan. 'I thought they were tranquillisers.' Johnston was packed off home in disgrace, suspended from international football for a year, told by Scotland he would never play for them again and consoled only by the rustle of bank notes as a Sunday newspaper paid him a large sum for his 'story'.

Scotland's morale lay in ruins. There were complaints about the poor training facilities, complaints about the hotel, complaints about MacLeod. It was a demoralised team which laboured in its next match to an embarrassing draw against Iran. Scotland's goal was farcical, scored by Eskandarian against his own team as he and his goalkeeper fell to the ground and he thrust out a desperate foot.

Holland, meanwhile, were proving as enigmatic as they had looked before battle began. There was, to begin with, a manifest conflict in approach and temperament between their managers, Ernst Happel, the dour Austrian, and Jan Zwartkruis, an Air Force Officer who had managed the team before Happel and who had known most of the players for years, having run the Army team. In a remarkable outburst at Holland's training camp—where the Dutch players were restless, too—he criticised Happel for treating his men 'as footballers, rather

1. Italy's team manager Vittorio Pozzo instructs his players before the start of extra time in the 1934 Final

2. World Cup Final 1938. Italy's Alfredo Foni clears with an overhead kick

3. World Cup Final 1958. Svensson, Sweden's keeper, challenged by
seventeen-year-old Pelé

4. World Cup 1958. Northern Ireland's airborne keeper Harry Gregg fails to stop Uwe Seeler equalising for West Germany

5. World Cup 1966. Portugal's Eusebio gets in his shot against Bulgaria

6. World Cup Final 1966. Wolfgang Weber's last-ditch equaliser for West Germany against England. Ray Wilson and Gordon Banks stretch in vain

7. World Cup Final 1966. Was it a goal? Roger Hunt exults as Geoff Hurst's shot beats Tilkowski to come down from the underside of the bar

8. World Cup 1974. Johan Cruyff scores a splendid second goal for Holland against Brazil, at Dortmund

9. World Cup Final 1978. Mario Kempes leaps between Dutch defenders Willy Van de Kerkhof and Erny Brandts

10. World Cup 1982. Italy's Bruno Conti trying to foil Argentina's Osvaldo
Ardiles with a back flick

11. World Cup 1982. Gerry Armstrong blasts the ball past Spanish goalkeeper
Luis Arconada for Northern Ireland's winner

12. World Cup 1982. Germany's Karl-Heinz Foerster and Harald Schumacher tangle in their efforts to keep the ball from the opposing Spanish attacker

13. World Cup Final 1982. Italy v. West Germany. Italy's Dino Zoff misses a high cross while defending his goalmouth

14. World Cup 1986. Preben Elkjaer scores Denmark's winner against Scotland at Neza

15. World Cup 1986. Diego Maradona swerves past England's Terry Fenwick on his way to a remarkable solo goal, his and Argentina's second

16. World Cup 1986. Gary Lineker puts England back in the game against Argentina, heading John Barnes' left wing cross

17. World Cup Final 1986. Jose Luis Brown exploits Toni Schumacher's error and heads Argentina into the lead against Germany

18. World Cup 1990. Scotland's Jim Leighton can't hold Careca's shot for Brazil

19. World Cup 1990. David Platt scores England's spectacular winning goal against Belgium in extra time

20. World Cup 1990. Andreas Brehme's deflected free kick for Germany sails over Peter Shilton's head into England's goal

21. World Cup Final 1990. Andreas Brehme scores West Germany's World Cup winning goal against Argentina

22. World Cup 1994. Romania v. Columbia. A clash between artists: Ilie
Dumitrescu of Romania and the dreadlocked Carlos Valderrama of Colombia

23. World Cup Final 1994. Brazil's superb centre-forward, Romario, the star of the tournament, kisses the Cup he did so much to help win

24. World Cup 1998. David Beckham sent off by referee Nielsen: England v. Argentina.

25. World Cup Final 1998. A dejected Ronaldo leaves the field after the Final: should he have played?

26. The 2002 World Cup Final. Germany's Carsten Ramelow stretches desperately to try to intercept Brazil's Ronaldo

27. Ronaldo whirls away in triumph having scored Brazil's second goal of the World Cup Final, beating the prostrate Oliver Kahn

than as human beings'. He may have had a point in so far as Happel's treatment of Jan Jongbloed, the 37-year-old goalkeeper, was concerned. Jongbloed, furious when Happel almost casually told him he'd been dropped after the game against Scotland, had to dissuade his wife from coming to beard Happel in his den.

Initially, it was supposed that Happel would experiment with a new system which placed five men in midfield, roughly in the shape of an X with the key player in the centre. This had been tried in May against Austria in Vienna with Wim Van Hanegem in the middle. Afterwards, however, the big, 34-year-old inside-left had been told by Happel that he could not guarantee him a place in Argentina and he had therefore become the last Dutch player to withdraw.

Held to a goalless draw by Peru, Happel dropped Aarie Haan, restored to midfield for this World Cup, from the team to play Scotland and chose Johan Neeskens though he was known not to be fit. Indeed, he did not last many minutes. The Scots at last brought Graeme Souness into the side. Asked whether he thought Scotland could score the three goals they needed against Holland Jongbloed replied, 'Yes, but not in ninety minutes.'

Score them, however, they did, including what many considered the finest goal of the competition; it took a desperate rally by the Dutch to pull the score back to 2–3 and stay in the competition. Scotland at last, and too late, had cast off their complexes to play splendid football. The Dutch, by contrast, played a sour, negative game, with much harsh tackling and excessive emphasis on the offside trap.

They owed much to the splendid play at sweeper of Ruud Krol—their 1974 left-back—who rescued them time and again. His former partner at full-back, Wim Suurbier, was surprisingly put at centre-back against Jordan, though he himself had never claimed to be strong in the air, where Jordan was at his strongest.

This, in any event, was a new Scotland, driven on from midfield by Souness and the exuberant little Archie Gemmill. Rioch, too, looked far more enterprising, hitting the angle of post and bar after only five minutes. The Dutch went into the lead when Johnny Rep was brought down by Kennedy and Alan Rough the goalkeeper, and Rob Rensenbrink scored from yet another penalty. But Johan Neeskens had already left the field, after a lunging tackle on Gemmill, and the Dutch team laboured. Just before half-time, Jordan headed down Souness's clever lob and Dalglish equalised. When Souness was fouled, after half-time, Gemmill in turn scored a penalty to make it 2–1.

This, though, was as nothing to the goal with which he made it 3–1, an astonishing slalom which took him from just outside his penalty area round three bemused defenders to end with a slashing shot past Jongbloed. A twenty-five-yard shot by Johnny Rep finally beat the vulnerable Rough to give Holland their second goal and take them into Group A. In Glasgow the cruel word went round that 'Micky Mouse is wearing an Ally MacLeod wrist watch'. A characteristically crass report by the Scottish Football Association, who confirmed MacLeod in office by a casting vote, seemed to put most of the blame on the Scottish journalists.

Certainly they had been mindlessly euphoric. Certainly the London Press had done Scotland a disservice by competing for sensational revelations from the players, but the players themselves had been disaffected and greedy. There was an especially displeasing episode when Don Masson went to Ally MacLeod to say that he, too, had taken 'pep' pills, only to withdraw his story when MacLeod marched him in to the Scottish officials.

Group III

In Mar del Plata, Brazil blundered their way into the second round, thanks chiefly to two shocking errors by their opposition. They were an unhappy ship—appropriately commanded by Admiral Heleno Nunes—from the first. Rivelino was overweight and unhappy; there were tense relations between Coutinho and another of his most gifted players, the little, attacking midfielder, Zico, unhappy at the long spell in training camp which prevented him seeing his baby son. Reinaldo, the clever, sharp mulatto centre-forward, reduced by an infinity of cartilage operations, had been under a cloud since making good-hearted if ingenuous remarks about Brazil's political prisoners. There was no Luis Pereira to play sweeper. The 1974 captain had virtually withdrawn from the team after a poor season with Atletico Madrid. He was also afraid, he said, that if he played badly against Spain he'd be accused in Brazil of 'throwing' the match.

Brazil began indifferently against Sweden in Mar del Plata, then played still worse against Spain and Austria. The Swedes running themselves to subsequent extinction, scored first. Reinaldo equalised for Brazil with delightful finesse when the first half was in injury time, but the Welsh referee, Clive Thomas, whimsically decided to blow for full time precisely as the ball was going into the net for what would have been Brazil's winning goal. The Brazilians protested. The Swedes retorted that as the corner kick sailed over they had relaxed when they heard the final whistle. Thomas incurred the disapproval of FIFA not for this, however, but for covering his face theatrically with his hands when Bo Larsson almost put through his own goal.

For the next game, against Spain, who had been beaten 2–1 in Buenos Aires by an unexpectedly lively Austria, Brazil omitted

Rivelino, whose supposed unfitness would become a bone of contention, Rivelino subsequently insisting he was injured, Coutinho that he was not. Without his heavy-thighed, heavily moustached, sombre and irascible presence in midfield, Brazil were much diminished. Dirceu, who now filled the left midfield position, was much eulogised by the end of the competition, but despite abundant energy and a strong left-footed shot, he seemed prosaic by comparison with the likes of Rivelino and Gerson.

It was a stupendous mistake in the second half by Julio Cardeñosa, the little Spanish midfielder, which permitted Brazil to draw 0–0. When the tall Real Madrid centre-forward Santillana flicked a high ball on to him, Brazil's defence was left in chaos; even the greying Leao was out of goal. Perhaps if Cardeñosa had not had so much time, he would have scored, simply have put the ball into the empty net. Instead he hesitated pitifully, and was lost. By the time he shot, the black Amaral had scuttled back to clear from the line. Some players, observed a Buenos Aires paper, became famous for the goals they scored. Cardeñosa had achieved fame through the one he missed. It says something for Cardeñosa's character and skill that in Spain's final game, in Buenos Aires, he should be the inspiration of their win against Sweden.

Brazil's, and Coutinho's, bankruptcy was shown by the fact that he used a right-back, Toninho, as his outside-right. Shades of Julinho, Garrincha and Jairzinho!

Against Austria, once more at Mar del Plata, Brazil won 1–0 because a centre from that same Toninho, now at right-back was allowed to drift over his head by the tall Austrian stopper, Pezzey. Roberto, on the far post, had infinite time to control the ball and score. So Coutinho, who had been burned in effigy in the streets of Mar del Plata by enraged Brazilian fans and relieved publicly of full powers by the egregious Admiral Nunes, survived—with his team. Calm elegance had given way to a haunted anxiety. He banned foreign journalists from his Press conferences and sometimes refused to give conferences at all. He would be shamefully traduced by Nunes before the game against Poland, as a man of 'scarce technical abilities', the team had been saved by its players and by 'wise officials'. If they were so wise, you wondered, then why had they appointed a man of 'scarce abilities' in the first place?

The Final Groups

The two final groups would be made up by: Italy, Holland, West Germany and Austria, in Buenos Aires and Cordoba; Argentina, Peru, Poland and Brazil in Rosario and Mendoza. The second was clearly the weaker, although Argentina won it only by goal difference. The question of goal difference had already caused extreme confusion when it seemed that Brazil might finish level on points with other teams in its group for second place; and level on goal difference, too. FIFA's rules on the subject were extremely vague, but Brazil's lucky win against Austria made the matter academic, for the moment.

Goal difference rendered Holland's 5–1 win over Austria in their opening Group A game in Cordoba of colossal importance. Quite how the Austrians, who had played so well in their first two matches and would play so well in the last two, collapsed so ineptly was a mystery.

The Dutch, much happier on the Cordoba surface than Mendoza's, gave a glorious display of Total Football. They successfully introduced two young players, the midfielder Pieter Wildschut and the tall centre-back Erny Brandts, who headed the first goal after five minutes from a free kick. Resenbrink at last justified the hopes placed in him with an irresistible display, scoring another penalty, beating men at will, brilliantly making goals for Rep and Willy Van de Kerkhof. Aarie Haan returned to the midfield, though Neeskens was again absent.

By contrast, Italy and West Germany played a stultifying goalless draw. 'The Germans', remarked Franco Causio next day, 'built the Berlin Wall in Argentina.' Though Dino Zoff made a wonderful save from Bernd Holzenbein in the first half, and West Germany fashioned several chances late in the second, the German attitude was cravenly defensive, Rummenigge more full-back than winger. Only two spectacular goal-mouth clearances by Manny Kaltz from Roberto Bettega—much less incisive than usual—prevented Italy from deservedly winning. Maier, moreover, was once exceedingly lucky when he completely misjudged a lob by Cabrini which came back from the post, though he atoned with a fine save from Bettega's header.

The Italians, however, were running out of steam. Their next game in the River Plate Stadium against Austria saw them begin superbly but fade embarrassingly. That lack of stamina which had bedevilled Italian football so long was all too manifest. After the disastrous Dutch game Enzo Bearzot was to complain violently of the referee, but in this game the Belgian Francis Rion's refereeing greatly favoured Italy. Towards the end, when the tired Italian defenders were going through the old repertoire of obstruction and tripping, he should have given Austria at least one penalty (Senekowitsch the blond Austrian manager, said two) and taken several Italian names.

The goal with which Italy won the game after fifteen minutes, however, was a gem. Cheekily crossing his feet, Paolo Rossi found Franco Causio on his left, outpaced Obermayer, the big blond Austrian sweeper, to the return ball and beat Koncilia to score. Other heroes, however, were evidently tired, not least Bettega and the blond Romeo Benetti.

The 'reprise' of the 1974 World Cup Final between West Germany and Holland, at Cordoba, provided one of the best games of the competition. West Germany, recalling Abramczik and so playing with two wingers, took the lead after only three minutes when the little Schalke 04 man dived bravely to head the ball past Schrijvers, after the keeper could only block one of those fierce free kicks for which Bonhof was famous, but which he so seldom produced in Argentina. Holland equalised through Haan with one of *his* specialities: a thirty-five-yard drive to which Maier did not move. Similar inattention by the Dutch defence allowed Dieter Muller to regain the lead for West Germany with a simple headed goal, twenty minutes from time, but with only seven left, René Van de Kerkhof threaded his way through the German penalty area, beat Maier with his shot, and Russmann's attempt to push it out with his hands failed.

In Rosario, Argentina defeated Poland 2–0 with difficulty. Kempes not only scored both goals but, punching off the Argentine line from Lato, enabled his team to keep their 1–0 lead.

Kempes headed the first goal from Bertoni's left-wing cross, with some complicity from the Polish defence. Jacek Gmoch remarked that Tomaszewski had been unsettled by the proximity of the crowd and, indeed, this was much more of a tight traditional soccer stadium than River Plate's. Eighteen minutes from time, Kempes scored the second goal after a spectacular, sustained run to the by-line by little Ardiles.

At Mendoza, an improved Brazil easily accounted for Peru, whom they always beat, two of the goals being scored from long range by Dirceu. The meeting of Brazil and Argentina in Rosario thus became crucial.

Luque returned for this game, greatly diminished. Not only had his shoulder been hurt, his brother had been horribly burned to death in a car accident. Within ten seconds, Luque had cruelly hacked down the Brazilian half-back Batista, who would be fouled still more brutally in the second half by Villa. Both teams, one French critic remarked, 'were finally the prisoners of their fears, and totally destroyed one another'. Palotai of Hungary was a flaccid referee.

This left Brazil, holding a goal advantage over Argentina, to play Poland at Mendoza, Argentina to play Peru (beaten by Poland) in Rosario. Brazil were scheduled to kick off in the afternoon, Argentina in the evening. Predictably, the Brazilians protested; predictably, their protest was turned down.

Brazil, beating Poland 3–1, gave their best performance of the tournament, though an Argentine critic disdainfully remarked that they won because 'they imposed a conquering temperament which allowed them to overcome their defects and lack of talent.' Poland, in fact, would have been ahead at half-time had they taken their chances. As it was, Brazil went into the lead with one of their right-back's, Nelinho's, extraordinary free kicks, Lato equalised just before half-time. After it Brazil hauled themselves up by their boot-straps, gained control, beat a tattoo on the Polish goalposts and scored twice more through Roberto. It was a game poorly refereed by the Chilean, Juan Silvagno, but then who refereed well?

Italy's Artemio Franchi presided over a Referees' Committee which largely emulated the three wise monkeys. They had given no specific instructions to referees on how to officiate, he said, each must be left to do so in his own way. Such an abdication of responsibility by the Committee led to a serious lack of control, above all in the failure to book offenders for grave fouls, and had its all too appropriate climax in the ineptitude of Sergio Gonella of Italy in the Final.

Brazil's success meant that Argentina had to beat Peru that evening by at least four goals to reach the Final. They beat them by six in a game which has left bitter memories. Before it the Peruvian captain, Hector Chumpitaz, said he realised that it was Peru's task 'to safeguard the decency of the competition'. After it, Quiroga the goalkeeper, actually born in Rosario, published an open letter defending himself and his team. It was a game in which Peru opened briskly, their right-winger Munante hitting the post, their left-winger Oblitas shooting just across the goal. Then the team collapsed and lay down abjectly before the opposition. Why? Claudio Coutinho, Brazil's disappointed manager, attacked them bitterly, said that their players would feel no pride when they heard their national anthem in the next World Cup. Argentine newspapers reported that the Brazilians had tried to offer money to Peru to play well. Some thought they were bribed, some thought they were simply frightened by the torrid atmosphere. Whatever, it was a shabby way for Argentina to reach the Final.

There, they would meet the Dutch, conquerors of Italy in Buenos Aires. Falling behind after eighteen minutes when Erny Brandts, lunging ahead of the encroaching Bettega, not only put through his own goal but disabled his goalkeeper, Schrijvers. Holland recovered in the second half to win. Brandts, remarkably, scored their traumatising equaliser, five minutes after half-time, a left-footed player, up for a free kick, swinging his right foot at the ball and sending it hurtling into the left-hand corner past Zoff. '*Che culo!*', what luck, remarked the Italian defender, Claudio Gentile, the following day. 'I'd never have believed it. He was in the middle of three of us, and the fellow shoots with his head down. He didn't even look up.'

The second goal came from a terrific, thirty-yard shot by Aarie Haan, which Zoff reached, touched but couldn't stop. Later, sunning himself on a beach in Sardinia, Haan said he thought Zoff should have stopped his own shot, but not Brandts's. The game was ill-tempered and abominably refereed by the Spaniard, Angel Martinez. Bearzot insisted that his players were intimidated, that Haan had committed the worst foul of the World Cup on Zaccarelli. Bad it unquestionably was, but it was the immediate sequel to a painful foul by Benetti on Haan himself as he went up the wing. Later, Benetti should have been sent off when he elbowed Neeskens in the face.

In Cordoba, Austria surprisingly beat a flaccid West Germany 3–2. There were rumours that certain German players did not wish to be bothered with the Third Place game. Schoen himself, at the subsequent Press conference said 'I do not want to mention any names, but I was utterly disappointed with our defence, which made things easier for our opponents to score goals.' Helmut Senekowitsch of Austria then chivalrously impugned the West German players' attitude. 'I deplore the fact that Schoen will be retiring from his professional career after seeing his team defeated in this manner.'

The Final   Argentina v. Holland

Would Holland win, without Cruyff? Their form had been mercurial; no European team had won the World Cup in South America, but they seemed to be running into form and Argentina's defensive weaknesses remained manifest. Four years earlier, inspired by Cruyff, Holland had made the merest mouthful of the Argentinians; but that was not in Buenos Aires. Meanwhile, Brazil, with long shots by Nelinho and Dirceu, right footed and left footed, beat Italy 2–1 to take third place after falling behind to a goal headed easily by Causio.

Would Neeskens play on Kempes in the Final? Would Ardiles play at all? The answers turned out, respectively, to be no and yes though Ardiles, that fragile, sleek-haired, ebullient tango-figure, who had hurt an ankle, would not last the game. 'The Dutch,' Paolo Rossi had admiringly observed, 'change positions as easily as they'd take a cup of coffee.' They marked the Argentinian strikers man to man while the Argentine defence continued to mark zonally and, no doubt, live dangerously. Each team was capable of blood-chilling excesses. Would Gonella be strong enough to control and contain them?

He would not, so much was obvious before a ball had even been kicked. The Argentinians took the field five full minutes late, a most arrant piece of gamesmanship, then, having done so, complained about the bandage René Van de Kerkhof, the Dutch winger, was wearing on his forearm. The Dutch, especially Neeskens, a Spanish speaker, protested violently that Van de Kerkhof had worn the bandage in several preceding games, but Gonella upheld the protest. The Dutchman was obliged to leave the field, where he simply covered that bandage with another.

Subsequently Passarella explained, 'We could not allow ourselves to concede any advantage. Luque saw the danger the bandage could be and I as captain had the obligation to protest.'

'Clearly,' said René Van de Kerkhof, 'but why did they let us wear it in the other games?'

The Dutch team, thus incensed, committed in the opening minute the first of some fifty fouls, a crude one by the young defender Poortvliet. To say that Gonella favoured the Argentinians was true to the extent that he was a weak, fearful referee who quickly allowed the game to slip out of his feeble grasp, tending to penalise the away team. Thus, he twice allowed Argentina's defensive midfield player, Gallego, to handle the ball deliberately without booking him, and if there was the benefit of a doubt it usually went to Argentina. Nevertheless, the attitude of the Dutch team itself was scarcely benign.

The game was a dramatic rather than a distinguished one, turning in the end on a couple of saves by Fillol and three marvellous slaloms by Mario Kempes, distinguished not only by his skill, speed and courage but by his remarkable composure. Both defences in the first half were curiously vulnerable. Four times, at the Dutch end, Passarella came upfield and was 'forgotten', three times Jongbloed saved and once the ball whistled just above the bar. At the other end Johnny Rep pounced when Jansen's cross was headed straight out to him, only for Fillol gallantly to save: as he did again, with his legs, when Neeskens nodded the ball down to Rensenbrink. What each team manifestly lacked in midfield was a true creator. Argentina had in Gallego a defender, in Kempes an attacker, in Ardiles a busy, venturesome halfback. Holland had the muscular versatility of Willy Van de Kerkhof, Neeskens and Haan. There was no Van Hanegem or Overath, as there had been in 1974, and despite the current heresy that such 'generals' were obsolete, the effect of their absence was manifest in the quality of play.

Kempes it was, much too vaguely marked by Willy Van de Kerkhof, given room and time to run at the defence, who scored the first half's only goal. There were seven minutes left to half-time when a four-man movement on the left was concluded by Luque—who had pulled the sweeper Krol out with him—crossing to Kempes. Only Haan stood between him and Jongbloed and, riding Haan's desperate tackle, he ran on to drive the ball home with his formidable left foot. It was right on half-time that Fillol made his crucial save from Rensenbrink, served by Neeskens. From a player cast out by Menotti but restored, a goalkeeper so vulnerable to crosses in the opening games, Fillol had grown into Argentina's rescuer.

He began the second half by saving a thundering shot from Johan Neeskens, hit from far outside the box. Holland now had a grip on the game, but they were not making any clear chances; the much-maligned Argentine defence proved surprisingly resilient when at bay. After fifty-nine minutes Holland took off Johnny Rep, no favourite of Happel and replaced him with the tall Dirk Nanninga, the object plainly being to attack Argentina in the air. Seven minutes later Argentina substituted Ardiles, obviously not wholly fit, with Larrosa, who'd taken his place against Peru.

Holland pressed on. Neeskens forced his way through, to be shockingly brought down by Galvan, who was shown the yellow card; but when he fouled Rensenbrink in the box—an obstruction at the least—no whistle blew. Now Holland moved up Erny Brandts, pulling back Willy Van de Kerkhof; and at last, with two tall men hungry for crosses, the equaliser carne.

Haan began the movement with a sweeping long ball from left to right. René Van de Kerkhof controlled it, slipped round Tarantini, centred; and Nanninga rose splendidly to head into the goal.

There was still time for Passarella to elbow Neeskens in the face, then, in the very last minute, for Krol perfectly to put Rob Rensenbrink through. The Argentine defence was scattered, but when Rensenbrink shot, he hit the left-hand post and, did we but know it, the Cup had passed from Holland.

In extra time it was logical and legitimate to expect the Dutch to go on dominating what looked an exhausted Argentine team, but somehow (will we ever know quite how?) Menotti roused his men, as Alf Ramsey had at Wembley. The Dutch restored Brandts to defence, and suddenly found themselves under pressure; Argentina were running and probing again. With fourteen minutes of extra time played, one to go, Kempes received from the lively Bertoni, forced his way through the defence again, almost lost the ball to the brave Jongbloed, managed to retain it and made the score 2–1.

That was that. The second period saw Holland throwing men up in desperate quest for a second equaliser, leaving great gaps in which the Argentinians frolicked. Luque, taking the ball from Krol, was once clean through, only for Jongbloed to frustrate him; but with five minutes left, another marvellous burst by Kempes and a one-two with Bertoni allowed the winger easily to score the third. The stadium now was a volcano of joy; the streets of Buenos Aires would be thronged all night by ecstatic thousands. If it had not been a famous victory, it had been a thrilling one, and if Holland deserved sympathy for losing their second consecutive World Cup Final, perhaps Argentine football deserved its honour, for the players it had given us over the years.

Kempes was not the least of them.

RESULTS: Argentina 1978

Group I

Argentina 2, Hungary 1 (HT 1/1)
Italy 2, France 1 (HT 1/1)
Argentina 2, France 1 (HT 1/0)
Italy 3, Hungary 1 (HT 2/0)
Italy 1, Argentina 0 (HT 0/0)
France 3, Hungary 1 (HT 3/1)

| | | | | | GOALS | | |
	P	W	D	L	F	A	Pts
Italy	3	3	0	0	**6**	**2**	6
Argentina	3	2	0	1	**4**	**3**	4
France	3	1	0	2	**5**	**5**	2
Hungary	3	0	0	3	**3**	**8**	0

Group II

West Germany 0, Poland 0 (HT 0/0)
Tunisia 3, Mexico 1 (HT 0/1)
Poland 1, Tunisia 0 (HT 1/0)
West Germany 6, Mexico 0 (HT 4/0)
Poland 3, Mexico 1 (HT 1/0)
West Germany 0, Tunisia 0 (HT 0/0)

| | | | | | GOALS | | |
	P	W	D	L	F	A	Pts
Poland	3	2	1	0	**4**	**1**	5
West Germany	3	1	2	0	**6**	**0**	4
Tunisia	3	1	1	1	**3**	**2**	3
Mexico	3	0	0	3	**2**	**12**	0

Group III

Austria 2, Spain 1 (HT 1/1)
Sweden 1, Brazil 1 (HT 1/1)
Austria 1, Sweden 0 (HT 1/0)
Brazil 0, Spain 0 (HT 0/0)
Spain 1, Sweden 0 (HT 0/0)
Brazil 1, Austria 0 (HT 1/0)

| | | | | | GOALS | | |
	P	W	D	L	F	A	Pts
Austria	3	2	0	1	**3**	**2**	4
Brazil	3	1	2	1	**2**	**1**	4
Spain	3	1	1	1	**2**	**2**	3
Sweden	3	0	1	2	**1**	**3**	1

Group IV

Peru 3, Scotland 1 (HT 1/1)
Holland 3, Iran 0 (HT 1/0)
Scotland 1, Iran 1 (HT 1/0)
Holland 0, Peru 0 (HT 0/0)
Peru 4, Iran 1 (HT 3/1)
Scotland 3, Holland 2 (HT 1/1)

| | | | | | GOALS | | |
	P	W	D	L	F	A	Pts
Peru	3	2	1	0	**7**	**2**	5
Holland	3	1	1	1	**5**	**3**	3
Scotland	3	1	1	1	**5**	**6**	3
Iran	3	0	1	2	**2**	**8**	1

Group A

Italy 0, West Germany 0 (HT 0/0)
Holland 5, Austria 1 (HT 3/0)
Italy 1, Austria 0 (HT 1/0)
Austria 3, West Germany 2 (HT 0/1)
Holland 2, Italy 1 (HT 0/1)
Holland 2, West Germany 2 (HT 1/1)

| | | | | | GOALS | | |
	P	W	D	L	F	A	Pts
Holland	3	2	1	0	**9**	**4**	5
Italy	3	1	1	1	**2**	**2**	3
West Germany	3	0	2	1	**4**	**5**	2
Austria	3	1	0	2	**4**	**8**	2

Group B

Argentina 2, Poland 0 (HT 1/0)
Brazil 3, Peru 0 (HT 2/0)
Argentina 0, Brazil 0 (HT 0/0)
Poland 1, Peru 0 (HT 0/0)
Brazil 3, Poland 1 (HT 1/1)
Argentina 6, Peru 0 (HT 2/0)

| | | | | | GOALS | | |
	P	W	D	L	F	A	Pts
Argentina	3	2	1	0	**8**	**0**	5
Brazil	3	2	1	0	**6**	**1**	5
Poland	3	1	0	2	**2**	**5**	2
Peru	3	0	0	3	**0**	**10**	0

Third place match

Buenos Aires

Brazil 2	**Italy 1**
Leao; Nelinho, Oscar,	Zoff; Scirea, Gentile,
Amaral, Neto; Cerezo	Cuccureddu, Cabrini;
(Rivelino), Batista,	Maldera, Antognoni
Dirceu; Gil	(Sala, C.), Sala, P.;
(Reinaldo), Mendonça,	Causio; Rossi, Bettega.
Roberto.	

SCORERS
Nelinho, Dirceu for Brazil
Causio for Italy
HT 0/1

Final

Buenos Aires

Argentina 3	**Holland 1**
(after extra time)	
Fillol; Olguin,	Jongbloed; Krol,
Galvan, Passarella,	Poortvliet, Brandts
Tarantini; Ardiles	Jansen (Suurbier);
(Larrosa), Gallego,	Van de Kerkhof, W.,
Kempes; Bertoni,	Neeskens, Haan; Rep
Luque, Ortiz	(Nanninga),
(Houseman).	Rensenbrink,
	Van de Kerkhof, R.

SCORERS
Kempes (2), Bertoni for Argentina
Nanninga for Holland
HT 1/0 FT 1/1

SPAIN
1982

The 1982 World Cup, top heavy with its twenty-four teams, ill-organised by its host country, ill-augured from the farcical moment of the draw itself, beset by heat and by displeasing incidents, none the less ended in a dramatic crescendo. That Italy should win seemed impossible at the outset, improbable after their three dull games in the opening round, yet splendidly appropriate by the end of a Final in which the 'disgraced' Paolo Rossi emerged as the Italian catalyst, the most dazzling star of the tournament.

The draw was made in Madrid in January. The egregious João Havelange, Brazilian President of FIFA, who had wished the twenty-four team World Cup on the game as the price of his election in 1974—when the votes of the Afro-Asian block sustained him—praised Spain for having accepted the challenge in the spirit of Don Quixote. Proceedings then took place very much in the spirit of Sancho Panza. One of the revolving drums from which the teams, each represented by a ball, were drawn stuck. A ball broke. Neuburger, the West German representative, rebuked one of the blue-clad orphans who were making the draw. The balls representing Scotland and Belgium were extracted too early, thus defeating the whole elaborate object of the exercise which was to keep South American teams apart.

It was hard to find favourites, though the West Germans looked good. Paul Breitner had returned to international football, now as captain and a dynamic midfield player. Hansi Muller, in the same section, had much matured, though he had problems with his knee. A little 21-year-old right-winger, Pierre Littbarski, quick, clever and daring, had forced his way into the team. Karl-Heinz Rummenigge, European Footballer of the Year, was among the best strikers in the game, and the giant Horst Hrubesch had proved a fine centre-forward when Germany won the 1980 Nations Cup.

But Bernd Schuster, perhaps the chief star of that team, a driving, blond midfielder, had had such trouble with his knee when playing for Barcelona that there was no hope of having him. A tour of South America, in which Brazil and Argentina had been met, had been most encouraging.

Argentina were still under the able managership of Menotti, and he had a wonderful new weapon in Diego Maradona. Twenty-one years old, thick-thighed, enormously quick in thought and movement, a superb finisher and a fine tactician, Maradona was a host in himself, and with him, from the youth team, had emerged the swift centre-forward, Ramon Diaz. Osvaldo Ardiles had returned from his triumphs at Tottenham to reinforce the midfield, but the team had looked tired in Buenos Aires before it left for Europe.

Since the highly doubtful custom of an opening game would be adhered to, Argentina would open the ball in Barcelona against Belgium, who had qualified with France, at the expense of Holland, runners-up in the two previous World Cups; and of Eire, victims of shocking refereeing decisions in both Paris and Brussels.

The twenty-four-team complement meant that the competition would be more than ever a madman's flytrap. There would be no fewer than six groups, made up of only four teams each. The first two in each group would qualify for the so-called second round, to be played entirely in Madrid and Barcelona, by four groups of three teams each. Points would decide; and if not points, then goal-difference. If this in turn was dead level, the complications became so infinite that almost Talmudic exegeses could, and eventually did, ensue. It could even come down to which team had done better in the previous round.

The four semi-finalists then played off on a knock out basis, not in Madrid and Barcelona as you might expect, but in Barcelona and Seville, thus giving an enormous advantage to the Barcelona-based teams, the more so as France and West Germany, the eventual semi-finalists, found themselves held up till the small hours of the morning in a chaotic Seville airport.

Add to this the ravages and depredations of the Mundiespana Organisation, to which the Spanish Federation handed over the organisation of hotels and tickets, and the recipe was complete for a World Cup which further compounded its anomalies with a timetable that left excessive delays between staggered games without properly parcelling out the periods of rest. Michel Hidalgo, the French team manager, was especially bitter about this; and about the obligation to play under such intense heat that his players risked sun stroke.

Brazil's Zico, before the competition, accused Argentina of being a one-man team. Maradona, the one man, retorted that the Brazilians had no forwards which, by contrast with Zico's stricture, proved substantially correct.

Brazil brought with them almost a surfeit of midfield players. Claudio Coutinho, their 1978 manager, had not only gone, the poor fellow had been drowned. His successor, Tele Santana, was much better attuned to the inner rhythms and patterns of Brazilian football. Players, now, were encouraged to attack and express themselves as the samba beat out from the terraces. But the plethora of midfield players—Zico, bearded Dr Socrates, the lanky magician Cerezo, and Falcao, back from Rome—was not complemented by fine players up front. Pelé, Garrincha, even Tostao and Vavà, were mere memories.

Britain had three entrants. England were among those present for the first time since 1970, but wouldn't have been there at all had it not been for the enlarged tournament, enabling two teams to qualify from their group. Apart from a fine, unexpected performance in Budapest, inspired by the veteran West Ham inside-forward, Trevor Brooking, who scored two splendid goals, England's performance under the shaky managership of Ron Greenwood—obsessed by the waning charms of Kevin Keegan—had been pitifully mediocre. Not till Don Howe, Arsenal's coach and the England right-back in the 1958 World Cup, was called belatedly was the defence decently organised.

Scotland, too, had a manager clearly past his substantial best in Jock Stein, who had never recovered from an appalling car crash on his way back from Glasgow Airport. Unlike England, the Scots had qualified not by default but on abundant merit, winning a group which included Portugal and Sweden; and gallant little Northern Ireland, who slipped into second place under the aegis of Billy Bingham, their outside-right in the 1958 World Cup.

Among the interesting outsiders were the Cameroons in Group I, the Algerians in Group II, and Kuwait in Group IV. Immense sums of money had been poured into their preparation, supervised by the little Brazilian coach, Carlos Alberto Parreira, who in 1983 would be appointed manager of Brazil themselves.

Remoter still seemed the chances of El Salvador, who had qualified despite the fearful civil war devastating the country; their rivals Honduras, drawn in Group V with the hosts Spain; and New Zealand, who had narrowly got the better of China, competing in a World Cup for the first time.

The opening match may not have been a distinguished one, but at least it produced a goal for the first time for twenty years. The surprise was that the Belgians should score it, the more so as they left out the 37-year-old Wilfried Van Moer, inspiration of their midfield in the Nations Cup finals two years before. His place went to a completely new cap, the blond 24-year-old Vandermissen. But instead of shadowing Maradona, as was widely expected, Vandermissen, who did well, was only one of several Belgians who passed Maradona on to one another with such good effect that the presumed star of the game was seldom seen to effect, apart from one fine free kick which hit the crossbar.

Overall, the Argentines seemed weary, as they had in Buenos Aires. Some thought that the effect of the lost Falklands War weighed upon them. Be that as it may, Kempes, hero of 1978, looked a fish out of water on the extreme left; Diaz, who'd later be criticised by his colleagues, was out of form in the middle; and the defence lapsed horribly when a long cross from the left by Vercauteren was allowed to reach the unmarked Vandenbergh, who was able to score almost at leisure and pleasure.

The Italians next day opened their programme at Vigo, and played an unimpressive draw against the Poles, who'd knocked them out in Stuttgart in 1974 in a game which has ever since produced claims and counter-claims of attempted bribery. Paolo Rossi, a hero of 1978, looked explicably out of touch and practice.

He had disgraced himself by being involved in the Italian fixed odds betting scandal while on loan from Lanerossi Vicenza to the Perugia club. A game at Avellino had been drawn 2–2, Rossi scoring twice. His alleged complicity led to a three-year suspension, subsequently reduced to two. The mythical words of the old Chicago White Sox (or Black Sox) scandal of 1919, 'Say it ain't so Joe' (or Paolo), became the apposite catch-phrase. It seemed impossible that the ingenuously boyish Rossi could be involved in such chicanery, but he cut a poor figure at the tribunal in Milan and out he went, returning in time for only three Championship games with his new club, Juventus.

Both that game and the one between Peru and the Cameroons at Coruna ended in a goalless draw. Tardelli hit the Polish bar, and Zbigniew Boniek, the key Polish midfielder, explained his poor form on the grounds that he was overwhelmed by having to play against his future colleagues of the Juventus team.

In their next game, once more at Vigo, Italy were most fortunate not to give away a penalty when the notorious Claudio Gentile brought down Peru's swift winger Oblitas, only for Eschweiler, the referee, to turn a blind eye. To give him his due, Eschweiler had just been winded by the ball.

Bruno Conti, the elusive little Roma winger, one of the relatively few newcomers to Enzo Bearzot's team, scored the Italian goal after eighteen minutes; Diaz equalised seventeen minutes from time.

The handsome young Italian players were the delight of the Galician girls, who hung around, admiring, outside their training camp, but within it, matters were tense. The team had played appallingly badly in Braga, Portugal, on their way to Spain, and the violent, sometimes malicious, criticism by the Press, not least about the size of their bonuses, provoked a head-on collision.

It had only just been avoided in Argentina, largely through the good offices of the ebullient little public relations officer, Gigi Peronace, but Peronace had died sadly of a heart attack in Bearzot's arms just before the team set out for the Mundialito tournament in Montevideo in December 1980. Now there was no buffer. The players refused to talk to the Press except through their veteran goalkeeper, Dino Zoff, renowned as the most taciturn of all, and they maintained their ban right to the very end.

Fortunately for them, the Poles continued to play still less efficiently and could well have lost to a bright and eager Cameroons team, which had a splendid goalkeeper in N'Kono, who would stay on in Spain, and a forceful centre-forward in the French domiciled Roger Milla. In the end, Poland were glad of a goalless draw, but they came vibrantly to life in their third game, crushing a feeble Peru, 5–1, the two redheads Boniek and Buncol, and the incisive left-winger, Smolarek, running rings round the flat-footed Peruvian defence.

Against the Cameroons, Italy showed again how much they missed the cool attacking skills of Roberto Bettega, lost to them through injury. True, the sometimes prodigal Conti missed one astonishingly easy chance, but the goal with which Graziani put them ahead on the hour came only because N'Kono slipped; and the Cameroons equalised right away. Later, some Italian journalists attributed their team's fine form thereafter to the fact that the weather in Galicia had been so cool, by contrast to that elsewhere. But the muscle stimulant administered to the team may have had still more to do with their undoubted and somewhat untypical energy.

England made a very good beginning against France in Bilbao. They scored after only twenty-seven seconds, the quickest goal in the story of the competition, flagged briefly in the second half when Alain Giresse split the defence with a through pass to Soler, but ran out clear 3–1 winners in the end.

Bryan Robson scored the first two English goals and had he not injured a groin in the ensuing game, England might have done vastly better. A Geordie, developed by West Bromwich Albion and sold at a massive fee to Manchester United, Robson had the energy, strength, talent and temperament to make him one of the most complete midfield players since Johan Neeskens.

His first goal was banged in when Coppell took a long throw in on the right and Terry Butcher came up from centre-half to flick the ball on at the near post. His second was a brave piece of opportunism when he beat a hesitant French defence to head in. Things went better for Robson and for England when he moved from the left of midfield into the centre where he felt so much more at home. On the left, 'I seem to get lost a bit in the game.'

It was appallingly hot. 'We sat there in cold towels in the dressing-room at half-time,' said Ray Wilkins, the Manchester United inside-forward, 'and the heat came off us like steam.'

Neither Trevor Brooking nor Keegan played. Neither would—until the very last match. Brooking had pelvic trouble. Keegan, perhaps providentially, had trouble with his back.

The most extraordinary game of the group took place in Valladolid, between France and the Kuwaitis, who had opened impressively against a flaccid Czech team in the same city.

Towards the end of a game which they had clearly lost, Michel

Platini, out of form against England but dominant against Kuwait, sent little Giresse through a Kuwaiti defence which stopped because someone had blown a whistle on the terraces behind their goal. Giresse scored, the Russian referee gave a goal and the Kuwaitis protested with great vehemence. Up in the stand, their Prince and President, splendid in a pink burnous, seemed to be beckoning them off the field. But as the players prepared to abandon it, down he came to persuade them to stay on. The Russian referee inexplicably changed his decision, disallowing the goal, and the match was finished.

Afterwards, the ebullient Carlos Alberto, a Peter Sellers figure, tried to minimise the incident, insisting that the Prince had been trying to keep the players on. 'So when he goes like this,' said a sceptical German journalist, beckoning, 'he is telling the players to stay on the field?'

The Kuwaitis narrowly lost their last game in Bilbao to a strangulated English side which had done rather better against the Czechs, the lithe and gifted Trevor Francis exulting in the excellent long passes of Tottenham's Glenn Hoddle, a highly gifted but enigmatic player who, after a fine debut and goal against Bulgaria, had been dropped by Greenwood with the lapidary words, 'Disappointment is part of football.'

But the major cataclysms of the opening round came in Group II where West Germany, losing, astonishingly, to Algeria, then came to what was scarcely a gentleman's agreement with Austria, whom they beat 1–0 with an early headed goal by Hrubesch in a match which was a travesty of effort and football, one which threw into stark relief the weaknesses of the reorganised tournament. The Algerians had every right to make their bitter protest, every reason to feel more bitter still when they were waved aside.

The truth is, however, that after their superb beginning in Gijon, the Algerians ran out of steam against Austria, could not master the clever, strong, experienced attackers Hans Krankl and Schachner, and were beaten 2–0. Clever Lakhder Belloumi, African Footballer of the Year, had an excellent game against the Germans. He created the first goal after fifty-three minutes with a chip over the burly goalkeeper Schumacher, Majder scoring, and himself got the winner made by the speedy Assad; the Algerian wingers set Germany's defence many problems throughout. Yet Jupp Derwall, the bewildered German manager, had some reason to murmur afterwards, 'I just don't understand.' In torrid heat, his team had had far more of the play, gaining sixteen corners against four.

So to the disgraceful game in Gijon, again, when the West Germans and Austrians had their *Anschluss*; and the World Cup Committee did nothing. Michel Hidalgo suggested they be given the Nobel Peace

Prize; the French manager had come to take notes on the Austrians, whom France would meet. He did not take a single one.

It was the Brazilians who, in this first phase, excited and electrified everybody, their wonderful midfield play compensating for the lack of truly good forwards: there was no substitute for Reinaldo, the immensely gifted young centre-forward sabotaged again by knee injuries. The voo-doo drumming wife of Bob 'Dynamite' Roberto drummed away, his rival Careca was hurt and sent home, but Roberto wasn't the answer. The benign surprise was Falcao, ignored four years previously by Coutinho, brought in after a fine season with Roma, and used on tour because it was known Cerezo would be suspended for the opening game. So gloriously did the strong, quick, intelligent, adventurous Falcao play that he could not be left out. The four-man midfield gave opportunities to him and the other talented three to break often into attack.

The opening game against Russia, in Seville, though abominably refereed by Lamo Castillo of Spain, who denied two plain penalties to the Russians and one to the Brazilians, was of the highest order; one of the best of the competition. Russia took the lead when Valdir Peres, latest in the line of inept Brazilian keepers, allowed Bal's long shot to bounce gently through his palsied arms. But the sheer exuberant skill and originality of the Brazilians was not to be gainsaid. A quarter of an hour from time, the loping Socrates, tirelessly ubiquitous, now in the firing line, now covering for Junior, his attacking left-back, struck the equaliser with a stupendous shot. An equally fine one by Eder, after Falcao had dummied, swerved in to give Brazil victory. The Russians, under the old Dynamo centre-forward Constantin Beskov, eternal revenant, had played well; but not quite well enough.

The Scots were their usual blend of talent and error. They, too, main-tained their tradition of inadequate goalkeeping. Four years after his fail-ures in Cordoba, Scotland still hadn't found anybody better than Alan Rough. They could hardly fail to beat the clumsy New Zealanders, though after going into a three goal lead, they managed to give away two goals before collecting themselves. The goal scoring ability of the Ipswich midfielder, John Wark, forever stealing into good positions, two of which he exploited, was their chief attribute.

Jock Stein warned them there would be no gifts against Brazil in Seville; nor were there. The Brazilians played gloriously well to win 4–1, but the Scots made a rousing game of it in heat which eventually exhausted them. They even took the lead after eighteen minutes with a magnificent goal by their right-back, David Narey, bursting through an astonished Brazilian defence to score with a fine shot after clever preparatory work by Hartford and Wark. But even a five man Scottish midfield could not extinguish the fires of the Brazilians. A typical, beautifully swerved free kick from outside the box by Zico curved round the wall and Alan Rough for a thirty-second-minute equalising goal.

Three minutes after half-time, Oscar came up from centre-back to leap above the Scots defence and head Junior's corner past Rough. 'From then on,' said Stein afterwards, 'we were really chasing the game.'

They never caught it. Eder, the erratic but sometimes devastating winger, lobbed Rough elegantly for the third goal, Socrates neatly turned a ball to Falcao, who shot in off the post for the fourth.

So Scotland had to beat the Russians in Malaga to qualify; and how very close they came to it. Joe Jordan, in his third World Cup, was brought back into the team to lend his robust methods; Dalglish, also playing his third World Cup, a disappointment once again, dropped out. Graeme Souness of Liverpool worked with great flair and industry in midfield, scoring a coruscating individual goal worthy of the best Brazilians; but weak goalkeeping and a bizarre defensive collision condemned the Scots to a 2–2 draw, and elimination.

An error by the usually immaculate Tbilisi defender, Chivadze, gave Jordan his opening goal after fifteen minutes. Steve Archibald charged down his clearance, Jordan scored from twelve yards. But Chivadze atoned by equalising after Rough had saved from Gavrilov, and another Tbilisi man, the elusive Shengelia, gave Russia the lead eight minutes from the end. Souness' marvellous goal squared the score, but it was not enough.

Northern Ireland, in the meantime, were surpassing themselves. Spain, favourites in the Valencia group, benefited from some ludicrous refereeing decisions, and at least one FIFA official, interviewed on television, admitted how important it was for the World Cup's finances that Spain should stay in the tournament.

Violent, unpunished play by Barcelona at the huge Nou Camp stadium in the Cupwinners' Cup had led to well justified fears that Spain would play it rough and hard without much let or hindrance. Their team, under the naturalised Uruguayan, José Santamaria, had pitifully little to offer, its two key players, the midfielder Zamora and the winger Juanito, being both out of form.

Spain began abominably in Valencia against Honduras, who, with Costly defiant in defence and Gilberto, a Spanish league player, skilful in midfield, horrified them with a seventh-minute goal by Telaya. Dull, blunt, baffled by Honduras' orderly defence and neat breakaways, the Spaniards could do little but fling themselves down and appeal for penalties, eventually getting and converting one through their quick little winger, Lopez Ufarte, after sixty-six minutes. A humiliation.

In Saragossa the following day, Northern Ireland boldly brought in the barely 17-year-old Norman Whiteside, a Manchester United centre-forward who thus became the youngest player ever to figure in the World Cup Finals, and held the fancied Yugoslavs to a goalless draw. Whiteside, never overawed or intimidated by any occasion or opposition, played with his characteristic aggression and courage; he was booked in the second half. But the Irish also had skill in midfield in Martin O'Neill and Sammy McIlroy, while Gerry Armstrong, no more than a Second Division reserve centre-forward with Watford, emerged as a surprisingly dangerous and effective right-winger.

Spain could thank Lund, the Danish referee, for their 2–1 win against Yugoslavia; he gave them a fourteenth-minute penalty, this time converted by Juanito for a foul (admittedly a bad and cynical one) clearly committed outside the box. Moreover, Ufarte missed the first spot kick, Juanito then succeeding him to score. Pantelic, the Yugoslav keeper, had, it must be said, clearly moved.

Honduras went next day to Saragossa to hold the Irish as they had held the Spaniards. Gerry Armstrong scored after only ten minutes, after McIlroy sent an in-swinging free kick against the bar, but the Irish lost their grip on the game and Laing, the substitute, equalised on the hour, a mere two minutes after he had taken the field.

Four days later, they confronted Spain in Valencia and, against all the odds, gallantly beat them with another goal by Gerry Armstrong; one of the most remarkable results of the competition. For their pains, the Irish were kicked, intimidated, and given nothing by a lamentable referee, Ortiz of Paraguay. Making light of that, the intense heat, and the ludicrous expulsion of Donaghy simply for pushing an opponent away, when so much worse had been allowed, the Irish still prevailed.

The closest the Irish came to losing this match, it might be said, was when they almost missed their flight from Saragossa. So dehydrated were Sammy McIlroy and Sammy Nelson that it took them more than two hours to produce specimens for the drug test.

Gerry Armstrong, nicknamed 'Don quick quote' by Sammy Nelson for his facility with the Press, was again the scorer after forty-seven minutes. Billy Hamilton, the powerful Burnley centre-forward, went roaring up the right. Luis Arconada, the much lauded Spanish goalkeeper, strangely out of form in the World Cup, merely pushed out his cross; Armstrong banged the ball in. But though the Yugoslavs beat Honduras 1–0 with still another penalty, by Vladimir Petrovic, Spain sneaked into the second round.

In Group III, Argentina and Maradona woke up after their demise against the Belgians. Maradona was irresistible, displaying his whole, vast catalogue of talents. Hungary, who had volleyed home ten goals against El Salvador, three of them by Kiss, who played only the last thirty-four minutes, were outclassed. Maradona scored two of the goals, Diaz didn't play, and Hungary scored only after the Argentines were four ahead. Suddenly, Menotti's team looked as if it might keep its Cup.

Not least because the Belgians were plainly flagging. Astonishingly, the Salvadorean team which had conceded ten against Hungary gave them a long, hard run for their money, succumbing to a single goal by the blond Coeck, scored after eighteen minutes with a shot which the keeper, Mora, should have saved. True, El Salvador played a massed defence, but Gonzalez, a fast and eager forward, still gave the Belgians some awkward moments. In the concluding game of the Belgians and Hungarians, the latter needed only a 1–0 win to qualify on goal diffe rence, but got a 1–1 draw, Czerniatynski eventually equalising Varga's first-half goal. Belgium were through.

It was now that Italy would take wing. When they literally did so, flying to Barcelona for the second round, Federico Sordillo, the new Football Federation President who'd bitterly criticised the team after Braga, told Enzo Bearzot that his job was safe after the World Cup. Bearzot replied that he didn't want it if he was to be stabbed in the back. The allusion was clear. His 'Brutus', the serpentine Italo Allodi, a wheeler-dealer of the transfer market and friend of referees, mysteriously placed in charge of the national coaching centre at Coverciano, had long been the foe. Indeed, it was from a managers' conference in Coverciano that a pipsqueak Second Division coach from Varese violently assailed Bearzot, saying that all Italian managers should repudiate him and his methods. Allodi would in due course be eased out; but nobody at this point gave Italy a prayer of winning the World Cup.

Were they not drawn in the same group as Maradona's Argentina; and with a Brazilian team which had played the best World Cup football since Brazil themselves took the trophy in 1970? Total Football might virtually be dead, Brazil might lack a centre-forward—the burly, black, volcanic Serginho looked inept by comparison with his midfield—but the attacking powers not only of the midfield but of defenders like Junior were immense. There was, however, some slight doubt whether those defenders could defend as well as they attacked.

The other, salient, factor was that Italy finally found themselves obliged, by the exigencies of the competition, to come out and score goals. The Brazilians do that naturally; it was Coutinho's attempt to restrain them which made them so poor in 1978. Italians are natural ball players, attackers, but the brute sterility of their Championship obscures the fact. What nobody could know or predict was that Paolo Rossi would suddenly burst into form.

No England player did so. The pulled muscle which sharply reduced the effectiveness of Rummenigge, the noises of dissension

which came, as always, from the West German camp—where the
manager, as always, was criticised not only by players but by his own
assistant—gave them a manifest chance in their first match. Craven
tactics threw it away.

They were perfectly, if unwittingly, summed up next day by the hapless, thin-skinned Ron Greenwood at the training camp outside Madrid
in Navacerreda. He was astonished, he said, that none of the journalists present had singled out one of England's main achievements in the
previous day's goalless draw at the Bernabeu Stadium. Silence; till
Greenwood triumphantly explained, 'We didn't let Kaltz get in any
crosses.' Silence, again. England had excelled; to the extent that they
had managed to prevent the West German right-back from putting the
ball into their goalmouth! When Bearzot heard about it after the World
Cup, he smiled and said that in the Final, his team simply hadn't
worried about Kaltz.

It was indeed a dreary game. Bryan Robson, clearly far from wholly
fit, had a good nineteenth-minute header which Harald Schumacher
turned over the bar, Rummenigge actually hit the bar five minutes
from the end, Paul Breitner had one marvellous run down the right,
another down the left, but it was a sterile evening. With the blond
Foerster brothers tackling furiously, to the eclipse both of Francis and
the largely ineffectual Paul Mariner, with Uli Stielike there to intercept, or if necessary foul, behind them, England were no more effective than West Germany. Littbarski was belatedly brought on in the
second half but the giant Hrubesch, to his unconcealed fury, was not
brought on at all. There was no Brooking to get hold of the English
midfield; nor was Glenn Hoddle used, when his passes might have
created an opening or two.

Not to use him even in the last, decisive, game at Bernabeu against
Spain, when the industrious little right-winger Stevie Coppell had to
withdraw, seemed sheer self-defeating folly. Instead, Mariner kept his
place and the quick Tony Woodcock was picked in a three man attack;
Brooking and, of all people, Keegan were suddenly thrown on after
sixty-three minutes. Brooking, hardly picked up for twenty minutes,
made such a difference that you wondered what would have happened
had he been able to play before. He'd been secretly sent to Germany for
a futile back operation. Keegan, embarrassingly rusty, missed the easiest of headed chances right in front of goal, finally to cook England's
goose. He'd been secretly sent to Germany for a futile back operation.

The Spaniards, who had lost 2–1 to West Germany, Arconada's feeble
goalkeeping betraying them again, were surely there to be taken. But an
England team in which Howe's careful negativity was not complemented
by Greenwood's supposed (long gone) attacking flair, was simply not
bright or good enough.

The Spaniards began as uneasily as might have been expected, yet they had at least three fine chances in the game to score. Miguel Alonso missed one in each half, Satrustegui another, after he had dribbled through the English defence. But none of the misses was as appalling as Keegan's, six minutes after he had taken the field, and Bryan Robson put the ball on his head. By contrast, Brooking, too, had earlier made a fine chance when he turned his man, but when he shot, Arconada, almost perversely, made one of the few fine saves he brought off throughout the tournament. So England were out, and West Germany went on.

Northern Ireland went out, too, but with considerably more glory even though their eventual fate was to concede, exhausted, four goals to France just as they had done in 1958. Austria were their initial opponents in Atletico Madrid's Calderon Stadium. The heat was suffocating, but Ireland would surely have won the game were it not for a serious defensive error: failure to clear an easy ball enabling Austria, early in the second half, to equalise the goal strongly headed by Billy Hamilton after a characteristic slalom down the right by Gerry Armstrong (who said, afterwards, that the way the Austrian defenders stood square on facilitated his task).

Made more effective by the arrival of their substitutes, especially the lively Kurt Weltzl in attack, Austria took the lead in the grinding heat through the other substitute, Hintermaier, driving in a free kick pushed to him by Herbert Prohaska. But another header by the resilient Billy Hamilton, looking anything but the Third Division footballer he'd been the previous season, gave the Irish the draw which was the least they deserved.

Since Austria had lost their match against France to a superb free kick driven home by the slender Genghini, they were out. And so alas were the Irish, after France, with Michel Platini at last in his most commanding form, beat them 4–1 at the Calderon.

France still lacked a decent goalkeeper, but Marius Trésor, at sweeper, had come emphatically back into commanding form, and there was so much talent in the midfield that it was second only to Brazil's. The black Tigana had been brought in with Genghini to give it greater drive and elegance, while Platini was able to float dangerously and gracefully between midfield and attack where Dominique Rocheteau, now more centre-forward than winger, and either Soler or Six, were able to capitalise on many chances made.

Giresse and Platini showed that each could be either executioner or prompter when, after thirty-three minutes, Platini got to the by-line and pulled the ball back for the stocky little Giresse to score. The Irish might have ridden the punch but, just after half-time, a bad error by McCreery let Rocheteau through on the left, and the 37-year-old Pat Jennings compounded it by letting Rocheteau's far from irresistible low shot fly between him and his right-hand post.

A sinuous run and a clever cross by Tigana, a flying header by Rocheteau, brought yet a third French goal. The splendid young Whiteside, shrugging off the possibility of an easy, laid off ball from the left, taking on and beating his opponents, crossed to confuse Ettori and give Armstrong the Irish goal; but Giresse headed, untypically, a fourth to France. Ireland were out, just as in 1958, exhausted but honoured.

Italy's first game in Barcelona, at the smaller Español Stadium where the fates had whimsically decreed that they play, while far less popular games took place in massive Nou Camp, was against Argentina. To the general surprise, they won it in style, with one major proviso: the appalling excesses of Claudio Gentile, set to mark—in every sense of the word, it seemed—Maradona, were a blemish on the match, the tournament and Italy's eventual success.

The curious blind spot which led Enzo Bearzot to indulge the brutalities of Romeo Benetti in Argentina, now led him to be similarly indulgent to those of Gentile who, clobbering, holding, hacking and impeding Maradona out of the game, may be said to have won Italy the match. The accessory after the fact was the atrocious Rumanian referee, Nicolae Rainea, who emulated the three wise monkeys.

After a terrible first half, in which there was but one shot of note, executed by Ramon Diaz, turned over the bar by Dino Zoff, Italy at last came out to play in the second half. Rossi was still out of form, still to explode. Indeed, on the occasion of the second Italian goal, he would miss the simplest opportunity. But those around him, encouraged by the eclipse of the ill-treated Maradona, dominated the second half.

Bruno Conti, the fast, resilient little winger from Nettuno, on the Mediterranean coast, was in lively form. He it was who began the movement for the first goal. Giancarlo Antognoni produced one of his jewelled passes and Marco Tardelli, even more effective than he had been four years earlier in Argentina, struck the ball home.

The big, inelegant but always willing Graziani started the move for the second goal. He put Rossi clean through, Rossi surprisingly failed to beat Fillol, but when his shot rebounded Conti retrieved it on the left to pull the ball back and enable the attacking full-back Cabrini to score.

A goal six minutes from time by Passarella, a dubious one from a free kick when the Italians were still organising their wall, was all Argentina got from the game. It may well have been a bad mistake for Menotti to send Maradona—who once grazed the post from a free kick—so far upfield and into Gentile's clutches, but he was entitled to expect protection which was never forthcoming from Rainea.

Brazil, in turn, then beat Argentina in another World Cup meeting between these implacable rivals. Though they scored after only eleven minutes, when Eder's insidious free kick came down from the underside of the bar and Zico thumped the ball in, it was an hour or so before Brazil became truly dominant. Argentina had their best period early in the second half, when they seemed likely to get an equaliser.

Gradually, the superb Brazilian midfield took over the game. One of Zico's killing passes set the excellent Falcao free on the right. The black Serginho rose to the cross and headed in, thus briefly giving the lie to the Brazilian critic who had said, 'When Serginho plays, the ball is square.' There was still a third Brazilian goal to come, scored by the rampant full-back Junior, exploiting a still more dazzling pass by Zico.

A wild, disgraceful foul by Maradona on Batista, the foul of a spoiled, frustrated boy, had Maradona sent off five minutes from the end. Passarella should have gone earlier for an equally spiteful, painful foul on Zico, whom Batista replaced. A minute from the end, Ramon Diaz gave Argentina back a little dignity with a goal, but it was small consolation.

Now, it seemed sure, Brazil would sweep Italy aside and qualify for the Final, where the Cup would be theirs for the taking. It did not happen. This was where Paolo Rossi came suddenly and sensationally to life; this was the game which 'should' have been the World Cup Final. The game in which Brazil's glorious midfield, put finally to the test, could not make up for the deficiencies behind and in front of it.

It took only five minutes for Rossi to score, and put Brazil on the ropes. The Italians, indeed, resumed where they had left off. As in the second half of their match against Argentina, they were untypically but exuberantly committed to attack, and they scored through Rossi after only five minutes. Valdir Peres, the Brazilian keeper, had cause to reflect how prescient he had been when he said before the match that his chief fear was lest Rossi should suddenly come to life.

The goal was simple in execution, but showed Rossi's amazing ability to scent a chance no one else would have imagined, to take on (almost) protective colouring; and to put the chance away. This, significantly, was the first of his several headed goals, although he is only a small fellow. But these headed goals were not those of a Hrubesch, a Kocsis, a Dean or a Lawton. They were tucked neatly away because Rossi had timed his run so perfectly that the defence was caught unawares.

On this occasion, Rossi, who only the previous minute had failed to control a ball in the penalty box, glided in Cabrini's immaculate cross from the left, after the full-back had been sent away by Conti from the right.

Only six minutes later, however, the Brazilians were level. Zico, whose fate it was to be delivered to Gentile's tender mercies, and to have his shirt ripped off him for his pains, eluded him this time and, with one of his beautifully angled passes, released Socrates. The shot, with so narrow an angle, was remarkable; a bullet between Zoff and the post.

Despite Gentile's presence and a certain lack of response around him, with the very notable exception of Falcao, Zico was shining. After twenty-four minutes, however, a further lapse in Brazil's defence brought another goal: for Rossi. A careless pass under no pressure at all by Toninho Cerezo to Junior was intercepted and exploited by a grateful Rossi. 2–1 for Italy.

Once again the Brazilians, who needed only a draw to get through, seemed to have got it. Twenty-three minutes into the second half, after Rossi had wasted a chance for Italy, Junior found Falcao, who dribbled across the penalty area, saw a gap, shot, and beat Zoff. 2–2: a magnificent left-footed shot which set the seal on Falcao's remarkable performance.

Brazil took Serginho off and brought on the right-winger Paulo Isidoro—'Now the ball is round again,' said a Brazilian critic—but Zoff's fine goalkeeping denied them. Abraham Klein, the Israeli referee, kept the game admirably under control, but should really have given a penalty at either end. Zico had faded, but Giancarlo Antognoni was in admirable form in the Italian midfield, once giving Cabrini a solid opportunity which he spurned.

After seventy-four minutes, Zoff almost lost a ball from Cerezo, but recovered to snatch it away from Paulo Isidoro. In the very next minute, Italy had won the game. Again, it was Rossi's electric opportunism which did the trick. Brazil could only half clear a corner, Tardelli drove the ball back, it broke to Rossi, and into the net it inevitably went. A final, splendid save by Zoff, flinging himself at a header by Cerezo, and Brazil were out. Falcao was so distressed that he wanted to give up the game, and certainly had no will at all to resume playing for Roma, whom in fact he would help to win their Championship.

Poland qualified in the other Barcelona group, which was of a far lower standard, immeasurably less dramatic. The Russians went badly off the boil, not least their famous blond Ukrainian striker, Oleg Blokhin, once European Footballer of the Year, who was accused by his manager of talking rather than playing.

In the opening game, the Poles, with Boniek in magnificent form playing as an out and out striker, beat Belgium 3–0, all the goals coming from Boniek himself. Everything he did all evening seemed to succeed, whether it be a shot, a header or a pass, while he was well abetted by the durable Lato, a midfielder in Belgium by now, though a hero, as right-winger, of 1974.

Vandenbergh did once volley against the bar, but in general Belgium gave the heavy Polish defence surprisingly little trouble. Lato made a superb goal for Boniek after only four minutes: a run, a pulled-back cross, an immaculate first-time shot into the roof of the net.

Certainly the Belgians seriously missed the commitment, drive and exuberant overlapping of their bearded right-back, Gerets, who had suffered a bad head injury in their third game. But something else seemed radically to have gone amiss with the side which had done so well two years earlier in Italy, reaching the Final of the Nations Cup. Van Moer did play against Poland but he was, perhaps inevitably, no longer the fine force he been in 1980 and François Van Der Elst took his place after half-time.

'My first goal after three minutes killed the Belgians,' said Boniek afterwards, 'and they just lost control of the game. They made incredible mistakes, leaving wide gaps in defence as they concentrated on attacks down our crowded middle.'

Boniek got his excellent second goal after twenty-six minutes when Buncol headed Kupcewicz's cross back to him, and he himself headed skilfully into the goal. His hat trick was achieved after eight minutes of the second half, Lato enabling him to beat the famous Belgian offside trap and score with some ease. A bad, bleak night for Belgium, who next lost to the Russians.

This time, fielding a much changed team, however, they did a great deal better than in the first game. Indeed, but for two very bad misses by the usually prolific Vandenbergh in the second half, they would have had a deserved win. Russia's nervousness and uncertainty were personified by the usually adept Shengelia, for whom little would go right. Even their winning goal, three minutes after half-time, was a freakish affair. Yuri Gavrilov got to the by-line and pulled the ball back. The Armenian, Oganesyan, snatched at his volley but the ball went home.

This meant that the old, deadly rivals, Poland and Russia, contested the semi-final place. There could have been no finer, more depressingly apt commentary on the stupid organisation of the tournament than the moment when, late in the second half, Poland's Smolarek received a good through pass, but instead of racing for goal dribbled deliberately into a corner, where he hung on to the ball to waste time. Poland needed only a draw and a draw, to the infinite boredom of all who watched the game, was what they got.

In the first half, Poland pulled forwards back into the midfield and battened down hatches to resist the Russian offensive. Having succeeded, they themselves began to throw men forward and occasionally threaten goals, but the fine, careless rapture of the Peruvian and Belgian successes was, perhaps not surprisingly, no longer to be found. Blokhin winged his way through the match, the Georgian full-back Sulakvelidze struck a good chance over the bar, Oganesyan missed another, to the manifest disgust of Blokhin. Dassaev, the talented young Russian goalkeeper, made a couple of capable saves from Matysik and Boniek, and the game petered out as a draw. Alas for Poland and Boniek, he had foolishly got himself cautioned a second time, which put him out of the semi-final against Italy at Nou Camp.

Perhaps he would have had another frozen game, overawed by the presence of his future Juventus colleagues, but the fact was that without him, Poland were little threat to an Italian team now playing immeasurably better than they had in the initial game at Vigo. Above all Rossi, anonymous that day, was now in formidable form. He would cleverly score both the Italian goals.

With Gentile, like Boniek, suspended, Italy boldly kept in the team the 18-year-old Internazionale defender Bergomi, who had been thrown in at the deep end against Brazil and performed with remarkable coolness. Here, not for the first time, was proof that the much maligned Enzo Bearzot was indeed prepared to give youth its fling; just as he had in Argentina, where he picked Rossi and Cabrini for the tournament.

Bergomi was very much the protégé of his captain, the veteran keeper Dino Zoff, whom he idolised. Capped for the first time at only seventeen, in April 1981 against East Germany in Leipzig, it was still an ordeal for Bergomi to step on to the field in so vital a World Cup match, against Brazil. Another of his idols, curiously enough, was Gianni Rivera, from whom he now took the record of being the youngest Italian to play in a World Cup; as a boy, he had supported Milan, rather than Inter.

'I can't do it any more,' he complained helplessly to Zoff, soon after he had come on the field in Barcelona. 'I can't breathe, my legs are trembling.' Zoff reassured him; and Bergomi returned, encouraged, to the task of marking the huge black Brazilian centre-forward Serginho; one he accomplished so well that, as we know, Serginho was eventually substituted.

Now, against the Poles, he was first assigned to the quick, evasive little inside-forward, Buncol, then to Lato, who, in the absence of Boniek, was used as a striker. This might have been an excellent idea eight years earlier when he and Gadocha caused such havoc in opposing defences and Lato himself finished as top scorer of the German tournament, but those days were long gone.

Lato's forte now was lurking in the midfield with intent, away from the close marking, making chances for his strikers, and occasionally breaking forward into the action himself. Once picked up, there was little he could do.

But if the Poles couldn't create and couldn't attack, there was one thing they could abundantly do; and that was kick. On this occasion at least, the biter was bit. Without Gentile, and with little facing them in attack, the Italian defence seldom transgressed. The Poles, by contrast, took no prisoners, and one of their victims was the unfortunate Giancarlo Antognoni, whose injured foot would cause him to miss the Final at the very time when, after so many controversial years in the Italian national team, he seemed truly to be running into form, to be reaping the full fruits of his fine technique and quick, strategic mind.

Only twice in the game, at a distance of fully half an hour, did the Poles carry any threat to the Italian goal. After thirty-four minutes, a free kick by Kupcewicz scraped the outside of a post. After sixty-four, Buncol got in a header which Zoff took with no trouble at all. The Poles failed utterly to free Smolarek, their one real hope of goals in the absence of Boniek. Their midfield players tended to hold the ball too long, thus denying Smolarek, well marked by the Italian stopper Collovati of Milan, the chance to burst into his dangerous, incisive runs. Gentile simply wasn't needed, though Gaetano Scirea, playing more cautiously than was his wont at sweeper, hung back to make quite sure nothing went wrong rather than breaking upfield as was his usual style.

The first Italian goal arrived after twenty-two minutes. Antognoni drove a free kick into a mass of bodies in the penalty area from the right. Rossi it was who got to the ball with the inside of his right foot—almost, indeed, with his heel—deflecting it neatly past Mlynarczyk.

His second goal was a great deal more spectacular. It came after seventy-three minutes and was begun by the long, lanky Internazionale centre-forward Altobelli, nicknamed Spillone, the Big Pin. Having come on only four minutes earlier as substitute for the injured Graziani, Altobelli cleverly sent Bruno Conti away on the left: each, by an odd chance, had once played with the little southern Third Division club of Latina.

Conti, perfectly at home on either wing, sped away and launched a long, perfect centre. Paolo Rossi, who had once again rendered himself invisible to the defence, ran in from the right, met the ball on the far post and headed inexorably home. By comparison with the two previous, hectic, dramatic games against the South Americans, it had been a peaceful passage for Italy.

Peaceful was the last word you could use about the remarkable semi-final between France and West Germany in Seville. The French were clearly now in form. It was odd to reflect how very nearly they had gone out of the World Cup in Valladolid in their last game of the first round against the Czechs, who had played poorly throughout and had been reduced to ten men when, in a match ineptly refereed by the Italian, Casarin, Vizek was sent off for a stupid foul on Soler. Equally stupid was the foul by Bossis which gave the Czechs and Panenka an equaliser from the penalty spot five minutes from time when they should long since have been dead and buried. But there was still time for Nehoda to get in a header which the little right-back Amoros, shrewd enough to pop up on the left-hand post, headed off the line.

Platini that day had been, but for one fine run, unrecognisably poor. Now, despite trouble with an injury, he was in fine fettle; the midfield was flourishing, and as an attacking force the French team looked substantially better than West Germany, badly hampered by Hansi Muller's knee injury and Rummenigge's pulled muscle, not to mention the absence of Bernd Schuster.

Jupp Derwall was still under severe criticism. 'What this team needs,' said Horst Hrubesch, 'is an iron hand.' Well, that was just what it used to have when little Sepp Herberger was in charge, but what it had never had since his tall, gentle successor, Helmut Schoen, had taken over and changed the whole pattern and attitude of play. The huge excitements of Total Football, so superbly played by the West Germans in the Nations Cups of 1972 and 1976, the World Cup of 1974, might be a memory, but the basic design was the same.

But the defeat by the Algerians, the shoddy accommodation with Austria, lay like a shadow across the team's performance in the present World Cup: and worse, in Seville, was to come. If Stielike's injured spine had not prevented him being a highly effective sweeper, Muller's knee clearly rendered him inoperative, and took away from the midfield the only player but Breitner capable of springing surprise. As for Rummenigge, the muscle he had pulled—for the first time in his life—on June 16 was so far from being healed that it was known he could not play the whole semi-final, if any of it.

Still, Littbarski, after being strangely and controversially left out of most of the England game, was back in the side and in form while the massive, blond Briegel, a human Panzer division in himself, another revelation of the 1980 Nations Cup, was formidably versatile, though as a back-four man now rather than the midfielder he had so effectively been in Italy.

The defence, indeed, was generally extremely strong. Schumacher rivalled Dassaev as the best goalkeeper of the competition, Karl-Heinz Foerster was an implacable centre-half and if Kaltz was a better right-back going forward than when staying in defence, his value as an overlapper was considerable.

In the event, Derwall restored to the side the Hamburg inside-forward Magath, who had not been especially effective so far, while Rummenigge would not appear till five minutes into extra time. At centre-forward Fischer, the smaller, quicker man, was preferred to Hrubesch, as he had been against Spain, the huge Hamburg player getting on only after seventy-two minutes in place of Magath. Perhaps Jupp Derwall consoled himself that on the other two occasions West Germany had won the World Cup, they had each time lost in the first round, just as they had in Spain.

For the French, the choice of their team was much easier; though like Brazil, they did have something of an embarrassment of midfield talent. Platini, Genghini, Tigana and Giresse were all chosen; four artists, running the risk that there was no real hard man, no tackler, no Tardelli, shall we say, among them. Ettori played in goal; an inadequate figure, but France were no better off for goalkeepers than Brazil . . . or Scotland.

The heavy Lopez, sweeper by choice, forced by the presence of Trésor to play as an unwilling and permeable stopper, did not start the game, but he would come on for the maltreated Battiston, himself a substitute for Genghini, after fifty-nine minutes. Up front, Dominique Rocheteau would be partnered this time not by Soler but by a survivor of 1978, Didier Six. It had been expected that if Six did play it would be in place of Rocheteau, who had strained the outer ligaments of his right knee, in the match against Northern Ireland.

Luck, by their own journalists' admission, had been with France. Losing that first game to England in hot Bilbao had been a blessing in disguise. They had finished second in the group which had placed them in Madrid with Austria and Northern Ireland, rather than West Germany, who awaited them now, and Spain. Absent against Austria, Platini's impressive return against Ireland laid to rest the whispers that the team played better without him and his enormous, manifold talents as goal maker and goal scorer, his beautifully struck free kicks, perfected in hours of practice shooting past lines of life-sized wooden dummies.

The match may be said to have turned on a horrifying incident in the fifty-seventh minute. At that point the score was level at 1–1, as it would be till extra time. Patrick Battiston, who had just come on as substitute for Genghini, raced through the middle on to a beautifully executed pass which turned the defence. Out of his goal raced the burly Schumacher. Battiston beat him to the ball, but Schumacher thundered into him, brutally smashing him to the ground with a blow of the forearm, and callously leaving him, minus two teeth, so badly hurt that there were fears he would die; fears compounded by the idiocy of the Seville police who had banned the Red Cross from the pitch. Battiston had to lie there for three long minutes before he could

be treated. It was this incident, above all, which would make most neutral observers supporters of Italy in the World Cup Final. No penalty
was given.

The French were obliged once more to reorganise their side, bringing
Lopez on for Battiston. Schumacher should undoubtedly have been sent
off, which would almost surely have condemned the Germans to defeat,
but Corver, the Dutch referee, had not seen the incident and his linesman, incomprehensibly, did not enlighten him. As an embittered Michel
Hidalgo, the French manager, complained afterwards, he was also obliged
to use up his remaining substitute so that he did not have a fresh man to
send on in extra time.

It was the Germans who took the lead after seventeen minutes. Though
Giresse had been quite eclipsing Breitner in midfield, Breitner it was who
suddenly and cleverly sent Fischer through. The centre-forward's shot
rebounded from the knees of Ettori, but little Pierre Littbarski, following
up, drove the ball into the goal.

It took the French ten minutes to gain a merited equaliser to this goal.
A cleverly floated free kick by Giresse had the German defence in turmoil: Bernd Foerster fouled Rocheteau, and Platini, first planting a con-
ciliatory kiss on the ball, then put it on the penalty spot, sent Schumacher
the wrong way, and scored.

Ettori, belying his previous form, rose to the occasion when his
colleagues seemed angered and unsettled—not surprisingly—by
Schumacher's outrageous foul. His two excellent saves saw to it that the
game went into extra time.

Platini and Giresse were still in lambent form, but the necessary
reshuffle, the arrival of Rummenigge, ultimately gave West Germany
an edge. Marius Trésor gave fresh hope in the second minute of extra
time when he acrobatically—and quite unmarked—converted another
teasing free kick by Alain Giresse. Six minutes later, though Rummenigge
was now on, Giresse seemed to have made matters sure. Splendidly
served by Platini, his powerful shot beat Schumacher and went in
off a post.

The Germans, however, as England might well remember from
Leon in 1970, are seldom so dangerous in a World Cup as when they
are two goals behind. After 112 minutes, Derwall's gamble in putting
on Karl-Heinz Rummenigge abundantly paid off. A chip from
Littbarski, a tap by Rummenigge, and the ball was home. Six minutes
later, West Germany, against all odds and logic, were level. Bernd
Foerster crossed, the giant Hrubesch nodded back, and his fellow
centre-forward Klaus Fischer, the man who had kept him out of the
initial team, scored. A glorious shot from little Amoros came back from
the German bar.

So, abominably, irrationally and unforgivably, a World Cup semi-final would be decided, for the first time ever, on penalties. One hopes, without any great conviction, that it will also be the last. The excuse that time was of the essence hardly holds. It was the mindless organisation of the tournament which left *longueurs* between so many matches. But the manifold idiocies of World Cup committees should perhaps occasion no surprise by now.

Penalties, at all events—with their synthetic drama—it would be. Giresse, Kaltz, Amoros, Breitner and Rocheteau all scored. Next, Uli Stielike; but when the German sweeper shot, Jean-Luc Ettori saved. Stielike flung himself to the ground in despair; little Littbarski was the only one who came to console him.

Stielike, clinging to Littbarski, did not even watch as Didier Six took the next penalty; and Schumacher saved! Littbarski himself now scored. So, inevitably, did Platini; and Rummenigge. But when Maxime Bossis, the full-back, shot, Schumacher saved again; and it was all down to the next penalty, taken by none other than Horst Hrubesch, the man who had called Derwall a coward for leaving him out of the team without facing and telling him.

Hrubesch scored; and West Germany were in their fourth World Cup Final.

The taste, however, was exceedingly sour. Hidalgo, a man by nature quiet and moderate, furiously condemned Corver's flaccid refereeing. Both he and Platini insisted that Rummenigge's goal was an outrage: 'Scandalous', Platini called it, pointing out that both he and Giresse had been fouled before Rummenigge scored; he himself in a manner 'which must have been seen by everybody but the referee.' Hidalgo properly condemned Schumacher's vicious assault on Battiston. 'We have been eliminated brutally,' he insisted, 'I would say, scientifically.'

Now came the chaos of Seville airport, where already exhausted players had, as Hidalgo later complained, been obliged to sit on their suitcases while plane after plane took off. Paul Breitner made a scathing attack in his excellent Spanish—he had played for Real Madrid—on the gross ineptitude of the Spanish organisation. Whichever team had won would have been at a severe disadvantage against the Italians, who had not had to leave Barcelona, not had to play extra time, and not had to play in the evening.

Before the Final, a reprise of the extraordinary semi-final between West Germany and Italy in Mexico City twelve years before, there was the mammoth irrelevance of the third-place match, which took place, whimsically, in Alicante. Poland played without Smolarek, France without most of their team, including Platini, Giresse, Rocheteau and, of course and alas, Battiston, about whose injuries Schumacher spoke with such cold-blooded indifference that he cut a worse figure still. An eventual, clearly obligatory, visit to Battiston merely threw the goalkeeper's crass behaviour into still greater relief.

For what it mattered, Poland won the game 3–2, thus taking their second third place in the space of three World Cups. Girard, brought into the depleted French midfield, scored a fine individual goal after thirteen minutes, but the pitiful goalkeeping of Castaneda allowed first Szarmach, a hero of 1974, then Majewski, after the keeper missed a corner, to make the score 2–1 in the minutes before half-time.

Castaneda, in the depths of a nightmare, gave Kupcewicz a goal direct from a free kick immediately after half-time, and though Tigana's admirable pass launched Couriol for the second French goal seventeen minutes from the end, the Poles ran out winners.

Who would play in the Final? Rummenigge? Antognoni? Fischer? Hrubesch? Frantic attempts to get the unlucky Antognoni fit were in vain; when the teams took the field, the Fiorentina inside-forward was sitting behind the Press Box at the Bernabeu Stadium. In the event, Enzo Bearzot decided daringly, even if it may not at first have seemed so, not to attempt to replace Antognoni with a similar player—and who was there? Certainly not the still inexperienced Dossena and certainly not the pedestrian, defensive Marini—but to give the 18-year-old Bergomi another chance. Since Derwall, after immense *Sturm und Drang* in the German camp, decided to let Karl-Heinz Rummenigge start the game, Bearzot was able to put Bergomi on him. The young Inter defender's cool resourcefulness might have allowed him to dominate even a fully fit Rummenigge, but the hobbling player we saw in the Bernabeu Stadium presented him with an easy evening.

To the tender mercies of Gentile was confined, not Rummenigge, but the little winger Pierre Littbarski. The Germans chose Dremmler in their midfield again, Hansi Muller as a substitute who eventually came on for Rummenigge a mere nine minutes from the end, and Fischer rather than Hrubesch at centre-forward.

After the fiasco of Gonella's refereeing in Buenos Aires four years earlier, it was no reassurance to learn that the uncertain Brazilian, Senhor Coelho, would be given the job. The obvious choice was Abraham Klein, the Israeli who had made such an excellent job of the potentially cataclysmic Italy-Brazil game, just as he had made such a fine job of the Argentina-Italy game in the River Plate Stadium in the previous tournament. But the Referees' Committee, pleased with itself and as incompetent as ever, compromised pathetically by assigning Klein to . . . the replay. Which, in parenthesis, was scheduled for Barcelona, another decision calculated, if it were implemented, to create the maximum confusion given the insufficiency of Spanish administration and communications. Breitner had not been wrong.

Coelho had made a poor fist of refereeing the match between West

Germany and England on the same ground; there was no reason
to hope that he would do any better in the colossal tension of a
World Cup Final. Mean-spirited, over physical, negative, largely
unadventurous, a throwback to the times of Sepp Herberger rather than
to the more adventurous, open times of Helmut Schoen, the West
German team was well-equipped to retort to anything the Italians
threw at them in kind. So, predictably, we saw a wretched first half,
in which each team was chiefly concerned to stop the other playing.
True, the Italians squandered a penalty kick, but that was one of the
very few decent chances created in forty-five minutes which were
given their tone when Bruno Conti, almost immediately, fouled and
felled his man.

The best you could say for Senhor Coelho was that he wasn't as bad as
Signor Gonella, but then he did not have to compete with the frenzied
atmosphere of the River Plate Stadium, its huge crowd united behind the
home team.

Perhaps a fit Rummenigge would have scored as early as the fourth
minute. When Breitner centred and Fischer moved the ball on,
Rummenigge, turning on the ball, had perhaps more time than he
realised. His shot was hurried, and a bemused Italian defence was glad to
see it fly past the post.

Three minutes later Graziani was tackled and, falling, exacerbated
the shoulder injury which had forced him off the field in the semi-final
against Poland. Though Bearzot would clearly have preferred to use a
substitute much later, given the possibility of extra time, he knew
that he had the right man in waiting. On went the Big Pin, Altobelli,
who had done so well when he took Graziani's place against Poland.
He might not be so robust, but his technique and movement were
substantially better.

Gradually, the game began to be something rather more than a mosaic
of ill will and sullen fouling. After twenty-four minutes, one of those fouls,
a singularly futile one, gave the Italians a penalty. Altobelli crossed, little
Conti went in for the ball and the gigantic Briegel, his direct opponent,
lurched in and brought him down. A penalty, instantly and correctly
given. Up in the stand sat Antognoni, whose powerful right foot would
have taken it. Instead, it fell to the left foot of the left-back Cabrini who
sent his shot feebly wide of the post. It was a tribute to the morale of the
Italians, of Bearzot's benign influence over them, that they should not
then go to pieces.

The rest of the first half was eminently forgettable, though Stielike's
dreadful foul on Oriali, four minutes from half-time, is easily remembered. As the stocky little Inter midfielder, a busy, straightforward man
of all work, raced for goal, Stielike brought him down on the edge of
the box with a violent body check. It was a foul worthy of expulsion,

one which, in the context of the coming English season, would have led to automatic dismissal. But all the Italians got was a free kick of no value. Stielike, amazingly, was not even shown the yellow cautionary card.

The closest the Germans came to scoring was ten minutes earlier, when Fischer would have scored but for a splendid saving clearance by Collovati. A couple of minutes before half-time, Kaltz, who had frightened Greenwood to death but scarcely troubled Bearzot and Italy at all, finally got over a centre but Dremmler shot over the bar.

So to half-time and, it is said, a veritable *Götterdämmerung* in the West German dressing-room, with Stielike violently condemning the choice of the injured Rummenigge, and Rummenigge in turn allegedly asking another German player to hit him!

The game would finally and fortunately be unblocked after eleven minutes of the second half, and it was most appropriate that Rossi should be the scorer, Tardelli the very motor of the team in midfield, the man who took the initial free kick. Perhaps it was less expected that Gentile, who could always play good football when he wanted, should himself be centrally involved.

By an immense irony, it was a foul by Rummenigge—dropping deep into his own territory—on Oriali, who deserved some consolation, which made the goal possible. Tardelli very quickly and percipiently nudged the ball to Gentile on the right. Gentile's cross found the German defence uncharacteristically bemused. Past Altobelli and Cabrini it went, but not past Rossi. Once again, the little centre-forward had exquisitely timed his run. In he dashed from the left, untrammeled and unobserved, to head inexorably past Schumacher. Now, at least and at last, the Germans would have to come out looking for a goal; and one hoped the Italians would not retire into their shells to avoid one.

They didn't. The good, progressive habits briefly inculcated in Barcelona would endure. On the hour, Dremmler was booked for a foul on Oriali; ironic, again, when one considered what Stielike had disgracefully got away with. Dremmler lasted only another couple of minutes; then Derwall brought his sharpest critic, Horst Hrubesch, on. The Italians simply moved Collovati on to Hrubesch instead of Fischer and played on, untroubled, happy with the space that the increasingly anxious Germans were now vouchsafing them, making light of their lack of a midfield general in the steps of Antognoni, Rivera and Mazzola, and getting little trouble from Littbarski, locked in the bulldog grip of Gentile.

Hrubesch, quickly into the game, had a header pounced on by Zoff—better on his line than when it came to dealing with crosses, perhaps no surprise at 40 years of age. Then Zoff, under great pressure, grasped a cross by Briegel at the second attempt.

The killer goal came four minutes later, in the sixty-eighth minute. Conti began the movement, Scirea broke out of defence up the right to make the extra man, and sweetly exchanged passes with Paolo Rossi. Over came the ball and just as Tardelli seemed to have lost possession, he struck it with an acrobatic shot which tore past a wholly helpless Schumacher. It was a goal worthy to win a World Cup Final; and there was still another Italian goal to come.

Ten minutes from time, the massive Briegel goes thundering into the Italian penalty area, where he topples like a forest giant. The ball is played out to little Conti, who roars away up the right with inexhaustible energy—the energy, perhaps, conveyed by that muscle stimulant. More than half the length of the field he goes, till at last he pulls the ball across the German goal. The German defence is scattered to the winds. Altobelli, the Big Pin, coolly stops the ball, advances, and beats Schumacher in his own good time. 3–0.

By now, Hansi Muller is on, but it is not the Muller whom one knew and admired in 1980. Still, he it is, when Conti brings down Briegel on the left, who takes a free kick. The Italian defence fails to get it away and Paul Breitner, on what once was his home ground but by now must seem very alien territory, swoops to beat Zoff, and give Germany what may laughingly be described as a consolation goal.

Italy, as in 1970, have bested West Germany in a World Cup; though this time it is the Final, rather than the semi-final. There is time for Bearzot, sentimentally, to send on the veteran Franco Causio in place of Altobelli to give him a World Cup medal. Then the game is over, the Cup is Zoff's, and there is nothing left to do but for the ineffable Madrid police to club the photograhers who are trying to take pictures of the scene.

So the 1982 competition ended in a manner wholly inconceivable a mere couple of weeks before. That Italy deserved their trophy, that Paolo Rossi was the player of the tournament, that it would have been a sorry thing for the game had West Germany won; all this is quite undeniable. Yet the competition left behind many imponderables.

Predictably João Havelange, whose fault it chiefly was and who had wished his twenty-four-team monstrosity on the world, insisted that it had been a splendid success even if he could scarcely avoid rebuking the disgraceful Spanish organisation, the disgrace of Mundiespana, with their over-priced accommodation and their inept distribution of tickets. It was also fairly plain that Colombia would never be able to put on a twenty-four-team World Cup; but then, how many countries could? In due course the United States would lobby for the 1986 tournament, but it was Mexico who suddenly and—in terms of logic rather than advantage—inexplicably emerged as favourites to put it on again, despite the fact that they had had it in 1970, despite the horrors of high altitude, and the fact that the country was $80 million in the red.

Brazil had seemed, after the inevitable withdrawal of Colombia, the obvious choice, even if its debts were more than $100 million, but the bitter enmity between Havelange and the President of the Brazilian Football Federation, Giulite Coutinho, led, astonishingly, to Havelange setting his face against the tournament being played in his own country; and eventually having his way.

Havelange alone was not to blame for the twenty-four-team tournament. Artemio Franchi, the Italian President of UEFA, the European body, had been against it from the first, but he was betrayed by the European countries who pursued their own narrow advantage, enticed by the fact that most of them would have a double chance to qualify.

England were among those who slipped through because the field was enlarged, demonstrating that it was not merely the Afro-Asian bloc which benefited from the expansion.

It was significant that while various minor Third World countries gave a reasonable account of themselves, none of them survived beyond the third round. The victory of Algeria over West Germany was almost an historic one, but as we have seen, the Algerians quickly came down to earth against the Austrians. The pity of it was that the World Cup, no longer an elimination contest since 1938, could not reward such feats of giant killing with the qualification they clearly deserved.

The twenty-four-team complement meant that the World Cup dragged on for a weary month; the wearier because Spain was hit by an unpredictable heat wave, forcing some teams, such as Northern Ireland and Austria, to play in an afternoon heat of 110 degrees. No wonder Hidalgo of France complained as he did about the advantages offered to teams chosen heads of series, who did not have to travel out of their 'centre' cities.

Tactically, it was hard to draw many lessons from the World Cup. If Brazil were the 'moral' victors, they could scarcely complain about their defenestration by Italy; they had to blame their own sloppy defensive mistakes, their own inadequacies up front. In 1970, Brazil had won the World Cup despite a weak goalkeeper and an indifferent defence. But then, they had not only a superb midfield but a magnificent attack, with Pelé incomparable and wonderfully inventive; Tostao, a clever and resourceful centre-forward; Jairzinho the latest in what seemed an endless line of superlative outside-rights.

Suddenly, however, it dried up. Jairzinho himself had been at centre-forward in 1974, and at centre-forward, Tostao—or perhaps the unfortunate Reinaldo—seemed the last of the line.

It had been generally agreed that Argentina would never have won the

1978 World Cup anywhere but Argentina, and their disappointing performances in Spain gave fuel to such an argument. The fading of Kempes, the inability of young Diaz and, above all, Maradona to live up to their promise, the indifferent World Cup of Ardiles, condemned the Argentines to elimination. Only a Maradona at his best could have saved them, and with the exception of the Hungarian game, Maradona was never at his best.

The British attempt was similarly disappointing. Once again the parts of the Scottish team were greater than the whole. Against Brazil, well though they played, they were shown to be tactically and technically well below the level of the world's best. Northern Ireland, who had been their runners-up in the qualifying group, surpassed themselves, shrewdly managed by little Billy Bingham, though in the event, they were once again shown, as in 1958, to be living above their means.

England, like Scotland in 1974, were knocked out without losing a single game, but one might have had more sympathy with them had they sometimes tried harder to win them.

Those of us who thought that Ron Greenwood should have been politely thanked and put out to graze in 1980 after his abject performance in the Nations Cup Finals, and that Kevin Keegan should have been similarly despatched, saw no reason to change our views. The English, in effect, played two good games; against the French, who would later on transform, and the Czechs, both well beaten in Bilbao. The rest was anticlimax and insufficiency, though it is still legitimate to speculate what a fully fit Bryan Robson and a fit Trevor Brooking might have done.

For Bearzot, the World Cup success was a wonderful vindication against his spiteful critics in the Press, the Brutus who, as he complained, lurked at his back. Should he have quit while he was ahead, retired at once from a job which he had done so well, in which he had twice confounded his malign detractors? Perhaps, but the temptation to stay on was too much for him and, away from the benign rigours, the blessed privacy of training camp, the *azzurri* quickly slid down the slope with a string of bad results in the Nations Cup.

Never mind. Bearzot had proved his point and won his triumph; in his own quite different way, the most successful Italian team manager since Vittorio Pozzo. And Pozzo, though he dealt with highly temperamental players, never had to put up with such a vindictive Press, never had a Brutus at his back.

For all the rancid memories of what Gentile did to Maradona in Barcelona, one had to feel happy for Bearzot: a good man who, for the moment at least, had splendidly routed all his enemies.

RESULTS: Spain 1982

First round

Group I

Vigo, La Coruna

Italy 0, Poland 0
Cameroons 0, Peru 0
Italy 1, Peru 1
Cameroons 0, Poland 0
Poland 5, Peru 1
Italy 1, Cameroons 1

	P	W	D	L	GOALS F	A	Pts
Poland	3	1	2	0	5	1	4
Italy	3	0	3	0	2	2	3
Cameroons	3	0	3	0	1	1	3
Peru	3	0	2	1	2	6	2

Group II

Gijon, Oviedo

Algeria 2, West Germany 1
Austria 1, Chile 0
West Germany 4, Chile 1
Algeria 0, Austria 2
Algeria 3, Chile 2
West Germany 1, Austria 0

	P	W	D	L	GOALS F	A	Pts
West Germany	3	2	0	1	6	3	4
Austria	3	2	0	1	3	1	4
Algeria	3	2	0	1	5	5	4
Chile	3	0	0	3	3	8	0

Group III

Barcelona, Alicante, Elche

Argentina 0, Belgium 1
Hungary 10, El Savador 1
Argentina 4, Hungary 1
Belgium 1, El Salvador 0
Belgium 1, Hungary 1
Argentina 2, El Salvador 0

	P	W	D	L	GOALS F	A	Pts
Belgium	3	2	1	0	3	1	5
Argentina	3	2	0	1	6	2	4
Hungary	3	1	1	1	12	6	3
El Salvador	3	0	0	3	1	13	0

Group IV

Bilbao, Valladolid

England 3, France 1
Czechoslovakia 1, Kuwait 1
England 2, Czechoslovakia 0
France 4, Kuwait 1
France 1, Czechoslovakia 1
England 1, Kuwait 0

	P	W	D	L	GOALS F	A	Pts
England	3	3	0	0	6	1	6
France	3	1	1	1	6	5	3
Czechoslovakia	3	0	2	1	2	4	2
Kuwait	3	0	1	2	2	6	1

Group V

Valencia, Saragossa

Spain 1, Honduras 1
Yugoslavia 0, Northern Ireland 0
Spain 2, Yugoslavia 1
Honduras 1, Northern Ireland 1
Honduras 0, Yugoslavia 1
Spain 0, Northern Ireland 1

	P	W	D	L	GOALS F	A	Pts
N. Ireland	3	1	2	0	2	1	4
Spain	3	1	1	0	3	3	3
Yugoslavia	3	1	1	1	2	2	3
Honduras	3	0	2	1	2	3	2

Group VI

Seville, Malaga

Brazil 2, Russia 1
Scotland 5, New Zealand 2
Brazil 4, Scotland 1
Russia 3, New Zealand 0
Scotland 2, Russia 2
Brazil 4, New Zealand 0

	P	W	D	L	GOALS F	A	Pts
Brazil	3	3	0	0	10	2	6
Russia	3	1	1	1	6	4	3
Scotland	3	1	1	1	8	8	3
New Zealand	3	0	0	3	2	12	0

Second round

Group A

Nou Camp, Barcelona
Poland 3, Belgium 0
Belgium 0, Russia 1
Russia 0, Poland 0

	P	W	D	L	GOALS F	A	Pts
Poland	2	1	1	0	**3**	**0**	3
Russia	2	1	1	0	**1**	**0**	3
Belgium	2	0	0	2	**0**	**4**	0

Group B

Bernabeu, Madrid
West Germany 0, England 0
West Germany 2, Spain 1
Spain 0, England 0

	P	W	D	L	GOALS F	A	Pts
West Germany	2	1	1	0	**2**	**1**	3
England	2	0	2	0	**0**	**0**	2
Spain	2	0	1	1	**1**	**2**	1

Group C

Sarria Stadium, Barcelona
Italy 2, Argentina 1
Brazil 3, Argentina 1
Italy 3, Brazil 2

	P	W	D	L	GOALS F	A	Pts
Italy	2	2	0	0	**5**	**3**	4
Brazil	2	1	0	1	**5**	**4**	2
Argentina	2	0	0	2	**2**	**5**	0

Group D

Calderon, Madrid
France 1, Austria 0
Austria 2, Northern Ireland 2
France 4, Northern Ireland 1

	P	W	D	L	GOALS F	A	Pts
France	2	2	0	0	**5**	**1**	4
Austria	2	0	1	1	**2**	**3**	1
N. Ireland	2	0	1	1	**3**	**6**	1

Semi-finals

Nou Camp, Barcelona
Italy 2, Poland 0

Seville
West Germany 3, France 3
After extra time, West Germany won on penalty kicks

Third-place match

Alicante

Poland 3	**France 2**
Mlynarczyk; Dziuba, Janas, Zmuda, Majewski; Lato, Kupcewicz, Matysik (Wojcicji), Buncol; Boniek, Szarmach.	Castaneda; Amoros, Mahut, Trésor, Janvion (Lopez); Tigana (Six), Girard, Larios; Couriol, Soler, Bellone.

SCORERS
Szarmach, Majewski, Kupcewicz for Poland
Girard, Couriol for France
HT (1–2)

Final

Bernabeu, Madrid

Italy 3	**West Germany 1**
Zoff; Scirea; Bergomi, Gentile, Collovati, Cabrini; Tardelli, Oriali; Conti, Rossi, Graziani (Altobelli, Conti).	Schumacher; Stielike; Kaltz, K-H. Foerster, B. Foerster, Briegel; Dremmler (Hrubesch), Breitner; Littbarski, Rummenigge (H. Muller), Fischer.

SCORERS
Rossi, Tardelli, Altobelli for Italy
Breitner for West Germany
HT (0–0)

MEXICO
1986

At the end of the 1982 World Cup, João Havelange, the President of FIFA, flew directly to Mexico City in a plane owned by Emilio Azcarraga, head of Televisa Mexicana. It was then that Colombia, the designated hosts of the 1986 World Cup, might just as well have thrown in the towel.

Immensely rich, enormously influential, owner not only of Televisa but of the Spanish International Network in the USA, employer of Guillermo Canedo, former President of the Mexican Football Federation, Azcarraga was a man with much in his gift. 'My conscience is clear,' Havelange would later say. 'Other people may write or say what they like.' But the fact remains that whatever the deficiencies of Colombia as host, Mexico appeared a remote outsider.

Initially, it had seemed that the nightmare scenario of a 24-team World Cup would be visited only on those countries large and rich enough to support it. Colombia clearly couldn't. In retrospect, given the appalling level of violence there, the penetration of football by drug dealers, the brutal intimidation of referees, perhaps it was as well Colombia was bypassed.

But Mexico? Mexico, with the familiar problems of height and heat, of oxygen debt and the expensive need to acclimatise? How could the World Cup possibly go there, again? But go there it did, and it became clear that no other country had a chance. The United States, who'd be allotted the 1994 World Cup, put in a bid, but when the FIFA World Cup committee met in Stockholm in May 1983, it was not even discussed. Such was the hegemony of Havelange over the committee not even the presence of Henry Kissinger in the American delegation was of any avail.

In the event, the World Cup was a good one, despite the weather conditions and the altitude, despite shocking pitches in Monterrey and Mexico City, despite the lamentable introduction of penalty kicks to decide games which had not been resolved in extra time.

It will always be remembered as Maradona's World Cup. Seldom has a player, even Pelé, so dominated the competition. There were the two amazing goals he scored, whatever the pitch, in the Azteca Stadium against England and Belgium. The notorious goal he punched, in the same stadium, against England, attributing it later to 'the hand of God'. In an era when individual talent was at a premium, defensive football more prevalent than ever, Maradona—squat, muscular, explosive, endlessly adroit—showed that a footballer of genius could still prevail. Yet, irony of ironies, when it came to the Final, when Argentina met West Germany, Maradona was relatively subdued. Even then, he produced passes of devastating effect and flair.

The odd thing is that for many months, he seemed likely not to play at all. He had trouble, we were told, with the cartilage of his right knee. There were two alternatives. Either he had the operation he needed, which would put him out of the World Cup. Or he would play, and risk breaking down at any moment.

In the event he played, twisted and turned in his electric way, showed no sign of pain or trouble, and never had the operation. A mystery which has never truly been explained.

It seemed fairly clear that Italy would not hang on to their title. The heroes were tired, Enzo Bearzot among them. His flair for 'detoxifying' Italian players from the effects of their debilitating Championship had waned, as had such players as Paolo Rossi. Gentile was no longer there to maltreat and mark opposing forwards. Gianluca Vialli of Sampdoria, who shaved his head before the tournament, had shown high promise as a striker, but his international experience was scant. Perhaps Bruno Conti, so admired by Pelé four years earlier, could pick the team up and inspire it, but the task was great.

West Germany, as ever, had to be respected, if only for their amazing record and resilience in World Cups. In charge of them now was their old hero and captain, Franz Beckenbauer. Going wholly against their traditions, the DFB, the West German FA, had installed him as team manager though he had never taken any of their mandatory courses. It was hoped that his sheer prestige would be an inspiration—a hope which would be justified in two successive World Cups.

But the team hardly looked inspired. Karl-Heinz Rummenigge had been beset by injury. Without him, the quick centre-forward Rudi Voeller might find life hard. Lothar Matthaus was not yet doing, in midfield, what he would later, so commandingly, do for West Germany and Internazionale. There were the customary squabbles in training camp, 'Toni' Schumacher, the controversial goalkeeper, complaining when the younger Stein was preferred to him, and laming a colleague in training.

Brazil were favoured by the bookmakers, but so many of their star midfield players were injured that they were an enigma. Zico's left knee, Falcao's right knee, Cerezo's left thigh, Socrates' general condition left them a vulnerable side. Tele Santana had returned to manage them; and they too had had ructions in training camp.

When Renato Gaucho, the powerful, fast Flamengo right-winger, a known night-owl, had come back after curfew, Santana had thrown him off the squad. This so upset his friend and Flamengo team-mate Leandro, one of the country's finest defenders, that when the team flew off from Rio to Mexico, he didn't turn up.

Uruguay, who had looked impressive on a damp night in Wrexham, were wildly undisciplined when they played Mexico in Los Angeles. They had players of high skill, such as Enzo Francescoli, the attacker voted South American player of the year, the right-winger, Alzamendi, and the striker, Da Silva. Would they play or would they kick? Their manager, Omar Borras, was a kind, pleasant, intelligent man who'd been landed with the job after previously teaching physical education at the University of Montevideo and looking after the team's training. In the event, he'd find his inflammable players too hot to handle.

Mexico, the hosts, had lost badly to England in Los Angeles just before the tournament. But they weren't at full strength and could call on one of the most prolific strikers in European football: Hugo Sanchez of Real Madrid. A qualified dentist, little Sanchez was a marvel of swift opportunism, superb reflexes, uncanny anticipation. The somersault with which he greeted each goal had become famous in Spain, and beyond.

Under the managership of Alex Ferguson, once an aggressive centre-forward with Glasgow Rangers, subsequently to be manager of Aberdeen and Manchester United, Scotland did not look a very happy ship. Surprisingly, Ferguson had left out the elegant Liverpool centre-back, Alan Hansen. This reportedly enraged his club colleague, Kenny Dalglish, then at the height of his playing powers, and expected to play a major part in what would be his fourth World Cup, even if his previous three had been strangely disappointing. But Dalglish withdrew, with an injury, which meant the Scots, always so resilient when it came to qualification, so disappointing when it came to the Finals, lacked two of their most accomplished players.

England, in qualifying, owed a substantial debt to Northern Ireland, who'd shown amazing resilience in beating the gifted Romanians both at home and away. Their astonishing 1–0 victory in Bucharest was largely brought about by a marvellous goalkeeping display by the 40-year-old Pat Jennings, but in both games, the whole was immensely greater than the parts. Sammy McIlroy was an inventive midfielder, Norman Whiteside was confirming the promise he had shown as a tough 17-year-old in the Spanish World Cup. Once more, Billy Bingham, right-winger in the legendary 1958 team, was proving himself a true guerrilla general.

Not exactly what you could say of Bobby Robson, England's manager, strangely given to morose or indecisive moments. His team had thrashed Turkey home and away, but only managed to draw with Romania in both matches. The Romanians and their able young manager, Mircea Lucescu, World Cup skipper in Mexico in 1970, protested bitterly when England could only draw at home in their decisive match against Northern Ireland, who thus qualified at the expense of the Romanians. There were accusations of a fix.

These, I am sure, had no objective basis, though talking with certain of the England players it was plain they'd prefer the Ulstermen to get through, rather than the 'Communist' Romanians. Such feelings, at what might be called a pre-conscious level, could have their effect on how a team played, without any actual desire to take its foot off the accelerator. At all events, the Irish got their draw and went to Mexico. Since they'd twice beaten the Romanians fair and square, one could scarcely grudge them their success.

England had played in Mexico City the previous summer, very soon after the shocking disaster of Heysel Stadium, when Liverpool's fans ran riot before a European Cup Final, and 39 Juventus fans were killed. By an irony, Italy were one of England's opponents, but the Italian players behaved with impressive generosity and understanding.

Now the England team had various problems to solve. There was the question of Bryan Robson, and there was the question of Glenn Hoddle—the first very dear to Bobby Robson's heart, the second tolerated rather than welcomed. That Bobby Robson, in an outburst of over-compensation when England were in pre-tournament training camp in Colorado, should extol Hoddle convinced very few. A year earlier, Robson had grudgingly picked Hoddle to play—absurdly and wastefully—wide on the right flank.

In the 1985 Mexican tournament, a tacit conspiracy among the other England players had enabled Hoddle to move into the middle, where he could exploit his fine technique and his superb passing ability. Now Robson was proclaiming that while he'd never thought anyone could equal Johnny Haynes, the inside-left with whom he'd played for Fulham and England, now he had to confess that Hoddle had done so. It was interesting to see that the Road to Damascus passed through Colorado Springs.

Bryan Robson had dislocated his shoulder, and plainly needed an operation before he would be fit to play again. Bobby Robson, talking manifest nonsense about a shoulder which could easily come out going easily back in again, insisted against all logic on continuing to use him.

In Los Angeles, Bryan Robson collapsed and was taken off the field. The shoulder had gone again—for the third time. Bobby Robson denied it. It was an inept cover-up and Robson, most embarrassingly, had to admit in his turgid and ingenuous World Cup diary that he had lied to the Press. When the shoulder went for the fourth time, in the match against Morocco, Bryan Robson was at last, and belatedly, out of the World Cup. Irreplaceable as he doubtless was, to keep him so long in the team in such circumstances was inexplicable in any rational terms.

Hoddle's case was a classical one, in the history of English football: the brilliant, unorthodox footballer—Charlie Buchan, Len Shackleton, Stanley Matthews—who worries the mediocrities. Such distinguished talents as Michel Platini and Sandro Mazzola eulogised Hoddle, dismissing any criticism of him on the grounds that he didn't tackle, 'close down', defend. But he would have his hour.

The French themselves still had Platini, Tigana and Giresse. Even if their manager, Michel Hidalgo, had lamented earlier in the year that most of his players couldn't successfully operate two against one, though he excepted Giresse and Platini. The French had recalled the swift little centre-forward Jean-Pierre Papin from Belgium, where he'd been scoring goals for Bruges. In this World Cup, he would perhaps miss more than he got, but his future would be a coruscating one.

Was there not some way of abolishing opening matches, one wondered, as yet another ground its mediocre way to the final whistle? This time, the Italians played Bulgaria and had enough chances to win with ease. But after the Mexican crowd had loudly whistled Cañedo and their President, the Italians threw away what should have been a comfortable win. 'Spillone' Big Pin Altobelli scored just before half-time, but with six minutes left, the clever Bulgarian attacker Sirakov headed a centre by the right-back Zradvkov past the uneasy Galli.

Strange things then began to happen. In Leon, in Group C, France could squeeze through only 1–0 against a very modest Canadian team managed by the former Blackpool and England goalkeeper Tony Waiters. Papin scored the only goal after Paul Dolan, the Canadian goalkeeper, missed a cross; there were just 12 minutes left. Platini was strangely subdued.

Mexico began by beating, at the Azteca, a Belgian team which had very unhappy memories of their last World Cup encounter there in 1970, when they justly felt cheated. This time, with the tall, strong Mexican skipper Tomas Boy ruling the midfield, Mexico won fair and square, 2–1. Belgium, who gave away both goals on defensive errors, played so feebly that their later successes came as a vast surprise. Sanchez, from a couple of yards out, headed Mexico's second goal.

The real shock was the Soviet Union's 6–0 thrashing of Hungary at Irapuato in Group C. The Soviets had looked a dull team in the spring, when they lost a friendly at home to England in Tblissi. But they sacked Malafaev, replacing him as manager with the inspiration of Dynamo Kiev, Valeri Lobanovski, who filled the team up with his Kiev players; and a fancied Hungarian side was crushed.

Over the years, Hungary have manifested a strange inferiority complex *vis-à-vis* the Soviets. Now, Yakovenko was feebly allowed through to score after just a couple of minutes. The versatile midfielder

Aleinikov scored a second with a shot from outside the box barely two
minutes later; and the Hungarians collapsed. As the unfortunate
Lobanovski would himself, later in the tournament, with intestinal
troubles.

In Guadalajara, in Group D, Brazil were lucky to squeeze through
against Spain, their attack led by the precocious young Emilio Butragueño,
nicknamed El Buitre, the Vulture. His father, an impassioned Real Madrid
fan, had put his son's name down as a member of the club almost as soon
as he was born. He could scarcely have dreamed the boy would turn into
such a skilled, talented, intelligent player, technically exceptional, able to
glide past defenders and make goals out of nothing.

This time, he didn't score, and Brazil's goal, scored by Socrates eight
minutes from the end, was blemished by what seemed his offside position,
after the clever centre-forward, Careca, had shot against the bar. Brazil,
it's true, could have had a couple of penalties, but against that a shot by
Michel which hit the underside of the Brazilian bar seemed plainly to
have crossed the line. Brazil brought in two effective new midfielders,
Elzo and the blond Alemao, while Junior, moved up from full-back, was a
driving force. The Spaniards lacked two key midfielders, Gordillo and
Caldere, who were ill.

England made an inept beginning. Much had been hoped for from
Mark Hateley and Ray Wilkins, the two players signed by Milan, but
their form had badly deteriorated since the autumn. Wilkins now sat in
front of his defence, playing square balls and seldom getting forward.
Hateley, who, it's true, had undergone a knee operation, was, against
Portugal, a blunt instrument.

The Portuguese, in hot and humid Monterrey, had been in a state of
virtual rebellion, accusing their officials of failing to treat them 'like people with a head and heart', of grabbing all the sponsorship money, of
being too mean to arrange proper international fixtures as preparation.
By contrast, the Poles, also in England's group, had seemed relaxed and
happy.

The long grass of the Monterrey stadium scarcely helped good football, but this was scant excuse for England's poverty; least of all for the
deciding goal they gave away. It was a true chapter of blunders. First,
on the left, almost on the goal line, Kenny Sansom, England's left-
back, somehow allowed Diamantino to squeeze past him. Terry
Butcher, the centre-back, perhaps because he couldn't visualise such a
thing happening, failed to cover. The cross came in, and Gary Stevens,
the right-back, failed to materialise on the far post. An easy goal for
Carlos Manuel. Paolo Futre, coming on late for Portugal, twice ridiculed Fenwick, and should have had a penalty when the defender
brought him down.

So England's long unbeaten run, owed largely to the magnificent goalkeeping of Peter Shilton, came to an end. They should have gone out in their next game, three days later, against Morocco, but Bobby Robson's famous luck held; even if, in his ensuing Press conferences, he might have been well advised not to dress it up as just reward.

That luck was proof against the departure of Bryan Robson, with his shoulder dislocation, and Ray Wilkins, who, quite uncharacteristically, threw the ball at the referee in frustration, five minutes from half-time, and was ordered off.

The Moroccans, who had a dazzling midfielder in the left-footed Timoumi, and an elegant striker in Aziz Bouderbala, should have taken the game over and won it. But like many a team before them, they paid England exaggerated respect. They cravenly went into their shell, content with a draw; and England survived.

Not, however, before a veritable rebellion in the dressing-room at half-time, when players demanded of the coach, Don Howe, that he should tell them what to do. In most emphatic terms.

Back at their hotel in Santillo, the players expressed their bitter dissatisfaction with their tactics. Bryan Robson, wearing a harness to play, wanted to go on. Wilkins, insisting he'd never meant the ball to hit the referee, thought Robson should continue. No one else seemed to—including, at last, Bobby Robson. The predominant view among the players was that Trevor Steven, the accomplished deep right-winger, Peter Reid, the tough little Everton midfielder, and Steve Hodge, who'd come on against Morocco as substitute, should form the midfield against Poland with Hoddle, in a match which would make or break.

In the event, it made. With these three playing, England looked a rejuvenated team, dominating the midfield, with Gary Lineker emerging, at last, as so much more than an accomplished rabbit-killer.

The son of market traders in Leicester, a fine all-round sportsman, adept at both cricket and snooker, Lineker had long shown anticipation and speed, but was curiously wasteful of so many chances, tending to lack composure and control. Of his temperament, there was no doubt at all. He gloriously gave the lie to the myth that a successful sportsman must be aggressive. He never got booked. He never retaliated. He was a shining example to any young footballer taught to 'get his retaliation in first' and to despise the rules.

Scoring all three goals against Poland, Lineker suddenly became a hero. He would end as top scorer of the World Cup, ahead, even, of Maradona, and a £3 million transfer to Barcelona awaited him.

Against Poland, the England team were simply transformed. The Poles had drawn with Morocco and beaten Portugal, with a breakaway goal by the powerful left-winger, Smolarek. Another dire game. Lineker, who had missed two good chances against Portugal, was off the mark in only eight minutes, revelling in the support he got from little Peter Beardsley, another player belatedly called into the team.

Glenn Hoddle, in his own half of the field, began a move carried on by four other players, concluded when Trevor Steven set up his Everton colleague Gary Stevens, the right-back, whose cross Lineker duly despatched. England, in fact, could already have been a goal down, but when Fenwick culpably let the red-haired Zibi Boniek through, Shilton yet again came to the rescue.

Lineker would score twice more. After another six minutes, Beardsley released Hodge, and again Lineker did the final execution. The third goal came when the big Polish goalkeeper, Mlynarczyk, fumbled Trevor Steven's corner, and Lineker accepted the gift.

Beardsley, mysteriously left out of the first two games after excellent performances before the World Cup, had been a revelation—mobile, incisive, intelligent, quick in thought and movement, modestly insisting, 'If we win the World Cup, it won't matter which eleven play. The eleven that don't play will be as happy as the eleven who do.' In the event, England wouldn't win the World Cup, but there was no doubt that Lineker has never had a more unselfish, space-creating partner than Beardsley, happy to take opponents away from him.

Scotland lost their first, Group E, match in Neza, to Denmark, appearing in their first World Cup finals. This, though they had been the first of all foreign teams to master the game, presenting English football with something of a challenge, reaching two Olympic Cup Finals before the Great War. After the Second World War they again had a notable team, packed with such skilful players as Carl Praest and John Hansen, but the depredations of foreign clubs and their own insistence on amateur status sabotaged the national side for years.

Now, there was a galaxy of stars; not least Michael Laudrup, son of a well-known former player, Finn Laudrup, an attacker of tremendous, fluent gifts but slightly suspect temperament, a Juventus player like Hansen and Praest before him.

Frank Arnesen and Soren Lerby, clever, versatile midfield players, had gone, very young, to Ajax Amsterdam, then moved about Europe. Morten Olsen was a sweeper of shrewd versatility, Preben Elkjaer a fast, strong, left-footed centre-forward, who would score the only goal of the game against the Scots. But he was lucky when the ball rebounded to him from Willie Miller's legs as he went through on Arnesen's pass; and even then his shot clipped the post.

With such accomplished players as Graeme Souness, who'd been a star in Spain, and Gordon Strachan in their midfield, Scotland never gave up the ghost, but the loss of Dalglish had drawn the teeth from their attack.

Strachan did score in the ensuing game against West Germany, in

Queretaro, but again, a defeat by the margin of a single goal was Scotland's fate. The Germans, who'd snatched a draw against Uruguay with Klaus Allofs's goal six short minutes from the end, used Karl-Heinz Rummenigge as a late substitute for the second time. By then, however, all the goals had been scored. Strachan spun to beat Schumacher with an inspired shot inside the near post after 17 minutes, and Scottish hopes rose. Only, alas, to be dashed.

Perhaps all would have been well had the clever little Rangers winger, Davie Cooper, only been brought on earlier, for the Germans could do little with him. In the event, he had just over a quarter of an hour, by which time Voeller and Allofs had surprised the Scots twice, the huge, blond Briegel constantly thundering down the left. For Scotland, Strachan never stopped running and prompting.

That same day, the Danes obtained a victory over Uruguay almost as resounding as would be their subsequent defeat by Spain: 6–1. True, the violent Uruguayans had Bossio sent off after 19 minutes, when Denmark were only one goal up; but in their next game, they'd hold out against Scotland, though Batista was sent off in less than a minute.

In Neza, Uruguay simply wilted, while Denmark took wing. Laudrup, who'd fashioned Elkjaer's opening goal, dummied and dribbled his way perpetually through Uruguay's defence, generously setting up Elkjaer and the rest. Elkjaer ended with a hat trick; Laudrup himself scored only once, but it was a marvellous goal, scored after he'd danced past two defenders.

In the last game of their pool, Denmark confirmed their dazzling streak, beating West Germany 2–0 in Queretaro. Not that this was quite the real thing. Both teams fielded several reserves, the Germans leaving out four first-choice players. It was a Danish victory which presaged their remarkable success in the European Championship Final in Gothenburg in 1992. Little Jesper Olsen, from a penalty, and Eriksen scored the goals.

Scotland's goalless draw against Uruguay, in Neza, condemned them to go home; and left them in a state of fury. While Omar Borras protested that his players had been victimised by FIFA, Ferguson retorted, 'Uruguay are a disgrace. They have no respect for other people's dignity.' Perhaps; but the fact remained that a dubiously reconstructed Scottish team looked clumsy and naive against Uruguay's ten men. The omission of Souness from midfield did nothing to improve a team which looked technically maladroit and tactically inept by comparison with Uruguay, who'd now go on to face Argentina in Puebla—a knock-out game of potential chaos.

The Argentines were now under the management of Dr Carlos Bilardo, a sombre man of many parts; a medical doctor, once engaged in serious research, a left-half for the notoriously tough Estudiantes de La Plata team of the late 1960s. His head had left its mark, in Buenos

Aires, above Nobby Stiles's eye, just as his assistant, Carlos Pachamé, had split open Bobby Charlton's shin, in the 1968 Intercontinental Cup game.

No one in Argentina seemed to like Bilardo's methods, least of all the President, Alfonsin, who publicly criticised them. So, said Bilardo, did his own father, but people in Argentina didn't understand the modern game. He had no real strikers or wingers at his disposal.

The World Cup won, Bilardo would boast that Argentina had taught new tactics to the game; a sweeper, two markers, five men across midfield, and a single striker. In fact, they'd not used such tactics in their laborious passage to the Finals—a very lucky home win against Peru had scraped them through in their last game—nor did they in their opening World Cup games. It was only when the young centreforwards Pasculli and Claudio Borghi had failed to satisfy Bilardo that he made a virtue out of necessity, introducing his new methods.

The team had to do without the fearsomely competitive Daniel Passarella, who succumbed, soon after his arrival in Mexico City, to colic and calf injuries. This gave—a romantic story—an unexpected chance of fame to a very different personality, the solid, amiable José-Luis Brown, a 28-year-old central defender who hadn't even got a club when he set out for Mexico. He'd played in Colombia, come back to Argentina, but nobody had signed him. Playing *libero* behind two central markers, the modest Brown would prove a bulwark; and the Final would see him spring a dramatic surprise.

A bruisingly combative South Korean team was beaten 3–1 at the Olympic Stadium in Mexico City. Maradona, roughly dealt with, took the best possible revenge by setting up all three goals, two scored by the tall, elegant Jorge Valdano, who could play centre-forward or on the wing. Weak goalkeeping by the Korean, aptly named Oh, doomed his team, who did, though, score the final goal with a rocketing shot by Park Chung-Sun.

Next, at Puebla, came Italy; and a draw. This time it was his Napoli colleague, Salvatore Bagni, whom Bearzot set to mark Maradona. Not the gentlest of players; but gentler than Gentile. Italy had little Galderisi and tall Altobelli up front, again, and went ahead from Altobelli's penalty after only six minutes, when Garre handled.

But with Maradona showing splendid sleight of foot, and the strolling, bearded Batista complementing him cleverly in midfield, Argentina stayed afloat. Eventually, after 33 minutes, Valdano centred from the right and Maradona—with no Gentile to mark him slipped in to equalise. A sublimely insidious shot, low into the far corner. Which left the Italians with the ungrateful task of beating the Koreans in their third game; memories of the North Koreans, Middlesbrough and 1966 were still painfully alive.

In the event, the South Koreans gave Italy an embarrassingly good run for their money. 3–2 was the margin, with Altobelli scoring twice but hitting the post from a penalty, the third Italian goal going in off the hand of the unlucky Cho Kwang-Rae. The Koreans equalised the first Italian goal, just after half-time, Choi demonstrating again their shooting power. A late goal by Kyung-Hoon made the score respectable, but Italy, playing Vialli only for the last two minutes, had at least survived.

Argentina, in their final group game in the Olympic Stadium, overcame Bulgaria 2–0, Valdano scoring once again; the clever, busy midfielder, Jorge Burruchaga, got the other. Borghi led the attack once more. Hope remained that he'd fulfil his undoubted talent; but life, and football, would alas turn sour.

In Group B, Belgium still showed few signs of what was to come. They won only once, a meagre 2–1 against Iraq, the elegant Sicilian-Belgian Enzo Scifo scoring their first goal. Paraguay, with two goals by the dashing Cabañas, once a partner of Romerito in the New York Cosmos attack, drew with the Belgians, 2–2. Paraguay beat the dogged Iraqis 1–0, through Romerito's goal, and held Mexico 1–1, with another goal by Romerito, a hero in Brazil. Iraq thus went out. Mexico beat them 1–0.

Now the competition lurched out of its protracted, over-complicated, initial phase, and became a knock-out affair. The French and the Soviets were predictably there. They'd drawn 1–1 in hot, humid Leon. Vasili Rats, a versatile left-footed player of Hungarian origin, smashed in a tremendous drive from 30 yards early in the second half, but the forceful young Luis Fernandez, a newcomer to the French midfield, equalised eight minutes later. France then easily disposed of the shell-shocked Hungarian side, while Oleg Blokhin was briefly recalled to score for the Soviets against Canada. They won 2–0, but Canada bowed out undisgraced.

The game which seemed all too likely to go up in smoke and flames was that between Argentina and Uruguay, eternal rivals of the River Plate, in Puebla. In the event, thunder and lightning came not from the players but from the elements. In the second half, a storm played about the pitch; the rain came down in torrents, but nothing could overshadow Maradona's glorious talents.

Bossio did his best to mark him, in a Uruguayan team well domesticated by a fine Italian referee, Luigi Agnolin, whose father had refereed before him. Stringent measures and threats by the World Cup committee, which had banished a defiant Omar Borras from the bench and fined him into the bargain, had their calming effect. Though Uruguay lost in the end only to Pasculli's forty-first minute goal, they might have conceded several more.

Maradona was irresistible, his swift and sudden spurts, his magical passing, his effortless control too much for Uruguay to master.

Valdano, who eventually set up Pasculli's goal, should have headed in an inviting cross from Maradona; instead he put it wide. Maradona's run began the move which led to the only goal; he struck the bar with a dipping free kick; he had a goal disallowed in the second half which seemed quite valid. Unable to kick him, Uruguay were obliged to endure him.

Brazil, meanwhile, Argentina's other, old, rivals, had been getting up steam, playing the kind of football they'd produced in Spain. The lean, swift Josimar, brought into the team as an attacking right-back against a bewildered Northern Ireland, had given them new options. He scored their second goal in Guadalajara, in a 3–0 success. The third goal, and Careca's second, was made by Zico, who came on, to huge applause, as a substitute after 67 minutes. Pat Jennings was yet again in defiant form, but even he could not rescue a disappointing Irish side.

Poland were next, in the same stadium—where Pelé's Brazil had excelled in 1970. This time, the margin was 4–0, with two penalties and another goal for the adventurous Josimar; 'The Pope is Polish but God is Brazilian' was the joke before the match. There were early moments when the Pope seemed likely to prevail, for the Poles began in style, 'Jackie' Dziekanowski hitting a post, Karas hitting the bar, Boniek lobbing the keeper, Carlos, only for the ball to finish on top of the net, not in it.

At last Brazil shook off their lethargy; Alemao and Junior began to take over the midfield. Careca was brought down, Socrates took but two steps forward to despatch the penalty; Poland wasted chances and Brazil finally prevailed.

At the Azteca, Mexico saw off the Bulgarians with little trouble. 'Bulgaria,' wrote the magazine *World Soccer*, 'were a disgrace to football. One almost wondered why they had even bothered going to the trouble of coming to the finals.' 100,000 saw the acrobatic Negrete volley in Mexico's spectacular first goal, and put over the corner from which Servin dived to head the second. Back after brief suspension, Hugo Sanchez showed in fits and starts. For him, it would be a disappointing World Cup.

The most remarkable game of this so-called Second Round would take place in Leon between the Belgians and the Soviets, bringing memories of the Italy v. West Germany semi-final of 1970, which also produced seven goals. Little the Belgians had done thus far prepared one for what they'd do now. Nor had the Soviet defence yet looked so porous.

Belgium had squeezed into the Second Round only because, under the strange new dispensation of this World Cup and its lopsided 24 teams, they were one of the four third-placed group teams with the 'best' record. Injuries to Erwin Vandenbergh and René Vandereycken, both sent home in consequence, and poor form by seemingly established players obliged Belgium's experienced manager, Guy Thys, to bring in fresh faces, such as those of Grun and Vervoort, pairing Claesen and Veyt in an experimental attack.

But much of the credit for Belgium's success went to a couple of veterans: tall, strong Jan Ceulemans, the attacking midfielder, whose mother had persuaded him to turn down AC Milan, and the 30-year-old sweeper, Michel Renquin, whom Thys had doubted before the tournament. Perhaps the chief revelation was the 20-year-old Anderlecht defender, Stéphane De Mol, precociously composed.

Though Belgium played with great spirit to win, it might be said that the game turned on their second equalising goal. There was a quarter of an hour left and the Soviets led 2–1, both their goals having gone to the rampant striker, Igor Belanov, of Dynamo Kiev. The Soviets' version of Total Football seemed likely to prevail when Vervoort's long pass came to Ceulemans, standing all alone. The Soviet defence looked for an offside flag, but the linesman, Sanchez-Arminio, kept his flag down. Ceulemans duly scored, but the match went into extra time, and the evidently shaken Soviets gave away further goals—to young De Mol, with a far-post header, and Nico Claesen. Belanov's penalty, three minutes from the end, gave him the consolation of a hat trick, but his team were out.

At the Olympic stadium in Mexico City, Bearzot lost his nerve, and Italy went out with a whimper. Though Michel Platini, by general consent, was not in his finest form, probably still suffering the effects of the tendinitis which had long been troubling him, Bearzot decided he must sacrifice a man to mark him, and brought in the Inter defender, Giuseppe Baresi, older brother of Franco, who would grace so many future Italian teams. To make room for Baresi, Bearzot contentiously dropped the inventive Di Gennaro; and handed the initiative to France.

They took it. They beat Italy, in fact, in a major competition for the first time since 1920. If, as Bearzot insisted, Baresi had always played well against Platini in the Italian Championship, this was neither the day nor the apt occasion. Italy throughout looked a team weary in mind and body, and this time there was no Paolo Rossi to lift them from the canvas.

Platini, Baresi or no Baresi, put France ahead after only 13 minutes with an elegant chip over the hapless Galli. Fernandez, in dominant form throughout, had begun the move; Dominique Rocheteau, so hugely gifted, so sadly prone to injury, had made the final, killing through pass.

Fernandez was here, there and everywhere, now clearing Conti's shot from the line, now hitting the Italian bar from some 35 yards. Bearzot did bring Di Gennaro on in place of Baresi at half-time, but by then France had a grip of the game. Their second goal, 11 minutes into the second half, went to the willing young Stopyra, who'd replaced Papin; the culmination of a sustained, inventive move. When Jean Tigana eventually put Rocheteau clear, he in turn selflessly found Stopyra, who drove into the bottom left-hand angle of the goal. Italy, the holders, were well and truly out. The inevitable recriminations followed, and Altobelli said he never wanted to play for the *azzurri* again. Bearzot would give way now to Azeglio Vicini, his assistant.

As for England, their rejuvenated team flew past Paraguay at the Azteca, as they had flown past Poland. 3–0 again was the score, despite some brutal tactics by a Paraguayan defence too heavy to hold Lineker— at least by legal means.

Yet again, England owed so much to the magnificent goalkeeping of Peter Shilton. A feeble header out by Alvin Martin, one of England's big, slow centre-backs, was whacked at goal by Canete, but Shilton turned the rising ball over the bar. The other centre-back, Terry Butcher, then blundered, with a casual back pass to Shilton. Mendoza ran on to it and squared the ball precisely to the feet of Canete, who was gallantly thwarted once more by Shilton.

Football being the predictably perverse game it is, England proceeded to score. Hoddle to Hodge, on the left, Hodge to Lineker, Lineker into the vacant goal. Almost at once, Lineker volleyed Beardsley's cross with precise power, but Fernandez tipped the ball gymnastically over the bar.

In the second half, the inadequate Syrian referee, Al-Sharif, failed to control the increasingly abrasive Paraguayans, given to spiteful fouls and endless protests. In one particularly vicious foul, Delgado, the centre-back, chopped Lineker across the throat, and forced him off the field for treatment. With wry philosophy, Lineker observed later, 'It was an accident. At least, I hope it was.'

England took swift revenge. With Lineker still absent, Butcher's shot, from Hoddle's corner, bounced off Fernandez's chest; Beardsley did final execution. Then 17 minutes from the end, Lineker had the satisfaction of his second goal. Hoddle launched Gary Stevens of Spurs, on as a substitute, Stevens crossed low from the goal line, and Lineker was there to score. Argentina would be next—the first time they'd met since the Falklands War.

In Monterrey, which Lineker was so glad to leave—'The awful dehydration just saps your strength away. In the last twenty minutes you feel weak'—West Germany squeezed through 1–0 against Morocco, with an eighty-ninth-minute goal.

The Moroccans had beaten Portugal 3–1 in Guadalajara to reach this stage. A triumph for them, as their manager, José Faria, said happily: 'Lots of people expected us to lose, and lots of people lost because of that. We are the first team from the Third World to win its group. We could go home now. It is just one big party for us. It's as if we have already won our title.'

Truth to tell, the Portuguese were clearly a demoralised side, torn apart by endless arguments with their officials. But at least, in this game, the Moroccans gave rein to their undoubted talents, so sadly masked in the games against England and, subsequently, West Germany. Abderrazak Khairi, their midfielder, shot two goals in the first half; the elusive Timoumi made a third for the veteran centre-forward, Krimau Merry, just after the hour. The response by the blond Diamantino, who came on only as a substitute, was irrelevant.

Franz Beckenbauer would castigate the Moroccans for their negative play in Monterrey; just as he'd dismiss the Danish tactics as 'primitive'. José Faria responded that he'd intended to bring on two fast attackers in extra time—a somewhat unconvincing riposte.

Yet Morocco surely had enough gifted players on the park over the 90 minutes—Krimau Merry, Timoumi, Bouderbala—to have troubled an unconvincing German team more than they did. Not till Beckenbauer brought on quick little Pierre Littbarski for a disappointing Rudi Voeller at half-time did the Germans begin to show much form.

The day was hot, the game was dull. Zaki, Morocco's excellent goal-keeper, made a splendid save from Karl-Heinz Rummenigge—playing a whole game at last—just before half-time, but chances were at a premium. He saved well again, with his legs, from Lothar Matthaus, three minutes from the end, but a couple of minutes later Matthaus had the last word.

A free kick to West Germany, a gap in the Moroccan 'wall', and Matthaus, needing no invitation, crashed the ball through it and low past Zaki, who couldn't have seen it.

The following day, in Queretaro, produced an astonishing game between Spaniards and Danes. Whatever Beckenbauer said, the Danes had played some wonderful football. But they'd be without Frank Arnesen, and here Matthaus comes into a last-minute picture, again. In the ninetieth minute of the Denmark-West Germany match, Arnesen had taken a kick at him and been sent off, and suspended. Ironically, Klaus Berggreen, who'd committed a painful and disgraceful 'professional' foul on Charlie Nicholas in the win against Scotland—he'd 'had to do it', he said—was able to take part.

Alas, it would be another four years before João Havelange relin-quished his crass opposition to the 'professional foul' rule, which he'd forbidden the Football League to adopt in 1982. And even then, he'd fail to get it right, fail, in his imperceptive way where football was concerned, to appreciate its import and subtleties.

The whole essence of the rule, as applied in England, was that it punished by expulsion defenders whose fouls outside the penalty box would otherwise allow them to escape. By applying the rule to the penalty area as well, FIFA and Havelange vitiated its significance and relevance.

This game, meanwhile, seemed to turn on a single moment's aberration. The culprit was little Jesper Olsen, the blond left-winger who played at times for Ajax and Manchester United. Strangely enough, it was Olsen who got the first goal of the game. Berggreen, of all people, procured the penalty, when Gallego was ruled—to Spanish fury—to have brought him down. Olsen scored.

Two minutes from half-time, he gave Spain their equaliser. Quite what got into his head when Hogh, his goalkeeper, rolled him the ball, who can say, but he whimsically rolled it across his own penalty box. Emilio Butragueño doesn't look such gift horses in the mouth. The teams went into the dressing-rooms at 1–1, and Denmark would never be the same.

Now Butragueño became a torment to them; his swerves, his accelerations, his sudden, unexpected appearances in striking positions, would perplex and undo them.

Some 12 minutes into the second half, Victor, the sturdy, busy midfielder, took a corner, Camacho knocked it on to the far post, and Butragueño, unmarked, proved he could score with his head as well as his elegant feet. Denmark collapsed, though not before Zubizarreta, the Spanish goalkeeper, had dealt with an attempt by Elkjaer.

Sixty-eight minutes had gone when Spain obtained the first of two penalties. Significantly, it was for a foul on the rampant Butragueño, who raced down the left, cut into the box, and was felled by Busk. That fearsome centre-back, Goicoechea, put away the penalty. Denmark broke now and then, but overall Spain simply overwhelmed them.

Eloy, a fast, skilled little winger, ran down the right to create Butragueño's first goal. With two minutes left, Butragueño was brought down in the box once again, this time as he took on Morten Olsen, and this time he himself scored from the penalty spot. No one had done as much in World Cup finals since Eusebio, against the North Koreans, in 1966.

So to the quarter-finals, the first of which pitted France against Brazil in Guadalajara in a memorable game, blemished only by the fact that it was shamefully resolved on penalties.

This too was a match which probably turned on a single incident: a missed penalty 17 minutes from the end. Missed, of all people, by little Zico, of the usually unforgiving spot kick. That would have made it 2–1 to Brazil, who had looked, till France equalised, as though they were going to come through in a canter. Up to that moment, moving with beautiful economy and grace, the Brazilians seemed always to have it in their power to raise their game at will, and prevail.

Dr Socrates, strolling about the field in samba rhythm, was never hurried, always inventive, occasionally breaking into a brisk trot. On the quarter-hour, receiving from the mobile Careca, Socrates struck a shot which Joel Bats, France's brave but inconsistent goalkeeper, could only beat out. Socrates returned the compliment, and Bats had to plunge desperately at Careca's feet.

France's defence, suspect in the air, none too certain on the ground, were having far more trouble than the craven Italians ever gave them. Three minutes later, they were penetrated. Muller, the quick mulatto winger, an outstanding talent but an eternal maverick, nonchalantly combined with Junior. Careca put Junior's ball past Bats. Later, leaving Bossis for dead, he enabled Muller to shoot against the base of the post.

One-way traffic; but it wouldn't last. A few minutes from half-time, a French team lucky still to be in the game suddenly drew level. Amoros, a dynamic attacking full-back, gave the ball to little Alain Giresse. On it went to Dominique Rocheteau, who crossed from the right. The ball took a deflection to the far post and reached Platini. Quite marginal till then, he had no trouble in scoring. So the teams went in at 1–1.

That goal, coming as it did at such a crucial psychological moment, brought France emphatically back into the game and took a good deal of the virtue out of Brazil. By the end of ordinary time, it would have been fair to say that neither team deserved to lose.

Bats had his adventures. Twice in the second half he blocked shots from the incisive Junior. He would save headers from Zico, Socrates and, in extra time, Socrates again. For good measure, he got his hand to a powerful drive by Alemao. And it was Bats who first conceded and then saved Zico's penalty. When Branco, Brazil's attacking leftback, dashed into the box after a swift exchange with Zico, Bats brought him down.

Zico, master of the dead-ball kick, decided to take the penalty with his right foot. It wasn't good enough. Bats redeemed himself, hurtling to his left to save.

Extra time came. Somewhat surprisingly, a clearly tiring Socrates was kept in play by Tele Santana. Carlos, in the Brazilian goal, now had plenty to do, as France showed that the Brazilian defence were far from impregnable. He blocked resiliently when Tigana came through on a superb exchange with Rocheteau. He thwarted Bossis, shooting after a sustained run out of defence. He was lucky, near the end of extra time, when Bellone, chasing Platini's pass, was clean through, though possibly offside. The winger, however, though plainly fouled by Carlos on the edge of the box, failed to benefit from a dubious 'advantage' played by the referee.

So, deplorably, to penalties. Two years' hard work by both teams would now be decided by an irrelevant lottery. Santana had cause to regret keeping Socrates on when the doctor missed the first penalty for Brazil. Stopyra scored for France, Alemao for Brazil, and Zico, this time, converted his kick. Bellone, in off post and keeper, and Branco scored in turn, then it came to Platini. Another dead-ball expert; and another failure, on the day. He shot over the bar! Perhaps his readiness to leave the field early against Italy, just as a tempting free kick had been awarded to France on the edge of the box, became explicable.

Bats to the rescue. He flew gloriously across his goal to save the kick from Julio Cesar, the Brazilian centre-back; and Luis Fernandez put Brazil out of their misery. Sad that either team had to go out, especially thus.

Shadows of the Falklands War hung over the ensuing game at the Azteca between England and Argentina, though the Argentine players, out at the luxurious sports club where they were in training, were detached and composed. The tall, elegant Jorge Valdano easily parried barbed questions by Latin American reporters. Journalists, he said, had a habit of befouling sporting issues. Argentina didn't need the issue of the islands to motivate them. Reaching the quarter-finals and playing against a team with one of the finest traditions in the game was enough.

The England players, one assured him, felt the same. '*A ellos conviene*,' he answered, drily—'It suits them to do so.' The reporters roared.

Decent, honest José-Luis Brown said, 'We all had cousins, fathers, nephews in the Falklands, and some of them didn't come back. Lamentable things, but we shan't be thinking of them.' England, he believed, were a team that let you play, that gave a surprising amount of room to the Paraguayan attackers, Romerito and Cabañas. He expected 'a very beautiful game'.

And Maradona? 'You've just got to play him the way you see it on the day,' said Terry Butcher, who, on the day, would be one of the players Maradona danced round for his amazing second goal. 'You can't possibly say do this, do that, because he can improvise, he can get out of a hole. No matter how many people are around him, he can somehow come out with the ball. You can try to crowd him out, but that might leave other sectors weak. They've got other class players.'

The bearded Batista, who had wandered the midfield to such effect, was confident that Argentina could dominate that area.

England weren't as comfortably ensconced as the Argentines, though the Americanised hotel where they were now quartered was a great improvement on the hovel they'd been put in when they arrived in Mexico City. Evidently the Football Association had had scant belief in the team's chances of reaching the Second Round. There was no air-conditioning in the first hotel, which stood by a motorway. So, for that matter, did the second, which lay under a flight path for good, or bad, measure.

Bobby Robson, still gloomily defending England's performance, even in the earlier games, disputing a foreign journalist's claim that they had 'started slowly', said 'I've got 24 hours to devise a way to stop Maradona. It won't be easy. Other teams have already tried everything. They've assigned one man to mark him, they've closed down space, they've let him go while attempting to cut off his service. To no avail . . . Let's just say that without Maradona, Argentina would have no chance of winning the World Cup. That's how great he is.'

At least it was a more cheerful Robson than a year earlier in Mexico City, when he'd told the English Press, 'You people provide the pressure. If you people didn't exist, my job would be twice as easy and twice as pleasurable.'

Only now did Argentina deploy the players and the formation which would become so famous and familiar. With Garre suspended, Olarticoechea, previously a substitute, took up the wide role on the left, and stayed there. Pasculli, who had both scored and missed against Uruguay, dropped out. Enrique came into the central midfield to mark Glenn Hoddle; Ruggeri and Cuciuffo close-marked Beardsley and Lineker. Brown played sweeper, behind them. England's attack struggled through the first half to make any kind of impact. The match, surprisingly, had been allotted to an inexperienced Tunisian referee, Ali Ben Naceur, who, in the event, would prove as badly out of his depth as had his Syrian predecessor in the England v. Paraguay game.

England didn't close-mark Maradona, who did relatively little damage before half-time. But then, England had just one promising moment, when the Argentine keeper, Neri Pumpido, slipped as he challenged Beardsley for a through pass. Beardsley, however, could only hit the side netting.

Just five minutes after half-time we saw what one might call the obverse side of Maradona, Buenos Aires urchin incarnate. If there was an urchin effrontery about his marvellous sorties, his effortless ridiculing of opponents who tried to stop him, his flicks and touches, so there was about what happened now.

Maradona bored his way into the heart of the English defence, but lost the ball. Valdano couldn't retain it either, and Steve Hodge, in a moment of fatal insouciance, hooked it over his head, meaning it for Shilton. Ninety-nine times out of a hundred, Shilton would doubtless have got it. This was the hundredth, and this was Maradona. Up he went with Shilton, up went his hand, into the net went the ball. The linesman did not object. The referee gave a goal—the worst scored against England since Silvio Piola punched one over his shoulder in Milan in 1939. But at least that wasn't a World Cup match, and at least England eventually equalised.

Later, brazen and shameless, Maradona was all mock innocence, talking about 'the hand of God'. For England, it was rather the hand of the devil. Four minutes later, Maradona would score again, a goal to bring the house down and to treasure. But an Italian journalist, later that day, said to me, 'England were still in a state of shock, like a man who's just had his wallet stolen.' Apt enough, for Maradona's first goal was an act of theft.

The second was astounding, a goal so unusual, almost romantic, that it might have been scored by some schoolboy hero, or some remote Corinthian, from the days when dribbling was the vogue. It hardly belonged to so apparently rational and rationalised an era as ours, to a period in football when the dribbler seemed almost as extinct as the pterodactyl. And if the English defenders were, indeed, still in a state of shock, Maradona would do very much the same again in his country's next game, against Belgium.

Getting the ball towards the right, far away from goal, Maradona began hurtling through the England defence. A body swerve left Stevens helpless, another feint had Butcher—well might he say that Maradona was irrepressible—careening off in the wrong direction. Fenwick, who'd later elbow him, was negotiated with ease. Finally, as a fourth defender converged on him, Maradona casually beat Shilton. What could he do for an encore? We'd have the answer in the semi-final.

After 65 minutes, Bobby Robson, seeing that Trevor Steven and Steve Hodge were getting nowhere down the wings, brought on the two-footed if erratic Chris Waddle, and took off Peter Reid, who'd had trouble with his ankle. Waddle was not yet the all-around, sophisticated player he'd later become with Marseille; he'd not convinced in the early games, but it was a valid risk.

After 74 minutes, John Barnes came on for Trevor Steven; and the recovery truly began. Barnes was, and remained, a tantalising enigma, a black player of enormous natural talent, son of the Jamaican military attaché in England, who'd been spotted by a Watford fan as a teenager, playing park football.

He had power, pace, control, a swerve, a fine shot. In Rio, two years earlier, he had scored a stupendous solo goal, then made a second for Mark Hateley, to give England victory over Brazil. Since then, he had been disappointingly inconsistent, though there were those who blamed Bobby Robson for demanding, allegedly, that he stay too close to his own full-back.

No such instructions restrained him now. From the first, he ran superbly at and past the Argentine defence. Giusti, on the right flank, was no true full-back, and couldn't cope with a true winger, least of all one of such talents. Ten minutes from time, five after he'd come on, Barnes roared past Giusti, delivered a perfect centre, and Lineker headed it into the goal. Three minutes from the end, Barnes did it again. Once more, Lineker moved in on the cross, but just as it seemed he must score again, must have the equaliser, it transpired that Lineker himself was in the net, the ball had gone by him. Tapia, Argentina's own substitute, meanwhile struck a post.

Afterwards, in the Stygian gloom of a bar in their hotel, England's players spoke gloomily of their defeat, of the punched goal and the inadequacy of the Tunisian referee. Shilton pointed out wryly that when a free kick was chipped to Barnes, he'd have had an excellent chance, had the ball not hit the referee, who had bizarrely stationed himself on the end of the Argentine wall! 'He said, "Sorry, sorry",' remarked Steve Hodge. 'Too late!'

So England went home with a genuine hard-luck story, though had Maradona not scored his 'hand of God' goal and had the English team remained unchanged, it's hard to imagine them scoring. Lineker's six goals, meanwhile, would make him the tournament's top scorer, and Barcelona beckoned.

West Germany were through; they'd beaten Mexico in Monterrey, but only on penalties. The Mexicans, who'd grown as the tournament went on, held them to a 0–0 draw, and went down only on penalty kicks. Thick grass, heat and humidity played their dire part again. Not for nothing had Zibi Boniek derided the quality of football played in the Monterrey group, advising spectators to stay at home and watch its games on television. True, it was all relative. As Gary Lineker remarked drily of the bad Azteca pitch, 'It didn't seem to affect Maradona.'

Toni Schumacher, the villain of Seville four years earlier, the terror of the training camp before the 1986 World Cup began, was unbeatable in the West German goal. The West Germans played a dourly cautious game, which Franz Beckenbauer tried to excuse, unconvincingly, on the grounds that they were away from home, in front of a partisan crowd. More significantly, Berthold was sent off after 65 minutes.

But with Hugo Sanchez ineffectual, Tomas Boy forced to go off after a tackle by Andy Brehme, playing in midfield, after only half an hour, Mexico were no real threat. Aguirre, who had forced a good save from Schumacher late in the game, was sent off after 99 minutes by the weak Colombian referee, Palacio. When it eventually came to penalties, only Negrete could score for Mexico. Quirarte and Servin both had their kicks saved by Schumacher, who'd now renew acquaintance with Patrick Battiston, the player he could have killed in Seville.

Belgium and Spain drew too, in Puebla. The Belgians, whose French- and Flemish-speaking layers seemed to have found a *modus vivendi* after reported early squabbles, went ahead through the dominating Ceulemans after 34 minutes, though Renquin's abject miskick a quarter of an hour earlier should have given Julio Salinas a goal.

Thereafter, Belgium's tall, lanky, confident defenders gave even Butragueño scant scope. Belgium's goal came against the run of the play, but was admirably made and taken. A left-wing cross by the persistent Vercauteren, a diving header by an unmarked Ceulemans, and the Belgians led. Curiously enough, Ceulemans, seven minutes after half-time, spurned the chance to sew up the game for his team.

Nico Claesen broke away—something the Belgians did so well—and found Ceulemans, once more left alone, some 12 yards out. Commendably but fatally unselfish, Ceulemans turned the ball on to Veyt, who missed by a fraction.

This spurred the Spaniards into a long period of pressure. With only six minutes left, Victor pulled a free kick back to the substitute, Señor, who drove in a tremendous first-time shot from a good 30 yards. It took such a shot to beat Jean-Marie Pfaff, in marvellous form in the Belgian goal.

Two weary teams went on to extra time; and penalties. Pfaff came into his own again. As each Spanish kick was taken, he did his best to gain the upper hand, and appeared to succeed. Eloy's second Spanish penalty was saved dramatically by Pfaff, leaping to his right. So Leo Van der Elst, a Belgian substitute, was able to qualify his team by driving in their fifth penalty.

Now for Argentina, and Maradona. Alas for the Belgians, they were no more successful in coping with him than England had been. There was to be no repetition of the opening game of the 1982 World Cup in Barcelona, when Belgium's defenders, playing a game of Pass the Parcel, handed Maradona on to one another, effectively subdued him and so, surprisingly, won the game. In the immortal if apocryphal words of Samuel Goldwyn, we had all passed a lot of water since those days.

The Belgians survived the first half in the hot Azteca; you could not put it any higher than that. Their attack was as impotent as England's

had been until the arrival of Barnes. Their massed defence watched anxiously when, at the start, the Argentines confidently and casually played
'keep ball'. Jorge Burruchaga, in midfield, had clearly found new confidence and authority, a splendid foil to Maradona. Jorge Valdano was
equally self-assured up front. But a greasy pitch as much as the many
Belgian defenders kept Argentina out. When Valdano did get the ball
into the net, he had clearly used his arm; and this time, Argentina found
no indulgent referee.

Just now and again, Belgium showed signs of life, and initiative. Enzo
Scifo, the Belgian-born Sicilian who'd done disappointingly little thus far
in his team's midfield, had flashes of class. Jan Ceulemans, predictably,
was not over-awed. But half-time came without a goal. It was clearly time
for Maradona to do something.

And he did. Two things, in fact: two marvellous goals, which even
the resilient Jean-Marie Pfaff could do nothing about. Six minutes
into the second half, Enrique and Burrachaga combined on the right.
As the ball came across, Maradona glided into the penalty area, bisecting two defenders, and beat Pfaff with the outside of his remarkable
left foot.

That goal was good enough. The one that followed, a dozen minutes
later, was extraordinary, a solo of sublime inspiration; and no one had,
metaphorically, robbed the Belgian defence of its wallet. He did not run
as far as he had done against England, but this made his goal only the
more remarkable. There was so little space, around the edge of the box,
as he swerved, dashed and dummied by four bemused defenders in turn,
finally to shoot past Pfaff.

Belatedly, Guy Thys gambled, taking off his sweeper, Renquin, and
putting on a winger in Philippe Desmet, but Desmet proved no John
Barnes. Indeed, Argentina could well have scored a third, Maradona
shooting just wide, then giving a simple chance to Valdano, who blazed
high over the top. Belgium, perhaps, had lived beyond their means,
exceeded all their hopes, made a virtue out of necessity by replacing
injured players with youngsters.

A tournament in which history threatened to repeat itself, when poor
refereeing—oddly enough, by the Argentine, Esposito—had helped to
lose them their first game against Mexico, had ended honourably. If that
was the word for the resourceful Belgian right-back, Eric Gerets, suspended and cast out by Milan in 1984, when found guilty of match-fixing
with Standard Liège. Guy Thys, anyway, had confirmed himself as a
resourceful international team manager. But what could even he do
against a Maradona?

In Guadalajara, Battiston renewed acquaintance, less painfully,
with Toni Schumacher; and West Germany again won a semi-final
against France. This time without recourse to penalties. Grindingly effi-

cient as ever, West Germany confounded their detractors to reach yet another World Cup Final, against the odds. If Berthold, after his expulsion against Mexico, was suspended, France lacked Dominique Rocheteau, who had an injured hamstring. Bellone took his place—in so far as anybody could.

This would not be as dazzling and dramatic a match as Seville's. Franz Beckenbauer used Rolff to shadow Platini; Michel employed Fernandez to keep an eye on Rummenigge, who this time lasted just 56 minutes. Schumacher and Battiston shook hands before the kick-off. The German keeper would have a happier game than Joel Bats.

Wearied by the extra time against Brazil—the Germans, though down to 10 for so long against Mexico, had at least prevailed in 90 minutes— the last thing France wanted was to concede a bad early goal. But after a mere 10 minutes, they did. Bossis fouled Rummenigge just outside the box. Magath touched the free kick aside, and Brehme, scorer of decisive World Cup goals, roared in to hit it round the wall. Bats, probably seeing it late, dived for the ball, but it squirmed off his chest and rolled under him, into the net.

France were not down and done for. Neither Platini nor Giresse, now 34, would excel in this game, but three minutes after the goal Platini headed a ball to Giresse which he volleyed only a little wide. Later, Tigana and Platini again put Giresse through a German defence which was plainly negotiable, but Giresse muffed his shot.

Next minute, the fifteenth, France threw away their best chance of all. Michel Platini, still capable of doing damage even on an off day, struck a volley from the right-hand side of the box. It was too hot even for Schumacher to hold. The ball rebounded to the big central defender, Bossis, just 6 yards from goal. An empty goal. He shot over the top.

Bats, twice using his feet, did something to atone for his mistake. He kept out thus a shot by Rummenigge—still plainly not quite fit—and another from Rolff. Forsaking his role as Platini's marker, Rolff ran on to a touch by Klaus Allofs, shot from 8 yards out, and was frustrated. When Magath shot again, Bats got to that too. It was Rolff once more who brought another fine save from Bats with a 30-yard bullet early in the second half; the goalkeeper turned it over the bar.

Yet Rolff almost emerged as the villain of the piece. A dreadful pass back was snapped up by Bellone, but his shot from the edge of the 6-yard box was charged down and, after some tense seconds, West Germany escaped.

Stopyra, nastily fouled early in the half by the blond German stopper, Foerster, had recovered sufficiently to carve a way through the German defence, after 63 minutes, only for Schumacher to save splendidly at just 8 yards' range.

It remained for Rudi Voeller, who'd come on seven minutes earlier in place of a struggling Karl-Heinz Rummenigge, to rub salt into French wounds. In the very last minute, he moved on to a left-wing cross from Allofs, expertly lobbed over Bats, ran by him, and found the empty net. Another World Cup Final for West Germany. Another disappointment for France.

Winning the third-place match, in Puebla, where the Belgians were beaten 4–2, was scant consolation. They did it without Platini, and despite a rash of missed chances by Jean-Pierre Papin, still some way from becoming the famous opportunist who'd cost Milan a fortune when they signed him. Jan Ceulemans was again one of the best players afield, cutting in from the right to beat Rust, Bats's deputy, for the first Belgian goal, after 11 minutes.

Thereafter, each team missed an abundance of chances, the score at 90 minutes being 2–2. In extra time, a goal by Genghini, a midfield star of 1982, and a penalty by Amoros won the game for France. At home, Platini became a scapegoat.

For the Final, Maradona was clearly the favourite. Yet, in the event, Argentina won without his ever reaching the heights he had in previous games. Won with surprising difficulty, not to say strange carelessness, almost contriving to throw away a game they seemed to have in their pockets. The West Germans, resilient as ever, made up with sheer morale what they lacked in tactics and technique.

The $64,000 question was, inevitably, who would mark Maradona? Beckenbauer decided it should be Lothar Matthaus, thus taking a double gamble. First, because for all his versatility, Matthaus was essentially a midfielder, rather than a marker, a defender. Secondly, because his creative gifts were thus denied a team which badly needed them.

Worst still, it was Matthaus's unpleasant foul on Maradona, a direct consequence of the marking role he'd been given, which led straight to the first Argentine goal. Twenty-two minutes had gone when Maradona's neat backheel left Matthaus in limbo. He retorted by chopping Maradona down from behind. Burruchaga took a long, high free kick from the right. It was a goalkeeper's ball, one which, at almost any time, you would have backed Schumacher to take. This time, he didn't. Mistiming his exit, he allowed the ball to float above his outstretched hands. Unmarked on the far post, left by defenders who'd perhaps placed excessive trust in their keeper, lurked José-Luis Brown. A free header, and the ball was home.

To go a goal behind was the last thing such a cautiously deployed German team wanted. So packed with defenders were they, you had the impression that even the man with the bucket and sponge must be a centre-back in drag. Michel Platini, asked the day before the Final whether he'd be going to see it, had replied that he wouldn't; there'd be nothing to learn. He was probably right. However much Bilardo would boast, subsequently, of the tactical innovations which circumstances had forced on him, the game had gone backwards since the exhilarating days of Total Football. Moreover, the goals scored in this Final were curiously sloppy, in defensive terms.

Dull stuff it was, for a long time. After 33 minutes, the Germans had a nasty moment when Maradona broke through, Schumacher kicked out at the ball, it rebounded from Maradona's chest, and flew not far wide of the goal. West Germany clearly had to do something drastic, and when they came out again for the second half, it was with Rudi Voeller replacing not one of the posse of defenders but the left-winger, Klaus Allofs. Hardly a daring stroke.

Four minutes into the half, a West German team now forced to go for goals found itself in numerical inferiority to Argentina, two defenders against four attackers. Foerster's desperate tackle on Burruchaga, within spitting distance of the goal, saved his side.

Now José-Luis Brown went down with an injured shoulder, left the field for treatment, came back again and, characteristically, loyally, played on in pain for the rest of the match. With Passarella indisposed, who else could play sweeper?

Briegel, the huge, blond Siegfried figure, was bullocking his way down the left from time to time, but this apart, the West Germans had sadly little to offer. Ten minutes into the second half, hoist with their own petard, West Germany succumbed to a counter-attack.

Enrique, in ebullient form, found Valdano, quite unmarked, on the left. Valdano ran on to beat Schumacher with ease. Those who accused the keeper of hesitation on this and Argentina's winning goal were being somewhat harsh. On each occasion, Schumacher was left exposed. Valdano's goal was just reward. Best player on the field, he also closed down the incursions of the massive Briegel.

Six minutes later, Beckenbauer made another change. Again, he did not take off a defender. It was Magath, the midfielder, who gave way to Dieter Hoeness, a tall centre-forward, powerful in the air, brother of Uli, star right-winger of the Total Football team of the 1970s.

Obsessed with Maradona, the Germans were giving far too much room to other Argentines, notably Enrique, who revelled in the extra space. But after 28 minutes of the half, the Germans were suddenly and unexpectedly back in contention.

Brehme took a corner, Rudi Voeller flicked on with his head, and in came Rummenigge, the old Rummenigge, to do final execution.

West Germany had risen from the ashes. Now, at long last, Matthaus deserted his ungrateful task against Maradona to move into midfield, and direct the play. Eight minutes from the end, another corner, another

German goal; the scores were squared after 82 minutes.

Again, the flag kick, was Brehme's, though this time the headed flick on was from Berthold. Voeller, who had set up the first goal, now, with another header, scored the second. The unthinkable had happened. Argentina had let the game slip out of their grasp. It if went to extra time, what hope of holding out, with Brown a virtual cripple?

Re-enter Maradona. With six minutes to play, his exquisite pass sent Jorge Burruchaga through. Burrachaga kept his nerve, and Schumacher was beaten again. The Cup, very properly, was Argentina's.

Overall, it had been a good World Cup, rising above the oppressive conditions in Mexico, and the dubious way it had been allotted there. The Mexicans themselves had risen above the shocking disaster which had devastated the centre of Mexico City, an earthquake to recall that which had devastated Chile before the 1962 World Cup. The Mexican people had shown warmth, enthusiasm, generosity. The English 'hooligans' had been little or no problem. Diego Maradona had been as great a hero as Pelé in 1970.

The great, yellow Camel cigarette balloon floating ominously outside the Azteca stadium had, meanwhile, been the very symbol of commercialism. It was defended by Havelange on the bizarre grounds that *he'd* never smoked, and FIFA needed the money for a 24-team World Cup. The tournament had risen above that misbegotten formula too. In 1990, it would not be so lucky.

RESULTS: Mexico 1986

First round

Group A

Mexico City, Puebla
Italy 1, Bulgaria 1
Argentina 3, South Korea 1
Italy 1, Argentina 1
Bulgaria 1, South Korea 1
Italy 3, South Korea 2
Argentina 2, Bulgaria 0

	P	W	D	L	GOALS F	A	Pts
Argentina	3	2	1	0	6	2	5
Italy	3	1	2	0	5	4	4
Bulgaria	3	0	2	1	2	4	2
South Korea	3	0	1	2	4	7	1

Group B

Mexico City, Toluca
Mexico 2, Belgium 1
Paraguay 1, Iraq 0
Mexico 1, Paraguay 1
Belgium 2, Iraq 1
Mexico 1, Iraq 0
Belgium 2, Paraguay 2

	P	W	D	L	GOALS F	A	Pts
Mexico	3	2	1	0	4	2	5
Paraguay	3	1	2	0	4	3	4
Belgium	3	1	1	1	5	5	3
Iraq	3	0	0	3	1	4	0

Group C

Leon, Irapuato
France 1, Canada 0
Soviet Union 6, Hungary 0
France 1, Soviet Union 1
Hungary 2, Canada 0
France 3, Hungary 0
Soviet Union 2, Canada 0

	P	W	D	L	GOALS F	A	Pts
USSR	3	2	1	0	9	1	5
France	3	2	1	0	5	1	5
Hungary	3	1	0	2	2	9	2
Canada	3	0	0	3	0	5	0

Group D

Guadalajara, Monterrey
Spain 0, Brazil 1
Algeria 1, Northern Ireland 1
Northern Ireland 1, Spain 2
Brazil 1, Algeria 0
Algeria 0, Spain 3
Northern Ireland 0, Brazil 3

	P	W	D	L	GOALS F	A	Pts
Brazil	3	3	0	0	5	0	6
Spain	3	2	0	1	5	2	4
N. Ireland	3	0	1	2	2	6	1
Algeria	3	0	1	2	1	5	1

Group E

Neza, Queretaro
Denmark 1, Scotland 0
West Germany 1, Uruguay 1
West Germany 2, Scotland 1
Denmark 6, Uruguay 1
Scotland 0, Uruguay 0
Denmark 2, West Germany 0

	P	W	D	L	GOALS F	A	Pts
Denmark	3	3	0	0	9	1	6
West Germany	3	1	1	1	3	4	3
Uruguay	3	0	2	1	2	7	2
Scotland	3	0	1	2	1	3	1

Group F

Monterrey, Guadalajara
Portugal 1, England 0
Morocco 0, Poland 0
Poland 1, Portugal 0
Morocco 0, England 0
Morocco 3, Portugal 1
England 3, Poland 0

	P	W	D	L	GOALS F	A	Pts
Morocco	3	1	2	0	3	1	4
England	3	1	1	1	3	1	3
Poland	3	1	1	1	1	3	3
Portugal	3	1	0	2	2	4	2

Second round

Leon
Belgium 4, Soviet Union 3

Azteca, Mexico City
Mexico 2, Bulgaria 0

Guadalajara
Brazil 4, Poland 0

Puebla
Argentina 1, Uruguay 0

Olympic Stadium, Mexico City
France 2, Italy 0

Monterrey
West Germany 1, Morocco 0

Azteca, Mexico City
England 3, Paraguay 0

Queretaro
Denmark 1, Spain 5

Quarter-finals

Guadalajara
France 1, Brazil 1
France win 4–3 on penalties

Monterrey
Mexico 0, West Germany 0
West Germany win 4–1 on penalties

Azteca, Mexico City
Argentina 2, England 1

Puebla
Belgium 1, Spain 1
Belgium win 5–4 on penalties

Semi-finals

Azteca, Mexico City
Argentina 2, Belgium 0

Guadalajara
West Germany 2, France 0

Third-place match

Puebla

France 4   Belgium 2
(after extra time)

Rust, Ayache, Battiston, Le Roux (Bossis), Amoros; Bibard, Ferreri, Tigana (Tusseau), Genghini, Vercruysse; Papin, Bellone.

Pfaff; Gerets, Renquin (F. Van der Elst). De Mol, Vervoort; Scifo (L. Van der Elst), Mommens, Ceulemans; Veyt, Claesen

SCORERS
Ferreri, Papin, Genghini, Amoros (penalty) for France
Ceulemans, Claesen for Belgium
HT (2–1)

Final

Azteca, Mexico City

Argentina 3
Pumpido; Brown; Ruggeri, Cuciuffo; Giusti, Enrique, Batista, Burruchaga (Trobbiani), Olarticoechea; Valdano, Maradona.

West Germany 2
Schumacher; Jakobs; Brehme, Foerster, Berthold, Briegel; Matthaus, Magath (D. Hoeness), Eder; Rummenigge, Allofs (Voeller).

SCORERS
Brown, Valdano, Burruchaga for Argentina
Rummenigge, Voeller for West Germany
HT (1–0)

ITALY
1990

Once again, West Germany met Argentina in the Final, but this time, the Germans had revenge of a sort. It was probably the worst, most tedious, bad-tempered Final in the history of the World Cup. Diego Maradona was half crippled; Claudio Caniggia, Argentina's dashing blond striker, was suspended—the result of a mere handball. The Germans, utterly uninspired, won through a penalty which should probably never have been given, but most neutral spectators were just glad to be done with the game. This time, the tournament did not escape the consequences of its elephantiasis.

Afterwards, intent on disavowing the real cause, FIFA emitted a series of insensate suggestions for 'improvement', everything from larger goals to fewer players. A committee consisting of the great and the good was set up. The mountain eventually parturated a mouse, in the spring of 1992, in the shape of a half-baked rule forbidding goalkeepers to handle back passes. The British associations had enough votes on the International Board—four against FIFA's four—to block the motion, but they sold the pass; or the back pass.

The tournament had its consolations, even if the greatest disappointment of all was the form of Holland. The Dutch had brilliantly won the European Championship in West Germany two years earlier, beating the Germans themselves in the semi-final, thrashing the Soviets in the final, inspired by the dazzling trio of Milan players, Marco Van Basten, Ruud Gullit and Frank Rijkaard, these last two coming from Surinam.

Van Basten, perversely omitted by the revered manager, Rinus Michels, from Holland's first line-up in Germany, was a protean centre-forward: strong, fast, highly intelligent, a superb finisher with foot or head. The goal he'd volleyed in the final against the Soviets was surely among the finest ever seen in an international match.

Gullit was the complete footballer: tall, powerful, astonishingly nimble for so big a man, a powerful shot, devastating in the air. But since the 1988 Championship, he'd had a series of grave operations on his right knee, and was in doubt almost till the eve of the tournament.

Rijkaard had been bought by Milan at the insistence of its determined little manager, Arrigo Sacchi, despite the opposition of the club's wealthy President, Silvio Berlusconi, owner of the television Channel 5. Berlusconi insisted the club prefer Claudio Borghi, the Argentine striker who'd played in the 1986 World Cup. Sacchi's view prevailed, and Borghi, drifting from club to club across South America, gradually and sadly faded from view.

Michels, now, was not the manager. That role had gone to the blond Leo Beenhakker, who'd had much success in Spain, most recently with Real Madrid. But he never won the admiration of the highly critical Dutch journalists; nor did he seem able to get the best out of his players. It was whispered that Michels, still in office in the Dutch Federation, overshadowed him and made his function difficult.

It's still hard to know quite what went wrong; why Van Basten, for example, played as poorly as he did. 'I think there were too many troubles inside the team,' Van Basten subsequently told me, 'inside the Federation, inside everything.' The nature of those troubles stays obscure.

Holland were drawn in the Sardinian-Sicilian group with England, the Republic of Ireland and Egypt, making them strong favourites to come through. They'd beaten England out of sight in the 1988 European Championship, where England had lost all three games, played abysmally, and Bobby Robson had become an Aunt Sally for the English Press.

Lurid revelations about his private life, which surely had nothing to do with the case, had allegedly induced the Football Association to tell him that whatever happened in the World Cup, they would not be renewing his contract. Robson promptly reached an agreement with PSV Eindhoven which, in the circumstances, he was fully entitled to do.

The English team had limped into the World Cup finals, Robson's famous luck holding in Katowice, where Peter Shilton's superb goalkeeping had yet again been the key to survival. Had Poland won, England would have been out. In the very last minute, even Shilton could do nothing about a tremendous long shot from Tarasciewicz which flew above his head, and twanged against his bar. 'Is this your proudest moment, Bobby?' asked a journalist, when the game was over. Strangely, there seemed no irony in the question.

Far more entitled to be proud was the manager of the Republic of Ireland, that same Jackie Charlton who'd played centre-half in the England team which won the 1966 World Cup. A resilient, combative Geordie, devoted to shooting and fishing, he found a full-time national manager's job perfectly suited to his rhythms and desires, where in Robson's case it simply gave him, it seemed, time to brood. Charlton's long-ball tactics were not for the purist. They had given small scope to perhaps the most gifted of Ireland's players, the creative Liam Brady, who'd played long years in Italy. Nor did the dubious qualification of several Irish players commend them to everybody. Ray Houghton, a Glaswegian, had scored the goal which beat England at Stuttgart in the 1988 European Championship.

But to see the Irish reach the World Cup finals at all was a minor miracle; and once there, they would fight their corner manfully. Beaten by Spain in their opening game, they'd had revenge in Dublin and taken three points from Northern Ireland, finishing in second group place, a point behind the Spaniards.

Italy, the hosts, had such colossal pressure on them that one doubted from the first whether they could resist it. An essential part of Enzo Bearzot's 'detoxifying' process—which had worked in two out of three World Cups—was that the players should be as far from the pressures of home as possible. Now, they were being interviewed within an inch of their lives.

There were ifs and buts about the team. Roberto Baggio, who'd emerged at Fiorentina as the most gifted Italian attacker for many years, after shocking ill-luck and a series of operations, clearly didn't please his manager, Azeglio Vicini. Vicini wanted him to play up front; Baggio preferred to lie deeper.

In attack, there were other enigmas. What could be expected from Gianluca Vialli, who, since his brief appearances in Mexico, had matured into the most powerful, dangerous striker the Italians ever had, developing from a left-winger into a two-footed player able to score from any position? But he'd injured his right foot, and both his form and his condition seemed uncertain.

Then what of 'Toto' Schillaci, the little Sicilian who'd emerged strangely late in his career, with Juventus? For years he'd hoped, and failed, to get away from Messina and Serie B, though his own city was Palermo. There, when Toto was due to play a European game in Turin for Juventus, his brother was arrested for stealing car tyres. Juventus kept the news from Toto till after the game.

Small, swift and dynamic, he'd had a splendid season for Juventus, but had still to prove he could flourish at international level, let alone in a World Cup. Though Sacchi had won glory with Milan, using zonal defence and what he called 'pressing' tactics, Vicini stuck to a sweeper.

Carlos Bilardo was still in charge of Argentina, Franz Beckenbauer of West Germany. At home, Bilardo remained a target. Once again the country's President, now the volatile exhibitionist Menem, had publicly criticised him. Menem, like many others, couldn't understand why Bilardo wouldn't pick Ramon Diaz, the centre-forward who'd won a Championship medal with Inter and now, with Monaco, had outwitted Argentina's defence in a friendly.

The conventional wisdom was that Maradona's veto was responsible. Though he and Diaz had once been great friends, playing in the Argentine youth team which had won the world title, they'd been at daggers drawn since Diaz, supposedly, had criticised Maradona. The new reality was Caniggia, transferred from River Plate to Verona, where he found himself on the edge of an unpleasant drugs scandal. There were anxious weeks, but he was finally absolved. Another Argentine player was convicted.

The Germans had abundant talent in midfield, where such players as Andy Moeller and Tomas Haessler had emerged, while Lothar Matthaus was clearly one of the most commanding generals in the game. They'd qualified one point behind the Dutch, with whom they'd drawn at home and away.

Scotland, ever resilient in the qualifiers, were present yet again, though they'd finished four whole points in their group behind Yugoslavia, inspired by the elegant Dragan Stojkovic. Scotland, now, were managed by the decent, studious, intelligent Andy Roxburgh, a former schoolmaster, a well-qualified coach, in sharp contrast to some of the flamboyant figures who had managed other Scottish World Cup teams. Could he, some wondered, get the best out of his players? But then, what Scottish manager had done that yet in World Cup finals? At least he had brought them thus far.

England were obliged to play all their group games in Cagliari, for fear of the hooligans among their fans. To say now that the Italian authorities over-reacted would be to put it mildly. Long before the England supporters arrived, with their bare chests, their tattoos and their Union Jacks, there were, it seemed, *carabinieri* on every corner, peering out of trucks, cradling their machine-guns. There'd be a riot before the match against Holland, a storm in Rimini before the match between England and Belgium in Bologna. On that occasion, at least, the English fans seemed hard done by. Several hundred of them, many asserting total innocence, were packed on to an aircraft which, just by coincidence, had exactly the number of seats to correspond with the arrests. Then all the fans, including many who'd simply and quietly been having a meal, were flown back to England.

Colin Moynihan, the Sports Minister, small but imperfectly informed, had been yapping round Cagliari, clearly suggesting that the Government's fiat, essential if English clubs were to return at last to European competition, would not be given. But when England so unexpectedly reached the semi-finals, *realpolitik* seemed to prevail. Suddenly and smilingly the Government gave its belated blessing. Whatever happened in Cagliari, the English clubs could now return.

The English players went to their training camp outside Cagliari in sour hostility to the Press. Bobby Robson himself, clearly incensed by the assaults on his private life, appeared to have set the tone. The irony was that sports journalists had nothing to do with such 'revelations', which they'd traditionally and wearily left to news reporters, whom they nicknamed 'The Rotters'. Bryan Robson, back again as captain, in his third World Cup, was also known to be distressed by allegations made outside the sports pages.

It was sad that the gifted young Paul Gascoigne should be dragged into all this, not least since, when Bobby Robson was iffing and butting about him, it was a handful of journalists who loudly trumpeted his claims. Gascoigne it was, however, in a notorious incident outside Bologna, at the England training ground, who hurled a cardboard cup of water at a journalist who was interviewing the little black defender, Paul Parker.

'Daft as a brush', Bobby Robson had called Paul Gascoigne and the words, alas, would come home to roost less than a year later at Wembley. There, playing for Spurs against Nottingham Forest in the FA Cup Final, Gascoigne launched himself into two suicidal tackles, the second of which left his right knee torn and useless. He'd be out of the game for over a year before he finally began to play again, in Rome, for Lazio.

Off the field, he could seem shy, simple, distracted. On it, he showed a flair, a superlative technique, a tactical sophistication, seldom matched by an English player since the war. Blond, thick-set, inclined to gain weight, Gascoigne might not have been fast, but, as admiring players would tell you, his sheer strength could compensate for that. He had a superb right foot, whether it was used for passing or for taking the kind of free kicks a Brazilian might envy. Over the generations, hundreds of fine players have come out of the north-east of England, but very few indeed have been the equal of Gascoigne.

Almost inevitably, he too found himself endlessly frustrated, fighting to gain a permanent place in the national team. When he should have been there, he could find himself playing for the England B team, forced out to the left wing. If he still contrived to do well, he might find Bobby Robson, afterwards, ignoring a spectacular goal, and preferring to stress the times he'd given the ball away. Which, to be fair, he did, at the cost of a goal, when the team played and drew in Tunisia, just before the World Cup began.

Gascoigne had played his way into the World Cup side with a glorious performance against Czechoslovakia at Wembley. Before the game, Bobby Robson had given an interview which must have put intolerable pressure on any less ebullient a character. This, he implied, was 'Gazza's' last chance. He must do it now, or fall by the wayside. Perhaps it was no surprise that, just before the teams took the field, Gazza was in the tunnel, eyes blazing, slamming a football furiously against the wall. He went out to play marvellously, having a hand in three goals, and scoring the fourth himself with an astonishing, sustained solo, almost worthy of Diego Maradona—who would again be present.

Brazil were going through another of their periods of trying to be more European than the Europeans, and it was clear that their manager, Sebastiao Lazaroni, the man who'd endowed them with a sweeper defence, had better win the World Cup, or else. Three goals conceded to East Germany in Rio hadn't suggested that a *libero* solved Brazil's defensive problems, and though the technical level of the team was high, the skill of Valdo undeniable, it seemed to lack the creative flair of the two previous World Cup teams.

Brazil qualified despite an astonishing attempt by Chile to cheat their way to the Finals. When the teams met in Rio in September 1989, at the Maracana, a girl threw a flare on to the pitch. Immediately Roberto Rojas, Chile's goalkeeper, collapsed, and was found to be bleeding. He was carried off the field, but investigation showed that he'd been quite unhurt, and had deliberately cut himself. He was banned for life; Chile were banned from the 1994 tournament, and fined £40,000. Chile's Federation President Sergio Stoppel, team doctor Daniel Rodriguez, manager Orlando Aravena, centre-back Fernando Astengo, plus the kit man and physiotherapist, also received bans of varying length.

As for Maradona, his presence had little effect in the remarkable opening match. Played at the San Siro stadium, which, like the Olympic Stadium in Rome, the Marassi Stadium in Genoa and the Communal Stadium in Florence, had been massively rebuilt, it saw the unthinkable happen: the World Cup holders beaten by an African team.

That team was Cameroon, who came to the World Cup in anything but a state of tranquillity. Their manager, Valeri Nepomniachi, was a Siberian who'd once worked under the great Lobanovski. But he spoke no French, had tenuous relations with his team at best, and was in stark contrast to the Frenchman Claude Leroy, who'd managed them with such success till 1988.

Joseph Antoine Bell, the veteran keeper who'd won his place back from his rival, Thomas N'Kono, spoke so disparagingly of the way things were being run that the officials put N'Kono back in goal, where he stayed. At 34, he was only a year younger than Bell.

Roger Milla was older than either of them. Just how old, nobody was quite sure. Thirty-eight was his official age, but he seemed to have been around for an awfully long time, playing for a wide variety of French clubs before, it seemed, retiring to play part-time football on the island of Réunion. This he enjoyed so much that Cameroon unexpectedly recalled him. He would do sensationally well, brought on as a second-half substitute to put bite and drive into an attack which never looked as dangerous without him—a view strongly contested by some of his colleagues, notably his fellow striker, Omam Biyik.

Omam Biyik it was who scored the only goal of Cameroon's sensational victory over Argentina, a game in which Milla came on only eight minutes from the end. The overall pattern of Cameroon's play

was quickly established: hard, even thuggish, at the back, lively and energetic in midfield, opportunist up front. A bruising game was made worse
by the draconian refereeing of Michel Vautrot, a French referee whose
large reputation would suffer badly in this tournament.

Perhaps it wasn't wholly his fault. FIFA, leaving it absurdly late, had
issued severe instructions to referees. At long last, and with pitifully little
notice and no consultation with the rule-making International Board, the
so-called Professional Foul rule would be introduced. On the eve of a
World Cup! Early in the tournament the controversial FIFA Secretary, the
Swiss Sepp Blatter, forever trumpeting the glories of football's liaison
with publicity and television, would make a stream of authoritarian
statements—till the Referees' Committee reminded him that it was *their*
business, not his.

Cameroon could hardly complain if two of their players were sent
off. They had fouled Maradona ruthlessly and painfully from the very
beginning. Strangely, and mistakenly, Carlos Bilardo had decided to 'sacrifice' Maradona in a central striking role, just as Menotti had done eight
years earlier in Spain, consigning him to the tender mercies of Gentile.
Equally strangely, Bilardo did not bring on the electric Claudio Caniggia
till the second half, when he should clearly have been on from the
beginning.

Maradona, who had just been made an honorary ambassador by President Menem, and was endlessly jeered by the Milanese crowd, dropped
deeper in the second half, took less punishment, and was able to assert
more influence. But overall, Cameroon were unquestionably the better
team, even if the goal they won with was the fruit of shocking errors in
the Argentine defence.

Caniggia's pace, and his ability to fall dramatically, unsettled the heavy
Cameroon defenders. Kana Biyik was sent off, perhaps a little harshly, for
fouling him after 62 minutes. It looked a good thing then for Argentina,
but five minutes later, Cameroon scored. Makanaky, he of the dreadlocks
and the endless activity, deflected a free kick from the left into the box.
Sensini seemed turned to stone. Omam Biyik was thus allowed to get his
head to the ball, but there still seemed little danger. But Neri Pumpido, in
goal, seemed as dazed as Sensini. The ball struck his knees and slithered
into the net.

'Without doubt,' said Bilardo, 'the worst defeat of my career.' But he'd
amply contributed to it.

The following day, in Rome, Italy opened their campaign in Group A
at the Olimpico against Austria, and made very heavy weather of it.
Admirable enterprise, endless pressure, good movement and original
ideas all added up to a mere one-goal win, against an Austrian side which
owed much to the goalkeeping of Lindenberger, and showed little
inclination to attack.

Those Italian journalists who had been muttering about the favours Italy would receive from referees had to eat their words when Russ brought down the splendidly creative right-winger, Roberto Donadoni, but the referee, the Brazilian Wright, refused a penalty.

So Italy had to wait till 16 minutes from the end before Toto Schillaci, who'd come on as substitute a mere three minutes earlier, scored their goal. He'd replaced the bigger, less mobile, Carnevale. Gianluca Vialli expertly went round the big Austrian sweeper, Aigner, on the right-hand goal line, pulled back a perfect cross and there was Schillaci, the man whose goose was supposedly cooked after a dreary display against Greece, to head it past Lindberger. Italy had impressed in everything except their finishing.

On the same day, in the glorious, futuristic new stadium in Bari, marvellous in its bold use of open space, Romania defeated the Soviet Union, again under the command of Lobanovski and full of seasoned players. It had looked an easy match for the Soviets, with Romania short of their most influential player, the remarkable George Hagi, an all-round midfielder with a superlative left foot, capable of both making and scoring goals.

But Group B was to throw up its second surprise. The Soviets would pay heavily for their miss in the second minute, when their much-lauded centre-forward, Protasov, sent through by Rats, allowed Lung to save. Zavarov missed in turn, Lung saved from Litovchenko and Aleinikov; and five minutes before half-time, the Soviet defence collapsed. Sabau, an alert midfielder, sent a through ball to the rapid outside-right, Lacatus. Aleinikov stretched but missed; Lacatus raced on and beat the Soviet keeper, Dassaev, with the outside of his accomplished right foot.

The Soviets' inability to take their chances had, not for the first time, proved expensive. Dobrovolski and Zavarov faded softly and silently away; Romania took up the running. What really knocked the stuffing out of the Soviets was the penalty wrongly given against them nine minutes into the second half by the referee, Cardellino. As Lacatus advanced on Khidiatulin, the Soviet defender handled, outside the box. Cardellino gave a penalty, and Lacatus himself hammered in the final nail.

In Bologna, the United Arab Emirates, newcomers to the World Cup, went down 2–0 to Colombia, without disgrace. The Arabs had sacked one Brazilian manager, the celebrated Mario Zagalo, for his open disparagement of their chances, and appointed another, Carlos Alberto Parreira. René Higuita, Colombia's spectacular, self-indulgent goalkeeper, got up to his customary trick, wandering far out of his goal, once heading a ball to safety. Nemesis was lurking.

The USA, benefiting from the absence from their qualifying group of Mexico—expelled after fiddling the ages of their youth players—and squeezing by little Trinidad, were in a World Cup finals for the first time since 1950. Few expected them to do well. Their manager, Bob Gansler, came out of the dour German–American League in the New York area, where skill was at a premium. He ignored gifted Latin players such as Hugo Perez, preferring beef to brains. Against the accomplished Czechs, in Florence, the Americans were unwise enough to try to play an attacking game. With little but courage to offer, they were thrashed 5–1, already 3–1 down when Wynalda was sent off for shoving Kadlec to the ground. Two of the Czech goals came from near-post headers to corners by the adroit Chavonec, sweeper or midfielder as required. It didn't look as if Gansler had done his homework.

Up north-west at Asti, Brazil's training camp was anything but happy. The players seemed at daggers drawn with everybody; even themselves, for the tough midfielder Dunga was at odds with the striker Careca. Each wanted, it appeared, to be the main man. Their hotel proprietor accused them of not paying for their drinks, their sponsors, Asti 90, of not fulfilling their supposed obligations. And there was the matter of the sweeper, Mauro Galvao, a bone of endless contention.

Despite all this, the Brazilians won their opening game in the fine new Stadium of the Alps in Turin. Careca, in incisive form, got both the Brazilian goals. Little Tomas Brolin, the young Swedish centre-forward, replied 11 minutes from the end after leaving the powerful Mozer standing with a remarkable turn.

Branco, once rejected by the obscure Brescia club, had something to prove, and he proved it, with an ebullient performance as raiding left-back. Mauro Galvao, the sweeper, took few risks.

In Milan, West Germany, whose fans had marauded their way across northern Italy, finally causing havoc in the city itself, made a devastating beginning at San Siro. Yugoslavia were crushed 4–1, with the three Inter players, Lothar Matthaus, Andy Brehme and the blond striker, Jurgen Klinsmann, more than comfortable on their home field. Matthaus scored twice with tremendous drives from afar, and still had enough stamina to nullify Stojkovic in the Yugoslav midfield. Clearly the West Germans were bent on reaching yet another final.

Scotland, in Genoa the next day, made their customary bad beginning, though this time it was a humiliation: defeat by little Costa Rica, who'd even lost in Wales, on their way to the World Cup. But their manager was the wily Yugoslav Bora Milutinovic, who'd got more out of Mexico in 1986 than most people had expected him to. Scotland's impotence in front of goal was manifest again, despite the presence of Mo Johnston, who would become the first major Catholic player ever signed by Rangers.

With the exception—significantly—of a Latin player, Tab Ramos, the USA had none to compare technically with those of Costa Rica, who'd qualified top of their CONCACAF group. Milutinovic was in his element. Once, when the game was halted through a player's injury, he actually drew a diagram to show his striker, Jara, what he wanted tactically. Illegal coaching from the touchline, but inspired impertinence!

The Scots couldn't exploit Costa Rica's indifferent prowess in the air, all their pressure producing only a handful of chances. Conjo, the accomplished Costa Rican goalkeeper, made a couple of good saves, Cayasso scored the only goal.

It came four minutes after the interval. A diagonal run by Marchena, a backheel by Jara, and Cayasso had scored. Scotland were in trouble again.

England, in Cagliari, hardly looked much better, though this time they at least managed not to lose to the Irish team which had beaten them two years before in Stuttgart.

In truth, England and Ireland's was a battle of the dinosaurs. NO FOOT-BALL, PLEASE, WE'RE BRITISH read the caustic headline in one Italian paper. It didn't worry Jackie Charlton. 'You need a point, we've got a point,' he said. A neutral spectator had to deplore the wretched technique and the lack of ideas. In a difficult wind, even Paul Gascoigne could not, after a promising start, rise above it all, and an early goal couldn't spur England to success.

After just eight minutes, a typical piece of opportunism by Gary Lineker enabled him to score. When Chris Waddle's excellent pass reached him, he used his chest to beat the Irish keeper, Pat Bonner, dashed on, pursued by Steve Staunton and McCarthy, and knocked the ball into the net.

Ireland's equaliser was a gift from Steve McMahon, the hefty mid-fielder who'd only been on for five minutes, substituting a disappointing Peter Beardsley. Ineptly, McMahon gave the ball away to Kevin Sheedy, whose ferocious left foot seldom misses such chances.

The ball was mostly in the air and Bryan Robson, troubled by a toe injury, not long recovered from a hernia operation, achieved little against the marking of the resilient Paul McGrath, as useful in defence as he was when going forward.

For England, the surprising consolation was that Holland didn't look much better. Indeed, Egypt well deserved to beat them rather than merely to draw, giving an exhibition of smooth, intelligent, creative football which, alas, they would not reproduce. The Dutch, by contrast, never flowed at all. Frank Rijkaard, his dislike of the centre-back position only too well known, 'didn't shine as he usually does', in the words of the *Corriere Dello Sport*; but that was predictable. Less so was the dull form of Marco Van Basten, who, but for one acrobatic strike at goal, did miserably little. The other Milan player, Ruud Gullit, though clearly still below full fitness, did reasonably well, but came off in a fury. 'I expected a completely different beginning. I'm disappointed. We must talk, we must find at once the reasons for this disappointing exhibition.' But perhaps they never really did.

Egypt, who'd given warning when they beat Scotland 3–1 in Aberdeen in a warm-up game, had the best players afield in Hossam Hassan, the muscular centre-forward, and Abdelghani, elegant in midfield, scorer of the penalty which gave Egypt their deserved draw, eight minutes from the end. The Dutch goal owed much to Rijkaard, who, for once moving upfield in his preferred style, dummied a cross by Van Basten which gave the big, blond substitute, Wim Kieft, an easy goal.

Five days later, again in Palermo, Egypt were unrecognisable from their first, ebullient, game. Fear had gripped them; or rather, it had gripped their manager, El-Gohary. He admitted he'd been obsessed by Ireland's strong, straightforward methods, that he had endlessly studied tapes, and believed this to be the most difficult game in the group.

The consequence was sterility and stasis. Jackie Charlton was openly scornful. 'I didn't like the way the Egyptians played. I didn't like their time-wasting tactics. I didn't like the game at all. We must take a little bit of the blame ourselves, because we didn't score goals; but at least we tried.'

In Cagliari the previous day, Bobby Robson, allegedly under pressure from his own players, had done what he'd sworn for eight years that he would never do: deploy a sweeper. The system, he felt, with substantial justice, was foreign to English players. But his own men, clearly overrating the Dutch threat, felt an extra defender vital. The irony of it was that Terry Butcher, given the Dutch formation, found himself, a left-footed central defender, virtually playing right-back.

The sweeper was the blond Derby County man, Mark Wright, a quick, resourceful defender whose international career had seemed to come to a sticky end when, at Wembley in a European Nations Cup match in 1986, a series of fearful errors had given Yugoslavia's Zoltan Vujovic chance after easy chance to score—all of them missed. Wright had remained prone to error, as we would see in the game against Cameroon, but on the occasion and in England's next game, he'd do well.

England, with Paul Gascoigne now showing that the World Cup was a fitting stage for him, deserved to win, and nearly did. Van Basten, till the belated arrival of Kieft, largely toiled alone, and the dynamic pace of England's fine young black centre-half, Des Walker, closed whatever gaps were created. They were few.

Gary Lineker, playing up front with John Barnes, was often in the picture, to varying effect. A move begun, early in the second half, by Gascoigne, with typical power and flair, was carried off by the adventurous Paul Parker. Lineker's strong shot rebounded from the body of Van Breukelen, the Dutch keeper. Four minutes later, a dazzling exchange with Barnes put Lineker clean through, but for once his left foot let him down. He sliced his shot wide.

Lineker himself clutched his head in despair when he crossed an inviting ball to the head of the substitute, the crop-headed Bull; but that went wide as well. Finally, when Gascoigne, on the right, twisted away from two Dutch defenders and centred, Lineker was in inches of making contact. England had looked transformed, Holland, again, a team in curious crisis.

Scotland, meanwhile, were showing the perverse resilience associated with them, gallantly beating the Swedes in Genoa, where Robert Fleck confirmed the superiority he'd asserted over Glenn Hysen, in the English league.

At Norwich, one had seen Fleck's pace in the home attack drive Hysen, in the Liverpool defence, to sheer distraction; eventually, and desperately, Hysen clumsily fouled Fleck, and was sent off. Now, Fleck would torment Hysen again. Once, when Hysen fouled him on the edge of the box, Ravelli, the keeper, needed two attempts to save McLeod's free kick.

The Scots had taken the lead after 10 minutes when their tall defender, Dave McPherson, flicked on a corner for Stuart McCall to score. Nine minutes from the end, when Roy Aitken was tripped in the box, Mo Johnston made it 2–0 from the penalty. Sweden had brought on their splendid old blond warhorse, Glenn Stromberg, a little earlier, and he scored for them five minutes from the end. But the good-natured Scottish fans deserved to dance in triumph.

Moreover, there was solace for Scotland in the fact that Costa Rica, in Turin, went down only 1–0 to Brazil, then beat the Swedes 2–1 in Genoa!

Hoist with his own petard, Sebastiao Lazaroni again used a sweeper defence against Costa Rica when he clearly needed to reinforce his attack. The result was frustration. The only goal was tinged with fortune. After 33 minutes, Mozer headed on a throw-in from the right, the ball glanced off the elbow of the Costa Rican stopper, Montero, and Muller was enabled to score.

The vials of wrath poured over Lazaroni's head. 'He has betrayed Brazilian football!' cried Mario Zagalo, whose own 1974 team had kicked without mercy. 'It is absurd to play with a *libero* and deprive the midfield of a player. And then, just two attackers is something quite incredible!' Zagalo went on to deplore the fact that the Corinthians midfielder Neto, 'the best player in the country', had been left behind. But when Neto did ultimately play, he'd make no impact.

In the event, Brazil came out head of their group, with maximum points; though their win over Scotland in Turin was deeply laborious. They seemed to be playing to get free kicks rather than to score from open play. The arrival of Romario, a famous centre-forward, did little good. He hadn't played since breaking his leg in March. Put right through, he allowed Leighton to save.

It was Muller, again, who broke the deadlock, coming on as a sixty-fourth minute substitute. Leighton couldn't hold a shot by Alemao, nor a second by Careca, following up. Muller, who'd replaced Careca, took his chance. Had Scotland been more adventurous in the second half, when they treated Brazil with exaggerated respect, they might have survived.

Sweden became disheartened and uneasy. Seeing this, the crafty Milutinovic sent on an extra attacker, Hernan Medford, who immediately missed a real chance. No matter. Flores headed in a free kick, and Medford himself trotted through, two minutes from time, to get the winner.

In Group B, Argentina, the holders, went down to Naples, Maradona's home ground, and beat the Soviets, thanks in no small degree to the right hand of Maradona. This time, it happened in his own penalty box. After 12 minutes, Oleg Kuznetsov's red head flicked on a corner from the near post. Maradona's hand clearly rose to stop the ball. The referee, none other than Fredriksson, the Swede who'd given Belgium a contentious goal against the Soviets in Mexico, saw nothing. Play went on; but Fredriksson, thereafter, would not.

Only a minute earlier, Neri Pumpido, Argentina's World Cup-winning goalkeeper, had broken his leg in a collision with Olartichoechea, giving way to Sergio Goycoechea. Cometh the hour, cometh the man. Goycoechea would emerge as a hero of the tournament. He'd got into the squad only because Carlos Bilardo decided finally not to bring the combustible second choice, Luis Islas. Thus can football history be made.

Argentina went on to win. The curse of Caniggia and expulsion alighted on the big, blond Soviet defender, Bessonov, guilty of tripping him, when the second half was but two minutes old. Already Troglio had headed a goal. Jorge Burruchaga, exploiting Kuznetsov's miscued back-pass, got another.

In Bari, Cameroon beat Romania, and Roger Milla scored both goals. This time, allegedly at the behest of the Cameroon President, to whom Omam Biyik, ironically, had dedicated his goal against Argentina, Milla came on much earlier. To be exact, after 58 minutes, when there was still no score.

Three minutes earlier, Hagi, whose powerful shot had been saved by N'Kono in the first half, and who had made two excellent, spurned, chances for his team, had been replaced. Twenty minutes later, Milla became the oldest player ever to score in the World Cup finals.

Did he foul Andone, after they collided and he kept his balance, going on to shoot past Lung? The referee thought not. At all events, Cameroon were galvanised. Three minutes from the end, Milla whipped home a second goal. In the very next minute, Balint scored for Romania—the Cameroon defenders protested as he was offside—but there was no time for Romania to save the game.

Milla now became a kind of icon. Explanations, more or less convincing, were given for his amazing durability, his bursts of speed. Carlo Vittori, a renowned Italian athletics coach, hedging his bets a little, said that Milla had the typical musculature of a West African who lived inland: not heavy, but ideal for speed. To this, he mysteriously added the powerful muscles of one who lived on the West Coast. Thus, said Vittori, Milla had the best of both worlds, principally the calves, which were his secret. 'Shorter and more flexible than the average, but with a much longer Achilles tendon. This gives extraordinary reflexes in the feet.' Indeed!

In their third group game, against the Soviets in Bari, Milla came on as early as 10 minutes from the interval, but Cameroon clearly weren't bothering. They'd already qualified, and were untroubled by losing 4–0. They still came top of their group, since Argentina drew with Romania.

In Rome, Italy received the United States, and found the going astonishingly hard. Maybe these big, strong college boys couldn't really play, but they could certainly defend; and indeed, in the second half, they very nearly scored. Only a spectacular double save by Walter Zenga, Italy's loquacious keeper, from Bruce Murray's free kick and Peter Vermes's shot, Ferri finally clearing from the line, rescued them.

When Giuseppe Giannini, the beautifully balanced, inventive little Roma play-maker, scored after only 11 minutes, it seemed the Americans were in for another drubbing. Vialli dummied on a long ball from Carnevale, letting Giannini through to elude Armstrong, beat Meola, and score his first goal for Italy for 18 months.

Vialli himself hadn't scored for a year. Nor did he when, after 33 minutes, Italy gained a penalty as Vialli himself was fouled by Caligiuri. Vialli struck his shot against a post.

Thereafter, though Giannini prompted splendidly, it was all frustration for Italy. Vicini still wouldn't use Roberto Baggio, and Schillaci came on only as a substitute, early in the second half. Italy's 1–0 win was a moral victory for the United States.

An injury to Vialli at last prodded an uneasy Vicini to pair Schillaci and Baggio from the start against the Czechs, whom Italy hadn't beaten for 37 years. It worked. In Rome, the two little men danced continuously through a bewildered Czech defence, each ending with a goal. '*Baggiomania!*' the Italian papers had cried, after a scintillating début against Bulgaria the previous autumn, in a friendly at Cesena. But Vicini had never truly taken to him. Like Bobby Robson in Mexico, he now blundered on his best team by accident.

Schillaci, with another header—a fairly rare occurrence—opened the score in the tenth minute. Giannini hooked a corner by Donadoni into the box and when the ball bounced in front of Schillaci, he headed it in. Baggio scored the second, 13 minutes from time, though the Czechs were bitterly unlucky when inept refereeing and lining cost them a perfectly good goal by Griga, their substitute, after 65 minutes.

The big centre-forward, Tomas Skuhravy, flicked on a left-wing cross and Griga shot home, but the Belgian linesman, Van Lengenhove, signalled a non-existent offside, and the French referee, Quinou, disallowed the goal. So, 12 minutes later, Baggio was able to wriggle his way through the Czech defence and end a glorious run by shooting past Stejskal. Italy were emphatically afloat again.

In the Cagliari–Palermo group, England's defender, Mark Wright, scored the only goal against an over-cautious Egypt, with a well-taken header from Paul Gascoigne's insidious free kick. Later, Egypt demanded a penalty when the ball made contact with Wright's arm in the box. When it ran loose, Hossam Hassan shot, but only to find the ever-resilient Shilton in the way. This time, England sensibly went back to a four-in-line defence against negative opponents, but their overall performance was mediocre—Egypt's worse. It was strange to hear Bobby Robson heap compliments on the Egyptian team afterwards, praising their so-called courage, saying how much better they'd been than when England beat them 4–0 in Cairo the previous season.

The fact is that that score was a travesty, England owing almost everything to an amazing display by Shilton, till Egypt finally cracked. In Cagliari, they'd extended him on only a couple of occasions.

Ireland completed their programme with a third draw, 1–1 against Holland, which was good enough to get both teams into the knock-out Second Round, as the drearily protracted, unnecessarily tiring, first phase ended. In Palermo, Ruud Gullit's dreadlocks flew to greater purpose. He and his fellow Milan players had flown in their personal physiotherapist, Ted Troost, whose ministrations seemed to have helped Gullit. After 10 minutes, his powerful right foot sent Holland ahead with an angled shot.

As the minutes fled by, Ireland went into all-out attack, seeking the equaliser, exposing themselves to Holland's breaks. But boldness paid off after 71 minutes, when Pat Bonner cleared far upfield, Van Aerle's back-pass slipped out of Van Breukelen's grasp, and there was the giant centre-forward, Niall Quinn, to snap up the chance. The Irish fairy-tale continued; now they must meet Romania in Genoa.

In Group E, played up in the north-east at Verona and Udine, Jan Ceulemans, brought on only at half-time to revitalise the Belgian attack against South Korea, stayed in, as powerful a presence as ever. The still older Eric Gerets had survived at right-back.

Belgium beat the dull Koreans 2–0, won 3–1 against a Uruguayan side which had cleaned up its act but, to vary the metaphor, seemed to have thrown out the baby with the bathwater. Gerets was sent off in that game just before half-time, for a second yellow card, but now the boot was on the other foot. By contrast with 1986, it was the Uruguayans who couldn't prevail against 10 men. The splendid Ceulemans scored a fine breakaway goal just after half-time, putting his team three up. Bengoechea alone replied.

Spain, talented but enigmatic, had a kind of revenge over Belgium for their unlucky defeat in 1986, beating them 2–1 in Verona in their last group game, which put them top. Previously, they'd drawn 0–0 with Uruguay and beaten South Korea 3–1, all their three goals going to the refulgent Michel: a right-footed volley, a searing free kick, a dashing solo. He scored the opening goal against Belgium, from a penalty.

West Germany, in Group D, got another five against the United Arab Emirates, but were surprisingly held to a draw by Colombia. No goals till the last two minutes, when Pierre Littbarski gave the Germans the lead, only for Rincon to shoot through Illgnerlegs to equalise. Yugoslavia, beating Colombia 1–0, the UAE 4–1, with two for Darko Pancev, joined these two teams in the next round.

Italy had gone wild about Schillaci, crazy about Baggio: Baggiomania, indeed. Schillaci, not exempt from that *vittimismo*, self-pity, which famously affected the Italian south, observed, 'I don't ask anything from life', when the French referee, Quiniou, refused him a plain penalty when he was brought down in the box against Czechoslovakia. Among the rich, sleek young men of the Italian team, he was a maverick, with his cropped hair, his prematurely aged face. 'I've had a lot of insults I don't deserve,' he complained. 'Now I hope people will realise I'm a lad who shouldn't be treated like that.' For the moment at least, he was being treated royally, though his fears would be realised in the years to come.

Schillaci scored yet again, against Uruguay in Rome. Vialli was fit, but he sat on the bench. A deeply defensive Uruguay held out in the first half. Seven minutes into the second, Vicini gave the big centre-forward, Aldo Serena, a thirtieth birthday present, unexpectedly send-

ing him on in place of the young midfielder Nicola Berti. It worked.
Italy began to pull Uruguay's defence about, and after 65 minutes,
Serena tapped a pass to Schillaci, who shot over the head of Alvez,
Uruguay's keeper, and into the net. Joy and surprise showed in Schillaci's ever-expressive face as he rushed, arm aloft, to receive his team-
mates' congratulations. Eight minutes from the end, Serena headed a
second in his familiar style.

In Genoa, Ireland drew yet again, and got through. The suspension of
Marius Lacatus was badly felt by a Romanian side which found Paul
McGrath a great stumbling block in midfield and Mick McCarthy a bulwark in the middle. Pat Bonner, in agile form, saved with one hand from
George Hagi 20 minutes from the end of normal time. With no goals in
extra time either, Bonner saved Romania's fifth penalty from Timofte,
and it was all down to Arsenal's veteran centre-half, David O'Leary, not
always Jackie Charlton's favourite player, and now brought on only in the
ninety-third minute.

Penalties were hardly O'Leary's speciality, but he trotted straight at the
ball, perplexed Lung in goal, and drove his shot home. Victory.

There was victory for England too, though they actually won their
game against Belgium in Bologna. The goal, superbly taken, was scored
by David Platt, who'd come on as substitute after 71 minutes, and struck
after 119.

If Gascoigne was the hare, then Platt was the tortoise. Both would find
Italian clubs. Rejected by Manchester United as a youngster, Platt fought
his way through from the shallows, at Crewe Alexandra, when he moved
to Aston Villa. Not blessed with Gascoigne's innumerable gifts, he had
something which served him as well: an enviable temperament. He
worked hard on his game and made himself into a player as valuable in
midfield as in defence—fast, intelligent, industrious, an exceptional finisher with foot or head.

Now he would justify what had seemed Bobby Robson's excessive
belief in him.

Playing with Wright as a sweeper again was a doubtful tactic,
since the Belgians played most of the game with only one striker.
With Bryan Robson indisposed, Lineker and Walker carrying injuries,
it was remarkable that England should last through the extra time. By
the end, Walker, who'd played outstandingly well, was reduced to a
hobble, potentially easy prey for Nico Claesen, who came on as
substitute.

Breaking through a weak tackle by Wright, Ceulemans hit the post in
the first half, Scifo with a swerving shot in the second. As against that,
John Barnes, who, like Lineker, missed one easy chance, had a good goal
disallowed for a phantom offside. A pity, since a splendid move—Parker,
Lineker, McMahon, Waddle, Lineker—deserved a goal.

So it was Platt who eventually and dramatically scored it. Needless to say, the irrepressible Gascoigne was behind it, battling to the end, though his legs were weary. Gaining a free kick on the left, he curled the ball to the far post, where Platt, in mid-air, volleyed a superb goal.

In Turin, Argentina managed somehow to beat Brazil, that 'somehow' best translated as the name Maradona. Futile, here, to put the blame on Lazaroni and his sweeper. In the first 20 minutes, Brazil had abundant chances to win the game. Goycoechea saved from Careca, a bitter critic of Lazaroni, in the very first minute. Dunga headed against a post; Goycoechea pushed Careca's angled drive against another in the second half, then made a glorious save from Alemao.

But teams who press and don't score risk condign punishment, especially when they have a Maradona against them. Even a Maradona reduced by his ill-used, swollen left ankle and other injuries to a trot. Used up front, he still found the will and the energy, eight minutes from the end, to thread his way irresistibly through the centre of Brazil's sweeper defence, ending with a glorious right-footed pass which Caniggia took across Taffarel, Brazil's blond keeper, with his right foot, turning to score with his left.

Maradona gave Caniggia great credit for the goal, saying it had been hard to score. Brazil, he said, had had 80 per cent of the play. Argentina needed to get things together.

Accusations flew. Branco, Brazil's left-back, accused the Argentine bench of handing him a bottle of drugged Gatorade! The trouble was, insisted Lazaroni, that Brazil no longer had great attackers. Some felt his tactics had deprived his strikers of the support they'd expected from their midfield. Branco would be proved right.

In Naples, where Argentina would now meet Italy, Cameroon despatched Colombia, with two more goals for Milla in extra time, one the product of a grotesque error by the eccentric Higuita.

Colombia could have won, in the first half, a game which only awoke in extra time. A slovenly back pass let Fajardo through, but he shot right at N'Kono. Tataw hacked Estrada down in the box, but got away with it. Rincon crashed a shot against the bar.

Milla, who came on after 54 minutes, and himself was one shoved down in the area, scored a dazzling first goal after 106 minutes. Taking a nicely angled pass from Oman Biyik, he sprinted past Perea, hurdled Escobar, and struck the ball wide of Higuita with his left foot.

Two minutes later, fiasco. Some 40 yards out of his goal, Higuita was mad enough to try to pass Milla. Instead, he lost the ball, and away went Milla, to find an empty net. The clever Valderrama, of the dyed blond dreadlocks, made a goal for Redin, but it was inconsequential.

Since Omam Biyik had so skilfully sent Milla away for the opening goal, it was sad when, on his return to France, green eyes rather than

Cameroon's green shirts seemed to be in evidence. Omam Biyik declared that Milla's substitutions had harmed the side, impairing its teamwork. If Milla had scored goals, it was because he'd always come on when the opposing team were tiring. Sour grapes indeed.

In perhaps the best World Cup game of all, one which would have made a far better Final than what was inflicted on us, West Germany beat Holland in Milan. Even the expulsion of Rudi Voeller and Frank Rijkaard after only 21 minutes, when Rijkaard spat at Voeller for allegedly insulting him, could not spoil things. It was surely the finest game the blond German striker, Jurgen Klinsmann, ever played for his country.

He gave them the lead after 50 minutes of a game played in a San Siro stadium which was home for Germany's three Inter players and Milan's three Dutchmen alike. Buchwald moved out of West Germany's sweeper defence to cross from the left, Klinsmann met the ball with his head, and guided it across Van Breukelen into the opposite corner. A little hard on the keeper, who'd only just made a notable save from Matthaus's header, itself set up by Klinsmann. Better still had been Van Breukelen's save from the adventurous Buchwald.

Klinsmann was rampant. Fourteen minutes from time, he dashed after a long cross-field ball from his club colleague, Brehme, and struck the ball against a post. Two minutes later, he was substituted, and applauded off the field. Brehme, six minutes from the end, neatly lobbed Van Breukelen to make the match safe; a disputed penalty two minutes from time by Ronald Koeman made no difference.

Costa Rica's brave saga came to an end in Bari, under a hail of Czech goals. Alas, Gabelo Conejo, who'd kept goal so bravely and well, who'd knelt to pray to the Madonna of the Angels before each game, couldn't recover from a kick on the ankle. Injections and laser treatment were in vain. He had to give way to Barrantes; and Barrantes was no Conejo. Especially when it came to crosses. The Czechs won 4–1, but Costa Rica had excelled themselves.

In Verona, Dragan Stojkovic had a remarkable game, scored two goals, and enabled Yugoslavia to beat Spain 2–1. The Spanish team, never much enamoured of its manager, Luis Suarez, nevertheless could well have won. Martin Vazquez, in midfield, was the outstanding player of the first half, and hit the post early in the second. Emilio Butragueño headed against a post, but it was Stojkovic who scored first, after 77 minutes. It was a coolly taken goal. Katanec turned back Vujovic's cross, Stojkovic killed the ball, dodged past a man, and beat Zubizarreta. Six minutes later, big Julio Salinas edged Martin Vazquez's cross-shot into the Yugoslav goal, which meant extra time.

Of this, just a couple of minutes had been played when Stojkovic curled his free kick round the Spanish wall, and inside the right-hand post. A goal good enough to win any game.

Neither Yugoslavia nor Argentina could score in their quarter-final in Florence. This, though Yugoslavia were down to 10 men soon after the half-hour, when Sabanadzovic committed his second bookable offence. This time, Maradona was a nullity. In suffocating heat, Stojkovic found his best ally in his heir apparent at Red Star Belgrade, the young blond Robert Prosinecki, splendidly creative in midfield.

But when the game went to extra time and penalties, it was finally too much for Yugoslavia's 10. True, even Maradona missed one of the penalties. So did Troglio, but Stojkovic hit the bar, and the resilient Goycoechea saved the kicks by Brnovic and Hadzibegic. Argentina scraped through.

In Rome, Italy won only 1–0 against the gallant Irish. Vicini's tactics were strange. He moved Bergomi out of the middle to mark Kevin Sheedy, and used Paolo Maldini, his attacking left-back, as a central defender! But the return to the right wing of Roberto Donadoni, now fit again, was important.

Ireland had their best moment after 26 minutes. The protean McGrath moved forward from his role in front of the back four, reached Quinn with a long, measured cross from the right, and Zenga flew through the air to catch Quinn's header.

Schillaci yet again was Italy's scorer—of a fine goal too. Giannini found Baggio, who gave it to Schillaci. Back to Giannini, left to Donadoni, whose strong shot Bonner could only block. Schillaci pounced to tap the ball just inside the right-hand post. In the second half, he'd hit the underside of the bar. When big Serena replaced little Baggio, Franco Baresi, Italy's elegant sweeper, put him through, but Bonner saved superbly with his legs.

Azeglio Vicini, nerves a-jangle, jumped off the bench to rebuke a linesman who'd annulled a goal by Schillaci for offside, protested to the fourth official, the Brazilian Wright, and then snapped, in the Press Conference, that 'certain decisions were inadmissible'.

In Naples, England started David Platt for the first time; unlucky Bryan Robson was now back in England. Once more there'd be a sweeper, in Wright, but this time things came badly unstuck. Cameroon, with four men suspended, had to rearrange their defence, but the alarming Massing was there, among others. Gary Lineker would state afterwards, rather than complain, that he'd been punched and kicked, several times.

England were favoured, but Cameroon nearly scored first, though Milla would not appear till after half-time. Makanaky crossed, Omam Biyik was there, but Shilton punched out his shot.

Four minutes later, Platt's opportunism gave England a somewhat illusory lead, rising to head in a left-wing cross by the powerful, adventurous full-back, Stuart Pearce. This at a time when England's defence was clearly uneasy.

Whatever Omam Biyik, who'd be thwarted time and again by an inspired Peter Shilton, felt, it was the arrival of a now shaven-pated Milla which galvanised Cameroon. On the hour, Platt was brought down by N'Kono. Mexico's Codesal, an inadequate referee, inexplicably praised afterwards by Bobby Robson, gave no penalty; but he would give two later to England, one almost immediately to Cameroon.

It was Gascoigne, showing fitful inspiration, who gave the kick away, Milla whom he brought down. Kunde, the big, resolute centre-back, beat Shilton from the spot though only just. With England's three centre-backs merely confusing one another, and Wright especially uncertain, Cameroon were ahead three minutes later. Ekeke, the substitute, had been on only a couple of minutes when Milla put him through, and he scored.

Bobby Robson took Butcher off, discarded his sweeper system, and at long last gave a chance to Trevor Steven, mysteriously out of favour till now, but due to respond with a fine performance up and down the right flank.

Eight minutes were left, and Parker was now competently looking after Milla when England equalised. Brought down in the box by Ebwelle, Gary Lineker himself calmly put away the penalty. Clashing with Milla, Mark Wright poured blood from a cut over his right eye, moved out of defence, and England faced extra time with ten sound men. Less compact than resilient, they still prevailed.

After 105 minutes, one of Gascoigne's jewelled passes put Lineker through. Again he was brought down, this time by N'Kono, and again he converted the penalty.

Next day, on a sunny hotel terrace above the waters of Salerno, Bobby Robson said, 'A flat back four saved us.' So it had; but it would be a sweeper defence again in the semi-final against West Germany. 'We've got here,' said Bobby Robson. 'I don't know how.'

The Germans themselves won on a penalty, the only goal of the match, in Milan again, against Czechoslovakia. All those tough games in blazing afternoon sunshine, not to mention the bloated, otiose first-round programmes, were taking their toll. Klinsmann was once more involved in a German goal. Straka brought him down as he dashed into the box, and Matthaus put away the penalty. Twice in the first half Hasek cleared from the Czech goal line.

Twenty minutes from time, Czech chances disappeared when Moravcik received his second yellow card: for kicking his boot off and into the air, when displeased with a decision! Kohl, an unimpressive referee, expelled him. The game died.

Before Argentina played Italy in the semi-final in Naples, Diego

Maradona made an ill-judged appeal to his Napoli fans, trying to play on
southern *vittimismo*. Support us, not Italy, he said. Look how badly you're
treated in the north! An appeal which would rebound on him, especially
after Argentina had won.

It was a defeat from which Azeglio Vicini would never recover, even
though it was only on penalties. From that moment, he was doomed.
His preference for Vialli over Baggio was illogical. His substitution of
Baggio for the creative Giannini made little sense. Yet were it not for a
goalkeeping blunder by Walter Zenga, he could still have got away
with it.

Playing in Naples seemed, for Maradona, the equivalent of Doctor
Theatre; curing him at least temporarily of his many physical afflictions.
Burruchaga, his faithful lieutenant, worked steadfastly beside him. After
eight minutes, Zenga had to dive to his shot.

Yet even without Baggio beside him, Schillaci would score the first
goal. After 17 minutes, he started a move carried on by De Napoli, Vialli
and Giannini, who chipped into the box, followed up, and got his head
to the ball. Vialli shot, Goycoechea blocked, Schillaci followed up to
score.

But as time went by, fear ate the Italian soul. The arrival of Troglio
after half-time gave Argentina more drive, but even they could hardly
have expected the kind of equaliser they scored.

Fifty minutes after Italy's goal, Maradona cleverly sent Olarticoechea
down the left. Over came a cross which seemed plainly a goalkeeper's
ball, but Zenga never reached it. Instead, fallibly, he allowed the blond
head of Caniggia to get there first. In went the ball, and Argentina were
level.

So it went to extra time; and to the abominated penalties. When
Donadoni took Italy's third kick, Goycoechea dived gallantly to his
left and got both hands to the ball. Maradona this time put his penalty away, and when Serena took Italy's fourth kick, Goycoechea
repeated his feat; a dive to the left, two hands to the ball, and Italy
were beaten.

Vicini replied bitterly to sharp criticism. He'd culpably recalled
Vialli, had broken up the Baggio-Schillaci tandem in consequence.
He'd used five defenders, thus handing the midfield to Argentina.
Vicini said he'd still put Vialli in, were the game repeated. He'd have
replaced Giannini with the powerful Ancelotti, had it not been for
Caniggia's goal. Zenga said it was 'impossible to save'.

The Turin semi-final went to penalties too. England's sweeper this
time was Terry Butcher, who seemed far more suited to the role than
Mark Wright. For much of the game, in which England played steadily
intelligent football, without creating many chances, the Germans looked
a tired team. Not least their fulcrum, Lothar Matthaus, anonymous for

the first half-hour, vigorously effective for 20 minutes, then evidently weary again.

Paul Gascoigne more than matched him, showing his familiar compound of strength, skill and originality. Alas, he would be reduced to tears—televised around the world—when a reckless tackle on Berthold got him booked for the second time in the tournament, condemning him to miss the Final, were England to reach it. Claudio Caniggia, foolishly handling the ball, knew already that this trivial foul would exclude him. Sad that offences should not be graded, when some were so much graver than others.

It was England who flagged at the start of the second half, but the goal with which West Germany led after 59 minutes was a freak. Tomas Haessler, the bright little midfielder—flanked this time by another, the fresher Thon—tapped a free kick to the formidable Andy Brehme. As Shilton came out of his goal, the shot hit Paul Parker, spiralled over the goalkeeper's head, and landed in the goal. Would a younger Shilton have got back to save it? Perhaps, but such questions do scant justice to a great goalkeeper.

England brought on Trevor Steven for Butcher, adopted a 4-4-2 formation, and equalised with ten minutes left. Parker crossed from the right; clumsy confusion between Kohler and Augenthaler, unthinkable in a German defence, let the ball pass across the face of the goal, and the unmarked Lineker put the chance away.

In extra time, both teams hit the post, Chris Waddle for England, the ever adventurous Buchwald for West Germany, while Shilton saved gloriously from Matthaus and Klinsmann. Penalties would settle it, and when Stuart Pearce whacked his into Illgner's flying body, the writing was on the wall. Thon then scored for Germany, Waddle sent his kick over the bar, and West Germany had reached another World Cup Final.

What a dismal one it would be. Argentina's sour, negative tactics were clearly conditioned by the crucial absence of Caniggia, and the physical condition of Maradona. At Argentina's training camp, out at Trigoria, Roma's ground, there was a violent incident when police stopped Maradona's brother, at the wheel of his Ferrari. A security guard was knocked down and kicked. A fitting prelude, perhaps, to what would happen in the Olympic stadium.

Altogether, Argentina had four players suspended; and two more would be sent off. That Codesal should be picked to referee the Final seemed to have more to do with the fact that his father-in-law, Javier Arriaga, was a member of the Referees' Committee than with any evident ability. Still, no referee would have welcomed a match like this.

Maradona was jeered throughout by a crowd incensed by his *faux pas* in Naples. West Germany dominated a dull, sterile first half. Rudi Voeller took none of four chances. He and Klinsmann, closely marked, looked tired.

After half-time, the game grew harsher. When Klaus Augenthaler was blatantly tripped in the box by Goycoechea, Germany had far stronger claims for a penalty than that which won the match. But when Monzon was expelled after 64 minutes for a shocking foul on Klinsmann, Argentina looked doomed. Twenty long minutes later, Sensini brought down Voeller in the area, and Codesal gave a penalty. Argentina protested furiously, and seemed to have a pretty good case. But a spot kick it was, and though Goycoechea dived perceptively to his right, Brehme's penalty flew inside the post.

Two minutes later, Dezotti grabbed Jurgen Kohler by the throat, as he tore after a ball which had run out of play; and followed Monzon to the dressing-rooms. A sad, crude end to a World Cup; but perhaps not an inappropriate one.

The third-place match between Italy and England in Bari had been a pleasant, meaningless contrast. England, without Gascoigne, did what they could. A fine header by David Platt equalised a goal by Baggio, the fruit of a moment's distraction by Shilton in his last England game. Seven minutes from time, Parker lost balance, tripped Schillaci, and that embattled little man concluded his World Cup by converting the penalty.

RESULTS: Italy 1990

First round

Group A

Rome, Florence
Italy 1, Austria 0
Czechoslovakia 5, USA 1
Italy 1, USA 0
Austria 0, Czechoslovakia 1
Italy 2, Czechoslovakia 0
Austria 2, USA 1

	P	W	D	L	GOALS F	A	Pts
Italy	3	3	0	0	**4**	**0**	6
Czechoslovakia	3	2	0	1	**6**	**3**	4
Austria	3	1	0	2	**2**	**3**	2
USA	3	0	0	3	**2**	**8**	0

Group B

Milan, Bari, Naples
Argentina 0, Cameroon 1
Romania 2, Soviet Union 0
Argentina 2, Soviet Union 0
Cameroon 2, Romania 1
Argentina 1, Romania 1
Soviet Union 4, Cameroon 0

	P	W	D	L	GOALS F	A	Pts
Cameroon	3	2	0	1	**3**	**5**	4
Romania	3	1	1	1	**4**	**3**	3
Argentina	3	1	1	1	**3**	**2**	3
Soviet Union	3	1	0	2	**4**	**4**	2

Group C

Turin, Genoa
Brazil 2, Sweden 1
Costa Rica 1, Scotland 0
Brazil 1, Costa Rica 0
Scotland 2, Sweden 1
Brazil 1, Scotland 0
Costa Rica 2, Sweden 1

	P	W	D	L	GOALS F	A	Pts
Brazil	3	3	0	0	**4**	**1**	6
Costa Rica	3	2	0	1	**3**	**2**	4
Scotland	3	1	0	2	**2**	**3**	2
Sweden	3	0	0	3	**3**	**6**	0

Group D

Milan, Bologna
Colombia 2, UAE 0
West Germany 4, Yugoslavia 1
Yugoslavia 1, Colombia 0
West Germany 5, UAE 1
West Germany 1, Colombia 1
Yugoslavia 4, UAE 1

	P	W	D	L	GOALS F	A	Pts
West Germany	3	2	1	0	**10**	**3**	5
Yugoslavia	3	2	0	1	**6**	**5**	4
Colombia	3	1	1	1	**3**	**2**	3
UAE	3	0	0	3	**2**	**11**	0

Group E

Verona, Udine
Belgium 2, South Korea 1
Spain 0, Uruguay 0
Spain 3, South Korea 1
Belgium 3, Uruguay 1
Spain 2, Belgium 1
Uruguay 1, South Korea 0

	P	W	D	L	GOALS F	A	Pts
Spain	3	2	1	0	**5**	**2**	5
Belgium	3	2	0	1	**6**	**3**	4
Uruguay	3	1	1	1	**2**	**3**	3
South Korea	3	0	0	3	**1**	**6**	0

Group F

Cagliari, Palermo
England 1, Ireland 1
Holland 1, Egypt 1
England 0, Holland 0
Egypt 0, Ireland 0
England 1, Egypt 0
Ireland 1, Holland 1

	P	W	D	L	GOALS F	A	Pts
England	3	1	2	0	**2**	**1**	4
Ireland	3	0	3	0	**2**	**2**	3
Holland	3	0	3	0	**2**	**2**	3
Egypt	3	0	2	1	**1**	**2**	2

Second round

Naples
Cameroon 2, Colombia 1

Bari
Czechoslovakia 4, Costa Rica 1

Turin
Argentina 1, Brazil 0

Milan
West Germany 2, Holland 1

Genoa
Ireland 0, Romania 0
Ireland win 5–4 on penalties

Rome
Italy 2, Uruguay 0

Verona
Yugoslavia 2, Spain 1

Bologna
England 1, Belgium 0

Quarter-finals

Rome
Italy 1, Ireland 0

Milan
West Germany 1, Czechoslovakia 0

Naples
England 3, Cameroon 2

Florence
Argentina 0, Yugoslavia 0
Argentina win 3–2 on penalties

Semi-finals

Naples
Argentina 1, Italy 1
Argentina win 4–3 on penalties

Turin
West Germany 1, England 1
West Germany win 4–3 on penalties

Third-place match

Bari

Italy 2	**England 1**
Zenga; Baresi; Bergomi,	Shilton; Wright
Ferrara, Vierchowod,	(Waddle); Stevens,
Maldini; De Agostini	Parker, Walker,
(Berti), Ancelotti,	Dorigo; Steven, Platt,
Giannini (Ferri);	McMahon (Webb);
Baggio, Schillaci.	Beardsley, Lineker.

SCORERS
Baggio, Schillaci (penalty) for Italy
Platt for England
HT (0–0)

Final

Rome

West Germany 1	**Argentina 0**
Illgner; Augenthaler;	Goycoechea; Lorenzo,
Berthold (Reuter),	Serrizuela, Sensini,
Kohler,	Ruggeri (Monzon),
Buchwald, Brehme;	Simon, Basualdo,
Littbarski, Haessler,	Burruchaga
Matthaus; Voeller,	(Calderon), Troglio,
Klinsmann.	Maradona, Dezotti.

SCORER
Brehme (penalty) for West Germany
HT (0–0)

USA
1994

Eventually it had to happen, and in Los Angeles, in July 1994, it did. A World Cup which, controversially but sensibly given to the United States, had attracted the most colossal crowds, ended not with a bang but with a whimper. A double whimper, you might say. For not only was it an ineffably dreary, negative, disappointing Final: it was, horrifically and inexcusably, decided on penalty kicks. It is telling that neither of the two World Cup Final's managers wanted a replay for the very good—or very bad—reason that each knew his players were exhausted. This was directly attributable to the bloated format, the burden on players compounded by the staging of so many matches in the oppressive heat of early afternoon. The competition, supposedly the most important in football, had again been prostituted to European television.

The title was won not by a dazzling Brazilian team, such as those of 1982 and 1986, but by a dull, functional one which relied heavily on the inventive brilliance of Romario and Bebeto up front, scarcely served by a pedestrian midfield. At least there was the consolation that Italy's duller team didn't win. It was deeply significant that, even after the *azzurri* had come so close to ultimate success, the great Italian soccer public still had little time for its team. And less time still for its manager, Arrigo Sacchi, whose perverse choices of tactics and personnel alienated the fans.

Greater blemishes still on the tournament were the horrific murder of the Colombian player, Andres Escobar, on his return home after his team's mysterious defeat by the USA; and the disqualification of Argentina's illustrious Diego Maradona, found guilty of taking a cocktail of drugs.

I was always convinced that, at least from a financial point of view, a World Cup held in the United States was bound to be a colossal success. The argument that soccer in America was a minor sport, that no real national competition had existed since the collapse of the North American Soccer League years earlier, seemed spurious to me. The colossal crowds which attended the soccer tournament in California during the 1984 Olympics had convinced me that American fans, 'event snobs' that they are, would flock in still greater numbers to the premier competition of them all. So, indeed, they would.

The engine behind America's bid and their subsequent preparation was a Californian lawyer called Alan Rothenberg, who had been pushed into office as President of the American soccer association by FIFA, who weren't satisfied with the previous incumbent. Rothenberg was a dynamic organiser, but in no real sense a football man. He refused to take a salary, but agreed to a payment after the World Cup was over. It was subsequently officially announced to be $7 million, though there were those who whispered it was even higher, a source of dismay to the army of unpaid volunteers who'd made the running of the World Cup possible.

The choice of stadiums was in several instances controversial. FIFA, as obsessed with novelty as were the American organisers, were misguided enough to go for the ghastly indoor Silverdome at Pontiac, near Detroit. In the first place, the perversity of choice cost the organisers a fortune. The grass had to be grown in California, after a regiment of scientists had pondered the best way to lay it. Enormous rectangles of turf were transported vast distances to be put down and glared on night and day by the stadium's electric lights. Malodorous, stuffy and oppressive, it was a venue which, amazingly, had no airconditioning to lighten the players' burden, and the space between touchlines and lower seating was minimal.

Orlando, in Florida, was another highly debatable choice. If the ideal stadium, the Joe Robbie, wasn't available at the time—and there was some dispute about that—then the Orange Bowl, where Germany had played Argentina in the previous year's mini-tournament, would surely have been far preferable to Orlando. There, the possibility of after-noon storms condemned the teams to play at noon in atrocious heat. It was alleged that, just as the organisers hoped to strike a deal with General Motors in Detroit, so they'd hoped to come to terms with the Disney organisation, located near Orlando. This, however, was an ambition which backfired. Disney wanted complete control over the ultimately vulgar and faintly ludicrous opening ceremony. The organisers didn't want to give it to them. Perhaps if they had we'd have been denied the diverting spectacle of famous stars falling through the platform of the dais and, in the case of Diana Ross, the singer, failing to 'score' in an open goal from just a few yards.

There were serious deficiencies, too, over the two Californian stadiums, at Stanford and Los Angeles. Neither would have been passed as adequate in most West European countries and, had the spectators been less malleable, there could have been serious consequences.

In the event, however, all was pretty peaceful. The elimination of England, and by extension their notoriously violent and provocative fans, may have had something to do with that. But the eager expectations of those dinosaurs of the American sporting press, fearful for the future of their native sports, that there would be rioting and mayhem, were utterly disappointed.

England's failure to qualify was a particularly abject one, made all the more so by the gallant achievement of the Republic of Ireland in reaching the finals for a second successive time. Graham Taylor, former guru of the long-ball game at Watford, and a most contentious choice to succeed Bobby Robson, staggered from one error to another.

Taylor had made a strange start in the autumn of 1990 when, before a European Championship qualifying match in Dublin against the Irish, he dropped Paul Gascoigne, preferring the small veteran midfielder Gordon Cowans (a choice all the more puzzling for a game in which the ball would spend a majority of the time in the air). Long afterwards, Taylor suggested that the deciding factor was Gazza's state of mind at the time, but this seemed pretty much of an afterthought.

Not that Gascoigne would at any stage in the World Cup preliminaries do Taylor and England proud. At Wembley, when it seemed that England were coasting to victory against Holland, Gazza received an elbow in the face from the Dutch midfielder, Jan Wouters, cracking his cheekbone. Wouters proclaimed his innocence, but there were whispers from Holland that Gascoigne's behaviour had been provocative. Out of the game for 16 months after an appalling knee injury in the FA Cup Final of 1991 between Spurs and Nottingham Forest—none the more bearable for being wholly his own fault—Gazza won the hearts of the Lazio fans when he moved to Rome, but failed in the two vital England away games of June 1993 against Poland and Norway. It was in Oslo that Taylor, with an allusion to the dangers of what he called Gazza's 'refuelling', would put the cat well among the pigeons.

England drew very luckily in Poland through a late goal superbly snatched by their substitute striker, Arsenal's Ian Wright. How the Poles hadn't killed them off earlier in the game, when they were rampant, was a mystery.

Taylor's tactics in Oslo were self-destructive to a degree. In fact he'd been constantly chopping and changing throughout his reign, reluctant to commit himself to the long-ball methods which had always seemed dearest to his heart. He seemed obsessed with the fact that Jostein Flo, a big striker, had been used by Norway to come in on crosses, from a right-wing position, and get his head to them. So with no time at all to do it, and with a botched bid for secrecy, Taylor radically changed his formation, decided to use a big centre-back, Gary Pallister, as left-back to mark Flo, and produced nothing but confusion. Des Walker, chosen despite serious questions about his form, erred again on the first goal which followed a free kick, and defensive blunders in the second half gave away a second.

When England, the following season, travelled to Rotterdam to play Holland, their chances were slim. It seemed remarkable that the inept officials of the Football Association had allowed Taylor to stay in office. In the American tournament of 1993, England had even lost to the USA, though they played far better to draw with Brazil and lose narrowly to Germany in the Silverdome. They lost in Holland, too, though there was bitter dispute about the goal that killed them off.

Ronald Koeman, the big, blond, Dutch sweeper scored it, directly from a curled free kick. But by that time he should have been off the field, for five minutes earlier he'd brought down England's David Platt on the edge of the penalty box when he was right through. The German referee, Karl Josef Assenmacher, surprisingly waved only a yellow card, and then allowed the Dutch defence to encroach on Tony Dorigo's free kick. Five minutes later, after England had charged down Koeman's free kick, Assenmacher had him take it again. And he scored. The elegant blond attacker, Dennis Bergkamp, got a rather soft second. But in Holland's favour it must be said that a goal by Frank Rijkaard, disallowed for offside five minutes before half-time, had in fact seemed perfectly legitimate.

Thus Holland, who'd been trailing Norway's surprising team, got through. But without the resplendent Marco Van Basten, whose ankle had required one operation after another, to lead their attack, and the dominating, versatile Ruud Gullit, they were badly depleted. Gullit didn't play that night against England. He'd played at Wembley, hadn't followed the instructions of Dick Advocaat, the much put-upon Dutch manager, and was furious when substituted. He refused to play for the team, though he came back before the World Cup began. He then flounced out of training camp after disagreeing with Advocaat's tactics and complaining that the atmosphere among his colleagues wasn't right.

Advocaat had a very hard time of it, the Dutch players maintaining their long record of intransigence. The word was that he'd be replaced for the World Cup by Johan Cruyff. Cruyff, however, couldn't reach agreement with the Dutch Federation and, *faute de mieux*, Advocaat stayed on. It's arguable, but had Gullit played rather than sulked, Holland might well have won their crucial game against Brazil in the finals, and gone on to beat Italy.

In the eliminators, Brazil showed themselves to be mortal indeed. They could only draw their first match 0–0 in Ecuador, then crashed to a 2–0 defeat by Bolivia on the breathless heights of La Paz. It was the first time Brazil had ever been defeated in a World Cup qualifying game. Predictably, Carlos Alberto Parreira became the whipping boy. Like his predecessor, Claudio Coutinho, he'd sworn to give a more 'European' aspect to his sides—which in practice again turned out to mean stifling initiative and encouraging harsh defence.

Gradually Brazil got things together. But things were still in the balance when it came to the last game against Uruguay, their eternal bogey team, in Rio. It was then that, finally, Parreira saw sense and restored Romario to the team. There'd been a stand-off between them since 1992, when Parreira had called Romario all the way from Holland, where he played for PSV Eindhoven, for a friendly against

Germany and then didn't start him. Romario came back against Uruguay, excelled, scored twice, and spared Parreira the shame of being the first manager to fail to take Brazil to the World Cup. Short, sturdy, superbly balanced, with a wonderful delicate touch, a terrific turn and devastating speed off the mark, Romario had the great attacker's gift of making goals out of nothing, and the further flair to make them for others.

Argentina had lurched their way to the States. Under a new manager in Alfio Basile, known earlier as a ruthless defender, they'd been humiliated in their group game against Colombia in Buenos Aires, losing 5–0 to a team which boasted the immense pace and thrust of young Tino Asprilla up front, and the wiles of Fredy Rincon in midfield. The score-line seemed too bad to be true and perhaps it was. As late as spring 1995, rumours insisted that this was one of the matches fixed by Malaysian gamblers. It left Argentina obliged to eliminate Australia—which they did, in another of those absurd play-offs with the winners of the Oceania group.

By this time, Argentina had Diego Maradona back. Quitting Italy after testing positive for cocaine, being suspended for a year, accused of involvement in supplying drugs—and of collusion with the Camorra—Maradona went home to Buenos Aires to work out his penance under the supervision of a judge. Somewhat ponderous in both play-offs against Australia, Maradona had made astonishing physical strides by the time it came to the finals. Claudio Caniggia, also banned for a year for cocaine use when playing for Rome, was free to play again on the verge of the World Cup.

There was also the elegant young midfielder, Fernando Rodondo, foolishly ignored by the authoritarian Carlos Bilardo in 1990, and opposed by Maradona because they'd clashed in a Spanish League game between Seville and Tenerife. But this time Maradona didn't get his way.

Italy had stumbled through the qualifying rounds under their much-criticised new manager, Arrigo Sacchi. Sacchi, who'd had such success with Milan, had never played at any decent level, but retorted to his critics, 'You don't have to have been a horse to be a jockey.' Controversially, he weaned Italy away at last from *catenaccio*, with its sweeper, and changed to the 4-4-2, defence in zonal line, formation which he'd employed at Milan. But by the time it came to the World Cup he was flirting with 4-3-3, and had made endless changes in personnel.

Short of forwards, he'd still decided to leave behind Gianluca Vialli, who'd lately recovered his form. He insisted on using the elegant, elusive Roberto Baggio up front, where he'd never been at home (then criticised him for being static in a friendly on the eve of finals!).

Franco Baresi, the veteran centre-back and skipper, had been persuaded to come out of international retirement, but he'd lost much pace and was a potential weak link.

On the face of it, it looked as if Ireland would never have a better chance of beating an uneasy Italian team. Charlton had lost his huge centre-forward, Niall Quinn, with a knee injury. But he'd found a very mobile new centre-back in Phil Babb, to complement the indestructible Paul McGrath, and a powerful young midfielder in the Cork-born Roy Keane, paired in the centre with Andy Townsend.

No France. They'd lost, almost incredibly, their two ultimate, home fixtures against little Israel and Bulgaria. Two very late goals by the swift, strong Bulgarian striker Emil Kostadinov at the Parc des Princes in Paris dashed the cup, and the World Cup, from France's lips.

The United States were managed by the wily, experienced Yugoslav, Bora Milutinovic, who'd worked wonders with Costa Rica in Italy, and done well with Mexico four years earlier. When he got his full team together, its best men returning from abroad, it looked decent enough. For most of the past four years, however, Milutinovic had had his lesser players in camp at Mission Viejo, playing a string of meaningless friendlies. Roy Wegerle, from England, Eric Wynalda, from West Germany, Tab Ramos, from Spain, and Ernie Stewart, from Holland, together with the resilient half-back John Harkes, from England, gave the team a backbone. Bora, who after all his years in the States still insisted on using an interpreter to translate from Spanish, and dodged questions with a sleepy ease, was not renowned for taking risks. But his tactics prevailed in a pre-tournament friendly against Mexico, which the USA won 1–0 in front of a crowd of 91,000.

The Germans would, if only for historical reasons, be strong challengers again, though they, like the Dutch, had just lost a friendly at home to the fighting Irish. Berti Vogts was still not a popular team manager. But his late decision to recall the veteran blond striker, Rudi Voeller, proved inspired. Severe knee injuries, however, had blunted the edge of the captain, Lothar Matthaus. No longer able to cut the mustard as a midfielder, he'd become a sweeper, but he was hardly a Beckenbauer: his defensive capacities were doubtful.

From a closely contested final Asian group in Qatar, South Korea, though beaten by Japan, came through yet again. So, unexpectedly, did Saudi Arabia who'd produce what might well have been the goal of the final tournament.

On 17 June, at Soldier Field, Chicago, Germany opened the tournament against Bolivia in Group C. Something of a shadow already hung over proceedings: FIFA had produced another of its unwelcome, last-minute surprises. The previous March, the law-making International Board had decided that a foul tackle from behind should automatically lead to expulsion. FIFA obtained permission to introduce the rule for the World Cup, though it was due only in July. (Ludicrously, FIFA attempted to make *any* tackle from behind a red-card offence but climbed down, claiming that they'd never meant it.) Ironically—a tribute perhaps to the good sense of referees—not a single player was expelled merely for an illegitimate tackle from behind.

It was marginally less dull a game than most World Cup curtain raisers. Germany, who used Karl-Heinz Riedle rather than Voeller, missed a number of chances, and somewhat luckily got the one goal of the match. Matthaus' long ball rebounded from Haessler to an unmarked Jurgen Klinsmann, who scored with some ease. In the same group, on the same day, in the Dallas Cotton Bowl, where temperatures would rise in some games to 106 degrees, Spain were held to a draw by the lively South Koreans. Spain took a 2–0 lead, but playing without their sweeper, Nadal, sent off after 25 minutes, proved too much for them in the end. The Koreans equalised in the last minute.

The following hot day, Ireland beat Italy. The first surprise, on an afternoon rich in surprises, was that the crowd of nearly 75,000 in Giants Stadium was essentially Irish, not Italian. Given the huge numbers of Italians resident in New York, not to mention the thousands who had come from Italy, it seemed inevitable that Italy would be playing virtually at home. Instead, Rutherford resembled a suburb of Dublin. The Irish, the most genial, good tempered and sporting of supporters, had somehow managed to acquire a huge preponderance of the tickets— many of them sold on the black market at disgracefully high prices (an inevitable corollary of a slack and mistaken ticket policy). But whatever an Irishman paid that day, he must have thought it cheap at the price. Italy, weighed down by Sacchi's obsessive tactical schemes, uneasy with their formation, might well have lost even had they not given away so bizarre a goal.

Little Ray Houghton, the Glaswegian Irishman, scored it after barely ten minutes, an early sucker punch. John Sheridan, a clever midfielder, played a high ball forward. Costacurta, one of Italy's two Milan stoppers, got his head to it, but without much power. Still less powerful was the header by his colleague and mentor, Franco Baresi. The ball dropped to Houghton, who took it on and then chipped it with his weaker left foot. To the joy of the Irish fans, and the despair of the outnumbered Italians, the ball sailed over the head of the poorly positioned keeper, Pagliuca, and into the net.

McGrath, in dominant form, blocked a fierce shot by Roberto Baggio in the first half, but little more was seen of Baggio who, outside the dressing rooms, said, with an obscenity, that his ligament trouble had had nothing to do with his poor form—though next day he changed his tune. 'You'll never beat the Irish!' sang the joyous Irish supporters, and apart from one good run and strong left footer by the elegant Beppe Signori, well saved by Packie Bonner, the Italians were seldom threatening. Indeed, it was Pagliuca who had to make a number of saves, not least from Tommy Coyne, running his heart out as the lone striker. Small wonder he'd collapse after the match on the team's bus.

Next day, in the same Group E, nicknamed the Group of Death, the muscular Norwegians beat Mexico with an 85th minute goal. It was a rather odd one: Jan Fjortoft, the big centre-forward, was fouled as he went for goal. Sandor Puhl, the Hungarian referee, sensibly played the advantage rule and Rekdal, a substitute, went on to score. Mexico, neat and intelligent, were terribly unlucky not to equalise in the final minute when their clever striker, Zague, put a diving header against a post. The rebound hit him on the head, only to be cleared by Norway's Berg.

What of Brazil in Group B? A stutter on the way to the finals, a 1–1 draw with little Canada, gave scant encouragement. Perversely, Carlos Alberto Parreira had left out the lively and inventive Valdo from his midfield and picked his Paris Saint-Germain colleague, Rai, who'd had a much inferior season. They began in Stanford with a 2–0 win against Russia.

The Russian squad was depleted and riven by a players' mutiny against the coach, Pavel Sadyrin, and the Russian Association, which, when Russia played in Greece, had condemned them to shiver in a third-rate hotel. The revolt, and the intransigence of the Russian FA, meant no Kanchelskis, Kolyvanov, Kiriakov, Shalimov and nearly Yuran, the Ukraine-born striker who fell out with the coach on the eve of the tournament. Ominously for the Russians, Brazil had scored eight times in a friendly against Honduras in San Diego, five goals being shared between Bebeto and Romario.

No fewer than a massive 81,061 fans saw the game, an indication of the amazing enthusiasm fans would show throughout this recordbreaking World Cup. With Romario quite irresistible, Brazil had little trouble in winning. He scored the first goal after 27 minutes, exploiting Bebeto's free kick, and was brought down after 53 minutes for Rai to convert the penalty. Yuran played, and was anonymous.

In the same group, Cameroon, 1990's revelation, held the Swedes to a 2–2 draw at the Pasadena Rose Bowl, watched by an astounding 83,959! Scant sign here of Sweden's later brio. Nor of Cameroon's subsequent collapse; financial problems had been devastating. JeanClaude Pagal, a 1990 player who didn't make the cut, travelled all the way from Martigues to Orly airport, Paris, to punch Cameroon's French manager, Henri Michel. Forty-two-year-old Roger Milla was in the squad again but didn't get on in this opening game, when Omam Biyik, his implacable critic after Italy, had an outstanding game and scored Cameroon's second goal. The 39-year-old keeper, Joseph-Antoine Bell, alternated horrible mistakes on crosses with outstanding saves. As a kind of inspired trade unionist, he it was who smoothed relations between players and officials. (He had been kicked out of the team in 1990 for his searing criticisms of the way things were being run.)

In the ghastly Pontiac Silverdome, the USA bravely held Switzerland to a draw before 73,425 in the first Group A match. Roy Hodgson, Switzerland's English coach, had fashioned a team which played beyond its evident means. Poor positioning by America's flamboyant goalkeeper, Tony Meola, allowed Bregy to give the Swiss a 39th minute lead from a free kick. But six minutes later, a still better free kick by Eric Wynalda levelled the score.

In the other Group A match, a staggering 91,856 packed the Rose Bowl to see Romania, inspired by Gheorghe Hagi of the sublime left foot, and the young centre-forward, Florin Raducoiou, beat the Colombians 3–1. Awful goalkeeping by Colombia's Cordoba was a help. 'Our players were tense,' said Colombia's coach, Pato Maturana. 'Since the Argentina game, people have talked and talked about us, and it made them nervous.' Worse, alas, was to come.

In Group F, two Arab teams alarmed their Lowlands opposition, each going down by just a single goal. In Washington, Holland prevailed thanks only to a fearful goalkeeping error by Saudi Arabia's Al Deayea, enabling Taument to find the empty net, after Saudi had taken a 19th minute lead. Jorge Solari, the Argentine coach appointed to manage Saudi late in the day, rightly said that Holland 'found it a lot more difficult than expected'. So, for that matter, did Belgium, who might not have come through 1–0 against a better goalkeeper than Morocco's uneasy Azmi.

Now to the second round of matches. Could Italy do better, in Giants Stadium again, against Norway? It looked unlikely when, in the first half, little Erik Mykland played a neat through-ball to Oyvind Leonhardsen, bisecting the Italian defence. Out of his goal in a panic rushed the unhappy Gianluca Pagliuca, handling outside the box to be very properly sent off. This meant, axiomatically, that the substitute keeper, Marchegiani, would come on. But who'd be pulled off, to make way for him? To the amazement of Italy's fans and the abiding disgust of the player himself, it was none other than Roberto Baggio. It was useless for Arrigo Sacchi to protest that, with just ten men, he needed players who 'would wear themselves out'. Or that Baggio would be valuable in the next game, against Mexico. The insult would be neither forgotten nor forgiven.

As it was, Italy played resiliently in defence, against a prosaic Norwegian team over-addicted to the long ball, and won the match 24 minutes into the second half from one of Beppe Signori's many clever left-footed free kicks. Dino Baggio, the powerful midfielder, soared aloft and headed in. 'Embarrassing,' said Erik Thorstvedt, Norway's keeper. As, indeed, it was.

But the Irish were in trouble, too. Orlando's heat was just too much for them. Mexico, dropping the veteran Hugo Sanchez from their attack, were far happier in the heat, which seemed especially to affect Ireland's right-back, Denis Irwin, moving across to replace the vigorous young Gary Kelly, who was much missed. Irwin was ridiculed by Garcia Aspe, on the wing, when he set up Garcia and Mexico's second goal after 66 minutes.

Jack Charlton had furious altercations on the touchline with officials, as did John Aldridge, belatedly brought on in time to score Ireland's only goal, six minutes from the end. Charlton was fined $14,900 and banned from the bench for the next game, Aldridge fined $1,850. Charlton felt he was being victimised for previous protests over heat and water breaks. 'Next time we'll play Mexico in winter and see what happens,' he declared. But the Mexicans had played well.

As, initially, did Argentina, though doom awaited them. Greece, who'd come through with a formidable but illusory qualifying record, were thrashed 4–0 at Foxboro, Gabriel Batistuta showing what a formidable striker he was and Diego Maradona evoking glories of old.

Next, again at Foxboro, they would play the Nigerians, who'd astonished Bulgaria, beating them with ease, 3–0, in Dallas. Small sign there of Bulgaria's future triumphs. Nigeria, despite uneasy relations between their gifted players and the Dutch coach, Clemens Westerhof, seemed set to replace Cameroon as the new Lions of Africa. The two powerful strikers, Rachid Yekini and Daniel Amokachi, were strongly supported by the talented left-winger, Emmanuel Amunike, with Oliseh doing skilful things in midfield. Westerhof, never one to mince his words, observed that it wasn't liaisons with women which tired his players out—it was the amount of night-time they spent looking for them!

Nigeria actually went ahead against the Argentinians and hope surged. Served by Amokachi, Siasia scored, though he was surely offside. But the lead wouldn't last. Inspired by Maradona, Argentina came back with two goals, both scored by Claudio Caniggia—seemingly rejuvenated by his long, enforced rest—within seven first-half minutes. Westerhof sneered at Argentina and Maradona. They wouldn't win the World Cup, he said, Nigeria would do better. Which proved correct.

Bulgaria climbed from the canvas, beating Greece in Chicago: remarkably enough, this was the first time Bulgaria had ever won a match in the World Cup finals. The Greek manager, Panagulias, dropped six of his team, but this made little improvement. It was a wretched game, though two of Bulgaria's future heroes were scorers: two penalties for Hristo Stoichkov and a goal for the big, blond, balding midfielder, Letchkov.

In Pasadena, the improbable happened: the USA beat Colombia 2–1 in a game which still awaits a full explanation. That the Colombians lay down and died now seems beyond all possible doubt. Why they did it is another matter. Out of fear? Out of gambling greed? What we do know is that they were unrecognisable, even if the Americans needed an own goal from Andres Escobar, after 35 minutes, to go ahead. Seven minutes after half-time Ernie Stewart made it 2–0, served by Tab Ramos. Valencia put in a rebound in the final minute. Escobar had little time left to live.

Maradona, astonishing in his stamina during the 95 minutes of the Argentina–Nigeria game, was, alas for him, obliged to take a dope test. On the last day of June it was officially announced that his urine contained no fewer than five different variants of the stimulant ephedrine. The Argentine Football Association withdrew him instantly from the tournament, before FIFA could suspend him. But the little man, inevitably swearing innocence, was allowed to stay on as a television commentator.

> Men are we, and must grieve when even the shade
> Of that which once was great has passed away.

Except that an embittered, 34-year-old Maradona had seemed so much more than the shade of the sublime player of previous World Cups. Now, alas, we knew why: ephedrine.

Meanwhile, the extent of Argentina's demoralisation was shown in their last group game in Dallas, against Bulgaria, who beat them 2–0 with goals by Stoichkov and, in the last minute from a corner, Siriakov (despite Bulgaria having Tzvetanov sent off after 67 minutes). 'I saw the match,' said Maradona, 'but I don't think it was Argentina playing out there.'

That, and the loss of Caniggia, with a toe injured in a training game before the tournament began, effectively knocked the stuffing out of Argentina. In the next round, they'd be easily eliminated by a Romanian team inspired by Hagi, with Dumitrescu, moving up front to replace Raducoiou, in wondrous opportunist form.

In Group F, strange things happened. Belgium, surprisingly, beat Holland; and, amazingly, lost to Saudi Arabia, even though there may have been some faint consolation in losing to one of the best individual goals ever scored in a World Cup. In Washington, the little Saudi, Owairan, received the ball in his own half, and set off on a

sustained and extraordinary run, beating one man, two, three four ...
FIVE! before shooting wide of Belgium's keeper, Preud'homme.
Paul Himst, Belgium's manager and once their star, blamed the heat for
what went wrong.

Against Holland, in Orlando, Philippe Albert, the Belgian centre-back,
came in from the right when Grun flicked on a corner, to shoot between
De Goey and his near post. Dick Advocaat said gloomily and somewhat
unconvincingly that the trouble had been his team used only three defenders against two strikers, 'and couldn't control them'. Ronald Koeman said
darkly, 'Things went wrong which weren't supposed to go wrong.' As they
so often do.

The Germans were making progress, but not without difficulty. Things
hadn't, after all, begun too well, with Thomas Berthold, the defender,
openly criticising Berti Vogts' tactics. Par for the course, really,
for a German World Cup team. Vogts swallowed his pride and said
such discussion might be good for the team. But not when the often
dissident blond midfielder, Stefan Effenberg, put a finger up to a
barracking crowd after Germany, fading badly in the intense heat
of Dallas, had only just scraped through against South Korea. He was
sent home.

Germany's somewhat fortunate 1–1 draw with Spain in Chicago
was notable for the return, as a substitute, of Rudi Voeller. Right
away, his partnership with Jurgen Klinsmann looked smooth and
menacing. It would reach its apogee in the ensuing second round,
when the two combined superbly, swiftly and lethally against a
Belgian defence which—in Chicago again—gave three goals away to
the pair. The Germans, though, were immensely fortunate not to
concede a penalty, late in the game, when Weber was plainly
brought down by Helmer in the box. Legalities aside—and the crass
decision led to Roethlisberger, the Swiss referee, being packed off home—
the Germans certainly didn't deserve to lose or draw. Exceptional goalkeeping by Preud'homme had kept Belgium in the game, and the
late goal Philippe Albert scored, though well taken, was something of a
surprise.

As for Spain, they'd scored a strange goal against the Germans: Illgner,
the German keeper, allowing Goicoechea's cross from the right to float
over his head and in off the far post. Klinsmann's bouncing header
equalised. Had Julio Salinas only kept his head, when through all alone
against Italy in the quarter finals at Foxboro, who knows how far the
Spaniards could have gone?

In Group E, Italy drew with Mexico, Ireland with Norway. Daniele
Massaro, the lithe, incisive Milan striker brought on as substitute,
scored Italy's goal and popped up in defence two minutes later. The
Italians could have had a penalty when Dino Baggio was shoved by

Perales. Right down to the other end went Mexico to equalise through their lively right-winger, Bernal. At which point Italy fell apart, survived rather than competed, and scraped into the next round only as one of the third-placed teams.

Watching Ireland draw with Norway at Giants Stadium was a penance. The Norwegians made no serious attempt to win the game till far too late. The Irish, Jack Charlton admitted, were obliged to work as hard as they did because they lacked explosive players. So Ireland went through, and dull, disappointing Norway went out. Coach Egil Olsen's loyalty to the long-ball game was an incubus in an America summer.

The Dutch, in Group F, made their way uneasily to the next round. Playing Morocco in torrid Orlando was no holiday. That risky, three centre-back defence still looked fallible, and was badly caught out when the Moroccans equalised Bergkamp's enterprising goal. Almost at once it was known that, in Washington, the Saudis were beating Belgium. But with 11 minutes left, Bergkamp made the winner for the substitute, the gifted Brian Roy.

The Colombians, coming to life too late, beat Switzerland 2–0 in Palo Alto, with Carlos Valderrama, he of the blond dreadlocks, inspiring their attacks. This surely was the real Colombia, a team which had the potential to reach at least the semis.

Over the rest of the tournament would hang the deep shadow of Andres Escobar's cruel assassination. It took place a few days after the Colombian team had arrived home in virtual disgrace. As Escobar and a woman friend were leaving a restaurant in Las Palmas, a suburb of Medellin, they were accosted by an aggressive group of men. There was an altercation, at the end of which Escobar was shot 12 times, the accomplices yelling, obscenely, 'Goal!' each time the murderer pulled the trigger. Arrests were made, but the mystery remained: not merely why Escobar had been shot but why Colombia had lost so abjectly to the United States; and whether the two incidents were connected. Before that game, Pato Maturana—who announced his resignation before going home, and into hiding—had withdrawn another player, Gabriel Gomez, who, like himself, had been sent death threats.

Two days before Cameroon were due to meet Brazil, their players arrived 90 minutes late for training in California. Joseph-Antoine Bell announced that if they weren't paid, they wouldn't play. It was rumoured that a suitcase packed with $450,000 in cash had arrived—illegally—from Yaounde. Whatever, the players did get paid, did play Brazil, and lost, 3–0. Dunga, strong, competitive but hardly creative, was the pillar of Brazil's midfield. No wingers—attacking down the flanks was left to the swift full-backs, Jorginho and Leonardo. In central defence,

the two Ricardos, both injured, had been replaced by Marcio Santos and
Roma's Aldair. A typical burst from Romario gave Brazil their first goal,
a header by Santos the second, a narrow-angled shot by Bebeto the
third.

Poor Cameroon. The Lions would go home with their tails between
their legs, annihilated 6–1 in Palo Alto by a Russian team which had
nothing to play for. Five of the goals were scored by just one man: the
centre-forward, Oleg Salenko, who would probably have been left out
had Yuran not squabbled, again, with Sadyrin. Salenko, who'd scored 16
goals for Logrones in the Spanish season, wouldn't even keep his place for
Russia after the World Cup. 'Please don't call me Superman,' he said.
Roger Milla, who had been called a Superman in 1990, did at least go
out, aged 42, with a goal.

At Foxboro, the Nigerians qualified to play Italy by beating hapless
Greece, goals going to Finidi George and, six minutes into injury
time, Daniel Amokachi. Clemens Westerhof, the coach, had sent him
a message that Bulgaria were winning 2–0 so goals were vital. 'He told
me to just get the ball and go through the Greek defence.' Which
Amokachi did.

Going into the second round, the cat was put among the pigeons by the
President of the Nigerian football federation, Samson Emeka Omeruah.
He wasn't scared of Italy, he told Italian journalists: 'We're the champions
of Africa; what are *you*? Italy is world famous for the Mafia and Fiat, not
for football.' An Italian TV team who tried to film the Nigerians in
training, near Boston, were slapped, shoved and threatened. 'They
jumped on us,' said a shaken Italian TV man. 'The police pretended not
to see anything. We're delirious, we're hysterical. These people are
crazy.'

How close the Italians came to defeat at Foxboro. How much they
owed to Roberto Baggio. And how inept was the refereeing of the
Mexican, Arturo Brizio. Italian critics savaged him, accusing him
of denying Italy two clear penalties and of sending the
unlucky Gianfranco Zola off for little or nothing. The gifted little
Sardinian attacker, who'd grown up at Naples in the lee of Diego
Maradona, should surely have had his World Cup chance much earlier.
As it was, he came on as substitute after 18 minutes of the
second half, to be expelled just 12 minutes later. The same critics
admitted that the hapless Brizio Carter blundered again when he didn't
send off Paolo Maldini, who'd replaced the injured Franco Baresi in the
centre of defence. Maldini, on 80 minutes, was clearly guilty of a 'last
man' foul, which demanded an automatic red card, when he hauled back
Yekini.

But, above all, it was the day when Roberto Baggio, that brilliant
enigma, took wing—and Italy with him. Neither started too well.

Indeed, Nigeria went into the lead after 26 minutes. Finidi George's corner bounced off Maldini's knee, Emmanuel Amunike banging the ball home. Not till Nicola Berti, ill at ease on the flank, was replaced by the muscular Dino Baggio, at half-time, did Italy really begin to click. He quickly hit the post from a pass by Signori. Just two minutes from the end of normal time, Mussi, unexpectedly brought in at right-back, gave Roberto Baggio the chance to slip the ball by keeper Rufai.

So it meant extra time in that exhausting heat. Yekini should have scored, but didn't. After 102 minutes, Roberto Baggio sent the other full-back, Benarrivo into the box. Eguavoen fouled him and Roberto Baggio's spot kick sneaked in, off the post.

At Palo Alto, before a crowd of 84,147, Brazil knocked out the USA by only 1–0. But some American critics ripped into Bora Milutinovic for what they regarded as his inexcusably craven tactics, failing to go out to try to win, even when Brazil were reduced to ten men with the sending off of their left-back, Leonardo, after 43 minutes. He'd crashed his elbow into the skull of Tab Ramos, the only really creative player the Americans had, and who, as a result of the incident, was obliged to go off with a nasty head injury. The Americans brought on Eric Wynalda, but he was a striker rather than a schemer, unable to produce the kind of pass whereby Ramos so nearly made an early goal for Thomas Dooley. As it was, the Brazilians always looked too sophisticated for the unadventurous Americans, and won the game in the way you might have expected, 16 minutes from time: Romario's run and killing through pass, Bebeto's calmly taken goal.

Holland knocked out Ireland, in Orlando, and here another manager had his critics for being too defensive. Jack Charlton was rebuked for cleaving to a one-man attack in sapping conditions. And when, only 17 minutes from the end, the tall striker Tony Cascarino did come on, the long-suffering, self-sacrificing Coyne came off. But in Charlton's defence, it must be said that two horrible defensive errors gave them a mountain to climb in those 90 degrees of heat and increasing humidity.

After only ten minutes the Irish left-back, Terry Phelan, whom Charlton had preferred to Dennis Irwin, headed a feeble back-pass to his keeper, Packie Bonner. Marc Overmars, the Dutch right-winger, raced on to the ball, and crossed for Dennis Bergkamp to score. To compound that, the usually resilient Bonner allowed a long shot from Wim Jonk to squirm nightmarishly through his hands, and Holland were two ahead. They stayed there.

Atrocious refereeing by the Syrian, Al Sharif, ruined a potentially marvellous game at Giants Stadium between Bulgaria and Mexico. Time and again, his crass decisions made you curse FIFA for their 'affirmative action', choosing referees on the basis of provenance, rather than prowess.

Both teams showed high potential. Emil Kostadinov and Hristo Stoichkov were a lethal pair of strikers for Bulgaria. The Mexicans, though somewhat old fashioned in their use of sweeper, dazzled with their passing, impressed with their imagination and ball control. They went one down when Yordanov put Stoichkov through and could have been two down when Kostadinov hit the post. But Emil Kremenliev, a Bulgarian defender, conceded a penalty, and Mexico were back in the game. Kremenliev had already been cautioned and should automatically have been sent off. Instead he stayed on, only to be expelled for quite a trivial foul, Al Sharif perhaps endeavouring to make amends. Was he doing that again when he expelled Luis Garcia, Mexico's incisive striker, for the second of two negligible fouls? It was ten men each now, and the game fell away. Even the penalty shoot out was a fiasco of misses, till Bulgaria put Mexico out of their misery.

Spain's 3–0 win against the Swiss, in Washington, perhaps flattered them but there was no doubt about their morale, their penetration, even if big Julio Salinas—snubbed by his team, Barcelona, resurrected by Clemente—played up-front on his own. It was a game in which the Swiss badly missed the left-wing pace and guile of Alain Sutter.

The deciding moment surely came on the quarter hour. Nadal, back from suspension in the Spanish defence, blocked a run by Stephane Chapuisat, the Swiss centre-forward. Was it or wasn't it a foul? Van der Ende, the referee, let play go on—for Fernando Hierro to score an extraordinary goal on the break.

So to the quarter-finals. Teams, inevitably, were tiring, and had not been helped by some insensitive scheduling. To make matters worse for the survivors, the semi-finals were scheduled for the same day. This gave a great advantage to the winners in Pasadena, who could stay put for the Final, while the New Jersey winners would have to fly 3,000 miles.

Spain should have beaten Italy, but three things thwarted them: a bad miss, a bad refereeing decision and Roberto Baggio's brilliance. Dino Baggio, that workhorse midfielder who'd been so surprising a marksman, gave Italy another priceless goal, after 26 minutes. This time it was a shot, not a header, a fulminating drive from some 25 yards after Benarrivo, overlapping down the left, had crossed the ball. Perhaps Zubizarreta should have got to it, but the shot was still spectacular and rich consolation for the fact that Abelardo, Spain's defender, saw only a yellow rather than a red card for a shocking early foul at the expense of Roberto Baggio's shin.

Conte, another workhorse, could have given Italy a second goal, but put a good chance wide. So José Caminero, a revelation in Spain's midfield, began to train his sights on the Italian goal. Thirteen minutes into the second half, he prevailed at last. Sergi got in a cross from the left. Otero was unmarked, but missed it, Caminero struck the ball, which hit the hapless Benarrivo and was deflected wide of Pagliuca. Spain got on top, but Salinas threw away their crucial chance. The Italian defence seemed curiously confused, waiting perhaps for an offside flag and whistle, allowing Salinas through alone, with just Pagliuca in his way. The keeper's extended left leg kept Italy in the World Cup.

Now Spain went forward in excessive numbers, forgetting Italy are the masters of the breakaway. Lazio striker Signori, a half-time substitute used by Sacchi wide on the left, sweetly lobbed Roberto Baggio through. Cool and adroit, Baggio went by Zubizarreta, and found the net from a difficult angle. 2–1, though there was still time for Tassotti, prone throughout to be drawn into the middle, to elbow Luis Enrique. 'I meant no harm,' Tassotti protested. 'I'll send him a telegram.' It wouldn't have pacified Luis Enrique. 'Tassotti acted like a killer,' he said. 'He looked around, and when he saw the referee and the linesman were distracted, he struck. He has ruined my World Cup, and Spain's.' Watching the incident on television, FIFA hit Tassotti with an eight-match suspension. Even Luis Enrique thought it was too much: 'A lifetime.'

Germany had seemed Italy's likely opponents in the semi-final, as they had been in Mexico, in 1970. But in the heat of Giants Stadium, before 72,416 astonished fans, Bulgaria defeated them. 'It was,' said Dimitar Penev, the Bulgarian manager, without exaggeration, 'the finest day in the history of Bulgarian football.' And a black day indeed for Germany.

Looking back on that game, which I watched, two factors seem to me to be salient. First, that the use of Lothar Mattaus as sweeper was as mistaken as it seemed to be in prospect. Second, that a large question mark was placed over man to man marking.

It had been a roller-coaster game, but it wasn't until very early in the second half that Germany went ahead. And it was Letchkov, the eventual hero, who tripped Klinsmann. Matthaus duly scored. The die seemed cast. Seventeen minutes from the end Moeller hit the post and Rudi Voeller put in the rebound, but Bulgaria breathed again: he was offside. So it was that, just a couple of minutes later, Bulgaria levelled the scores. Hristo Stoichkov, who'd been largely subdued by the German defence, was brought down by Buchwald. He took the free kick himself: a magnificent shot which sailed over the wall and into the right-hand corner.

Then, the *coup de grâce*. The high cross which came over from Bulgaria's right wing, 12 minutes from the end should have been a defender's ball. Towering above little Thomas Haessler, an attacking midfielder, Yordan Letchkov headed in. And Matthaus, the sweeper? Nowhere to be seen.

The Italian players, watching in their *ritiro* in New Jersey, amidst the spacious, green grounds of the Pingry school, were cheering not for either team but for ... extra time.

In San Francisco, on the same day, 81,715—the crowds remained astonishing—watched Sweden edge past Romania in a penalty shoot-out. Sweden played their usual four-in-line defence; Romania, as usual, employed a sweeper. Thomas Ravelli, the balding veteran Swedish goalkeeper, played his 115th game for his country. He was, by turns as usual, brilliant and erratic, and for ever the exhibitionist. After three minutes, Dahlin headed against Prunea's post. In Romania's midfield, Gheorghe Hagi's famed left foot constantly did clever things.

Brolin would score the opening goal, after 32 minutes of the second half, the result of a cleverly worked free kick. Stefan Schwarz, the midfielder who often used his powerful left foot to take them, feinted, Mild slipped the ball beyond the wall, and Brolin dashed in, to beat Prunea. But Florin Raducoiou, the young Romanian centre-forward, was on a day of grace. Just a couple of minutes from what would have been the end, Hagi, getting a return ball from a free kick, banged the ball into the box, it rebounded from the Swedish wall, and Raducoiou scored.

Romania took the lead after ten minutes of extra time, Raducoiou snapping up a ball deflected inadvertently by Sweden's stopper, Patrik Andersson. There were just five minutes left when the Swedish right-back, Roland Nilsson, centred. It should have been the goalkeeper's ball, but the giant Kennet Andersson soared aloft, and headed Sweden's equaliser. So, alas, to penalties. Survival indeed by Sweden, who'd been down to ten men after 102 minutes, when Schwarz was sent off for a second yellow card.

Mild promptly shot over the Swedish bar from the spot. Raducoiou converted, so did Kennet Andersson, Hagi, Brolin, Lupescu and Ingesson. But when Petrescu shot, Ravelli saved, and it was all square. Now, whoever missed would miss fatally. Roland Nilsson scored, Ilie Dumitrescu replied. Henrik Larsson succeeded. But when that elegant sweeper, Belodedici, shot ... Ravelli's left arm stretched out, reached the ball, and Sweden were in the semi-finals. Poor Romania: it was the second successive World Cup in which they had gone out on penalties.

The Dutch team which faced Brazil lacked both Gullit and Van Basten. There was no equivalent to Cruyff. Using Koeman to mark the effervescent Romario, and bringing Jan Wouters back to tail Bebeto,

Holland survived the first half. Brazil used Mazinho and Zinho wide on the flanks of midfield—the latter having his first really impressive game of the tournament. Brazil began to pick up steam, with Mauro Silva moving eagerly through from central midfield; now helping his defence, now starting attacks, he played a dominant role.

The Dutch defence, especially Ronald Koeman, was short of pace—a potentially lethal failing against the likes of Romario and Bebeto. And when, in ten minutes of the second half, those two put Brazil a couple of goals ahead all seemed lost for Holland. Was the second goal offside? The Dutch bitterly insisted that it was. Mauro Silva sent Bebeto flying through as Romario came running back from what was clearly an offside position. As the referee decided that he wasn't interfering with play, Bebeto ran on and scored.

Holland might have seemed down and out; their revival was a triumph of morale, helped no doubt by the fact that, for once, the Dallas weather was fresh and windy, rather than hot and stifling. A couple of minutes after Bebeto's goal Dennis Bergkamp got the ball from a throw-in on the left, worked his way cleverly through the Brazilian defence, and beat Taffarel: 2–1. Twelve minutes more, and the Dutch were level. Taffarel had earlier saved a powerful shot from Holland's black midfielder, Aron Winter. But when Marc Overmars sent in a corner, Winter's head met it on the edge of the six-yard box: the game was now wide open.

How ironic that it should be resolved by Brazil's veteran left-back, Branco, playing only because Leonardo was very properly suspended. Branco had given fair warning when one of his left-footed specialities from a free kick was turned over the top by De Goey. With nine minutes left, he tried again from thirty yards: a veritable missile which flew by De Goey, and put Brazil into the semi-finals. 'This will shut up the people who don't believe in me,' said Branco. 'I've played in three World Cups, and I think I deserved more respect.'

Sweden, in Pasadena before 84,569 fans, proved far less trouble. The Swedish players, after that extra-time against Romania, looked dead on their feet. To make matters worse, Jonas Thern, replacing the suspended Schwarz in midfield, was also sent off, after 18 minutes of the second half. Though Sweden had been under endless pressure, and had time and again narrowly escaped, there was still no score by then.

The Swedes owed a great deal to Ravelli, in his record-breaking 116th international, making saves from Bebeto, one of Branco's dreaded free kicks, and Romario, after Dunga's fine pass and Bebeto's cross. Many other chances were missed. 'We'll fly over the heads of the Brazilian defenders,' tall Kennet Andersson had promised, encouraged by the success of the Dutch attackers. But it didn't happen. Neither he nor an obviously weary Dahlin, ill-served throughout, could exploit their notable heading powers.

So, after the break, Parreira 'amnestied' the lanky Rai, who replaced the man who'd displaced him on the right of midfield—Mazinho. Scarcely had the second half begun than Rai was through, and Ravelli had to dive at his feet. It was again virtually a question of Brazil v. Ravelli. Thern's expulsion, for kicking at Dunga, was decisive.

Not till the 80th minute, however, did the Swedish citadel fall. Bebeto launched his attacking right-back, Jorginho, over came the cross, and little Romario somehow managed to drift away from the Swedish defenders, jump at the far post and head the winner.

From the Italian camp the news was that Beppe Signori would not start the semi-final against Bulgaria. A mortified Signori heard this from a reporter, rather than straight from Sacchi himself. It was a wound which would take some time to heal, and made him the second star to resent the ways of Sacchi—Roberto Baggio being emphatically the other.

The Bulgarians that afternoon at Giants Stadium bore no comparison with the team which had triumphed there against the Germans. They could do little or nothing about Baggio, 'The Divine Ponytail', as the Italians nicknamed him. From the start, Bulgaria's defenders were chasing shadows, clutching at straws. When the sweeper, Petar Houbtchev, made a pathetically maladroit attempt to tackle Baggio, advancing on him from an inside-left position, Baggio glided past, curling his shot exquisitely around another defender, Ivanov, and into the far corner of the goal. Borislav Mikhailov, the goalkeeper, had no hope at all.

Nor had he four minutes later. He and Bulgaria were delighted to escape when Baggio neatly moved the ball on to Albertini. The young Milan midfielder thumped a shot which canoned back from the foot of a post. Albertini was rampant. Receiving once more from the Divine Ponytail, he drove in a shot which Mikhailov turned over the bar. Next minute he would return the compliment with a perfect chip which sent Baggio himself through, to score his and the Italians' second goal.

Bulgaria were being overrun, and it was a surprise when they suddenly came back from the dead with a 44th minute penalty. Siriakov was brought down from behind by Costacurta and Stoichkov put away the penalty. Costacurta was booked, which meant he'd miss the Final. Finally, in that crippling heat, the Bulgarians began to play like international footballers rather than struggling mediocrities, while the Italians, by Sacchi's own admission, grew increasingly tired.

But justice was done. For twenty minutes or so, the Italians had played outstandingly good football, with Benarrivo and another new full-back, Roberto Mussi, constantly raiding down the wings. A large shadow hung over the Italian success: Baggio was obliged to go off with a strained hamstring. On top of that, he had broken a tooth. Would he, could he, possibly be fit in time? And what of Franco Baresi, indestructible veteran, making astonishingly fast progress after his knee operation?

ITALIAN TORMENT: WILL ROBY PLAY? was the headline on the front page of Rome's *Corriere Dello Sport* on the Friday. 'I hope to make it,' declared Baggio. 'I can't miss the Final of this World Cup, a World Cup which means more to me than ever.'

'Italy,' said Parreira, 'has grown with the days. It's not just Baggio. We've earned the right to play the Final through our consistency. Italy have earned it with their last, brilliant performances.' But by no means all Brazilians were as enthusiastic about his team as Parreira. Chico Maia, a radio reporter from Belo Horizonte, said he hoped Brazil would lose, and sounded an old, embittered song: 'We journalists consider it an error to Europeanise the play of our national team. We have a tradition, a credibility, and we're not disposed to sell it off or bargain it away.'

That day, there was the third-place match to be got out of the way, in Pasadena. The Swedes walked all over an utterly spent Bulgarian team which had flown 3,000 miles to meet them. The Bulgarians resisted for about half an hour. Then Brolin, advancing from midfield, headed in Ingesson's cross on the bounce. Thomas Ravelli then turned aside a tremendous shot by Stoichkov from outside the box. But on the half hour, the Swedes scored their second, Brolin's quick free kick being easily exploited by Mild. Seven minutes more, and Larsson, who was running riot, took another of Brolin's jewelled passes, danced on, evaded the keeper and scored Sweden's third. Kennet Andersson headed in Stefan Schwarz's cross to make it 4–0; a Swedish World Cup record.

So, a repeat of the 1970 Final, in which Brazil had brushed the Italians casually aside.

A strangely morose Sacchi had promised that he wouldn't on any account risk picking both Baggio and Baresi for the Final. Then, after fevered speculation all that Saturday, what did he do but pick both. Daniele Massaro, the Milan opportunist, who had been on the bench in the 1982 World Cup Final, would play up front. No place for a deeply disappointed Gianfranco Zola. He'd not had enough games, said Sacchi.

From the Brazilian camp, there were whispers that Romario, feeling a lingering groin strain, might not make the cut. He and Bebeto held the key, no one disputed that. This would be their 33rd international as a partnership, and they'd so far scored 57 goals for Brazil.

The teams were announced. Sacchi had gambled. Roberto Baggio and Franco Baresi would both be playing, Baresi just twenty-four hours after his operation. Brazil restored Mazinho to midfield, where Rai had replaced him in the second half against Sweden. Romario was there.

It was a game which never really got off the ground. Sacchi seemed not to have any real ambition to win it. Surely at some point in this protracted, debilitating game, Signori and his legendary left foot should have been brought on. And had Parreira only had the courage to bring on the big Corinthians' striker Viola earlier in the game, extra time might not have been necessary.

As for the midfield, Mauro Silva was the pick of them all. Solid, active, decisive and intelligent, rather than inspired, he was certainly the pivot of his team. And he was terribly unlucky not to score, 15 minutes from the end of normal time, with a right-footed cross-shot which Pagliuca fumbled piteously. The Fates looked after him, for the ball flew on to hit the post, then rebounded into his grateful arms.

It was a day on which Daniele Massaro's renowned finishing skills alas deserted him. So much so that you could almost, at the end, lay money on him missing his penalty—which he duly did. Franco Baresi, of all people, slipped him beautifully between Mauro Silva and Aldair after just 17 minutes—he shot straight at Taffarel. Taffarel would thwart the Italians twice again in extra time: once with a spectacular tip over the bar, when Roberto Baggio spun and shot from 25 yards; and from Baggio again, after a clever, quick exchange with Massaro. You might say that Sacchi could justify the choice of Baggio, despite the fact that he was so clearly walking—or trotting—wounded.

Dunga, known simply as a tackler, destroyer and grafter, had perhaps his most creative match for Brazil. In the absence of a Gerson or a Didi, somebody had to supply the attack; this he tried constantly to do, and not without success. There was, of course, always Branco and his free kicks. After 25 minutes, he banged one in hard and low. Pagliuca couldn't hold it, but Mazinho stumbled. Three minutes before the break, Branco struck another low, ferocious free kick, but this time Pagliuca held it capably.

Romario and Bebeto were always a threat, but could never quite make it count. Romario missed a fine chance to score after only 12 minutes, when Dunga crossed accurately from the right, but the little man could only head into Pagliuca's hands. In the second half, Pagliuca rushed out to kick away to safety a dangerous one-two between Romario and Bebeto. And just three minutes into injury time, Cafu crossed, Pagliuca made no contact, but Bebeto's attempt on the far post was so unusually weak that the keeper gathered with ease.

So, for all Viola's left-wing incursions, penalties it would be—a dire, disgraceful and dishonourable conclusion to the game's greatest competition, but one which sooner or later was surely bound to come.

Taffarel and Pagliuca wished each other luck. Baresi took the first kick—and shot over Tafferel's bar. Marcio Santos took the second—and Pagliuca stopped it. Albertini put his penalty away for Italy, Romario replied for Brazil. Evani, an Italian substitute, scored on his turn. More than 94,000 fans watched breathlessly and waited.

Now it was Branco's turn: who could imagine that left foot missing? Now, Daniele Massaro. And Taffarel saves. Dunga scores: Roberto Baggio must score to keep the shoot-out alive. Alas, the Divine Ponytail puts his shot high over the bar. Brazil have regained the World Cup—after 24 years. The samba beat is triumphant.

'I missed because I tried a powerful shot,' said Baggio. 'I went against my own nature. I shot towards Taffarel's right-hand corner, but I was worn out, I made a bad run-up to the ball, with my body too far backwards. Out of it there came a wretched shot; rubbish.'

But who could blame Baggio?

RESULTS: USA 1994

First Round

Group A

Detroit, Los Angeles, San Francisco
USA 1, Switzerland 1
Romania 3, Colombia 1
USA 2, Colombia 1
Switzerland 4, Romania 1
Romania 1 USA 0
Colombia 2, Switzerland 0

	P	W	D	L	F	A	Pts
					GOALS		
Romania	3	2	0	1	5	5	6
Switzerland	3	1	1	1	5	4	4
USA	3	1	1	1	3	3	4
Colombia	3	1	0	2	4	5	3

Group B

Los Angeles, San Francisco, Detroit
Cameroon 2, Sweden 2
Brazil 2, Russia 0
Brazil 3, Cameroon 0
Sweden 3, Russia 1
Brazil 1, Sweden 1
Russia 6, Cameroon 1

	P	W	D	L	F	A	Pts
Brazil	3	2	1	0	6	1	7
Sweden	3	1	2	0	6	4	5
Russia	3	1	0	2	7	6	3
Cameroon	3	0	1	2	3	11	1

Group C

Chicago, Boston, Dallas
Germany 1, Bolivia 0
Spain 2, South Korea 2
Germany 1, Spain 1
Bolivia 0, South Korea 0
Germany 3, South Korea 2
Bolivia 1, Spain 3

	P	W	D	L	F	A	Pts
Germany	3	2	1	0	5	3	7
Spain	3	1	2	0	6	4	5
South Korea	3	0	2	1	4	5	2
Bolivia	3	0	1	2	1	4	1

Group D

Boston, Dallas, Detroit, Chicago
Argentina 4, Greece 0
Nigeria 3, Bulgaria 0
Argentina 2, Nigeria 1
Bulgaria 4, Greece 0
Argentina 0, Bulgaria 2
Greece 0, Nigeria 2

	P	W	D	L	F	A	Pts
Nigeria	3	2	0	1	6	2	6
Bulgaria	3	2	0	1	6	3	6
Argentina	3	2	0	1	6	3	6
Greece	3	0	0	3	0	10	0

Group E

New York, Orlando
Ireland 1, Italy 0
Norway 1, Mexico 0
Italy 1, Norway 0
Mexico 2, Ireland 1
Italy 1, Mexico 1
Ireland 0, Norway 0

	P	W	D	L	F	A	Pts
Mexico	3	1	1	1	3	3	4
Ireland	3	1	1	1	2	2	4
Italy	3	1	1	1	2	2	4
Norway	3	1	1	1	1	1	4

Group F

Chicago, Orlando, Washington
Belgium 1, Morocco 0
Holland 2, Saudi Arabia 1
Belgium 1, Holland 0
Saudi Arabia 2, Morocco 1
Belgium 0, Saudi Arabia 1
Morocco 1, Holland 2

	P	W	D	L	F	A	Pts
Holland	3	2	0	1	4	3	6
Saudi Arabia	3	2	0	1	4	3	6
Belgium	3	2	0	1	2	1	6
Morocco	3	0	0	3	2	5	0

Second Round

Chicago
Germany 3, Belgium 2

Los Angeles
Romania 3, Argentina 2

Orlando
Holland 2, Ireland 0

San Francisco
Brazil 1, USA 0

Boston
Italy 2, Nigeria 1
after extra time

New York
Mexico 1, Bulgaria 1
Bulgaria win 3–1 on penalties

Washington
Spain 3, Switzerland 0

Dallas
Sweden 3, Saudi Arabia 1

Quarter-finals

Boston
Italy 2, Spain 1

Dallas
Brazil 3, Holland 2

New York
Bulgaria 2, Germany 1

San Francisco
Sweden 2, Romania 2
Sweden win 5–4 on penalties

Semi-finals

New York
Italy 2, Bulgaria 1

Los Angeles
Brazil 1, Sweden 0

Third-place match

Los Angeles

Sweden 4	**Bulgaria 0**
Ravelli; R. Nilsson,	Mikhailov; (Nikorov),
P. Andersson,	Ivanov (Kremenliev),
Bjorklund, Kamark;	Zvetanov, Houbtchev;
Schwarz, Larsson	Yankov, Letchkov,
(Limpar), Ingesson,	Kiriakov, Strakov
Mild; Brolin, K.	(Yordanov);
Andersson.	Kostadinov,
	Stoichkov.

SCORERS
Brolin, Mild, Larsson, K. Andersson for Sweden.
HT (4–0)

Final

Los Angeles

Brazil 0	**Italy 0**
Taffarel; Jorginho	Pagliuca; Mussi
(Cafu), Aldair,	(Apolloni), Baresi,
Marcio Santos,	Maldini, Benarrivo;
Branco; Mazzinho,	Berti, Albertini,
Mauro Silva, Dunga,	D. Baggio (Evani),
Zinho (Viola);	Donadoni;
Romario, Bebeto.	R. Baggio, Massaro.

Brazil win 3–2 on penalties

FRANCE
1998

For the third time in succession the World Cup Final was an anticlimax, though by no means as sterile as it had been on the previous two occasions. France, it might be said, won by default, though it was good to see the joy of their fans, who had been slow to come to life in the competition. Joy which, by and large, was untouched by the violence of their English counterparts, who disgraced themselves yet again in Marseille, the hooligan 'minority' proving as hard to deter or restrain, despite enormous policing efforts, as ever. Worse still were the brutal, nihilistic German right-wing thugs who almost killed a gendarme in Lens. And of course there was the usual scandal over match tickets. Thousands from Tokyo to London who thought they'd bought them found they were without them, vast numbers found their way on to the black market, the customary 'missing' tickets would prove to have been surreptitiously purloined. The inevitable consequence, some felt, of giving the host country such a massive allocation.

The disappointing quality of so many games, the inadequacy of several competitors, could be put down to the ultimate grandiose scheme of the FIFA President, João Havelange, who stood down at last just before the tournament after 24 controversial years in charge, only to give way to the FIFA Secretary, Sepp Blatter, the man of whom a German journalist once said, 'Sepp Blatter has fifty new ideas every day; and fifty-one of them are bad!'

Among his doubtful or disastrous ideas was the restoration of the kick-in for the throw-in after more than a century of disuse, the forbidding of kicked passes back to the goalkeeper and the insistence that from now onwards any foul tackle from behind be punished with sending off. This last, of course, had been tried and failed in America four years earlier, and despite Blatter's dictatorial outbursts early in the competition it was no more successful in 1998. It was plain that most referees' sheer common sense restrained them from sending players off in such doubtful circumstances, but the unfortunate result of Blatter's ukases was that the rule was applied so inconsistently—when it was applied at all.

Blatter's elevation to the Presidency was itself nothing if not controversial. It had seemed done and dusted in favour of the Swedish President of UEFA, Lennart Johansson, but when push came to shove his lead melted mysteriously away, so much so that, hurt and puzzled, he withdrew before the second ballot. How had this happened? We may never know. Accusations were made, but Blatter angrily brushed them all aside.

Meanwhile his authoritarian predecessor had decreed that the competition be enlarged yet again—this time to 32 teams. At least the number, by comparison with the previous 24, had a kind of mathematical logic, but it meant that the quality of the entrants was seriously diluted, while far too many games had to be played.

Over the Final itself, in the huge new Stade de France at Saint-Denis on the fringe of Paris, hung and still hangs the mystery of Ronaldo. No one has yet satisfactorily explained just what happened to him a few hours before the game. That it was some kind of seizure is clear enough. That he was in extreme torment and pain is equally clear. Roberto Carlos, the Brazilian left-back with whom Ronaldo shared his room, rushed for help, yet later, bizarrely, would accuse Ronaldo of lack of moral fibre. The 21-year-old centre-forward was taken post-haste to hospital but neither there nor in subsequent examinations in France and Brazil was anything found physically wrong with him. The clear inference was that his troubles were psychosomatic, brought on by the immense pressure which he'd had to endure, the more so as at no point in the tournament was he fully fit, strained thigh muscles severely inhibiting his lateral movement.

Yet to declare that there was 'nothing' wrong with him, as Brazilian apologists subsequently did, was ludicrous. Equally ludicrous seemed the decision of Brazil's veteran team manager Mario Lobo Zagallo not only to play Ronaldo but to keep him, despite his evident troubles, on the field throughout. Yet Zagallo continued to insist, even when back in Brazil, that he had taken the right decision. The Brazilians brushed aside accusations that the team's sponsors, Nike, who had certainly been responsible for the side taking on previously such a heavy programme, had insisted that Ronaldo play.

Voted the world's finest player in the latest FIFA poll, bought by Internazionale of Milan for a king's ransom the previous year from Barcelona—who themselves had paid a huge sum to PSV Eindhoven— Ronaldo's talents were beyond dispute. No more than a non-playing reserve in the 1994 World Cup, he has since eclipsed even Romario— ruled out, to his anger, by Zagallo on the grounds of his physical condition. Ronaldo had strength, superb ball control, exceptional pace. He could make goals out of nothing, or make them for his colleagues. But his background was one of wretched poverty. The son of a Rio drug addict, he wasn't even able to afford the bus fare to go for a trial with his favourite club, Flamengo, and found his way to lesser São Cristavão, moving thence to Cruzeiro of Belo Horizonte. He'd found it hard at first to settle down with Inter and had been publicly and insensitively criticised by the club's President, Massimo Moratti.

At the turn of the year Zagallo had had hard words for him in the first stages of that wholly superfluous, Havelange-inspired tournament, the so-called Confederations Cup in Riyadh, though later Ronaldo had struck form. The loss of Romario was a costly one for him. Bebeto, Romario's partner in the USA, couldn't give him the same support, though in the left-footed Rivaldo there was a better, more creative midfield player than any Brazil had had in 1994. The young Denilson had emerged as an attacking player with a left foot compared by Zagallo to that of the formidable Rivelino, but there were problems in central defence, while Claudio Taffarel, who at one stage had seemed likely to retire, was back, *faute de mieux*, in goal. For all that, Brazil seemed favourites to win again.

Perhaps they would have done, had Zagallo stuck to his original plan to leave out Ronaldo and deploy Edmundo, alias 'The Animal', the immensely talented but notoriously violent striker whom he'd brought back after banishment. (Edmundo had punched a Bolivian opponent in the previous year's Copa America in La Paz, but somehow Edmundo, eternally in trouble on and off the field, not least with his new club Fiorentina, was always pardoned.) Shortly before the Final began, journalists were astounded to receive team sheets with Ronaldo absent, Edmundo in his place.

The following year, an exhaustive reportage in the São Paolo magazine *Placar* at last shed at least some light on the mystery. Ronaldo, it said, at just after 2 o'clock on the afternoon of the Final had had a 'convulsion' in his room at the Château de Grande Romaine hotel, to the horror and alarm of his room mate, Roberto Carlos. The left-back rushed to summon Edmundo; he and others entered the room. Cesar Sampaio prised open the mouth of the rigid Ronaldo to make sure he didn't swallow his tongue. After about a minute and three-quarters Ronaldo came round, but then fell into a deep sleep.

Quickly the players called Dr Lidio Toledo, an orthopaedic specialist, who cleared the room and in turn summoned his colleague, the clinician Dr Joaquim da Mata. Zico, the assistant manager and ex-international star, heard what had happened. Zagallo still didn't know; Toledo didn't want to disturb him, as he was resting. Ronaldo meanwhile regained consciousness, and at 5 o'clock the doctors took him for examination to the Lilas clinic, where he was examined for over an hour and a half. Nothing was found to be wrong.

Arriving at the stadium at 8.10, Ronaldo insisted he felt fine and begged Zagallo, who'd not seen him since his 'convulsion', to let him play. The two doctors confirmed that he could. 'Imagine my situation,' Toledo would later say. 'Ronaldo says he is fine, and the doctor vetoes it. And the team loses.'

The charge against Zagallo then is not so much that he started Ronaldo, but that when it should surely have been clear that the player was in no fit state to take part he kept him on. Was Ronaldo given a 'blue pill', probably Valium, before the game? This hasn't been established, but if he was, Brazilian specialists who were later consulted said that this could have increased the possibility that he might fall ill, or even die, during the game.

There was one highly significant moment in the game when the

French keeper, Barthez, came out to gather a ball which was clearly his, assuming that the advancing Ronaldo would pull up. He didn't.

Professor Acary Souza Bulle Oliveira, a neurologist at the São Paolo School of Medicine, would later state that he was certain Ronaldo had had a convulsion—something denied by Internazionale's own doctor Piero Volpi—and that it was one of the easiest to diagnose. Another Brazilian neurologist, Professor Alex Caetano de Barros, engaged by Inter to examine Ronaldo in Rio, declared unequivocally that making Ronaldo play only seven hours after his fit was 'an absolute error, since the 24 hours after a convulsion are those when a recurrence is most likely. Ronaldo could have had another convulsion, in front of billions of spectators.'

Brazil's opponents in the Final seemed at the outset of the tournament to have little more than home advantage to recommend them. Until the finals of Euro 96 in England their team, under the aegis of Aimé Jacquet, had gone through a remarkably long run of unbeaten games. Dropping from his team two of the outstanding French attackers, Eric Cantona, because, said Jacquet, though he respected him, he didn't fit in with his tactics, and David Ginola, because he—already blamed for giving away to Bulgaria the goal that eliminated France from the 1994 World Cup—was a disruptive influence, all was optimism. But in England the French team sadly fell away, and in the interim years Jacquet had been at daggers drawn with France's principal sports paper, *L'Équipe*, on whom, immediately after winning the Final, he launched an embittered attack.

Germany, with their remarkable World Cup record, were initially viewed with a respect they hardly, in the event, deserved. It was evident that the loss through injury of their red-headed sweeper and European Footballer of the Year, Matthias Sammer, would cost them dear. Bringing back that contentious veteran Lothar Matthaus hardly seemed a good augury. Nor had Berti Vogts, though he and his team had won Euro 96, gained the love and trust of the German public. But Oliver Bierhoff, the centre-forward whorisen from the obscurity of struggling Ascoli to score twice in the Euro 96 Final and come top of the Italian Championship scorers in 1997/8 with modest Udinese, was still a force. The worrying thing was, as Vogts stressed, that so few youngsters were coming through.

Italy, having rid themselves of Arrigo Sacchi in midstream, were under the command of the 66-year-old Cesare Maldini. Father of Paolo Maldini, Italy's captain and outstanding defender, Cesare had for years been in charge of the successful under-21 side, sticking firmly to *catenaccio* (the door bolt) defending while Sacchi favoured four in line defence, even though at one point it look likely to cost him his job. Ding, dong the witch is dead seemed the refrain of Italian football when Maldini took over. *Catenacciaro* he might be but the career would at last be open again to talents, the unorthodox, the so-called *fantasisti*, such as Roberto Baggio—who had suffered under Sacchi at AC Milan as well as in the national team—and Chelsea's Gianfranco Zola.

And so it was for a time. In what was only his second match, Maldini scored a notable triumph at Wembley where a goal magisterially taken by little Zola—abetted by defensive errors—gave the Italians victory in the qualifier against Glenn Hoddle's England. But as time went by the dead hand of *catenaccio* strangled the Italian team, results degenerated, and eventually a well-organised England came to Rome, got a goalless draw and won the group.

In France, things continued to go wrong. Only a shocking refereeing decision, the concession of a late penalty in Bordeaux against a Chilean team which well deserved to win the game, saved the Italians. Despite the fine form of Roberto Baggio, Maldini perversely insisted on making Alessandro Del Piero his first choice even though the Juventus man was plainly out of form, never more obviously so than when he missed chance after chance against the Norwegians in Marseille. Zola was left out of the squad, to his bitter dismay. So vanished his chance to make up for the frustrations of 1994 when he was so unjustly treated by a poor referee.

Spain were again under the charge of little Javier Clemente, but his loyalty to past glories would cost him and them dear. There was plenty of new young talent to call on, such as the Real Madrid attacker Raoul, while Luis Enrique, long since recovered from that brutal assault in Chicago, was playing better and with more versatility than ever. But Clemente's obstinate attachment to the veteran keeper Andoni Zubizarreta would lose them the opening match against Nigeria and set Spain on a decline which could not be compensated even by the six-goal flourish of their last match in Lens against Bulgaria.

England? They and their new manager Glenn Hoddle, of blessed memory as so elegant an inside-forward, had rallied after the Italian fiasco, when he had rashly thrown in the maverick Matthew Le Tissier, Southampton's gifted striker, with no time to integrate him, and picked a vulnerable goalkeeper in Tottenham's Ian Walker. Hoddle's 3-5-2 formation with its wing-backs didn't please everybody, notably the defiant centre-half Tony Adams, rehabilitated from his drinking problem, but there was a good win in Georgia where Italy could only draw, a resilient performance in Poland where Italy were lucky not to lose, and finally that draw in Rome.

That was the game after which Mrs Eileen Drewery, the spiritual healer to whom Hoddle had turned as a teenager, announced that she had had a 'one to one with God' and had invoked Him to see that Ian Wright, late in the game, had hit the post rather than scoring, for fear of the mayhem which might have resulted. She didn't tell us whether she and the Almighty were responsible for the blatant headed miss by Christian Vieri at the other end which immediately followed.

Of Mrs Drewery's healing capacities there seemed small doubt. That she should have been foisted on the whole England party, producing inevitable divisions, seemed seriously unwise.

That other gifted maverick, Paul Gascoigne, perpetually in and out of trouble on and off the pitch, had an impressive game in Rome, which seemed to augur well for the trials to come. By the time it came to the pre-World Cup training camp, alas, Gazza was in anything but an ideal state. Yet on the Friday, a day before he was due to announce his final squad, Hoddle went on television to say that Gascoigne's physical condition was most satisfactory. Gazza, like the rest of us, could be forgiven for feeling that this meant a place in the World Cup squad.

It didn't. The following day Gazza, drunk on the golf course, was summoned to Hoddle's hotel room and told he was not among the elect. In his ill-judged and often crass autobiography, so surprisingly and contentiously ghosted by Hoddle's public relations aide David Davies, the England coach relentlessly revealed all. Gascoigne, he wrote, had smashed a lamp, kicked the furniture and looked as if he might attack him. Hardly surprising when the player had been treated like a Pavlovian dog.

Then there was Hoddle's bizarre attitude to Liverpool's 18-year-old prodigy Michael Owen, which led one to suspect that the England coach must have been feeling the hot breath of the gift horse on his face. The son of a professional footballer, Owen, though small and slight, had been a prolific goal scorer at every level since joining Liverpool as a boy. His debut at Selhurst Park against Wimbledon as a 17-year-old substitute, who promptly scored a goal will be treasured by all of us who were there. Yet Hoddle publicly announced that Owen was not a natural goal scorer, had much to learn—who hasn't, at any age?—and must improve his behaviour. Hoddle compounded such fatuities by preferring, in England's second match against Romania in Toulouse, the pedestrian Teddy Sheringham, who had in fact incurred his manager's ire with his louche behaviour in a Portuguese night club when the squad had been given a few days off.

When Owen eventually replaced Sheringham he galvanised the English attack, scored a dramatic goal and might have saved the game had not Graeme Le Saux clumsily let in his Chelsea team mate, Dan Petrescu, to score a strange winning goal. It was a defeat—prefaced in Marseille by the traditional violence of England's complement of hooligan fans—which condemned England to an eventual meeting with the powerful Argentine team, just what they had been hoping to avoid.

The Argentines, under the contentious managership of their old

World Cup captain Daniel Passarella, had eventually come through the debatably enlarged South American qualifying group after an uneasy start. Passarella had not been a popular manager, and some of his decisions, such as the exclusion of the country's most effective goal scorer, the Fiorentina striker Gabriel Batistuta, seemed hard to explain in terms of anything but personal antipathy. Once Batistuta did return, Argentina flourished. Ariel Ortega, the bright attacker who'd done so well in the 1994 World Cup yet had failed to hold a regular place in Spain all season in Valencia's attack, would support him skilfully, while another young star had emerged in the shape of the effervescent Marcelo Gallardo who, however, would be the object of Passarella's stony displeasure after a bright but inconsistent showing against Croatia.

The Croatians in the event surpassed themselves. When, just before the tournament, one of their two fine strikers, Alen Boksic, had to undergo a knee operation, thus breaking up his partnership with Davor Suker, Croatia's hopes seemed doomed. But in their distinctive red and white chequered tablecloth jerseys they would go all the way to third place. Especially satisfying for Suker, whose goals made up for the frustrating season he had passed sitting, for the most part, on Real Madrid's subs' bench.

The Africans, of whom so much was expected, would prove a disappointment; especially the Nigerians, who flattered so brightly to deceive under the managership of the ubiquitous Bora Milutinovic, sacked by Mexico after he'd got them most of the way to the Finals. Nigeria would surprise the Spaniards, outclass the Bulgarians, only and ultimately to take their foot off the accelerator with fatal results. Their victory in Paris over Bulgaria seemed almost a metaphor for sub-Saharan Africa; so much sheer talent, so little ultimately to show for it. Jay-Jay Okocha in midfield with his dyed hair, his refined technique, his passing and his penetration was a joy to watch. Yet only one goal—however beautifully worked—with the danger at the end that Emile Kostadinov (executioner of France in 1993's qualifier in this very city) might unjustly have equalised. A tiny Nigerian journalist afterwards was fuming at the lost opportunities. He proved prescient.

Scotland opened the ball in Paris against Brazil. Under the tutelage of the estimable and amiable Craig Brown, a former schoolmaster who'd been a promising Glasgow Rangers wing-half till the astonishing Jim Baxter arrived, had gallantly got them to the Finals: a triumph of persistence over lack of penetration. No one knew better than Brown that with the withdrawal of Duncan Ferguson, that lofty centre-forward, deadly in the air, but nicknamed Duncan Disorderly for his many peccadilloes, scoring power was at a premium. Even so, Coventry's Kevin Gallacher would surpass himself in this game, giving Roberto Carlos, the attacking left-back with the fulminating free kick and the defensive vulnerability, an awkward afternoon. There was lively support from Gordon Durie, whose error, alas, would eventually let Cafu in from the right to provoke the winning goal. John Collins was the hub of the midfield, a more sophisticated player since his time with Monaco.

This game was played in Group A, one of eight four-team qualifying pools from which the top two teams proceeded to the next eliminating round. Some were moved by the elaborate opening ceremony, but Scotland's defender Colin Calderwood complained afterwards of being obliged to stand around so long before the game.

The Scots had come a meritorious second in European-qualifying group 4, with home wins against Austria, the group winners, and Sweden, who came third two points behind them. They were perhaps unlucky to go behind only four minutes into the game when the midfielder Cesar Sampaio (a decade earlier an under-21 Toulon tournament player like Paul Gascoigne, David Ginola and his goalkeeping colleague, Claudio Taffarel, virtually exhumed for the tournament) scored with his shoulder at the near post from Bebeto's left-wing corner.

John Collins coolly equalised from a penalty when Sampaio, enjoying mixed fortunes, restrained Gallacher, but after 76 minutes Durie let in Cafu, and though the 39-year-old revenant goalkeeper Jim Leighton parried the shot, it bounced back past him off Tommy Boyd. Brazil had not convinced. Their attacking full-backs left gaps, and only when the young Denilson came on—football's most expensive player since his recent transfer to Real Betis—did the wheels truly turn.

There was no place in the 4-4-2 line up for the notoriously violent but highly gifted Edmundo, not yet rehabilitated by Zagallo after his Bolivian antics.

Scotland favoured a bold 4-3-3 formation, whilst England under Hoddle preferred 3-5-2 with wing-backs, though Tony Adams, arguably the key defender, would much have preferred a flat back four. Whatever England's hooligan followers were to do in the streets, England in Group G made a reasonable enough start against the Tunisians, with Manchester United's red-headed terrier Paul Scholes repeating the form he had shown in the previous year's Tournoi de France. Newcastle's Alan Shearer, who had missed much of the season with a severe injury suffered in a meaningless pre-season game at Everton, with nobody near him, powerfully headed the first goal. Scholes, though he'd seemed to be tiring, revived to score the second with a cleverly curled shot.

In Bordeaux against Chile, Italy set a pattern of unfulfilled promise. Roberto Baggio, in fluent form, set up an early goal for a new hero in Christian Vieri. A large, muscular centre-forward, dangerous both in the air and on the ground, Vieri had been a relatively late developer, growing up and learning the game in Australia where his father 'Bob' Vieri, a gifted maverick of Italian football in his own day, had gone to coach. Returning with the family to Italy, Christian knocked around a series of clubs, including Torino, before establishing himself with Atalanta, who sold him profitably to Juventus.

He flourished there, though perhaps sealed his own fate by vigorously complaining to the manager, Marcello Lippi, when left out of the team. His goals brought them success but, in their established fashion, they sold him at the end of season 1996/7 to Atletico Madrid after swearing he would stay.

There, though he took time to adjust to the new tenor of life, Vieri became top goal scorer of the Primera Liga and continued scoring when he got to France. Roberto Baggio seemed his perfect foil, but perversely Cesare Maldini favoured Alex Del Piero, and spurned the chance to line up all three together.

For the Germans, it was Jürgen Klinsmann's last hurrah. On the brink of retirement, after a short second spell with Tottenham Hotspur—whose Chairman Alan Sugar had excoriated him on his previous departure— he showed exquisite technique in the opening Group F game against the USA in Paris. The Americans probably came to France expecting too much—not least after a gallant draw in Mexico City when reduced to ten men—and were proportionately disappointed. Yet they by no means disgraced themselves, even though their coach Steve Sampson was the object of criticism by several players, not least those who were included. He would pay the price on returning to the States, but at least he didn't have to suffer the humiliation of Carlos Alberto Parreira. Winning World Cup coach in 1994, he was dismissed by the Saudi Arabians early in the 1998 tournament itself, a fate later to be suffered by Tsha Bum Kun, ex-player of renown, manager of a South Korean team which failed once again to win a World Cup Finals match after 44 years of trying.

Klinsmann headed the ball to Andy Moeller for the first German goal and sublimely scored the second, in virtually the same movement both controlling Oliver Bierhoff's right-wing cross, beating the close challenge of Thomas Dooley, then sweeping his shot past Kasey Keller, the agile Leicester City goalkeeper. It must be said, however, that the insertion of the fast, adventurous right-winger Frankie Hejduk brought the Americans strongly into the game, giving them an impressive period of sustained pressure.

Bierhoff, whose two goals had won Germany the Euro 96 Final at Wembley, and who had triumphantly led the Italian Serie A goal scorers of the season with modest Udinese, had emerged after years in the shadows; not least with Ascoli, with whom he'd even sunk into Serie B. Now, however, he looked a formidable threat with foot or, particularly, head. But Klinsmann would fade as the tournament wore on, Moeller was no longer the force of yore and the newer, younger players would disappoint.

Germany's next game was against Yugoslavia in Lens. The Yugoslavs had made surprisingly heavy weather of a 1–0 win at Saint-Etienne against an increasingly lively Iran, who missed an excellent chance to take the lead. In the end the game was decided only by a late goal from Sinesa Mihailovic (operating at centre-back rather than in midfield)—a devastating free kick with his famous left foot.

In Lens, Bierhoff had scant service. Yugoslavia were dominant for most of the game, taking the lead with a freakish goal when a low centre by Predrag Mijatovic—scorer of Real Madrid's winning goal in the recent European Cup Final—went in via the leg of the goalkeeper Kopke and the far post. A second goal arrived when Kovacevic's cross squirted beneath Kopke for the veteran Dragan Stojkovic, in lively vein, to score.

In his desperation Vogts sent on Lothar Matthaus, and gradually the Germans, famous for their deathbed recoveries, got back into the game. An own goal by Mihailovic, a header by Bierhoff, and they had breathlessly escaped.

Much was expected of Holland, despite the Dutch habit of falling at the last, or the penultimate, fence. Their manager, Guus Hiddink, had made his peace with 'Pit Bull' Edgar Davids, the midfielder who had been sent home as a dissident during Euro 96 and had inspired Juventus in the season just finished when transferred from Milan. He guaranteed bite and drive in the midfield. Patrick Kluivert, who had also left Ajax for Milan, was picked in the hope that he would put his recent troubles—notably a rape charge which was eventually set aside—behind him and find the form he'd scarcely shown all season. In the event the gamble would be justified, though in the opening game against Belgium Kluivert allowed himself to be provoked by an opponent (Staelens) calling him a rapist and was sent off. No goals were scored; Belgium hardly sought them. Playing 4-4-2 rather than the old Ajax-style three at the back, happy to have the dynamic little winger Marc Overmars fit and back again after his long absence through injury, Holland proceeded to thrash the hapless South Koreans 5–0 in Marseille. But their third game, against Mexico in Saint-Etienne, seriously impugned their defence, not least the centre-back Jaap Stam, for whom Manchester United had just paid a vertiginous £7.5 million. Stam's lack of pace on the turn led to at least three costly errors. Indeed, he came to the tournament after a thoroughly unhappy Dutch Cup Final for PSV against Ajax, who scored five goals. Against Mexico, at the last gasp, Stam let Luis Hernandez roar past him to score a dramatic equaliser. Against Yugoslavia he clumsily gave away a penalty when he couldn't catch Vladimir Jugovic, hardly the fleetest of adversaries. Against Croatia, in the third-place match in the Parc des Princes, he was outpaced up the flank by Roberto Jarni, who pulled the ball across for what turned into Croatia's opening goal. To be fair, Stam did have an honourable game against Brazil.

Dennis Bergkamp was his gifted, enigmatic self. Against Argentina he would score a goal of sensational aplomb and skill, a small miracle of virtuosity. Against Yugoslavia in the second round, late in the game, he committed a bloodcurdling foul on Mihailovic, compounding his initial offense by stamping on the Yugoslav's abdomen. The linesman was right on the spot, but no action was taken. A Dutch journalist once explained to me that Bergkamp had modelled himself on his hero, Marco van Basten, always well capable of looking after himself. The difference was that, whereas van Basten could wreak havoc by stealth, Bergkamp hadn't the same subtlety.

For the blond Hernandez, his untidy straggling locks secured by a white headband, the tournament would prove a vindication. Boca Juniors of Buenos Aires had sent him back to Mexico with his tail between his legs, but he and his team flourished in France. Indeed, had Hernandez taken his chance when Germany's keeper Andreas Kopke could only block a shot, it's doubtful that the Germans would have got even as far as they did, to succumbing to a spectacular Croatian goal by Roberto Jarni and to the deadly opportunism of Davor Suker. Hernandez's shot in Montpellier was on target, but close enough to Kopke for him to save, again.

The French were hard to figure out. Like the Danes, who were under the genial management of Swede Bo Johansson, they were continually changing their personnel, now using wingers, eventually disposing of them in favour of attacking wing-backs who, in the shape of Lilian Thuram, eventually supplied their various failing strikers. As for the multi-talented Zinedine Zidane, who would decide the Final, he, like Bergkamp, combined high technique with a combustible temper, though he would be suspended for his excesses after expulsion against Saudi Arabia, whereas Bergkamp would survive unscathed.

France, in Group C, comfortably won 3–0 in Marseille against a disappointing South Africa, playing in their first World Cup, despite the incubus of a 70 miles per hour mistral. Thierry Henry, the quick, promising Monaco right-winger, scored in that game and did still better with a brace in the next match against the Saudis but he would not, in the event, last the pace.

When France met Denmark in their third group game they dropped three players who were on a yellow card, knowing that these would be set aside after the first phase. A chance was given to 20-year-old David Trezeguet of Monaco, son of an Argentine player, who'd learned the game in his father's country, to solve the centre-forward problem, but neither he, Christian Dugarry (injured) nor the hapless Guivarc'h would provide the answer. France won 2–1 against a Danish side which did little of consequence, though it would greatly improve; especially when Michael Laudrup, absent against France, lined up beside his younger brother Brian.

England, rejuvenated by Owen's devastating pace, his superb eye for an opening, duly accounted for Colombia in Lens. A powerful shot into the near top corner by the hitherto disappointing Darren Anderton—so often out injured that his nickname at Tottenham was Sick Note—gave England the lead. On the half hour, David Beckham's typically clever right-footed free kick produced a second goal. Beckham himself had had to wait before starting in the England team. He could operate effectively on the right flank, but preferred to fill a more central, influential position, as he did on this occasion. But a tendency to childish petulance would let him and his team down badly.

As for the Scots, they should really have beaten Norway in Bordeaux. Against a team packed with English Premiership players and using only Tore Andre Flo up front, they eventually went behind to a goal scored by Riseth just after the second-half kick-off. But Craig Burley, exploiting a long high ball from Weir, the substitute centre-back, equalised. Later, Scots and Norwegian fans fraternised happily.

Alas, the Scots were doomed to repeat their World Cup disappointments, going down with a crash in Saint-Etienne to, of all teams, Morocco. Shocking errors by the usually rock-like blond centre-back Colin Hendry and the ever-unpredictable veteran keeper Jim Leighton presented the Moroccans with two of their three goals.

Brazil, who had brushed Morocco aside 3–0 in Nantes, surprisingly came to grief against the Norwegians in Marseille. Rekdal scoring the winner from a bitterly disputed penalty after 88 minutes. Cruel criticism was poured on the hapless American referee, who was eventually vindicated by an amateur video which conclusively proved Tore Andre Flo had indeed been fouled.

Bebeto—earlier in the tournament furiously rebuked by his veteran skipper Dunga—put Brazil ahead after Denilson, now starting the game in midfield, had somewhat luckily kept control to serve him. Norway had largely looked dull and defensive, but suddenly Tore Andre Flo came to life. He equalised after leaving Junior Baiano for dead and almost scored another with a powerful header; then came that penalty to prove emphatically that this Brazilian team was mortal.

The Japanese, playing in their first ever World Cup Finals, began honourably against Argentina in Group H, losing only 1–0 to a freakish goal by the prolific Gabriel Bati-Gol Batistuta, who later headed against a post. Argentina made heavy work of a Japanese team in which the lively midfielder Hidetoshi Nakata, with his luridly dyed hair, made a fine impression. He'd soon be back in Europe to play for Italy's Perugia.

The Japanese also played gallantly against Croatia, again going down by but a single goal, only to lose, bathetically, to little Jamaica. The so-called Reggae Boyz, shrewdly managed by the Brazilian Rene Simões, had surpassed themselves in the eliminators, materially helped, it is true, by a stiffening of Anglo-Jamaicans from the English game. No fewer than seven of them figured on the Jamaican roster for France. They had been cut to pieces in Paris by Argentina, when Darryl Powell got himself sent off at the end of the first half for a second caution. In Lyon, however, the Reggae Boyz substantially consoled themselves. In heavy rain, they went two ahead through enterprising dreadlocked midfielder Theodore Whitmore, a much-capped native Jamaican. Japan, poor finishers, could reply but once.

Spain, despite thrashing an inept, flaccid Bulgarian side in Lens 6–1 in what proved to be their last game at the tournament, never truly recovered from the fiasco of their defeat by Nigeria. That wily magician Bora Milutinovic, who had no easy job in reconciling the various factions in Nigeria's squad, sprang a benign surprise on them in the dressing room just before that game, showing them, on a screen the exhortations of their families. That may have helped. The ineptitude of poor Zubizarreta helped even more. Foolish in putting his trust in his aging keeper, too slow to bring in his younger talent, Javier Clemente gained nothing from the win over the Bulgarians, whose manager, the old inside-right Hristo Bonev, resigned instantly in disgust only to be reinstated for a while, months afterwards.

The Nigerians, freewheeling against Paraguay in the knowledge they'd already qualified, went down 3–1, so out went Spain. Alas, for Bora and Nigeria that freewheel turned into free fall and a resuscitated Denmark took them apart 4–1 in Paris in the second round, the Laudrups irresistible.

The Mother of all Matches, that between Iran and the USA, alias The Great Satan, played in Lyon, was in fact pleasingly free of violence on or off the field. This despite what *L'Équipe* described as 'Iranian paranoia' five days before the game when three Iranian players excoriated the showing of a film on French television which dealt with the misadventures of an Iranian doctor who returned to his country after the 'clerical' revolution. The intention, proclaimed Mohammad Khakpour, was to destabilise his team.

Paranoia indeed, for Iran looked anything but destablised in an exciting game. Despite facing an eight-man defence, the unlucky Americans twice in the first half hit the woodwork. Squealing, screaming, making most of the noise, the Iranian fans had their offensive banners taken away by security staff. Refused a clear penalty when Kasey Keller brought the lively Azizi down, the Iranians went ahead through Estili but

had the woodwork to thank again when Regis—enlisted at the last
moment on the basis of having an American wife—struck the post. A
breakaway goal by the quick, cool Mahdavikia made it 2–0; McBride's
reply three minutes later was academic.

The Americans then lost 1–0 to Yugoslavia, which to an outsider
seemed a perfectly decent performance. Delusions of grandeur seemed
to afflict them; what on earth did they expect from the tournament? Tab
Ramos, the player so badly injured by the elbow of Brazil's Leonardo—
back again as an attacking left-sided midfielder—was a pungent critic.
'From the start, this whole World Cup has been a mess,' he said. 'As long
as Steve Sampson and Clive Charles are around this team, I won't have
anything to do with it.' He did not have to wait long.

The Italians, profiting from their Chilean escape and from the
emergence of Roma's Luigi Di Biagio as the playmaker they so badly
needed, easily disposed of a Cameroon team reduced to ten men when
their big centre-back Kalla was sent off for his assault on Di Biagio, who
himself enterprisingly headed the opening goal. He always liked to be
constructive with Roma, he said. Christian Vieri added a couple more.
Then Austria, turgidly defensive yet occasionally dangerous, were beaten
2–1 at Saint-Denis, Vieri notching another goal, the Austrians scoring a
penalty via Herzog in the 90th minute immediately after Roberto Baggio,
coming on as a substitute, had scored Italy's second.

What of Brazil, the holders and the favourites? Whatever his problems
with Dunga, his lack of popularity with the fans, Bebeto had outshone
Ronaldo in the game against Norway and taken his goal well, also
surpassing Denilson. In defence, the parts seemed greater than the whole.
'At the back,' said Scotland's John Collins, 'notably in the central area,
they seem to be very nervous. If Brazil have a weak point, it's in that
area.' Zagallo himself admitted, 'The backs go up too much, in the belief
that people will fill in the gaps. But Dunga and Cesar Sampaio cannot
always do that. It's clear that Cafu and Roberto Carlos must observe a
certain discipline.' Something not always clear to Roberto Carlos.

But the way Brazil brushed Chile almost contemptuously aside in their
second round eliminator at the Parc des Princes suggested there was
abundant life in the old dog yet. Cesar Sampaio got another couple of
goals, Ronaldo scored two and hit the woodwork twice. Marcelo Salas,
though he did score Chile's solitary goal to make the score 3–1, did so
only after Ivan Zamorano's header had bounced off Claudio Tafferel. A
couple of minutes later Ronaldo, whose first goal had been a penalty,
made it 4–1. Brazil had re-established themselves as favourites.

In Marseille, Italy made heavier weather than necessary of beating a
Norwegian team which came out to play only in the last 20 minutes; and
very nearly equalised when only a magnificent save by Gianluca Pagliuca
(the keeper sent off against Norway in 1994 in Giants Stadium) kept out

Tore Andre Flo's header. Flo had been left alone up front by previously cautious Norway. Italy's winning goal came when Luigi Di Biagio cleverly launched Christian Vieri, who shrugged off Eggen and ran on to score. But Alex Del Piero missed two easy chances and the mystery was not only that Cesare Maldini kept him on the field so long, but that when he did substitute him it was not with Roberto Baggio but with Enrico Chiesa.

England's match with Argentina in Saint-Etienne was a classic of its kind, enormously dramatic, right up to its conclusion with the absurdity of penalties, itself compounded by the taking of the last, unsuccessful, English penalty by a player who had never taken one for his country before. There was, of course, a substantial and controversial history of meetings in World Cups between these countries, notably the affair of the 'animals' at Wembley in 1966 and Maradona's notorious Hand of God incident in Mexico City twenty years later.

The game had a dynamic beginning; two goals in the first 10 minutes, each of them a penalty. Argentina's was the first. When Diego Simeone broke through the English defence did David Seaman have to bring him down? Was Simeone's fall histrionic? Whatever the answers, Gabriel Batistuta scored from the spot. Only six minutes had gone, but four minutes later England were level, scoring the first goal conceded by the Argentine defence for just over eight games. Michael Owen raced through only to be brought down by Roberto Ayala. Again, was the tumble dramatic? Alan Shearer capably thumped in the penalty.

Another six minutes and Owen had put England ahead with a goal about which there was no doubt at all. His astonishing pace, his bold readiness to go it alone, took him past two desperate Argentine defenders, one of them Ayala, to beat Roa: 2–1.

Had England only been able to cling to that lead at least till half time, who knows what might have been? As it was, they conceded the equaliser just before the break. Argentina's elaborate free kick was most cleverly worked, but a more alert England defence would surely have countered it. From the bench, Daniel Passarella gave his orders, and as England laboured, a final pass from the gifted Juan Veron gave Zanetti the opening to shoot inexorably past Seaman.

All square, but two minutes into the second half England were effectively doomed. Brought down by Simeone, David Beckham, who'd been warned time and again by Hoddle about his moments of impetuous folly, suddenly kicked back at the Argentine as he himself was lying on the ground. It was not vicious, merely petulant, but it happened right under the gaze of the the referee, Denmark's Kim Nilton Nielsen. Off Beckham went, and England had their backs to the wall.

It was immensely to England's credit, due particularly to their indomitable defence, pivoting around Tony Adams and the powerful young Spurs centre-back Sol Campbell, that they held out for fully 70 minutes, extra time demandingly included. Campbell had the ball in the Argentine net but to no avail, since Shearer's elbow had connected with Roa's face. Batistuta, for once evading Adams, should have scored but untypically headed wide. Extra time brought no so-called Golden Goal, the innovation which was meant to curtail it, and so to the abomination, the prevailing irrelevance, of penalties.

Berti scored for Argentine, Shearer repeated his earlier success for England. Seaman saved Hernan Crespo's shot but then Paul Ince, the main force of the English midfield, was thwarted by Roa. Veron and Paul Merson, a substitute, scored in turn. Ayala made it 4–3, then poor David Batty had his shot saved. England were out, to contemplate what might have been in a match which would duly be mythologised. Heroic defeat. If only Hoddle had left it at that and eschewed his wretched diary.

In Toulouse, Holland began as though they would overwhelm Yugoslavia only to run into difficulties later on. Would they have won at all had it not been for Dennis Bergkamp's appalling foul on Sinisa Mihailovic, which forced that key defender with the devastating left foot off the field after 78 minutes, while Bergkamp inexplicably stayed on it? Bergkamp it was, exploiting Frank de Boer's inspired long pass, who eventually opened the scoring after the Yugoslav keeper Ivica Kralj had kept Holland at bay. But two minutes after the break Dragan Stojkovic's left-wing corner was headed in by Komijenovic: 1–1. Then Stam, out-paced by Jugovic, pulled him back by the shirt, only for Predrag Mijatovic—why not Mihailovic?—to thump his penalty against the bar. So Edgar Davids' strong, low shot in the 90th minute allowed Holland controversially to prevail.

Mexico, in Montpellier, put up a gallant show against an uneasy German team. Were it not for Hernandez's failure to score from point-blank range after Kopke had turned the excellent Arellano's shot against the post, and poor Lara's fateful 75th-minute error, the Mexicans could well have won. Lara miskicked Hamann's right-wing cross straight to Jürgen Klinsmann and in went the equaliser to Hernandez's 47th-minute goal. Oliver Bierhoff headed the winner but Klinsmann's words 'We try to instil fear' rang hollow. This was a waning German team.

France made the heaviest weather of beating a defiant, largely defensive, Paraguay in Lens, eventually squeezing through on the Golden Goal scored by their elegant experienced centre-back Laurent Blanc. Blanc scored in the 113th minute when avid Trezeguet diverted Robert Pires' cross to him. Neither of these two would last the course in a French team still looking for its identity. Paraguay's fiery idiosyncratic goal scorer José Luis Chilavert, famous for scoring from left-foot free kicks, pulled his distressed colleagues to their feet, then congratulated his excellent bald opposite number, Fabien Barthez, his chief rival as best keeper of the tournament and a major figure in the eventual French success.

In the Stade de France Nigeria simply and strangely collapsed against a Danish team inspired by the brothers Laudrup. Having strolled insouciantly through the previous irrelevant defeat by Paraguay, Nigeria seemed incapable of recovering their commitment and form. Overwhelmed in midfield by a Danish side which deployed only the newcomer Peter Moller up front, Nigeria crashed out 4–1.

Croatia, for their part, eliminated a mysteriously passive Romanian team. Sporting the ghastly bleached hair they'd assumed for their draw against Tunisia—the consequence of a wager with their coach Anghel Iordanescu—the Romanians never took wing in Bordeaux. On this hot afternoon, the symbolic moment perhaps arrived when Romania's talismanic skipper, Gheorghe Hagi, so effective against England, was substituted in his 114th and seemingly last international early in the second half.

The decisive goal had already been scored from the spot. Bogdan Selea, whose defiant goalkeeping had kept Romania in the game, could not keep out Davor Suker's penalty, right on the interval, after the highly effective midfielder Aljosa Asanovic had come down in a heap with Gabriel Popescu. Suker had to take the penalty twice. Romania felt the decision unjust, but correct or not the result was emphatically right. Only Stelea's fine goalkeeping had kept the score down. So wily old Miroslav Blazevic, who had once been manager of French captain Didier Deschamps at Nantes and had a few years back spent time in a French prison accused of corruption (he was absolved), had taken Croatia without Boksic to the quarter finals.

There, in Lyon, they took Germany apart; substantial revenge for the defeat by Germany in a bruising Euro 96 match. Berti Vogts, Germany's never popular manager, took the thumping 3–0 defeat very hard. 'There were some strange decisions made against us in the World Cup,' he complained. 'Maybe there was some secret instruction. Perhaps German soccer had become too successful and had to be punished.' Evidently, the Iranians did not have a monopoly on paranoia. Vogts in due course was obliged to eat his words.

A couple of minutes before the young German defender Christian Worns was sent off for body-checking Suker in the first half, Oliver Bierhoff should most certainly have gone for elbowing Soldo in the face. Rough justice, you might say.

It was Roberto Jarni, Croatia's protean attacking left-back, who gave them the lead with a spectacular goal, exploiting the greater freedom given him when Heinrich was moved inside to mark Davor Suker. Taking a pass across field from Mario Stanic, Jarni raced on to beat Kopke with a left-footed drive. It was just before half-time, which seemed a propitious moment for a Croatia who had gained new brio and thrust with the return from injury of Zvoni Boban.

Desperately, Berti Vogts put on Marschall and Ulf Kirsten to supplement an ineffectual Klinsmann, but it was Croatia who scored twice more, first through the lively Goran Vlaovic, survivor of a fearful cranial operation, then from Suker. This was a notable solo effort, Suker picking up a ball on the by-line, dodging the defence then shooting home.

A happy Blazevic explained his victory in terms of military history. In the Second World War Rommel, the Desert Fox, seemed unbeatable, but the Allies defeated him. 'Why? Because Rommel had no more petrol to put in his tanks. So me, I wanted to neutralise the German petrol! The German centres, if you prefer. If you don't get the ball, you can jump higher than anyone in the world, like Bierhoff, but you won't achieve anything.'

Italy, for the third consecutive World Cup, as Cesare Maldini wryly reflected, went out on penalties, this time to France at Saint-Denis. Given their persistent lack of ambition it was hard to sympathise with them, though easy to feel sorry for Luigi Di Biagio when his penalty hit the bar. Until this game, when he was somewhat effaced, he'd been Italy's most effective and constructive midfield player.

France set the pattern as early as the fifth minute when the big, blond, pony-tailed Emmanuel Petit, a much improved player since his transfer to Arsenal the previous summer, brought a dramatic one-handed save from the excellent Gianluca Pagliuca, then banged in a typical left-foot shot when the ball came out to him from a corner. With Del Piero once more mysteriously preferred to Roberto Baggio and once more so disappointing, France emphatically called the tune in the first half, though their finishing remained inadequate: just before the interval, a clever exchange with Deschamps put Youri Djorkaeff clean through only for him to pull his shot ineptly wide. Overall, there was a dull sterility about an Italian team that used Gianluca Pesotto to follow Zinedine Zidane around, though without ever subduing him.

In extra time, the Italians did once come close to a goal. Demetrio Albertini, at last producing the kind of pass for which he was once well known, sent through Roberto Baggio, who'd come on after 67 minutes. His cross shot flew just wide. So to penalties, and Italy's defeat. Afterwards, Cesare Maldini insisted that no errors had been made and bridled when an Italian journalist declared that France had had 70 per cent of the play. 'I'm happy with my team,' he said. 'They gave everything, to the last drop of sweat.' Soon afterwards be received the ritual ominous vote of confidence from Luciano Nizzola, the President of the Italian Federation. It was no surprise when not long afterwards it was announced that he would be replaced. The

World Cup winning goalkeeper of 1982, Dino Zoff, would leave Lazio to succeed him.

Brazil were given a very hard run for their money in Nantes by Denmark and again their defence looked vulnerable. Roberto Carlos may have been dangerous surging forward from left-back, but he was too easily drawn out of position and it was his clumsy attempt at an overhead kick which presented Denmark with their second goal. Their first arrived after a mere couple of minutes. Moller's free kick found Brian Laudrup with room and time to go to the goal line and pull the ball back for Martin Jorgensen to score.

Bebeto, with a flash of his old form, equalised nine minutes later, racing past Helveg to beat Peter Schmeichel. Poor Helveg was a culprit in the second Brazilian goal, too, losing the ball to Roberto Carlos. On it went to Ronaldo, then Rivaldo, who put Brazil ahead. Roberto Carlos's blunder allowed the vibrant Brian Laudrup to equalise on 50 minutes but 10 minutes later Denmark's dreams were shattered. They'd thrown caution to the winds when Dunga launched an unopposed Rivaldo, who shot home from 25 yards. Even then Denmark rallied, for after 89 minutes Rieper, a centre-back deployed now at centre-forward, headed against the bar.

It was Michael Laudrup's last international and he threw his boots into the crowd. Within days, alas poor Denmark, his younger brother Brian had retired in his turn.

Was Brazil's manager still 'Lucky Zagallo' (insisting now that his name be spelt with a double I)? It seemed questionable. Signs of pressure were evident and he'd not taken at all kindly to being flanked by another former Brazilian star in Zico, who had no coaching experience. An unkind French critic wrote: 'Sometimes when he speaks, with all the banalities and clichés, you have the impression his 50 years on the field have eroded his mental faculties.' But Brazil still clung to their Cup.

In hot Marseille there was a re-run of the 1978 Final, Holland against Argentina and this time in an exciting game the Dutch prevailed, just. The goal that won the match after 89 minutes, however, was worthy of winning any World Cup Final. It was scored by Dennis Bergkamp with superb virtuosity, almost casually controlling a searching, long diagonal ball from Frank De Boer, then, with the sole of his foot, taking it inside Ayala—once more the fall guy—before, with the same right foot, shooting past Roa.

It was barely a couple of minutes earlier that Ariel Ortega, ending his otherwise distinguished World Cup in shame, had been sent off. Had he not reacted so aggressively when booked for alleged diving in the area after a clash with Stam, Argentina would have kept their one-man advantage (Numan had been sent off after 73 minutes for his second yellow card; the tackle—how history repeats itself—was on Diego

Simeone). But Ortega, in his fury, butted the intervening Dutch keeper Van der Sar and off he went.

Patrick Kluivert, now under full sail, had put Holland ahead after just a dozen minutes when Ronald De Boer crossed from the left to the far post and Bergkamp expertly headed into Kluivert's path. Claudio Lopez, having his best game up front for Argentina, equalised five minutes later after Juan Veron had split the Dutch defence. Overall, Holland were the better team against an Argentina probably tired from the exertions against England. Next day, Daniel Passarella resigned as their coach.

So to the semi-finals and another reprise. Brazil against Holland, just as in 1994, though this time penalties would decide in the holders' favour. And the unexpected hero, pushing away the crucial spot kick by Philip Cocu, would be Claudio Taffarel, Brazilian goalkeeper *faute de mieux*.

Did Holland rely too heavily on Dennis Bergkamp? Against Brazil, he had an undistinguished day and the team suffered accordingly. A little ironic, given that manager Guus Hiddink had said beforehand that one of his side's strengths was that it didn't, like the 1974 team, rely too heavily on a single player such as Johan Cruyff, who for Hiddink had been below his best in that Final.

Significant, too, was the absence of that electric little winger Marc Overmars, not fully fit when put on as substitute against Argentina and now definitely out. He would surely have tormented the uneasy Brazilian reserve right-back, Ze Carlos.

Twice in the first half Kluivert sent headers just wide, emphasising the vulnerability of Brazil's defence in the air for which they'd pay so heavily in the Final. So it was Brazil who went ahead just after half time, Rivaldo producing a typical defence-dissecting through pass, Ronaldo dashing in from the right to score, after which he was rampant.

Four minutes from time, however, Cocu found Ronald De Boer, whose swift centre eluded both Brazilian centre-backs Aldair and Junior Baiano, enabling Kluivert to head home at last.   •

With Denilson, on after 70 minutes for Bebeto, improving the Brazilian attack, Brazil now called the tune. The resilient Frank De Boer kicked Ronaldo's shot off the line, stopped the centre-forward with a majestic tackle and blocked a dangerous shot by Rivaldo. So to penalties. Cocu missed, Dunga scored to make it 4–2 for Brazil, then Taffarel saved again, from Ronald de Boer. Holland were out with honour.

At Saint-Denis, Aimé Jacquet successfully shuffled the pack against Croatia, went without wingers, used attacking wing-backs, was rewarded by two fine goals from Lilian Thuram and saw France prevail despite the contentious expulsion of Laurent Blanc five minutes after Thuram had scored his second goal.

Earlier in the tournament Thuram's great friend and team mate at

Parma, Fabio Cannavaro, had said that Thuram lost 50 per cent of his efficiency when deployed at right-back rather than at centre-back. Tell that to the Croatians! With a 4-3-2-1 formation, Stéphane Guivarc'h being the one, against Croatia's 3-5-2, France rode the shock of Croatia's opening goal and reached the Final for the first time ever.

You might say that the course of the game was decided in one dramatic minute. After 46 minutes, Asanovic sent Davor Suker through to score for Croatia. A minute later or less, Zvoni Boban, previously a Croatian hero, lost the ball to Thuram, who thundered on, exchanged passes with Djorkaeff and equalised.

After 69 minutes Thuram, remarkably, did it again, taking the ball from Jarni and advancing to shoot past Ladic, this time with his left foot. Then came the expulsion of Blanc. Should it have happened? Was Slaven Bilic guilty of histrionics? He denied it fiercely after the game. 'He caught me here,' he said, pointing somewhere between throat and chest. 'I didn't want him to be sent off. I didn't want him to miss the Final, but that's his problem.' In retrospect, it may be said that Blanc, initially provoked, was foolish to raise his hand and that Bilic probably made a meal of it. One remembered that in Euro 96 Bilic had kicked Germany's Christian Ziege on the head as he lay on the ground and got clean away with it. In the end, though, France had won and Paris went wild.

The game had really turned on France's immediate equaliser and Croatia's evident moment of distraction. 'We gave our maximum,' said Davor Suker afterwards, 'but when we scored, we thought we were already in the Final.'

They were not, though they duly won the meaningless third-place match against Holland at the Parc des Princes. Then the stage was set at Saint-Denis for France, the home team, against Brazil, holders and favourites. And for the astonishing events which have still to be fully explained; Ronaldo's pre-match 'fit', the team sheet which excluded him and named Edmundo; the rumours, never substantiated, that there had been a fight in the dressing-room; the eventual, demoralised performance by a Brazilian team clearly distracted; the presence, till the end, of a Ronaldo so clearly a shadow of the player we knew him to be. It was cruelty to keep him on, and immensely destructive. Rumours flew that Nike, Brazil's demanding sponsors, had demanded that Ronaldo played. They were denied, not least by an angry Zagallo.

Before the Final, the former Dutch hero Johan Cruyff had declared, 'I said at the start of the tournament that I did not like this Brazilian team, and I still say that. It would be really bad for football if Brazil won with such poor play, because this team is imitated throughout the world.' France, he hoped, would win the Final. 'I am not going to say that they will, because Brazil are a strong team, but I hope so for the sake of football, because the play produced by Zagallo's team is really poor.'

On this important occasion it unquestionably was, though Cruyff's strictures seem in retrospect peculiarly harsh. In the event, it was not only the passivity of Ronaldo, who had but one valid attempt on goal, but the failings of the Brazilian defence which condemned Zagallo's team to defeat and extinguished for ever the myth of his good fortune. Zinedine Zidane took his two headed goals, one at each near post, wonderfully well; but how was he ever allowed to do so the first time, let alone the second, when Brazil's defence had surely received due warning?

After 27 minutes Emmanuel Petit, a powerful influence throughout, whizzed in one of his insidious inswinging corners from the right, and Zidane popped up on the post to head it in.

His second goal followed an abysmal miss by Stéphane Guivarc'h, allowed through by Junior Baiano's fearful misjudgement. The best you could say for Baiano was that he might have been fooled by the strong wind. Guivarc'h, however, came too close to Taffarel, who responded with a gallant one-handed save.

But almost at once, just before half time, Zidane repeated his initial coup with a header from Youri Djorkaeff's corner from the left. Playing with poise, confidence and fluency the French brushed off early Brazilian supremacy to take over the game. Once, in the 57th minute, Ronaldo almost casually made himself space for a shot which Fabien Barthez held at the near post, but that was largely the extent of the Brazilian threat.

With a quarter of an hour left Zagallo gambled desperately, throwing on Edmundo for Sampaio, but the French, though their usually impeccable centre-back Marcel Desailly had been sent off for a second yellow card after 69 minutes, stood firm. Indeed, revelling in the extra space afforded them, they fluffed another easy chance through the substitute striker Christophe Dugarry. A third goal did arrive, however, when Arsenal's Patrick Vieira, a lively substitute, sent his club colleague Petit through for an inexorable left-footed goal: 3–0. Joy for France after 68 years of World Cup striving; humiliation for Brazil. A shot against the bar by Denilson was their sole, meagre consolation. 'Will I stay on as coach?' asked Zagallo. It was a rhetorical question with only one possible answer. Within a few weeks, he was gone.

And in Paris, the streets had thronged with hundreds of thousands of joyous celebrants. Who could grudge them their delight?

RESULTS: France 1998

First Round

Group A

Saint-Denis, Montpellier, Bordeaux, Nantes,
Marseille, Saint Etienne
Brazil 2, Scotland 1
Morocco 2, Norway 2
Scotland 1, Norway 1
Brazil 3, Morocco 0
Brazil 1, Norway 2
Scotland 0, Morocco 3

	P	W	D	L	F	A	Pts
Brazil	3	2	0	1	6	3	6
Norway	3	1	2	0	5	4	5
Morocco	3	1	1	1	5	5	4
Scotland	3	0	1	2	2	6	1

Group B

Bordeaux, Toulouse, Saint-Etienne, Montpellier,
Nantes, Saint-Denis
Italy 2, Chile 2
Cameroon 1, Austria 1
Chile 1, Austria 1
Italy 3, Cameroon 0
Chile 1, Cameroon 1
Italy 2, Austria 1

	P	W	D	L	F	A	Pts
Italy	3	2	1	0	7	3	7
Chile	3	0	3	0	4	4	3
Austria	3	0	2	1	3	4	2
Cameroon	3	0	2	1	2	5	2

Group C

Lens, Marseille, Toulouse, Saint-Denis, Lyon,
Bordeaux
Saudi Arabia 0, Denmark 1
France 3, South Africa 0
South Africa 1, Denmark 1
France 4, Saudi Arabia 0
France 2, Denmark 1
South Africa 2, Saudi Arabia 2

	P	W	D	L	F	A	Pts
France	3	3	0	0	9	1	9
Denmark	3	1	1	1	3	3	4
South Africa	3	0	2	1	3	6	2
Saudi Arabia	3	0	1	2	2	7	1

Group D

Montpellier, Nantes, Paris, Saint-Etienne,
Toulouse, Lens
Paraguay 0, Bulgaria 0
Spain 2, Nigeria 3
Nigeria 1, Bulgaria 0
Spain 0, Paraguay 0
Nigeria 1, Paraguay 3
Spain 6, Bulgaria 1

	P	W	D	L	F	A	Pts
Nigeria	3	2	0	1	5	5	6
Paraguay	3	1	2	0	3	1	5
Spain	3	1	1	1	8	4	4
Bulgaria	3	0	1	2	1	7	1

Group E

Lyon, Saint-Denis, Bordeaux, Marseille, Paris,
Saint-Etienne
South Korea 1, Mexico 3
Holland 0, Belgium 0
Belgium 2, Mexico 2
Holland 5, South Korea 0
Belgium 1, South Korea 1
Holland 2, Mexico 2

	P	W	D	L	F	A	Pts
Holland	3	1	2	0	7	2	5
Mexico	3	1	2	0	7	5	5
Belgium	3	0	3	0	3	3	3
South Korea	3	0	1	2	2	9	1

Group F

Saint-Etienne, Paris, Lens, Lyon, Montpellier,
Nantes
Yugoslavia 1, Iran 0
Germany 2, USA 0
Germany 2, Yugoslavia 2
USA 1, Iran 2
Germany 2, Iran 0
USA 0, Yugoslavia 1

	P	W	D	L	F	A	Pts
Germany	3	2	1	0	6	2	7
Yugoslavia	3	2	1	0	4	2	7
Iran	3	1	0	2	2	4	3
USA	3	0	0	3	1	5	0

Group G

Marseille, Lyon, Montpellier, Toulouse, Lens, Saint-Denis
England 2, Tunisia 0
Romania 1, Colombia 0
Colombia 1, Tunisia 0
Romania 2, England 1
Colombia 0, England 2
Romania 1, Tunisia 1

	P	W	D	L	F	A	Pts
Romania	3	2	1	0	**4**	**2**	7
England	3	2	0	1	**5**	**2**	6
Colombia	3	1	0	2	**1**	**3**	3
Tunisia	3	0	1	2	**1**	**4**	1

Group H

Toulouse, Lens, Nantes, Paris, Bordeaux, Lyon
Argentina 1, Japan 0
Jamaica 1, Croatia 3
Japan 0, Croatia 1
Argentina 5, Jamaica 0
Argentina 1, Croatia 0
Japan 1, Jamaica 2

	P	W	D	L	F	A	Pts
Argentina	3	3	0	0	**7**	**0**	9
Croatia	3	2	0	1	**4**	**2**	6
Jamaica	3	1	0	2	**3**	**9**	3
Japan	3	0	0	3	**1**	**4**	0

Second Round

Marseille
Italy 1, Norway 0

Paris
Brazil 4, Chile 1

Lens
France 1, Paraguay 0

Saint-Denis
Nigeria 1, Denmark 4

Montpellier
Germany 2, Mexico 1

Toulouse
Holland 2, Yugoslavia 1

Bordeaux
Romania 0, Croatia 1

Saint-Etienne
Argentina 2, England 2
Argentina win 4–3 on penalties

Quarter-finals

Saint-Denis
Italy 0, France 0
France win 4–3 on penalties

Nantes
Brazil 3, Denmark 2

Marseille
Holland 2, Argentina 1

Lyon
Germany 0, Croatia 3

Semi-finals

Marseille
Brazil 1, Holland 1
Brazil win 4–2 on penalties

Saint-Denis
France 2, Croatia 1

Third-place match

Paris

Holland 1	**Croatia 2**
Van der Sar; Stam,	Ladic, Bilic,
Numan, F. de Boer,	Soldo, Stimac,
Davids; Jonk,	Stanic; Boban
Cocu (Overmars),	(Vlaovic), Jarni,
Seedorf; Kluivert,	Prosinecki (Tudor),
Bergkamp	Asanovic; Jurcic,
(van Hooijdonk)	Suker.
Zenden.	

SCORERS
Zenden for Holland
Prosinecki, Suker for Croatia
HT (1–2)

Final

Saint-Denis

France 3	**Brazil 0**
Barthez; Thuram,	Taffarel; Cafu, Junior
Leboeuf, Desailly,	Baiano, Aldair,
Lizerazu; Karembeu	Roberto Carlos;
(Boghossian),	Dunga, Leonardo
Deschamps,	(Denilson), Cesar
Petit, Zidane;	Sampaio (Edmundo),
Djorkaeff (Vieira),	Rivaldo; Bebeto,
Guivarc'h (Dugarry).	Ronaldo.

SCORERS
Zidane 2, Petit for France
HT (2–0)

JAPAN
2002

A World Cup redeemed by Ronaldo, you might say, just as the previous World Cup Final was blemished by his all too evident plight. Had Brazil not beaten Germany in the Final in Yokohama, the sheer mediocrity of the tournament would have been plain. Dramatic rather than distinguished, surprising rather than scintillating, its very Final was contested by two teams that at one point seemed unlikely even to qualify for the final stages. The Germans had been traumatisingly beaten 5–1 in Munich by England and eventually had to play off against Ukraine. Brazil, using no fewer than three different managers, losing to the likes of humble Ecuador, had looked in real danger of finishing no better than fifth in the elongated South American qualifying tournament, and thus be condemned to play off against Australia. In the event, they came fourth.

There is no doubt that Ronaldo made the difference, after nearly four traumatic years in which time and again, trying to play in Italy for Inter, he broke down with injury. Even in Japan he did not play a full game until Brazil's third, a topsy-turvy one in Suwon against Costa Rica. His explosive pace might have been somewhat diminished, but his tremendous skills, his finishing powers, were emphatically not. Although, in the Final, he missed a sitter, he went on in the event to score twice.

Fears over apportioning the Finals between Japan and South Korea proved baseless. If the eternal problem of ticket distribution reared its ugly head again, this was hardly the fault of the hosts, but manifestly that of Byrom, the England-based company run by two Mexicans, who had, somewhat controversially, been given the franchise by the FIFA committee headed by Scotsman David Will.

Controversial to a degree was the re-election in Seoul two days before the start of the tournament of the Swiss FIFA President, Sepp Blatter against an obscure African candidate, Issa Hayatou of Cameroon. Unsurprisingly he won by a landslide: 139 to 56. It was astonishing that UEFA, which provides 80 per cent of FIFA's funds, couldn't field a candidate of their own. Under withering allegations of corruption, incompetence (over the collapse of the ISL company which cost FIFA countless millions), favouritism (to such as the autocratic Jack Warner of CONCACAF), and profligacy (for the expensive programmes such as GOAL, which seem little more than sweeteners to the smaller countries), Blatter nevertheless achieved the backing of several major European nations, and of influential figures such as Germany's Franz Beckenbauer.

Scarcely had the smoke of the election cleared than Blatter had sacked the courageous FIFA Secretary, Michel Zen Ruffinen, who had questioned his competence. When the tournament was over, out too went the efficient Director of Communications, Keith Cooper, seemingly on the grounds of 'he who is not with us is against us'. Cooper had not been known as one of Blatter's critics, but in a chaotic organisation in which every member, big or small, had just one vote, the scope for suborning was always to be infinite. The ineffable João Havelange, Blatter's predecessor, had after all stayed impregnably in office for twenty-four disastrous years.

The favourites to win the tournament were indisputably France, the holders, and Argentina; and both bit the dust in the first group stage. Two years earlier the French, with Roger Lemerre succeeding Aimé Jacquet as manager, had added the European title to the World Cup, squeezing past Italy in the Rotterdam Final. By then, they had found the centre forward, indeed the two strikers, they'd plainly needed in 1998, in Thierry Henry and David Trezeguet, both of whom had figured in the 98 Finals but with limited impact. Zinedine Zidane, header of two goals in the 98 Final, had become the most expensive player in the history of the game when he moved from Juventus to Real Madrid and was widely seen as the most influential.

True, France had faltered somewhat in the weeks before the tournament, with two disappointing displays in Paris, a 0–0 draw against Russia and a 2–1 defeat by Belgium, though in neither case were they at full strength. Argentina had romped home top of the South American qualifiers, though they'd lost in Brazil. They seemed to have talent in abundance: Juan Sebastian Veron to pull the strings in midfield, even if he'd had a largely frustrating first season with Manchester United; Hernan Crespo to get goals, even if it were at the expense of the previously prolific Gabriel Batistuta, who'd had an uneasy season with Roma; gifted emerging youngsters such as the creative little midfielder, Pablo Aimar; tough defenders such as Roberto Ayala. In prospect was one more in the series of World Cup matches against England, due to take place in the spectacular domed arena of Sapporo, built with the technological help of NASA, its pitch wheeled slowly in and out of the stadium.

With memories of Alf Ramsey's 'act as animals' words after the 1966 quarter final at Wembley, of Diego Maradona's Hand of God goal at the Azteca twenty years later, of David Beckham's petulance that led to his expulsion at Saint Etienne in 1998 and the gallant English resistance into extra time, this was a match loaded with significance.

Beckham, alas, long since rehabilitated, even glorified, would have to make extraordinary efforts to play at all. A brutal double-footed tackle by an Argentine (oh, would it not be!) in a European Cup match against Deportivo La Coruna at Old Trafford had broken a metatarsal bone in his left foot, leaving pitifully little time for it to heal. In the previous game against Deportivo, Beckham had been the victim of an almost equally shocking foul by Diego Tristan, the Spanish international striker. That it was so inadequately punished by the referee may well have led to Aldo Pedro Duscher's appalling challenge.

Beckham's metamorphosis from pariah to hero had been remarkable. After the 98 World Cup, he was sometimes viciously abused by young

thugs at matches. By the time it came to the 2002 Finals, he was a role
model, a cynosure even of the Japanese. He and his wife Victoria, 'Relatively' Posh Spice, an utterly ordinary singer in the factitious Spice Girls,
led lives of monumental vulgarity, whether it be their wedding in Ireland,
during which they sat on thrones, or the flamboyant 'charity' party they
put on soon after the 2002 tournament. It was common, almost customary, to sneer at Beckham for his alleged stupidity, but this merely cheap-
ened those who did so. What Beckham clearly possessed was what he
needed: football intelligence. Paul Gascoigne, far and away the most
gifted and creative English footballer of his generation, could behave like
an idiot when off the field. One doubted whether Beckham's critics could
score from the halfway line with that extraordinary right foot, deliver
crosses of absolute precision on to the heads of his colleagues, or conjure
goals from insidious free kicks as he did.

Not least when, in the final seconds, his free-kick goal gave England
the luckiest of home draws against Greece in their last qualifying match,
thus escaping the necessity of a play-off. And this from a free kick which
should never have been awarded, the veteran striker Teddy Sheringham
having cunningly obtained it.

England's manager by then was the enigmatic Swede, Sven-Göran
Eriksson, enlisted on a salary of £2 million a year after the failures of
Kevin Keegan and Howard Wilkinson. The emotional Keegan had
instantly resigned after his absurd tactics and a goalkeeping error by
David Seaman at Wembley—far too slow to react to Dietmar Hamann's
free kick—had condemned England to a 1–0 defeat by Germany.
Keegan's fatuous decision to use the one-paced defender Gareth
Southgate in central midfield had been a disaster. Wilkinson's choices
were no better when he took England to Helsinki and a laborious 0–0
draw with Finland, though England should have been awarded a goal
when Ray Parlour's drive clipped the underside of the bar and bounced
over the line. Wilkinson added insult to injury by proclaiming that
England had no chance of qualifying and should think instead about
the 2006 tournament.

Eriksson had coached successfully in Italy—Roma, Fiorentina,
Lazio—and in Portugal at Benfica. A calm, quiet man, much respected
by his players, he made a spectacular beginning when he took England
to Munich and their 5–1 win over a German team which became
increasingly demoralised, unable to deal with the electric pace of
Michael Owen. This suddenly resurrected England's hopes of qualification, and confirmed the exuberant promise Owen had shown in
1998. In the interim, he had suffered greatly from hamstring problems,
which at times had seemed intractable, and had forced him to go to an
unorthodox German specialist in search of a cure. Whatever the merits
of Beckham—who might be said to have made the very best of

essentially limited talents, a lack of pace, elusive skills and heading prowess—Owen seemed the outstanding member of the team. This, though Beckham, with his constantly changing hairstyle, was the salient public figure.

In the run-up to the Finals, however, the England team fell disconcertingly away, an uninspired 2–0 win against Albania, being followed by a home draw with Greece—who themselves came close to winning. Eriksson himself meanwhile became surprisingly embroiled in a relationship with a Swedish television presenter, Ulrika Jonsson, a woman scarcely known for her reticence, who during the 98 Finals had been brutally knocked down and kicked in a Paris bar by her boyfriend, former England centre-forward Stan Collymore. As the 2002 Finals approached, it seemed that Eriksson's luck had run out.

Not only was Beckham seriously injured, but one of his best young midfielders, Steven Gerrard of Liverpool, a powerful player, adept in launching his team-mate Owen with long passes, was forced to drop out with an injury. All of which made it the more surprising that Eriksson obstinately turned his back on a former Liverpool man, Steve McManaman, even though he had played exceptionally well for Real Madrid in the semi-final and Final of the European Cup. Though never at his best when played on the left flank, McManaman, on the right, where he might have relieved Beckham during games, still looked an impressive player and his experience was large. Yet Eriksson chose to take to the Far East the Newcastle United midfielder Kieron Dyer, though his own injuries had put him out of the game for months.

In the event, Dyer would make only substitute appearances in the Finals, and one, controversially, was as a substitute on the left flank of midfield in what proved to be England's last game, against Brazil.

Brazil, so often champions, arrived under the controversial aegis of Luiz Filipe 'Big Phil' Scolari, brought in after the failures of Wanderley Luxemburgo—accused after his dismissal of various finagles and tax offences—and the former World Cup goalkeeper, Leao. Scolari's credentials were somewhat dubious. As manager of Gremio, he had openly encouraged his players to commit fouls so long as they were outside the penalty area. The Brazilian concept of The Beautiful Game was deeply alien to him, and he had no time for the talismanic veteran striker Romario, who had been Brazil's saviour in the past and was still scoring goals for Flamengo. But having qualified, Brazil's World Cup group didn't look too taxing. It included Costa Rica, Turkey and China, who had qualified under the managership of Bora Milutinovic, the latest of no fewer than five countries he had coached in the World Cup finals, though hardly the strongest.

Italy's chances seemed good though, not untypically, their pre-World Cup friendlies had seen them *in diminuendo*. This, said their critics, was of no import; it merely followed the perennial pattern. Inspired by the thrust and invention of Francesco Totti, playing just behind the front line, still strong in the powerful presence up front of Bobo Vieri, the Italians had come so close to winning Euro 2000.

They were now under the new management of the veteran Giovanni Trapattoni, winner of championships with Juventus and Inter and successor to Dino Zoff, who'd resigned soon after Euro 2000, incensed by the coarse criticism of the Milan owner and by 2002 President of the Council, Silvio Berlusconi. 'Trap', brought up as player and coach on the negativity and caution of the Italian *catenaccio* ('door-bolt') system, had never been the most adventurous of coaches, but he seemed ready to be tactically more flexible.

It was said during and after the finals, not least by Franz Beckenbauer, a World Cup winner as both player and manager, that the European teams were tired, that they had played too much football, much of it in the European Champions Cup. Indeed, soon after the Finals, UEFA decided to abolish the second league stage of the European tournament, no doubt to the relief of the players but not to the directors of several major European clubs which would lose a great deal of money as a result.

No doubt many of the leading Europeans were indeed tired but then, when in past World Cups have they not been? When Enzo Bearzot was in charge of Italy, he would concentrate on what he called the 'disintoxication' of his team, purging them, that is to say, of what he regarded as the poisons of the Italian Championship, with its pressures on his players.

The Republic of Ireland would excel themselves again, both in their path to the finals—for once successfully negotiating a play-off—and in the Finals, too. Had it not been for the banishment of their finest player, Roy Keane, on the eve of the tournament, they might have done better still.

That they were forced to play off at all was something of a scandal. They had performed gallantly in their group, twice holding Portugal to a draw, drawing in Holland, then beating the Dutch 1–0 in Dublin, despite being reduced to ten men, when the right back Gary Kelly was sent off. Thus they finished second to Portugal, and that should have been that, but FIFA's craven capitulation to threats from the Asian Confederation, who'd demanded an extra place, meant that the Irish, of all teams, were the victims of the compromise, condemned to a decider against Iran.

The victory over the Dutch, who admittedly missed a host of chances, was extraordinary, procured when the substitute Steve Finnan crossed from the left and the outstanding Jason McAteer scored. Holland's experienced manager, Louis Van Gaal, profligately threw on striker after striker but succeeded only in upsetting the balance of his team.

With McAteer again exuberant, Ireland then in Dublin beat an Iran team managed by that old fox of a coach, Miroslav Blazevic, and, without the injured Roy Keane, qualified after going down narrowly in Teheran. But when the team arrived for World Cup preparations on the Japanese island of Saipan, more noted for its red-light district than for its football facilities, the balloon alas went up.

Keane doubtless had a point when he angrily complained about a farcical training ground and what he deemed a too casual approach. Always a loose cannon, subject to violent moments on the field, long at loggerheads with the team's manager, Mick McCarthy, it was surely inevitable that when McCarthy summoned Keane to a reckoning before other members of the team, there'd be an explosion. So there was; Keane abused his manager furiously for a full eight minutes, making it inevitable he be sent home. Whether McCarthy had been wise to upbraid him in public, with its predictable consequences, is a moot point.

Even the Irish Taioseach, Bertie Aherne, and the efforts of the Irish FA failed to extract an apology from Keane, and Ireland had to do without him.

The opening match, on the last day of May in Seoul's imposing new stadium—the city's Olympic stadium would not be used—saw France, the holders, meet a Senegalese team every member of which was playing top-flight football in France and which, under the passionate manager-ship of the long-haired Frenchman, Bruno Metsu, had swept into the Final of the recent African Nations Cup in Mali, losing to Cameroon only on penalties.

There was an alarm for Senegal before the game when one of their key midfield players, the powerfully left-footed Khalilou Fadiga, was accused of stealing a gold necklace from a jewellery shop. In the event, the jeweller, getting the necklace back, decided not to bring charges and the authorities decided not to prosecute, on the charitable grounds that this might disturb Fadiga's concentration! The case had still not been cleared up when Senegal met France but Fadiga seemed anything but disturbed, emerging as a tireless midfielder, now winning tackles, now reinforcing the speedily elusive El Hadji Diouf, the solitary striker, up front.

Before the game, the 33-year-old France centre-back, Marcel Desailly, had reacted irritably when reminded that he and the whole of his back line were veterans now. But it would become all too clear, above all in the case of the now laborious central defender Frank Leboeuf, a strange choice by Roger Lemerre, given his indifferent international form and his far from convincing performances even in the French League for Marseille. Three times in the game, Diouf would surge past him with almost insulting ease, and on one of those occasions Senegal would score the game's only goal.

That came somewhat luckily on 29 minutes against a French team palpably missing two of its best players. Robert Pires, an all-round attacking midfielder, had broken down towards the end of a splendid season with Arsenal. Zinedine Zidane, perhaps the best player in the world, had been injured, would miss the next game, too, and would do little more than hobble through the traumatising third.

When Diouf, out on the left, easily negotiated Leboeuf, he pulled back a ball which ricocheted off Desailly's heel, couldn't be cleared by Emmanuel Petit, bounced off the leg and arm of the keeper Fabien Barthez, and was forced over the line at full stretch by the muscular Papa Bouba Diop. David Trezeguet and Thierry Henry—unhappy to be used on the left—both hit the woodwork, but then, so did Fadiga for Senegal. The French made numerous chances but took none of them, bravely opposed by the third-choice Monaco keeper Tony Sylva, who began shakily but looked safer and safer as the game went on. It was indeed a bitter-sweet night for a weary looking Patrick Vieira, playing against the country he had left when seven years old.

So Senegal led Group A. Next day, under the dome in Sapporo—not seen as ideal for soccer by various players—Group E favourites Germany thrashed a pitifully poor Saudi Arabian team 8–0, thus arguably gaining the confidence which would in due course surprisingly take them to the Final. The game was no contest. The Saudis were utterly vulnerable on their right flank where Germany's Michael Ballack made hay, his centres eagerly exploited with scant opposition by Miroslav Klose, who headed three of the goals.

In a game like that, the lack of a playmaker, such as the injured Mehmet Scholl, was irrelevant. Franz Beckenbauer had asserted that failing to top their qualifying group was the making of the German team since it had solidified in the two play-offs against Ukraine. Certainly the former star striker Rudi Voeller seemed a more inspiring manager than the disillusioned Berti Vogts, whose team had crashed to Portugal in Euro 2000.

Also in Group E, Ireland drew in Niigata with Cameroon, whose players had had their usual squabbles with officials over overdue wages and had arrived late in the Far East in consequence.

For most of the first half, however, they had Ireland under pressure, and went ahead on 39 minutes, Samuel Eto'o setting up his strike partner, Patrick Mboma. But the Irish recovered and with the excellent Matt Holland and Mark Kinsella making light of the absence of Roy Keane in central midfield, deservedly equalised in 80 degree heat on 52 minutes when Holland pounced on Raymond Kalla's headed clearance to score. Robbie Keane subsequently hit the post.

Back in Group A, Denmark's win in Ulsan over Uruguay, who'd sneaked in by beating Australia in a play-off, was something of a vindication for Jon-Dahl Tomasson, the striker who failed at Newcastle, flourished at Feyenoord and was already booked for Milan. He scored both his team's goals in the 2–1 win.

In Saitama next day, England, in Group F, made a wretched start, lucky to draw with Sweden even though Sol Campbell, with a header from a corner, had given them the lead. But on 59 minutes, clumsy defending by Danny Mills enabled the Swedish right winger Niclas Alexandersson to drive a left-foot shot past David Seaman. The rest of the game saw England desperately hanging on. Magnus Hedman, Sweden's keeper, surely had a point when he said, 'You put up the long ball and hope for the knock on to Owen, but that way of playing is dependent on chance.' Where indeed was the English playmaker, the new Paul Gascoigne? Young Joe Cole was still maturing.

Though David Beckham gallantly did his best, and used the ball with greater effect than his colleagues, it was inevitable he should fade after half an hour. The choice of Emile Heskey on the left flank seemed bizarre, given his ineffectuality, not least as West Ham's Trevor Sinclair—irrationally sent home but then recalled—had shown such lively form.

Argentina's 1–0 win against Nigeria was hardly scintillating, though nor was it encouraging for England. It was gained with a typically majestic header by Gabriel Batistuta, soaring above both friend and foe and well justifying his recall after, not for the first time, falling out of favour.

Under the dome of Sapporo, Italy made a comfortable start in Group G, against Ecuador, two smartly taken goals by Bobo Vieri—that awful right-footed miss against South Korea lay in the future—guaranteeing success. In Group C, the first of what would be two games between Brazil and Turkey proved a contentious affair. Two Turks were sent off, the first of them Aston Villa's centre back, Alpay, for pulling Luizao's shirt as the substitute striker went by him. The Korean referee, Kim Young-Joo, gave a penalty as well, though the foul certainly took place outside the box. Ronaldo scored. Rivaldo was later deviously involved in the expulsion of Hakan Unsal, who petulantly kicked the ball at him. It hit him on the knee but he fell, clutching his face, and Unsal was off; though technically he should have been, anyway.

Turkey had in fact led with a delightful goal, clever little Yildiray Basturk's floated pass setting Hasan Sas free to score, left footed. Ronaldo equalised with his first goal for Brazil for two years before his winning penalty.

In Group G, at Niigata, the white-booted Cuauhtemoc Blanco's penalty, after he himself had been fouled, gave Mexico deserved victory over Croatia, who had Boris Zivkovic expelled for the foul. Blanco was back after a prolonged absence caused by a brutal foul in a World Cup qualifier.

In Group D, South Korea finally made their debut on 4 June at Busan, with its 65,000 capacity the largest stadium in the country. The enthusiasm and anticipation were colossal; red shirts among the passionate crowd were the order of the day. Never in their forty-eight years of trying had South Korea won a game at a World Cup Finals, and it still rankled that North Korea had been the sensation of the 1966 World Cup. True, there had been a long gap after the disastrous South Korean debut in the World Cup in 1954, when in their opening match the side had lost 9–0 to Hungary. True also, there had been several subsequent draws; yet never a win. Home advantage now would surely bring victory against Poland.

Not least under the expert tutelage of Guus Hiddink, previously manager of the Dutch international side, Real Madrid and PSV. Appointed in January 2001, he had got the local Championship suspended to enable him to work for five months with those of his players, the majority, who played their football in the country. He was somewhat preoccupied that the few who didn't were largely not regular first teamers for their clubs, but he need hardly have worried. Little Jung-Hwan Ahn may have been in and out of the Perugia team in Serie A, but those of us who'd seen him when he did play knew how incisive he could be; and indeed, would be.

Before the game, Poland's veteran centre-back, Tomasz Waldoch, had reportedly said, 'We'll never lose a goal against an attack as weak as the Koreans. Maybe they will be a problem for other teams, but not for us.' Hubris punished by Nemesis. In fact Waldoch, and his fellow Schalke 04 defender, Tomasz Hajto, had rings run round them by the quick Korean attackers.

Emmanuel Olisadebe, Poland's little Nigerian-born striker, was unquestionably quick, and made a fine early chance for Jacek Krzynowek, but it was wasted, and there wouldn't be another. Instead, it was the Koreans who dominated the game, over eager at first, but increasingly dangerous once they cooled down. It would subsequently be suggested that their exceptional stamina might have had chemical origins, but none of their players failed a dope test.

On 26 minutes, when Lee Ful-Yong crossed accurately from the left, Hwang Sun-Hong, the striker, was left culpably unmarked, and beat Jerzy Dudek with ease. With Yoo Sang-Chul dynamic in midfield and the veteran sweeper Hong Myung-Bo marshalling the defence, the Koreans dominated. On 53 minutes it was Yoo who scored Korea's second goal, holding off two defenders. Only a string of saves by Dudek, not least late on, from the substitute Ahn, prevented more goals.

In Group H, in Saitama, co-hosts Japan drew 2–2 with Belgium. The evergreen 33-year-old Marc Wilmots scored Belgium's first with a spectacular bicycle kick. Japan's second goal was adventurously taken by their midfielder Junichi Inamoto, emerging from the shadows of a frustrating season with Arsenal in which he never played a Premiership game.

When Portugal met the USA in Suwon the following evening, in Group D, it seemed no great test for the talented Europeans. Instead, in the early stages, their feeble defence was swept aside by an ebullient USA team, which took a 3–0 lead.

Under their resourceful coach Bruce Arena, who had had great success in Major League Soccer with the Washington club DC United and had made an untypically positive transition from college coaching to the professional game, the Americans now had an internal harmony notably missing in 1998: though even then, under the much-contested coach Steve Sampson, their results were hardly as disastrous as seemed to be assumed. Moreover, two lively young attackers had emerged in the shape of the 20-year-old Landon Donovan, even though he was yet to make an impact at Bayern Leverkusen, and the little black left winger, 20-year-old DaMarcus Beasley.

In the opening phases, Portugal hardly knew what hit them. Even without their key playmaker, the injured Claudio Reyna, the American attack was full of energy, pace and penetration. Not least in the shape of their fourth-minute goalscorer, John O'Brien, who, after joining the Ajax Amsterdam youth scheme at the age of 16, had finally gained a place in their first team. 'I predicted John would have a great World Cup and he proved me right,' Reyna would enthuse.

When another player many years in Dutch football, Earnie Stewart, took a free kick from the left, Brian McBride's header was fumbled by the shaky Portuguese keeper, Vitor Baia, and O'Brien scored. The second American goal on the half hour was rather more fortunate, but rewarded sustained pressure. When Donovan, unmarked, hit the ball across from the right, it struck Jorge Costa and a surprised Baia could only push it on to the post, whence it entered the goal. Five minutes later Stewart missed a sitter, but a minute after that, Tony Sanneh's cross was headed in by McBride.

Three minutes more and at last Portugal scored, through Beto, following up his own rebounded header. But with the renowned midfielders Rui Costa and Luis Figo so ineffective, Portugal were dominant only in the last 20 minutes or so and even then their second goal came only when the unlucky Jeff Agoos defected Pauleta's cross past the excellent keeper, hefty Brad Friedel. A remarkable victory indeed.

A couple of hours later, in Ibaraki, the spirited Irish brought the Germans back to earth with a well-merited last-minute equaliser. Indeed, the game was two minutes into injury time when Niall Quinn, a second-half substitute, characteristically nodded on a high ball from Mark Kinsella, and Robbie Keane shot from seven yards. The German keeper, Oliver Kahn, did turn the ball on to a post but couldn't prevent it flying home. The German goal had been headed by Miroslav Klose on 19 minutes, when he exploited a long ball from Michael Ballack, with Ireland's defence in confusion.

On 6 June in Daegu, Senegal and Denmark played out in intense heat a somewhat untidy draw in which the accomplished but erratic Senegalese midfielder, Salif Diao, had a hectically uneven game. He gratuitously gave away the penalty from which Tomasson, whom he shoved, gave Denmark the lead, finished off a glorious move to equalise but got himself expelled for a wretched foul on Rene Henriksen.

In Busan, it was an equally ill-natured foul which saw French striker Thierry Henry being sent off after only 25 minutes. The Uruguayans didn't exploit their numerical edge, but the resulting goalless draw was a second nail in France's coffin.

So finally and apprehensively to Sapporo and the grand confrontation between England and Argentina. With England's fans still behaving impeccably, ridiculing all the pre-tournament fears and police preparations, Eriksson's team played by far its finest game of the tournament: a total contrast with the dull performance against the Swedes. One, moreover, which made Guus Hiddink's later, gratuitous dismissal of the England team as pedestrian and defensive seem unfair, even if they'd not be able to replicate such prowess.

It was in some sense the apotheosis of Nicky Butt, seen essentially as a competent journeyman midfielder for Manchester United somewhat in the image of 1966's Nobby Stiles. But here he seemed inspired, quite nullifying his club mate Veron, who was eventually substituted, and providing on 23 minutes the pass on to which an electric Michael Owen ran, shooting through the legs of his opponent Walter Samuel, only to hit the far post.

When young Owen Hargreaves was forced off, injured, it proved an advantage, since Sinclair's entry to the left flank enabled Paul Scholes to move off it into a far more congenial role which he filled with great brio, on 49 minutes forcing Pablo Cavallero into a spectacular save with an equally spectacular volley. The decisive goal came when Owen, as great a trial to the Argentine defence as he had been in Saint Etienne, was brought down by Mauricio Pochettino—standing in for the injured Roberto Ayala—as he was moving past him. David Beckham, who rose gallantly above his hardships, banged home the penalty. Revenge was exquisitely sweet.

On 57 minutes, England produced a scintillating 17-pass movement which ended with a searing volley by Teddy Sheringham, on as a substitute. Cavallero acrobatically turned it over the bar. But, having deployed his forces so shrewdly, Eriksson seemed to lose his nerve when, for the last ten minutes, he took off Owen, the terror of the Argentinians, to replace him not with another front runner in Darius Vassell or Robbie Fowler, but with of all things a second left back in Wayne Bridge, placed in midfield.

Thus handed territorial advantage—and, indeed, overall they had 65 per cent possession—Argentina assailed the English goal and it was Pochettino, the man who gave away the crucial penalty, who came so close to equalising, his point blank header from a corner being blocked dramatically by Seaman. So Argentina, joint favourites at the start with France, were, like them, in peril of the void.

In the other Group F game, in Kobe, Sweden, with two goals by Celtic's Henrik Larsson, accounted 2–1 for Nigeria while in Group B, Spain impressively won 3–1 against a Paraguay team managed by Cesare Maldini, Italy's coach in 1998. Fernando Morientes, strangely snubbed in the past, came on at half time to score twice and combine incisively with his Real Madrid partner, Raul.

Saturday would bring another surprise; Italy's defeat by Croatia in Ibaraki.

Two highly controversial refereeing decisions by England's Graham Poll—who, thought Italy's captain Paolo Maldini, should have been 'burnt at the stake'—led to Italy's defeat, yet in each case Poll was only confirming the decision of his Danish linesman, Lens Larsen. In the first case, there was no evident offside when Bobo Vieri scored on 50 minutes. Five minutes later, with one of his majestic leaps to Christian Doni's centre, he did, however, head Italy into the lead. On the second occasion, on 92 minutes, Marco Materazzi's long ball bounced past the Croat keeper, Stipe Pletikosa, only to be ruled out for an alleged jersey-tug by Pippo Inzaghi invisible to all but Larsen.

The fact remains that Italy's defensive blunders were the main cause of their defeat, and both were made by the hapless Materazzi, substituting for the injured Alessandro Nesta. On 73 minutes Materazzi allowed Robert Jarni's cross to reach Ivica Olic, one of the new faces in Croatia's team, and Olic scored. Then Materazzi was eluded by another lively newcomer, Milan Rapajic, who lobbed Gianluigi Buffon, too far out of his goal. Francesco Totti, largely marked out of the game, did hit a post, but Croatia had beaten the *azzurri*, just as they had in Palermo in the run-up to Euro 96. Totti complained furiously that Croatia's abrasiveness had gone unchecked.

Brazil's 4–0 win over China in Seogwipo, Korea, was flattering. The Chinese looked a decent, disciplined side and asked questions of the Brazilian defence. 'Sad to report, the genius of Ronaldo is gone,' wrote a journalist, who would have cause to repent. Ronaldo in fact played 71 minutes. Things would change. The next day, in Yokohama, Junichi Inamoto distinguished himself again with the only goal against Russia. After the tournament, his loan to Arsenal would become a loan to Fulham.

On the Monday, in Daegu, in front of another impassioned Korean crowd, South Korea were held to a draw in a fascinating match with the USA. An anti-American demonstration had been planned, but an appeal from the home country's President averted it. When little Ahn scored the Korean equaliser, however, he went into a provocative little 'skater's dance', evoking the much resented Olympic disqualification of a South Korean speed skater in favour of an American.

For most of the first half hour, South Korea laid siege to the American goal, in which the inspired Brad Friedel would perform wonders, not least the saving of a penalty. Yet it was the Americans who went ahead with a coolly worked goal, set up cleverly by John O'Brien for the forceful Clint Mathis, a player appreciated by Bruce Arena but warned by him about both his diet and his partying habits.

Curiously, given its previous resilience, the American defence conceded two careless late chances to the Koreans. Ahn flicked home a long left-wing free kick which should surely have been a defender's ball. And Tony Sanneh, the right back, allowed Lee Ful-Yong to leave him for dead, again on the left, before finding Choi Yong-Soo all alone, right in front of goal, only for Choi's shot to fly hopelessly over the bar.

In Jeonju, Portugal now came to life and annihilated the plodding Poles. Under heavy rain, Poland's defence looked as clumsy—not to say spiteful—as it had against South Korea. Hajto should certainly have been sent off for tripping then treading on João Pinto, who, with Pauleta, twisted and turned past the Poles at will. True, Poland had what seemed a good goal ruled out when 1–0 down, Kryszalowicz heading in only to be penalised for what seemed a non-existent foul on the shaky Portuguese keeper Vitor Baia. Overall, however, with Luis Figo at last fully operative, Portugal bestrode the field. Almost casually Pauleta turned Hajto to score, just as later he'd turn Waldoch for his third, having got his second meanwhile. Rui Costa exploited limp marking for the fourth.

On the face of it the revived Portugal should have stretched South Korea the following Friday, but in the event they signed their own death warrants. In Incheon, João Pinto's horrific, gratuitous foul on Park Ji-Sung, in the 27th minute had him properly expelled, which didn't stop his team mates shamefully mobbing Angel Sanchez, the Argentine referee. On 66 minutes Beto followed him on a second yellow card, somewhat more controversially, though the Portuguese rallied defiantly and all but scored when Sergio Conceicao hit the inside of a post on 88 minutes.

The Koreans made heavy weather of their advantage, though their goal, when it came, was a gem. Park Ji-Sung, who took Lee's cross from the left on his chest, turned past Conceicao then scored from an acute angle.

Curiouser and curiouser. The Poles, with nothing to play for, might have been expected to go down to a gung-ho American team whose coach Bruce Arena was shouting the odds about how sides like his had caught up with the supposed aristocracy. Instead, in Daejeon, the Poles quickly ran up a three-goal lead and cruised out winners at 3–1. Replacing their slow centre backs, revitalising their midfield, Poland were ahead in two minutes, Olisadebe, unmarked at a corner, cracking the ball in off the underside of the bar. Three minutes later, Kryszalowicz got a near-post goal. The third came from the substitute Marcin Zewlakow, heading in barely a minute after arriving as a 65th-minute substitute. Brad Friedel, again in resplendent form, saved his usual penalty, Landon Donovan volleyed in an 83rd-minute consolation, but by then, critics were erroneously tolling the knell for the USA.

France were down and out, brushed aside by Denmark in Incheon. True at various points Desailly and Trezeguet would hit the woodwork, but with Christian Pulsen stationed in front of the Danish back four, and Henry suspended, the French again paid the penalty for toiling on with the old guard; Lemerre's folly. On 22 minutes Dennis Rommedahl was given excessive space to score. Tomasson got the second, on 67.

In Suwon, there took place a strange game between Senegal and Uruguay. The Africans dominated the first half and went into a 3–0 lead. Shrewd substitutions in attack and a somewhat lucky goal right after the break brought Uruguay back into the game, to such an extent that they not only made it 3–3 but missed a simple headed chance to win, right on time. The best of the goals was that by Diego Forlan, whose father played in the 1974 World Cup as did that of centre-back Paolo Montero, whose carelessness led to the first Senegalese goal from a disputed penalty. Forlan chested down a clearance then hit an instant, glorious volley past Sylva.

Next day, in Osaka, England's display against Nigeria was a sad anti-climax after the win against Argentina. True, it was a roasting 34 degrees, but the goalless draw was still a disappointment. One consolation was another masterly performance in central defence by Rio Ferdinand, destined to leave Leeds for Old Trafford for a record £30 million not long after the World Cup ended. True, he made what one has almost come to recognise as his one gratuitous error per game, when Aghahowa might have a scored, but otherwise, he was impeccable. Teddy Sheringham, on as a sub for the ineffective Heskey, lofted a good chance over the bar and Paul Scholes had a shot tipped on to a post by the young Nigerian keeper, Vincent Enyeama, but by and large, this was pedestrian stuff, though Owen again looked lively.

Concurrently, in Miyagi, Argentina breathed their last, held by Sweden to a 1–1 draw. Batistutua described this as 'the saddest day of my long career'. Neither he nor his substitute, Hernan Crespo, could score from anything but Crespo's 88th minute follow-up, when Magnus

Hedman saved Ariel Ortega's spot kick. Previously, Anders Svensson's 59th-minute free kick had swerved past Cavallero. And quite why Henrik Larsson should receive a yellow card when badly fouled by Gonzalez, on his way through, was something known only to the referee, Bujsaim of the UAE. Still, Sweden had acquitted themselves well, transcending the brief battle between Freddie Ljungberg and Johan Mjallby when the latter had fouled him in a training game. Ljungberg, alas, subsequently had to drop out, injured.

On 13 June, in Oita, Italy stumbled again against Mexico, who had given them so much trouble in 1994, and the *azzurri* were lucky to survive. True, they had yet another good goal refused, when Pippo Inzaghi was certainly not offside when he scored, but overall, they were outplayed and only Mexico's poor finishing spared them. On 34 minutes, Borgetti twisted superbly in the air to lose Paolo Maldini and head Blanco's cross past Buffon. With Jesus Arellano causing chaos in the Italian defence, there should have been other Mexican goals. As it was, Alex del Piero was able to head a hardly deserved equaliser, on 85 minutes. 'Justice and God exist,' said Gianni Trapattoni, though one wondered why. Worse was to come.

In Suwon, Brazil defeated Costa Rica 5–2 in a game which emphasised both the power of their attack, with Ronaldo at last playing a full match and with great brio, and the fallibility of their defence. Truth to tell, while the Brazilians might have scored another three or four goals, the Costa Ricans and their elsuive forwards could have had at least another couple. So much for the blood-and-iron policies of Big Phil Scolari, which seemed to have been swept aside by the sheer élan and exuberance of his attacking players.

Brazil actually went into a 3–0 lead, the two opening goals being scored by Ronaldo, even if the first was somewhat surprisingly debited officially to the Costa Rican defender Marin. But within a minute of the third goal Manchester City's long legged Paulo Wanchope, combining with Mauricio Wright, had made it 3–1 and from that point, Jack was largely as good as his master. Or, defensively, as bad. Gomez's diving header made it 3–2, Brazil countered with two more goals, but right to the end the Costa Rican forwards were buzzing about the Brazilian goal. Twice they hit a post.

So to the second-round knock-out games. In Niigata England made surprisingly short work of Denmark thanks in large measure to untyp- ically inept goalkeeping by the Danes' Thomas Sorensen. Traumatising indeed was the goal he gave away on just four minutes, when Beckham took a left-side corner, Ferdinand stole in for a header on the right-hand post, and Sorensen somehow fumbled the ball over his own line.

Not surprisingly, this seemed to demoralise the Danes, and a second goal came on 24 minutes, when Sinclair crossed, Butt steered the ball through the legs of Thomas Gravesen and Owen pounced. Alas, he was later forced off the field, injured, but England would score again on half time when Sorensen failed inexplicably to keep out a far from irresistible, straightforward shot by Heskey. Butt had another fine game, but Denmark had simply foundered.

In Seogwipo the prosaic, pedestrian Germans plodded their way on towards—of all unexpected things—the Final. Whether they'd have beaten the Paraguayans had their vigorous young striker Roque Santa Cruz not been obliged to go off on 29 minutes, and had another lively young attacker, Nelson Cuevas, scorer of two goals in the previous game against Slovenia, been fit enough to come on before the very last minute, was debatable. By the closing phases, however, the Germans had worn the Paraguayans down and when their best attacker, little Oliver Neuville, swept in Bernd Schneider's right-wing cross on 87 minutes, it was hardly a surprise.

In Suwon, the gloriously resourceful Irish gave Spain a notable run for their money only to go down at the last to the brutal anticlimax of penalty kicks. The Spaniards never mastered the blond Damien Duff, operating excitingly first on the left wing, then on the right, and they were almost hoist with their own petard. Almost that is to say paid heavily for the tactical corwardice of their coach Camacho.

With his team still ahead from an early goal by the coruscating Morientes, he seemed to lose his nerve, took Morientes off, put on an inexperienced midfielder in Albelda, only to lose the still more dazzling Raul when Gary Breen clattered into him. Lose him, as it would transpire, for the rest of the tournament. Having used all his three substitutes, Camacho was obliged, when Albelda departed, hurt, at the end of normal time, to endure the whole of extra time with ten men. The Irish, to be frank, never made enough of that advantage.

During the game proper, they were awarded two penalties, one missed, one converted, though the spot kick gained by Duff and missed by Ian Harte seemed dubious. The second, by contrast—both came in the second half—was commendably given by the referee, Anders Frisk, when Fernando Hierro blatantly hung on to the shirt of the towering Niall Quinn. Robbie Keane calmly put it away.

Spain's goal was cleverly worked. Carlos Puyo and Luis Enrique combined at a right-flank throw in, Puyol crossed, Morientes glanced in his header. Roy Keane or no Roy Keane, the Irish central midfield of Matt Holland and Mark Kinsella was doughtily effective, as indeed it had been in previous games. The penalty shoot-out was something of a fiasco. Robbie Keane duly converted the first of them, but Holland, Connolly and Kevin Kilbane all missed. So Gaizka Mendieta, the little blond midfielder, had only to score to give Spain the game. His kick was a poor one, but it found its way over the line and Spain had survived.

In Oita, the inspired finishing of Henri Camara, at his most effective when he moved to the flanks, took unpredictable Senegal through against Sweden on a burning hot day. Unbeaten in 16 games, the Swedes were one ahead on just 11 minutes, when Tony Sylva, in one of his more impetuous moments, rushed out to collect a corner, didn't, and enabled Henrik Larsson to head home. At the end of the game Larsson announced it had been his last international.

On 37 minutes, Camara took a pass from Diouf and sent a strong acute angled right footer searing past Hedman into the corner of the net. In extra time, Anders Svensson hit a post, but it was Camara who scored the Golden Goal, snapping up a backheel from Pape Thiaw, springing into the box, and beating Hedman with, this time, a left-footed shot, which flew in off a post.

In Jeonju next day, American confidence in facing Mexico, a team they'd played so often, and often beaten, proved justified, transcending current form. Canny Bruce Arena man-marked both Blanco, playing a 'three-quarter' attacking role, and Gerardo Torrado. It was the USA's gung-ho aggression against Mexico's more subtle approach. On the American flanks, clever experienced Claudio Reyna and Eddie Lewis, the player who'd spent the previous season in Fulham's reserves and now kept out DaMarcus Beasley, were impressive. Yet again, the majestic Brad Friedel was a crucial factor, making three memorable saves, two in the first half, one in the second.

It was Reyna who set up an eighth-minute goal, hitting the line, pulling the ball back for Josh Wolff to find Brian McBride, who scored. Mexico should have had a penalty when John O'Brien handled in the box, but it wasn't given. So the Americans eventually made it 2–0, Eddie Lewis crossing precisely from the left for Landon Donovan to head in. Arena had a point when he advised Fulham to give Lewis more of a chance.

In Kobe, Brazil rode their luck against Belgium. On 35 minutes, the ever dangerous Marc Wilmots leaped to head in a cross by Jacky Peeters from the right. Alas, another inexperienced referee, Jamaica's Peter Prendergast, disallowed the goal for a phantom push. Not till the 67th minute could Brazil score, and that was when Rivaldo's left-foot shot was significantly deflected past the Belgian keeper, Geert de Vlieger. Three minutes from time Ronaldo, ebullient again, struck the second with a low drive: 2–0. But the watching England players were hardly intimidated.

In Daejeon, history, in a sense, repeated itself; the Italians went out to Koreans. This time, however, to South rather than North Korea, who'd beaten them at Middlesbrough in 1966. It was a defeat the Italians took bitterly. The word *vittimismo*, the feeling that the world is against you, sprung to mind. At the end of the match Francesco Totti, sent off on a second yellow card for diving when he arguably had been fouled, admitted that he, and others, childishly smashed up their dressing room.

Something which wasn't done by the England players afflicted in Mexico City by Diego Maradona's Hand of God goal in 1986. Nor, then, did we hear the agonised claims of corruption which rose from the Italian and Spanish camps after defeats by South Korea. Those of us who have conducted long, exhaustive inquiries into football corruption—notably by Italian clubs—know how easy it is to make such accusations, how hard it is to prove them.

Byron Moreno, the Ecuadorian referee, was called 'a disgrace' by the head of the Italian delegation, Rafael Ranucci, who knew South Korea 'were going to try something'. To his credit, Giovanni Trapattoni was restrained.

Yet in the case both of Italy and Spain, the games were surely there for the taking. Gianni Mura, in *La Repubblica*, opined that the Italians had been like a man who drives through a notoriously dangerous zone wearing a Rolex watch with his arm dangling out of the window. So Moreno's refereeing had become 'a great sheet', covering up a multitude of errors.

Italy lived dangerously from the fourth minute when Moreno rightly gave a penalty after Christian Panucci grasped Seol Ki-Hyeon's shirt. Ahn missed it, Gianluigi Buffon diving to save. Fifteen minutes later Bobo Vieri soared typically to head in Totti's corner at the far post. Only spectacular saves by Lee Woon-Jae thwarted Totti and Vieri. So it was that when the hapless Panucci blundered again, failing to cut out Hwang's pass, Seol scored with a left footer. That was on 88 minutes and two later Vieri, of all people, struck Damiano Tommasi's cross over the bar from five yards. In extra time the same player had a perfectly good goal refused for alleged offside, Totti was expelled and Ahn scored the Golden Goal on 116 minutes, running in front of Paolo Maldini to head in Lee Young-Pyo's left-wing cross. The incorrigible blowhard, Luciano Gaucci, President of Perugia, swore that the ingrate Ahn would never play for them again, although he subsequently changed his mind. Italy, emphatically and sullenly, were out, as were the victorious Koreans' co-hosts, who went down 1–0 to Turkey in Miyagi.

Three days later came the quarter-finals, and an English anticlimax. Might it have been different if only Michael Owen had been fully fit, rather than recovering from a groin strain? Yet, after defeat by Brazil in Shizuoka, England and Eriksson had scant excuses. Had they not, after the sending off of Ronaldinho, scorer of his team's embarrassing winner, fully 32 minutes to score against ten men? Didn't they have the gift of an opening goal from Michael Owen on 23 minutes, after a bizarre blunder by Brazil's central defender, Lucio? Wasn't Ronaldinho's winner in the 49th minute a present from David Seaman, stranded hopelessly and helplessly off his line as the free kick sailed into the open net? Ronaldinho said he meant it; others say he didn't. But Seaman had erred expensively

like this in the past, memorably in a Cup Winners Cup Final in Paris for
Arsenal against Zaragoza, when from much farther out still, Nayim's shot
soared over his head.

Seaman left the field in tears; a sad climax to what had previously, for
him, been a triumphant World Cup. Brazil equalised in first-half injury
time and in this instance, too, Ronaldinho was crucial. Shaking off Paul
Scholes after Beckham spurned a tackle, he then elegantly eluded Ashley
Cole before laying the ball on for Rivaldo to score.

Though Emile Heskey was on far better form, England, deprived of
Owen's dash and opportunism, had neither the skill nor the strategy to
penetrate what was after all a far from irresistible Brazilian defence.
Neither Scholes nor Butt was able to produce the unexpected, decisive
pass. No Paul Gascoigne of old, alas. Eriksson seemed to have no solu-
tions. Bringing Dyer on to the left flank was no help. It might have been
a moment to risk using Joe Cole, the one English player with the skills
and flair to make chances, even if consistency had not been his forte. So
it was that Seaman's blunder was fatal; but surely, given that long
numerical advantage, it need not have been.

Sven-Göran Eriksson hardly inspired his team at half time. 'We
needed Winston Churchill,' complained an England defender, 'and we
got Iain Duncan Smith.'

After Germany had squeezed through 1–0 in Ulsan against the
United States, surviving a plain penalty when Torsten Frings handled
Greg Berhalter's shot on the line, Franz Beckenbauer's contempt was
unrestrained. 'We should change everything about this team,' he
inveighed. 'Everybody apart from the goalkeeper Oliver Kahn [who
made several crucial saves] should be thrown out for the semi-final.' It
was indeed one more drab performance by a German team riding its
luck to excess. The skilful Claudio Reyna declared that the USA had
'played Germany off the park'. Indeed, their muscular approach to the
game had given the Americans territorial dominance, but they simply
couldn't turn it into goals.

Thus, the only one came from Germany's best outfield player, Michael
Ballack just two minutes after Kahn had punched out Eddie Lewis' fierce
drive in the 36th. An in-swinging free kick by Christian Ziege, and
Ballack's header went under Brad Friedel and in. Oliver Neuville ran
himself to exhaustion.

After South Korea's hugely controversial win over Spain in Gwangju
once more accusations flew of dirty work at the crossroads.

There was no doubt that the officials' decisions went disproportion-
ately against Spain, but once again, sympathy had objectively to be
limited. The Spaniards should still have been able to win, and so avoid
the fiasco of penalties. Spain were without Raul, still injured, but chances
were made. On 48 minutes came the first fraught moment. When

De Pedro's free kick was headed in, from a knot of players, by Ivan Helguera, the Egyptian referee, Gamal Ghandour, gave a free kick, though nobody knew quite why.

In extra time, on the decision of his linesman, Michael Ragconath, he quite wrongly decreed that the ball had crossed the right-hand goal line after Joaquin centred and before Morientes headed in; though it was possible that the Korean keeper, Lee Woon-Jae, had stopped when he heard the whistle. But in my opinion the most blatant mistake was when Joaquin himself took what proved to be the fatal penalty in the shoot out—when Lee Woon-Jae so clearly came off his line.

'I have reached the conclusion that Senegalese players use their elbow first in high balls,' said Turkey's coach, Senol Gunes—who was largely confounding his many critics—provocatively, before the teams met in Osaka.

Elbows or no, Senegal would succumb to a Golden Goal, splendidly scored on the half volley by Ilhan from Umit Davala's right-wing cross. Afterwards the young striker, used yet again as a substitute, claimed with reason that he should have been on at the start in every game. Top scorer for Besiktas in the Turkish Championship, he took the place against Senegal of a waning Hakan Sukur, who missed chance after chance but would ultimately come alive in the Third Place match: in tandem with Ilhan.

Senegal, however, had truly distinguished themselves in this World Cup; a team whose kit had initially to be paid for by Salif Diao, later to be bought by the team at large. But it was Turkey who played the good football, Yildiray Basturk elusive and neat as ever, Hasan Sas a clever soloist on the left. Overall, one of the tournament's benign surprises.

But even they could not stem the advance of Brazil, when it came to the semi-final in Saitama. Clearly there were scores to be settled from the first match. A plus for Turkey was that Ronaldinho, sent off against England for his foul on Mills, would not be there. In the event Ronaldo, who would score the only goal, would complain of maltreatment.

Ronaldo scored Brazil's winner against the Turks on 48 minutes, racing on to Gilberto Silva's pass from the left, stretching to make the contact which took the ball past the excellent keeper, Rustu Recher. He would save resourcefully from the exuberant right flanker Cafu, Ronaldo, Roberto Carlos and twice from Rivaldo. This was so much more the 'real' Brazil, no matter the dour philosophy of Big Phil.

Meanwhile, in Seoul, in the words of one headline, GERMAN ROBOTS GO MARCHING ON. This time, no referee or linesman could save South Korea. Germany, bruising opposition, again had Kahn's goalkeeping to thank, but theirs was the one goal, scored by Michael Ballack on 75 minutes, when he struck Oliver Neuville's cutback ball with his right and, when Lee moon-Jae saved resiliently, converted the rebound with his left. But his cynical foul on the impressive Lee Chun-Soo got him the yellow card which would keep him out of the Final.

Just as in 1982, but for different reasons, neutrals prayed that Germany would lose the Final. In Madrid it was a moral matter, after Toni Schumacher's repugnant foul on Patrick Battiston. Now it was because a German victory would distinguish not the Beautiful but the Ugly game.

In the interim, a Turkish team inspired by Ilhan won a livelier than usual third-place match against the South Koreans in Daegu. Sadly for the resourceful 33-year-old Korean skipper, Hong Myung-Bo, who had scored the decisive spot kick for his team against Spain, been saluted as the best in his role in the tournament, and was playing his last international match, it would end in tears. Or, if you like, begin with them, for it was only after 11 seconds that he carelessly lost the ball to Ilhan, who enabled Sukur to score.

Korea equalised on nine minutes with Lee Ful-Yong's inspired curling free kick but their back three constantly let them down. Ilhan made it 2–1. Ahn, dynamically twisting one way then the other, almost equalised, but on 32 minutes Sukur knocked the ball through for Ilhan to score again. The second half was largely as great an anticlimax as Song's 90th-minute consolation goal.

The Final, in Yokohama, was overall a better game than might have been expected. Above all, it represented the apotheosis of Ronaldo, after the trauma of 1998, and victory for a team which, unlike its rivals, at least was sporadically capable of playing spectacular football, not least because Ronaldinho was now exuberantly back from his suspension. Even without Ballack, the Germans to their credit carried the game to Brazil in the opening stages, though they made few clear opportunities. Sadly and strangely, their keeper, Oliver Kahn, voted best player of the tournament and faultless till then, gave away the opening, crucially important, goal with a blunder as bad in its way as Seaman's against Brazil. Ah, football!

For that matter Ronaldo, though he would emerge triumphant, could well have looked back on the Final with despair. Twice in the first half he failed with splendid chances, once forced wide by Kahn, once allowing him to block, when an exquisite angled pass by Ronaldinho had sent him clear. Almost on half time, the lively 22-year-old midfielder Kleberson had struck Kahn's bar.

As against that, early in the second half, belying his diminutive stature, Oliver Neuville let fly a tremendous 35-yard free kick which Marcos, the best Brazilian goalkeeper for years, flung himself to turn on to the post.

It was another of the ironies of this game that the German midfielder Dietmar Hamann, who had made such a dominating start, should be seriously at fault when Brazil took the lead on 68 minutes. Dwelling on the ball, he lost it to a determined tackle by Ronaldo, of all people, one which would have done credit to any midfield terrier. Ronaldo advanced and served Rivaldo, who shot. Kahn, vulnerable at last, and on this of all occasions, spilled the ball and Ronaldo, following up, sent it home. Well might Kahn, afterwards invested with the golden award, have reflected that all that glisters is not gold.

Eleven minutes later, when Kleberson, evident again, crossed from the right, Rivaldo's cunning dummy freed Ronaldo, despite the clutch of opponents around him, to beat Kahn again with a right-footed drive. So he and the Brazilians laid the ghosts of 1998.

For all the mediocrity of the tournament at large, this was arguably the best Final since 1986.

Japan may not have done as well as their co-hosts South Korea, but they made honourable progress, reached the quarter-finals, and lost there only to a 12th-minute goal by Turkey's Umit in front of 45,666 fans. In their third and last qualifying match, Japan had scored a notable 1–0 victory over Russia, in Yokohama, with yet another well taken goal by Yunichi Inamoto.

Transferred on loan from Arsenal to Fulham after the tournament, Inamoto confessed after he'd played his first half game for his new club in the Intertoto Cup at home (well, at Queens Park Rangers' stadium) against Souhaux, that his World Cup feats had restored the confidence he had partly lost in his deeply frustrating season at Highbury.

The Japanese coach, Philippe Troussier, however, felt that after exceptional efforts in the first three matches he was running out of steam against the Turks, and substituted him at half time.

There was no doubt that Japan's impressive World Cup progress was thanks in large measure to Troussier, however uncompromising his attitude could be, and it was a blow to Japanese football when he maintained his determination to leave the job when the competition was over. Clearly he had hoped he could then take over the French international team, following the dismissal of the hapless Roger Lemerre, but though he was on the short list, the job went to Jacques Santini.

It was much to the credit of the Japanese Football Federation and its understanding President, Shunichiro Okana, that Troussier survived the hostility of the media and the J League's President, Saburo Kawaguchi, to remain in office. His brusque uncompromising approach alienated the local press. When Japan won their group decider against Tunisia, 2–0, he dedicated the victory sarcastically to the Japanese media who had 'so motivated me to shut them up that I owed them that. Thanks to them, I always had to be good.' It was perhaps inevitable that he and the J League should clash, such were his demands on their players for training camps and tours.

But there was no gainsaying his remarkable achievements. Before the

World Cup Finals, he had taken his gifted Under-20 team all the way to the Final of the 1999 World Tournament, reached the quarter-finals of the Olympic tournament in Sydney in 2000, and three months later won the Asian Cup. 'Here,' he said, somewhat enigmatically 'the players have a natural energy comparable to that of Mount Fuji. But you have to canalise it and teach them the football played in Europe. They were too naive and not prepared for battle.'

Gradually his 3-5-2 formation grew battle hardened. He never hesitated to make changes during a game and had the tendency not to start with his best side. In the quarter-final against Turkey, he would deploy all three substitutes, one of them, Ichikawa, himself being replaced.

'Two years ago,' he observed, 'we had one star (plainly Hidetoshi Nakata). Now we have twenty.'

RESULTS: Japan and South Korea 2002

First round

Group A

Seoul, Ulsan, Daegu, Busan, Incheon, Suwon
France 0, Senegal 1
Uruguay 1, Denmark 2
Denmark 1, Senegal 1
France 0, Uruguay 0
Denmark 2, France 0
Senegal 3, Uruguay 3

	P	W	D	L	F	A	Pts
Denmark	3	2	1	0	**5**	**2**	7
Senegal	3	1	2	0	**5**	**4**	5
Uruguay	3	0	2	1	**4**	**5**	2
France	3	0	1	2	**0**	**3**	1

Group B

Busan, Gwangju, Jeonju, Daegu, Seogwipo, Daejon
Paraguay 2, South Africa 2
Spain 3, Slovenia 1
Spain 3, Paraguay 1
South Africa 1, Slovenia 0
Paraguay 3, Slovenia 1
Spain 3, South Africa 2

	P	W	D	L	F	A	Pts
Spain	3	3	0	0	**9**	**4**	9
Paraguay	3	1	1	1	**6**	**6**	4
South Africa	3	1	1	1	**5**	**5**	4
Slovenia	3	0	0	3	**2**	**7**	0

Group C

Ulsan, Gwangju, Seogwipo, Incheon, Suwon, Seoul
Brazil 2, Turkey 1
Costa Rica 2, China 0
Brazil 4, China 0
Turkey 1, Costa Rica 1
Brazil 5, Costa Rica 2
Turkey 3, China 0

	P	W	D	L	F	A	Pts
Brazil	3	3	0	0	**11**	**3**	9
Turkey	3	1	1	1	**5**	**3**	4
Costa Rica	3	1	1	1	**5**	**6**	4
China	3	0	0	3	**0**	**9**	0

Group D

Busan, Suwon, Daegu, Jeonju, Incheon, Daejeon
South Korea 2, Poland 0
USA 3, Portugal 2
South Korea 1, USA 1
Portugal 4, Poland 0
South Korea 1, Portugal 0
Poland 3, USA 1

	P	W	D	L	F	A	Pts
South Korea	3	2	1	0	**4**	**1**	7
USA	3	1	1	1	**5**	**6**	4
Portugal	3	1	0	2	**6**	**4**	3
Poland	3	1	0	2	**3**	**7**	3

Group E

Niigata, Sapporo, Kashima, Ibaraki, Saitama, Shizuoka, Yokohama
Ireland 1, Cameroon 1
Germany 8, Saudi Arabia 0
Germany 1, Ireland 1
Cameroon 1, Saudi Arabia 0
Ireland 3, Saudi Arabia 0
Germany 2, Cameroon 0

	P	W	D	L	F	A	Pts
Germany	3	2	1	0	**11**	**1**	7
Ireland	3	1	2	0	**5**	**2**	5
Cameroon	3	1	1	1	**2**	**3**	4
Saudi Arabia	3	0	0	3	**0**	**12**	0

Group F

Ibaraki, Saitama, Sapporo, Kobe, Osaka, Miyagi
Argentina 1, Nigeria 0
England 1, Sweden 1
England 1, Argentina 0
Sweden 2, Nigeria 1
England 0, Nigeria 0
Sweden 1, Argentina 1

	P	W	D	L	F	A	Pts
Sweden	3	1	2	0	**4**	**3**	5
England	3	1	2	0	**2**	**1**	5
Argentina	3	1	1	1	**2**	**2**	4
Nigeria	3	0	1	2	**1**	**3**	1

Group G

Niigata, Sapporo, Miyagi, Ibaraki, Yokohama, Oita
Mexico 1, Croatia 0
Italy 2, Ecuador 0
Croatia 2, Italy 1
Mexico 2, Ecuador 1
Ecuador 1, Croatia 0
Mexico 1, Italy 1

	P	W	D	L	GOALS F	A	Pts
Mexico	3	2	1	0	4	2	7
Italy	3	1	1	1	4	3	4
Croatia	3	1	0	2	2	3	3
Ecuador	3	1	0	2	2	4	3

Group H

Saitama, Kobe, Yokohama, Oita, Osaka, Shizuoka,
Japan 2, Belgium 2
Tunisia 0, Russia 2
Japan 1, Russia 0
Tunisia 1, Belgium 1
Belgium 3, Russia 2
Japan 2, Tunisia 0

	P	W	D	L	GOALS F	A	Pts
Japan	3	2	1	0	5	2	7
Belgium	3	1	2	0	6	5	5
Russia	3	1	0	2	4	4	3
Tunisia	3	0	1	2	1	5	1

Second Round

Seogwipo
Germany 1, Paraguay 0

Niigata
England 3, Denmark 0

Oita
Senegal 2, Sweden 1
(Golden Goal)

Suwon
Spain 1, Ireland 1
Spain win 3–2 on penalties after extra time

Jeonju
USA 2, Mexico 0

Kobe
Brazil 2, Belgium 0

Miyagi
Turkey 1, Japan 0

Daejeon
South Korea 2, Italy 1
(Golden Goal)

Quarter-finals

Shizuoka
Brazil 2, England 1

Ulsan
Germany 1, USA 0

Gwangju
South Korea 0, Spain 0
South Korea win 5–3 on penalties after extra time

Osaka
Turkey 1, Senegal 0
(Golden Goal)

Semi-finals

Seoul
Germany 1, South Korea 0

Saitama
Brazil 1, Turkey 0

Third-place Match

Daegu

Turkey 3	**South Korea 2**
Rustu; Fathi,	Lee
Alpay, Bulent, Ergun;	W.-J.; Yoo, Hong (Kim
B. Umit, Basturk	T.-Y.), Lee M.-S.; Song,
(Tayfur), Tugay, Emre	Park, Lee Y.-P., Lee
B. (Hakan Unsal);	C.-S., Lee E.-Y. (Cha);
Ilhan, Hakan Sukur.	Ann, Seol (Coi T.-U.).

SCORERS
Hakan Sukur, Ilhan 2 for Turkey.
Lee E.-Y. and Song for South Korea

Final

Yokohama

Brazil 2	**Germany 0**
Marcos; Lucio,	Kahn; Linke,
Edmilson, Roque	Ramelow, Metzelder;
Junior; Cafu,	Frings, Hamann,
Kleberson, Gilberto	Schneider, Jeremies
Silva, Roberto Carlos;	(Asamoah), Bode
Ronaldinho, Ronaldo,	(Ziege); Klose
Rivaldo (Juninho)	(Bierhoff), Neuville.
(Denilson).	

SCORERS
Ronaldo 2 for Brazil

Germany
2006

You might say this time that the 2006 World Cup—not for the first time —ended both with a bang and with a whimper. The bang was the head butt in extra time by the 34-year-old Zinedine Zidane into the chest of Italy's Marco Materazzi, who collapsed. The whimper was the way the Final, after a promising enough start, petered out on penalties: with Zidane, until then arguably the star turn of the competition, sent off in his last game for France.

Until then Zidane, in the image of the French team itself, had been an astonishing example of rejuvenation. It was known that before the tournament he had been at odds with the team manager, Raymond Domenech, an endearingly comic figure on the touchlines as he gestured, wriggled and cavorted, besuited and bespectacled. Zidane, who claimed to have been inspired in the depths of the night by a mysterious presence to change his mind about retiring from international football, had begun badly: in the image of the team itself.

So much so that, during the second game, against South Korea, following the uneasy draw against the Swiss, Domenech actually pulled Zidane off the field. That relations had reached a point of no return seemed implicit in the way Zidane strode off the field without a word or a look at his manager. Since he was suspended, after a second yellow card, from the ensuing game against Togo, when Domenech successfully started his striker David Trezeguet alongside his former Monaco team mate, Thierry Henry, Zidane seemed a figure of the past.

It was immensely to the credit of Domenech that he bit the bullet, buried the hatchet, choose what metaphor you wish, and so surprisingly brought Zidane back for the quarter-final against Spain. Zidane responded with a magisterial display, a compound of skill, flair, calm command, invention and powerful finishing. The goal at the end of the match against Spain with which he crowned the French victory was a marvellous achievement, technique compounded by power. As, indeed, was the massive free kick from left to right which enabled Thierry Henry to smash home his spectacular goal against Brazil. A Brazilian team whose supposed stars were utterly eclipsed by Zidane, who went on to score the penalty which, stroked in off the bar, put France ahead in the Final.

What, then, made him lose his head in that last game, and assault Materazzi? Whatever it was (three insults?), there was plainly no excuse for it, least of all for a player of such experience and with such huge responsibility. But then Zidane already had 'form'. He had been sent off in the 1998 tournament, which he would crown with his two headed goals in the Final against Brazil, in the match versus Saudi Arabia. And a flagrant offence in a European Cup game, playing for Juventus, had earned him a five-match suspension.

That Materazzi, a notorious hard case, had insulted him was beyond doubt, though the Italian himself denied that he had abused Zidane's mother, insisting that he himself had been verbally provoked by the Frenchman. Lip readers insisted that Materazzi had indeed been viciously abusive. It was suggested that Zidane was especially vulnerable at the time, because his mother was seriously ill. But whatever his explosive temperament, Zidane was surely a sufficiently experienced figure to know the old, if unwritten, rule: never retaliate. It is arguable that this is exactly what Materazzi hoped he would do.

In the event, it compromised any real chance of winning a game in which the Italians after such a bright, brisk start seemed to have gone into their shell. Moreover, the skill in taking penalties which he had shown in that game and its predecessor was lost to his team, who duly succumbed on spot kicks. A truly distressing way to end the most important football competition that there is, though, of course, we had been subjected to it in 1994, in Pasadena.

Once upon a time, in the dim and distant past, there had been such a thing as replays, but the increasing gigantism of a tournament which had been so much more manageable and less, in every sense, exhausting at 16 teams made such a thing impossible: to the abysmal cheapening of the World Cup itself.

This would be a World Cup of endless surprises, which gave it a special allure. Some were positive, some negative, none more so than the failure of the favourites, Brazil. True, Brazil's form in pre-tournament friendlies had been a little disappointing, but their panoply of stars, the way they had cruised through the attenuated South American qualifying group— beating the old foe Argentina in Rio, though losing to them in Buenos Aires—indicated heights which no other competitor was likely to reach. In particular, there was the effervescent Ronaldinho, fresh from a dazzling season with Barcelona, whom he had materially helped to win the European Cup, voted best footballer in the world.

But from the very first World Cup game against Croatia, Ronaldinho looked strangely out of sorts. Explanations were various, but as the tournament went on there was general agreement that—though he never publicly complained—he was being asked to fill a role foreign to him, no longer able to dictate his own terms, obliged to drop deep rather than to go wide. By the time it came to the crucial match with France, he would be unrecognisable as the coruscating figure who had inspired Barcelona. And there was scant help coming from Ronaldo, even though, in the course of the competition, he'd establish a new World Cup scoring record. Ronaldo, like Zidane for that matter, had had a muted season at Real Madrid. Against Croatia, he looked overweight, even ponderous. There was something of an efflorescence after the first couple of games, and he took his goals well against an incredibly naive Ghanaian defence, but when push came to shove in the defeat by France, he was reduced largely to a series of palpable dives.

Nor was Adriano, so powerful and prolific a year earlier in Germany in the Confederations Cup, remotely at his peak. He had had a poor season with Internazionale in Italy, and for the most part looked largely ineffectual now. The much younger Ronaldinho provided glimmers of hope, but surely should have been used much more often.

As for the full backs, the veterans Cafu and Roberto Carlos, far too much was asked of them as overlappers in a Brazilian team still turning its back on the tradition of great right wingers: Julinho, Garrincha, Jairzinho. The manager, Carlos Alberto Parreira, seemed too much in thrall to the likes of Ronaldo and too unimaginative to turn things round. For oneself, he had never been an international manager of true consequence, wedded in his earliest brief spell in charge to a misbegotten ideal of what he thought to be 'European' football, later absurdly falling out with the country's finest talent, Romario; though he recanted in time, as we know, to put Romario back in the side and thereby qualify by the skin of his teeth for a World Cup which Mario's goals did so much to win.

By contrast, the manager of Argentina, José Pekerman, seemed to have done a quietly effective job in producing a team inspired by the clever play-making of Juan Roman Riquelme, to whom Pekerman gave a regular role after years in which Riquelme had been a marginal figure. The more bizarre that, when it came to the crucial quarter-final against the German hosts, Pekerman should substitute Riquelme; whose qualities he'd always lauded, emphasising that a certain lack of speed was amply compensated by quickness of thought and inventive passing. An error compounded by failing, in that game, to make any use of the precociously incisive winger, 19-year-old Lionel Messi. Somehow the virtue seemed to have seeped out of Pekerman, who resigned after his team had gone out on penalty kicks. That game over, there was the beginning of a brawl, and distant memories of the England–Argentina quarter final of 1966, when frustrated Argentina players confronted their opponents, Gabriel Heinze prominently among them, and Leandro Cufre, a substitute who'd not even been used in the game, was given a red card for kicking the German defender Per Mertesacker. 'It was typical Argentinian,' said the digusted German midfielder, Torsten Frings, one of his teams's liveliest players. 'They completely lost their minds. We tried to calm them down, but it just shows they are bad sports and badly behaved. I hope their players get suspended'.

'I had three or four red marks on my thigh and then he kicked me again in the groin,' said Metersacker. 'I cannot understand that it turned into so much aggression. I asked him why he did that and then he completely lost it again.' Would things have been different had Riquelme not tired and been replaced by Pekerman? Even a tired Riquelme can still do the unexpected. A result which would have seemed unimaginable after Germany's first two matches.

Desperate for a successor as manager to Rudi Voller, whose team had failed wretchedly in 2002 in Portugal at the European Championship, the

Germans had turned to another famous striker of the past in Jurgen Klinsmann. This, though Klinsmann was based in California and commuted to
Germany. Nor did he endear himself to the critics with his unorthodox
appointments of assistants from outside the world of football. Results were
alarming. A 4–1 defeat by Italy in a Florentine friendly. A wretched performance just before the tournament began in a friendly with Japan, who
might well, in the opinion of German reporters, have scored six times rather than twice, and who deserved far more than the 2–2 draw they conceded
when the Germans scored two late goals. There was little more cause for
optimism after Germany's first World Cup match against modest Costa
Rica. True, they won 4–2, but their defence looked inept, the tactics were
criticised by the talented captain, Michael Ballack, and one of the few consolations was the form of the attacking, right-footed, left-back, Bayern
Munich's 22-year-old Phillip Lahm.

There would, however, be a sea change after Germany defeated Ecuador
—another Latin American team, admittedly, of no great substance—3–0,
when what might be called their Polish pair of attackers, Lukas Podolski and
Miroslav Klose, suddenly became incisive. Where Podolski had missed
numerous chances in the previous game against Poland—where both men
were born—now he put them away, and his newly found confidence reflected the new self-belief of the team as a whole. Klose, whom one had seen
score those four goals in Japan against Saudi Arabia, only to fade from international view thereafter, now emerged as a striker of power and menace. He
and Podolski had the game against Sweden in the second round won in a
dozen minutes.

Of Germany's World Cup organisation, presided over by the ubiquitous
Franz Beckenbauer, who had won the trophy both as player and manager,
it should be said that it was an outstanding success, making one all the more
grateful to that elderly New Zealander who had prevented the competition
going to South Africa. A country from which, on the eve of the 2006 tournament, came dire stories of communications chaos, raising serious doubts
whether they would be capable in time of playing hosts to a competition
suffering, beyond doubt, from an extreme case of gigantism.

Sweden had found their way, albeit briefly, into the second round, despite
the humiliation of being held to a goalless draw by little Trinidad and Tobago in Dortmund, in their opening group game. Chiefly thanks to phenomenal goalkeeping by the 37-year-old Shaka Hislop, who initially was not supposed to be playing at all. He stepped in only because the first choice, Kevin
Jack, was obliged to drop out at the last moment. The Swedes, despite the
presence of such as Zlatko Ibrahimovic and Henrik Larsson—destined carelessly to miss a penalty against the Germans—found Hislop unbeatable. On
shots and headers alike, high up, low down, point blank, he was equal to
everything; and Trinidad down to ten men for almost all the second half
once even grazed the Swedish bar. It was a privilege to be present.

Talking of Swedes, the hapless England manager Sven Göran Eriksson emerged from the tournament – inevitably at the usual quarter final stage – a much abused and excoriated figure. Yet though it is beyond doubt that he made an inept job of things, that he unpardonably picked the untried seventeen-year-old Theo Walcott—then hadn't the courage of his convictions even to play him—that he sacrificed the barely recovered Wayne Rooney who ultimately, even predictably, went up in flames, a salient question should be asked. Were, in that old phrase, the guilty men essentially those who inexplicably kept him in office, rewarding disloyalty with a massive increase in salary, accepting the evasive responses with which he had tried to deny his misbegotten office 'romance'?

Admittedly, having known him and respected his achievements in Italy, when Eriksson was appointed I was among the relatively few who applauded. Applause indeed was general when England, who had seemed hopelessly devoid of World Cup hopes, went to Munich to thrash Germany 5–1. But it proved to be a false dawn. They struggled at home in the subsequent qualifiers against Finland and would have lost to Greece, had Teddy Sheringham not won a phantom free kick, from which David Beckham equalised. Neither in the subsequent World Cup finals in the Far East, nor in the European finals in Portugal two years later, did Eriksson in the quarter-finals show any real initiative.

To compound such inadequacy, he was known to have talked once to Manchester United and twice to Chelsea about leaving his England post to manage them. His second, surreptitious colloquy with Chelsea should surely have earned him the sack. Instead, incomprehensibly, he was given another million pounds. The egregious chief executive of the Football Association was then Mark Palios who, having enjoyed what one might loosely call the favours of the secretary Faria Alam, tried to persuade the *News of the World*—through his chief Press officer Colin Gibson—to keep him out of the frame at Eriksson's expense. He failed, but when he then left the FA it was reportedly—quite inexplicably again—with £650,000 of supposed compensation.

During the World Cup tournament, Eriksson insisted that there was no kind of metaphorical 'marriage' between himself and David Beckham. It was hardly convincing. Eriksson, in fact, had long seemed obsessed with Beckham, at the expense of the efficiency of the team as a whole. Beckham beyond doubt had had a remarkable right foot, a kind of howitzer, capable of delivering insidious free kicks, corners and crosses; though less effective with penalties. Yet it is arguable that Beckham is essentially a one-trick pony, devoid of the true winger's qualities of pace, ball control, the ability to swerve outside the back, reach the goal line and pull back the most dangerous pass in football into the middle. Alternatively, to cut in and go directly for goal. Things which Shaun Wright Phillips, who began so excitingly against Ukraine but didn't make the cut, and Aaron Lennon who did, and scintillated in his two World Cup appearances as a substitute, unquestionably can.

In the event, England came to rely to an alarming extent on Beckham's free kicks and crosses – one of which, helped by a goalkeeping fumble, produced the meagre victory against Ecuador. This however to the exclusion of what a more natural winger could achieve in open play.

In England's largely mediocre World Cup qualifying group, both in Cardiff against Wales and in Belfast against Northern Ireland—humiliating victors—Eriksson tried to deploy Beckham in midfield as a kind of quarter-back, thus utterly distorting the tactics of his team.

Having picked Walcott, who was still to make his debut for Arsenal, Eriksson thus left behind several far more experienced strikers, one of whom could well have been used. This in turn made the Swede desperately rush Wayne Rooney into the fray, soon after he had injured his metatarsal, exacerbating this self-serving stratagem—which had infuriated Rooney's club manager, Alex Ferguson—by using Rooney in a lone role up front, one which he didn't fill even when fully match fit, and now surely made intolerable through the physical pressure it involved.

This is not to excuse Rooney's violent assault on Portugal's Carvalho which had him sent off, but it may go some way towards explaining it. Eriksson, however, could hardly be blamed for the ineptitude of England's aerial defence, goalkeeper Paul Robinson very much included, in the second half of the match against Sweden, which seemed well won at half time with a 2–0 lead; Joe Cole's gloriously volleyed goal from the left being among the most spectacular in the tournament—to be ranked with the superb volley from the right with which Maxi Rodriguez won Argentina's game against Mexico, and Thiery Henry's against Brazil, the product of Zidane's massive free kick from the far left.

Yet until their dogged 10-man resistance against Portugal in the quarter-final, England had not produced a single decent performance. Their opening match versus Paraguay was won—yes, from a Beckham free kick—when the opposing centre back Carlos Gamarra put through his own goal on three minutes. In the second round, things could well have gone amiss against Ecuador when John Terry's absurdly clumsy header let through Carlos Tenorio, resourcefully thwarted at the last second by Ashley Cole's tackle, the ball hitting the bar. There were fine goals from Steven Gerrard, but Frank Lampard was strangely ineffectual. In contrast, the much criticised Owen Hargreaves did vigorously justify Eriksson's faith in him with his driving performances.

It was a tournament with four Dutch managers. Marco Van Basten, a hero in his playing days, had the national team; Dick Advocaat, former national team coach in 2004, had South Korea, so reluctant to use striker Ahn, Guus Hiddink had Australia, Leo Beenhakker had Trinidad and Tobago. The Dutch went out to Portugal after a repugnant affair which one was unlucky enough to attend. A game in which a feeble Russian referee, Valentin Ivanov, flourished four red cards and a multiplicity of yellows; in which the illustrious Portuguese veteran Luis Figo should have been expelled for head butting but wasn't, while the Portugal playmaker, Brazilian-born Deco, was sent off but probably should not have been.

Certainly it might have made a difference had Ivanov early on expelled the ruthless Dutch right back Khalid Boulahrouz for a shocking foul on Cristiano Ronaldo, which he would repeat later in the game before belatedly being expelled. Not for nothing was he named The Cannibal. But, as we know, referees are notoriously reluctant to flourish red cards so early in a game. It surprised me, and not only me, that Van Basten should not have sent on Ruud Van Nistelrooy at all. True, the Manchester United striker had been in somewhat indifferent form, but Dirk Kuyt, who displaced him, looked, as Dutch journalists themselves believed, a good club player clearly out of his depth. To some extent, the game was redeemed by the splendid goal driven home after skilled ball play by Maniche.

Italy, of course, played under the shadow of the massive corruption scandal chiefly concerning Juventus, so many of whose players were involved in the tournament. There were those who believed that the urge to prove that there was still something good to be said about Italian football stimulated the team. Certainly the abrasive midfielder Gennaro Gattuso came out boldly on the *azzurri*'s return to Rome to demand a newer, cleaner *calcio*.

Yet Italy teams continue to show the cloven hoof. Thus, Materazzi may deny that he three times insulted Zidane's wife and mother as the Frenchman insists, yet he has always, not least in his Everton days, been a ruthless performer, guilty last season of an appalling foul playing for Inter in a European Cup match. And it was thoroughly crass of him to dedicate the fine goal he headed against the Czechs—his header against France was equally spectacular—to Daniele de Rossi, properly suspended for his vicious elbow in the face of the American Brian McBride.

That day, the Italians couldn't even beat an American team down to nine men, while they had ten. Materazzi, his fortunes in this tournament mixed indeed, was somewhat controversially sent off against Australia, who themselves couldn't beat ten Italians. Though the penalty whereby Italy eventually won was itself contentious. When Fabio Grosso fell over Lucas Neill's prone body, was it a foul?

In a remarkable piece of frankness after the game, Italy's midfielder, Gennaro Gattuso, declared: 'It was not a penalty. The referee would never have given it if he had not unfairly sent off Materazzi earlier.'

There is no doubt the Italians had their finest game against Germany when Marcello Lippi, bolder than he would ever be in the Final, after which, of course, he resigned, threw extra strikers and full backs alike into attack. When Grosso scored he was actually in a central striking position, total football indeed, while Alex Del Piero, with his well taken, well engineered second goal, did much to erase the unhappy memories of the two easy chances he so expensively missed in the European Championship Final against France in Rotterdam in 2000.

What did surprise and perplex was the failure of the Italians to maintain their first-half aerial bombardment against the French, when every high ball that came over the box—mostly from the right and the effective Andrea Pirlo—looked a potential goal, so vulnerable did the French defenders appear, especially the ever erratic keeper Fabien Barthez, controversially preferred by Raymond Domenech to Gregory Coupet. Nor did the Italian full backs overlap with the enthusiasm they had shown against Germany, though the French use of two wingers may have been an inhibiting factor.

One of those was the 23-year-old Franck Ribéry, who came to Germany with just a couple of caps, but proved a marvellous foil to Zidane in the games against Spain and Brazil, justifying perhaps, with his bold, electric runs, Domenech's decision to leave out an incensed Ludovic Giuly, who had been in such ebullient form for Barcelona.

Though he was comprehensively out-jumped by Materazzi for the Italian equaliser, this was a tournament in which Patrick Vieira, after an uneasy start, in common with his team, did much to justify his great reputation. He made a fine goal for Ribéry against Spain, and scored one himself, once again the old, dominant figure in midfield.

The Japanese were something of a puzzle. Against Australia, they went ahead with a goal which should never have been allowed, the Aussie keeper Mark Schwarzer being palpably fouled while the ball sailed into the net from the right; the referee, *rara avis*, actually had the grace to apologise afterwards. But just as they did in the 2–2 draw with Germany, the Japanese wilted in the closing minutes. Tim Cahill was given far too much space and time to put the Australians ahead, and John Aloisi, you might say, was allowed to go Waltzing Matilda through a flaccid defence to get the third.

It was something of an irony that, when Japan unexpectedly took the lead against Brazil with a cracking goal, the superb through pass which set it up came from Alex, the naturalised Brazilian!

Out of Africa, always something new, wrote the Roman Pliny. There were, indeed, new African teams present in Germany in the shape of Ghana—knocking at the door for decades past—Togo, Angola and the Ivory Coast, but of these only the Ivory Coast, a shade unlucky to lose their opening game in Hamburg to Argentina, made any real impression. Togo and their predicament was almost a paradigm, not merely of sub-Saharan football, but of sub-Saharan life at large.

Togo had performed small miracles by qualifying at all, but things began to fall apart in Egypt at the subsequent African Nations Cup when the lanky Emmanuel Adebayor, scorer of no fewer than 10 goals in the qualifiers, fell out bitterly and badly with the well liked coach Stephen Keshi. He was replaced in Germany by the German Otto Pfister, long experienced in African soccer, but such was the turmoil in the team that he was in and out of office three times. On the eve of the match against Switzerland in Dortmund, which I saw, the players unsurprisingly threatened to go on strike. It was the old, sub-Saharan story; they'd still not been paid their large bonuses for qualifying. Adreas Herren of FIFA warned them of the disciplinary dangers they faced and ultimately play they did; with complete commitment. Indeed, they should have equalised had they been given a plain first-half penalty when Adebayor was brought down by Patrick Muller. In the event, they were beaten.

I also saw Angola's strange game against their former colonists, the Portuguese. The match had hardly begun when the veteran Luis Figo, advancing from the left, was able to give Jamba, the big Angolan centre-back, a couple of yards start and still cruise past him to make the easiest of goals for Pauleta. And that was that. Portugal, thus encouraged, could score no more, but squeezed through on a mere 1–0.

FIFA used the tournament for a half baked, superficial initiative to 'kick out racism', whose irrelevance was sharply exposed when Italy played Ukraine in the quarter-finals. When the teams lined up, the respective captains, Fabio Cannavaro of Italy, who had an outstanding competition, (bar the error which led to France eventually gaining their penalty kick in the Final) and Andrei Shevchenko, whose tournament was largely disappointing, stood there reading pledges to expel racism from the game. But right at the end of the Ukrainian line stood their manager and former star attacker Oleg Blokhin; poker-faced, as well he might have been. It was only some weeks previously that he had made a venomous, unashamedly racist, attack on the use of black footballers in his region. What had FIFA or UEFA done about that? Present at the tournament was another manager, Spain's Luis Aragones, guilty of a gross and gratuitous piece of racism when, in an evident but clumsy attempt to motivate one of his players some while before the World Cup, he had referred to Thierry Henry of France as 'that black shit'. The Spanish Federation fined him, but if UEFA, not to say FIFA, were looking for someone to punish as an example, here surely was a clear candidate.

Aragones' Spain team came to the conflict trailing clouds of glory, long unbeaten. They began with panache, annihilating Ukraine 4–0, with a coruscating performance by the twenty-four-year-old striker, David Villa, fresh from a splendidly prolific season for Valencia in the Primera Liga, in which he finished behind only Samuel Eto'o of Barça as top scorer. Capped just five times before the tournament, he ran rings around Ukraine's ponderous defence, scoring a penalty in the first half and another goal in the second, until Raul eventually succeeded him on 55 minutes. The other well-known striker, Fernando Torres, was also in lively form, and scored the fourth goal.

Hopes were high, but the crass optimism of the Madrid sports daily *Marca*, with its pre-match headline before France were met in Hanover:

WE'RE GOING TO SEND ZIDANE INTO RETIREMENT, proved an empty boast. It was principally Zidane, with a glorious performance, who sent Spain out of the Cup, even though they went ahead on 28 minutes with a penalty converted by Villa. In vain did Aragones try to ring the changes early in the second half, when it grew clear that he had over-egged the pudding. Starting Raul, Villa and Torres all together simply hadn't worked. But taking off both Villa and Raul didn't work, either. Zidane ruled, finishing with a glorious last flourish of a goal. Spain went out, 3–1.

Condign punishment alone will 'kick out racism', whether it be in Spain, where Real Madrid's Ultras Sur maintain a vindictive presence at the Bernabeu, or in one of those Balkan countries where black players in visiting teams are routinely subjected to abuse. All the bland statements by all the international captains in the world, or World Cup, won't make the smallest difference, while the Blokhins of the game stand by, unrepentant.

As for the match between Italy and the Ukraine, it was a somewhat different affair than the score, a 3–0 win for Italy, would suggest, and cast some doubt on the solidity of the Italian defence. Ukraine had reached this stage after a depressingly dull goalless draw in the previous round with the Swiss, when their attack, even with the presence of the much-lauded Shevchenko, had looked ineffectual. Yet here they were against the supposedly far better organised Italians, making chance after chance, forcing from the *azzurri* keeper, the agile Gianluigi Buffon, save after save. Some four in all, including a double block when he was equal to the shot which followed the initial rebound. In addition, the Ukrainians hit the bar. It was, football being the tantalising game that it will always be, immediately after one of those saves that Italy went straight up the field, forced a corner and took it short, enabling Francesco Totti to make a simple goal for Luca Toni. Curiously enough, not one of those previous shots had been the work of Shevchenko, who did not oblige Buffon to save again, and without great difficulty, until the 86th minute.

For the Italian manager, Marcello Lippi, who in common with José Pekerman, Jurgen Klinsmann—tired of transatlantic commuting—and Pawel Janas of Poland resigned after the tournament, his success was also something of a consolation, since his son, an agent, had been embroiled and charged in connection with the corruption scandal.

Sven Göran Eriksson was due, before the tournament, to relinquish his post. Even for the fatuously indulgent members of the Football Association, his naive decision to fly with two equally credulous advisors to Dubai, where a fake sheikh, working for the *News of the World*, spoke to him about a job with Aston Villa, was rather too much. It did seem extraordinary that neither Eriksson, his agent nor the agent's lawyer should have suspected the ruse, since the journalist involved had perpetrated it several times in the recent past.

Subsequently, the Football Association's search for a successor to Eriksson took on dimensions of farce. It seemed at first that the job might go to Martin O'Neill, previous manager of Celtic, or Sam Allardyce, the manager of Bolton Wanderers, with Alan Cubishley of Charlton, who had just resigned, another possible candidate. That was until David Dein, the hyperactive Arsenal vice-chairman, who to give him due credit had brought Arsène Wenger to the club, manoeuvred his way on to the relevant committee, and pressed the case of Portugal's Brazilian manager, Luiz Flipe Scolari. The hapless chief executive of the FA, a former head of sport at BBC and ITV television, Brian Barwick, was duly despatched to Europe to approach Scolari. But Scolari, whether or not in all seriousness, said he and his family were deterred by the intrusion of the media, and would not be coming. Barwick, for his part, insisted, despite all circumstantial evidence, that no offer had been made to Big Phil at all.

At this point Dein, previously known as a king maker, was voted off the FA Board, and the job, rather than being filled after the World Cup was over, was surprisingly given to Eriksson's sidekick, Steve McClaren, the manager of Middlesbrough. Where, according to an interview given by the club captain, and subsequent manager, Gareth Southgate, McClaren had seriously lost his way early in the year, when Boro were thrashed at Highbury and at home by Aston Villa, obliging the senior professionals to fill the breach.

The enthusiasm of the German fans rose to crescendo as the tournament progressed and with it, after so poor a start, their team. But blessedly, the infinite prophecies of doom which had preceded the competition—a rabid invasion by Polish hooligans, violence by neo-Nazis, a risk of death to any black fans who found themselves in areas of the old East Germany—proved wholly groundless.

In the concluding stages of the tournament, immense numbers of German fans who couldn't get into the stadia congregated in areas with television screens set aside for supporters. There were instances of city centres being so crowded that people could not reach their hotels or use their cars. Far from being the dull anticlimax which third-place matches are, and which an unhappy Scolari claimed this one to be, the German public embraced it as if it were indeed the Final which had been denied them.

In Stuttgart, the German team—without its motor, Michael Ballack, less influential in the concluding stages than in the first, due to a painful injury—duly beat Portugal. Both goals were scored for them with fierce right-footed shots from the left by the blond Bastian Schweinsteiger, a player I'd admired in a largely mediocre German team in the 2002 European finals, but who, until then, had had a rather disappointing World Cup. Portugal replied late on when Figo, surely this time playing his final game for them, produced a perfect right-wing cross, enabling Nuno Gomes to head a simple goal.

So to the thousand natural shocks of the Final in Berlin. The early penalty—contentious as always, yet, to most of us, the foul by Materazzi on the flying Malouda seemed less of an offence than when Malouda was subsequently fouled by Zambrotta. Be that is it may, Zidane coolly chipped his spot kick in off the underside of the bar, while Buffon dived in vain.

The first-half action held promise of a memorable Final, but as we know, it was destined not only to peter out in penalties, but to be besmirched by Zidane's assault on Materazzi.

Barely five minutes had been played when Thierry Henry headed on a long kick which seemed to confuse the Italian defence, resulting in a desperate challenge by Marco Materazzi bringing down Florent Malouda. Zinedine Zidane took the penalty with almost casual aplomb, lobbing the ball in off the underside of the crossbar.

Italy, far from demoralised, at once went on the attack, and it soon transpired that the French defence was alarmingly vulnerable to high crosses from the right, especially from corners. First, a header from Materazzi almost provoked an own goal. Then in the ninth minute, from Pirlo's right wing corner, Materazzi soared majestically above the defence and fully atoned for conceding the penalty, beating a Fabien Barthez who looked very ill at case on the crosses. So much so that you wondered why, thereafter, the Italians did not try to exploit their obvious advantage in the air, though on 35 minutes, from another right-wing corner, Luca Toni's header did clip the French bar.

But if Gattuso prevented Zidane from dominating the game, though Zisou was always potentially dangerous, then Italy found Francesco Totti, previously a key man, largely ineffectual. Indeed, he was substituted on the hour in favour of Iaquinta. At the same time, somewhat surprisingly, Marcello Lippi sent on the previously disgraced De Rossi, who would ultimately be one of Italy's penalty scorers in the shoot-out. Flourishing, you might say, like the green bay tree.

In truth, it was a Final which fell away after the early excitement, and the longer it went on, the more likely it seemed to be doomed and destined to go to penalties. It was perhaps somewhat ironic that, in the first period of extra time, Domenech should replace Franck Ribéry with David Treseguet, later to miss that vital penalty.

No such victory can be called anything but an anticlimax, but it was hard to deny Italy's resilient captain, Fabio Cannavaro, his delight. Many thought rather than Zidane, the outstanding player of the tournament, and, given Zidane's violent aberration, perhaps on moral grounds, Cannavaro deserved the choices.

It was somewhat strange, when Zidane and the French team returned to Paris, to see him eulogised by President Chirac in what seemed more of a political gambit than a sincere encomium. Meanwhile, lip readers were abundantly heard, telling us what Materazzi was meant to have said to provoke Zizou; not least a supposed insult to his sick mother, which Materazzi denied. Provocation there unquestionably was, but football's iron law of never retaliate had been badly and dearly breached.

For what it is worth, the shoot-out saw David Trezeguet miss, Italy put all their penalties away and prevail. Yet how close the French had come to winning in extra time, when Zizou sent out a measured pass to the right, Willy Sagnol responded with a perfect cross, Zidane got his head to the ball, only for Buffon to flail it, one-handed, over the bar.

On his return to Paris, Zidane was eulogised, all sins forgiven, by a now lame-duck President, Jacques Chirac. The duck quacked, Zizou bent his head towards him, and for one hallucinatory moment, it seemed as if Chirac might suffer the fate of Materazzi. But the moment passed.

The World Cup over, managers fell like autmun leaves. It was known that Eriksson would be on his way. Even the pitifully inept Football Association, which had not only countenanced his surreptitious dealings with Chelsea, twice, and Manchester United—incomprehensibly rewarding him, after his second meeting with Chelsea, with what might be called a 'disloyalty bonus' of an extra £1 million a year —could hardly ignore the Swede's ludicrous trip to Dubai. There, he and two supposedly experienced advisors, one his agent, Athol Still, were duped by a notorious 'con man' journalist from the *News of the World*, well known for attiring himself as a fake sheikh and eliciting flagrant indiscretions from a variety of 'celebrities'. Eriksson showed interest in leaving the FA and taking over at Aston Villa. He also made disparaging remarks about some of his players. But though this meant the end of his managerial job, his colossal contract still ran, ludicrously, until 2008; unless in the meantime he secured another managerial role.

So the great survivor partially survived even his latest, shabby episode. Just as he had survived not only his dealings with Chelsea, but the scandal of his affair with a woman secretary, Faria Alam, at the FA, favours he had shared with the then chief executive, Mark Palios.

Palios had tried in vain to exclude himself from the imbroglio, using the chief public relations officer, the experienced journalist Colin Gibson, to approach the *News of the World*, offering his co-operation, were his own name to be excluded. An offer brushed aside. It also transpired that when David Davies, a senior FA executive, had interrogated Eriksson about his liaison with Alam, he had failed to confess to it.

Looking for a successor to Eriksson, the FA flew into an apparent panic. Other countries had the sound sense to wait till the World Cup was over to appoint new coaches. Not the FA Their appointments committee was invaded by the Arsenal vice chairman, David Dein, the man who to his credit had brought the hugely successful Arsène Wenger to Highbury, but had also been a fervent advocate of Eriksson at the time of his appointment and, reportedly, later. Disregarding what appeared to be a short list of club managers, among them Eriksson's adjunct, Steve McLaren of Middlesbrough, Dein pressed the claims of Portugal's Brazilian manager, 'Big Phil' Scolari.

Accordingly the relatively new chief executive Brian Barwick, a former television supremo who had seemed anything but comfortable in the job, was sent to pursue Scolari, winner of the 2002 World Cup with Brazil, in Europe. The result was a humilating rebuff, on the somewhat unconvincing grounds that Scolari and his family had been distressed by so much media attention. For his part, the hapless Barwick returned to London, insisting that Scolari had never been offered the job.

So, acting in absurd haste with every prospect of repenting at leisure, rather than waiting till after the World Cup, the FA appointed Eriksson's adjunct, McClaren. A choice hardly met with a fanfare of trumpets. Not least because a recent interview, given by the then captain of Middlesbrough, Gareth Southgate, had alleged that early in 2006, a time when Boro lost 6–0 at Arsenal and 4–0 at home to medicore Aston Villa, McClaren had been so affected that senior Boro players had temporarily to run the team.

Elsewhere, Marcello Lippi resigned, despite Italy's success. He had been under extra pressure, since his son had been inculpated in the sensational Italian inquiry into referee-fixing, as a member of the player-agency ruled by Juventus's arch manipulator, Luciano Moggi. Pekerman resigned the Argentine post before the tournament was over. He had taken his team a long way, both tactically and in World Cup terms; only, it seemed, to lose his way and his confidence when it came to the vital match against Germany.

Poland's Pawel Janas could hardly do other than resign, after so disastrous a tournament. Serbia's Ilija Petrovic went, too. Jurgen Klinsmann, weary, it seemed, of so much commuting, stood down, having emphatically if belatedly proved his point with Germany. Bruce Arena, after taking the USA to the Finals for the second consecutive World Cup, was actually dismissed. It seemed that the new chief executive of the US Association, the multi-talented Sunil Gulati, a distinguished academic, who once worked for the World Bank and now taught at Columbia university, wanted a radical change in approach, abandoning the prevalence of players who had come through the colleges, and looking for those of Latin American provenance. But Raymond Domenech of France, all white suit, spectacles and endless touchline agitation, defied probability by keeping his job on the back, one might say, of Zinedine Zidane's revival. A Zidane who was fined over £3000 and suspended by FIFA, while Materazzi, also suspended, had to pay over £2000. Hardly draconian punishments, you might believe.

FIFA's attention, we were told, would turn in the future to the matters of verbal abuse, à la Materazzi, and the plethora of deliberate diving. A book called *Foul* by the indefatigable investigative journalist, Andrew Jennings, published just before the tournament, made ferocious charges against FIFA panjandrums. But, as we have learned all too pungently in the past, Teflon is as Teflon does.

Meanwhile, as the tournament was followed by recriminations among England players who had previously stood up for Eriksson, with Frank Lampard, surprisingly ineffectual, declaring that Jermaine Defoe should have been picked and Michael Owen deploring long-ball tactics, Graham Poll, the English referee, became something of a figure of farce. In the hectic match between Australia and Serbia-Montenegro, he had somehow managed to forget that he had given a yellow card to the Serbian Josip Simonic in the 50th minute. In the 90th Poll gave him another, though Simonic should have been automatically sent of for the second bookable offence. As the teams left the field three minutes later, Simonic upbraided Poll, who this time did, indeed, flourish a belated red card! Sepp Blatter remarked consolingly, 'We should not forget that Graham Poll, in his previous matches, achieved fantastic things.' But there were those, not least aggrieved English managers, who remembered things less fantastic in the course of domestic games. While there stays in the mind the depressing picture of Poll being followed around the field by an abusive Wayne Rooney at Highbury without taking any action against him.

RESULTS: Germany 2006

First round

Group A

Munich, Gelsenkirchen, Dortmund, Hamburg, Berlin, Hanover

Germany 4, Costa Rica 2
Poland 0, Ecuador 2
Germany 1, Poland 0
Ecuador 3, Costa Rica 0
Ecuador 0, Germany 3
Costa Rica 1, Poland 2

	P	W	D	L	GOALS F	A	Pts.
Germany	3	3	0	0	0	2	9
Ecuador	3	2	0	1	5	3	6
Poland	3	1	0	2	2	4	3
Costa Rica	3	0	0	3	3	9	0

Group B

Frankfurt, Dortmund, Nuremberg, Berlin, Cologne, Kaiserslautern

England 1, Paraguay 0
Trinidad and Tobago 0, Sweden 0
England 2, Trinidad and Tobago 0
Sweden 1, Paraguay 0
Sweden 2, England 2
Paraguay 2, Trinidad and Tobago 0

	P	W	D	L	GOALS F	A	Pts.
England	3	2	1	0	5	2	7
Sweden	3	1	2	0	3	2	5
Paraguay	3	1	0	2	2	2	3
Trinidad and Tobago	3	0	1	2	0	4	1

Group C

Hamburg, Leipzig, Gelsenkirchen, Stuttgart, Frankfurt, Munich

Argentina 2, Ivory Coast 1
Serbia & Montenegro 0, Holland 1
Argentina 6, Serbia & Montenegro 0
Holland 2, Ivory Coast 1
Holland 0, Argentina 0
Ivory Coast 3, Serbia and Montenegro 2

	P	W	D	L	GOALS F	A	Pts.
Argentina	3	2	1	0	8	1	7
Holland	3	2	1	0	3	1	7
Ivory Coast	3	0	2	5	6	6	3
Serbia/Mont.	3	0	0	3	2	10	0

Group D

Nuremberg, Cologne, Hanover, Frankfurt, Gelsenkirchen, Leipzig

Mexico 3, Iran 1
Angola 0, Portugal 1
Mexico 0, Angola 0
Portugal 2, Iran 0
Portugal 2, Mexico 1
Iran 1, Angola 1

	P	W	D	L	GOALS F	A	Pts.
Portugal	3	3	0	0	5	1	9
Mexico	3	1	1	1	4	3	4
Angola	3	0	2	1	1	2	2
Iran	3	0	1	2	2	6	1

Group E

Gelsenkirchen, Hanover, Cologne, Kaiserslautern, Hamburg, Nuremberg

USA 0, Czech Rep. 3
Italy 2, Ghana 0
Italy 1, USA 1
Czech Rep. 0, Italy 2
Ghana 2, USA 1

	P	W	D	L	GOALS F	A	Pts.
Italy	3	2	1	0	5	1	7
Ghana	3	2	0	1	4	3	6
Czech Rep.	3	1	0	2	3	4	3
USA	3	0	1	2	2	6	1

Group F

Kaiserslautern, Berlin, Nuremberg, Munich, Dortmund, Stuttgart

Australia 3, Japan 1
Brazil 1, Croatia 0
Japan 0, Croatia 0
Brazil 2, Australia 0
Japan 1, Brazil 4
Croatia 2, Australia 2

	P	W	D	L	GOALS F	A	Pts.
Brazil	3	3	0	0	7	1	9
Australia	3	1	1	1	5	5	4
Croatia	3	0	2	1	2	3	2
Japan	3	0	1	2	2	7	1

Group G

Frankfurt, Stuttgart, Leipzig, Dortmund, Cologne, Hanover
South Korea 2, Togo 1
France 0, Switzerland 0
France 1, South Korea 1
Togo 0, Switzerland 2
Togo 0, France 2
Switzerland 2, South Korea 0

	P	W	D	L	GOALS F	A	Pts.
Switzerland	3	2	1	0	**4**	**0**	7
France	3	1	2	0	**3**	**1**	5
South Korea	3	1	1	1	**3**	**4**	4
Togo	3	0	0	3	**1**	**6**	0

Group H

Leipzig, Munich, Hamburg, Stuttgart, Kaiserslautern, Berlin
Spain 4, Ukraine 0
Tunisia 2, Saudi Arabia 2
Saudi Arabia 0, Ukraine 4
Spain 3, Tunisia 1
Saudi Arabia 0, Spain 1
Ukraine 1, Tunisia 0

	P	W	D	L	GOALS F	A	Pts
Spain	3	3	0	0	**8**	**1**	9
Ukraine	3	2	0	1	**5**	**4**	6
Tunisia	3	0	1	2	**3**	**6**	1
Saudi Arabia	3	0	1	2	**2**	**7**	1

Second Round

Munich
Germany 2, Sweden 0

Leipzig
Argentina 2, Mexico 1

Stuttgart
England 1 Ecuador 0

Nuremberg
Portugal 1, Holland 0

Kaiserslautern
Italy 1, Australia 0

Cologne
Switzerland 0, Ukraine 0
Ukraine win 3–0 on penalties

Dortmund
Brazil 3, Ghana 0

Hanover
Spain 1, France 3

Quarter-finals

Berlin
Germany 1, Argentina 1
Germany win 4–2 on penalties

Hamburg
Italy 3, Ukraine 0

Gelsenkirchen
England 0, Portugal 0
Portugal win 3–1 on penalties.

Frankfurt
Brazil 0, France 1

Semi-finals

Dortmund
Germany 0, Italy 2 after extra time

Munich
Portugal 0, France 1

Third-place Match

Stuttgart

Germany 3	**Portugal 1**
Kahn; Lahm,	Ricardo; Paulo
Nowtny, Metzelder,	Ferreira, Ricardo
Jansen; Schneider,	Costa, Fernando
Kehl, Frings,	Meira, Nuno Valente
Schweinsteiger;	(Nuno Gomes 69);
(Hitzlsperger 79);	Costinha (Petit 46),
Klose (Neuville 65),	Maniche; Cristiano
Podolski	Ronaldo, Deco, Simao;
(Hanke 71)	Pauleta (Figo 77)

SCORERS
Schweinsteiger 2, Petit own goal for Germany.
Nuno Gomes for Portugal

Final

Berlin

France 1	**Italy 1**
after extra time, Italy win 5–3 on penalties	
Barthez; Sagnol,	Buffon; Zambrotta,
Thuram, Gallas,	Cannavaro,
Abidal; Vieira	Materazzi, Grosso;
(Diarra 56), Makelele;	Camoranesi (Del
Ribery (Trezeguet	Piero 86), Gattuso,
100), Zidane,	Pirlo, Perotta
Malouda; Henry	(Iaquinta 61); Totti
(Wiltord 107.)	(De Rossi 61)Toni

SCORERS
Zidane (penalty) for France
Materazzi for Italy

Index